Lilian Leland

Traveling Alone

A Woman's Journey Around the World

Lilian Leland

Traveling Alone
A Woman's Journey Around the World

ISBN/EAN: 9783744798990

Printed in Europe, USA, Canada, Australia, Japan

Cover: Foto ©Andreas Hilbeck / pixelio.de

More available books at **www.hansebooks.com**

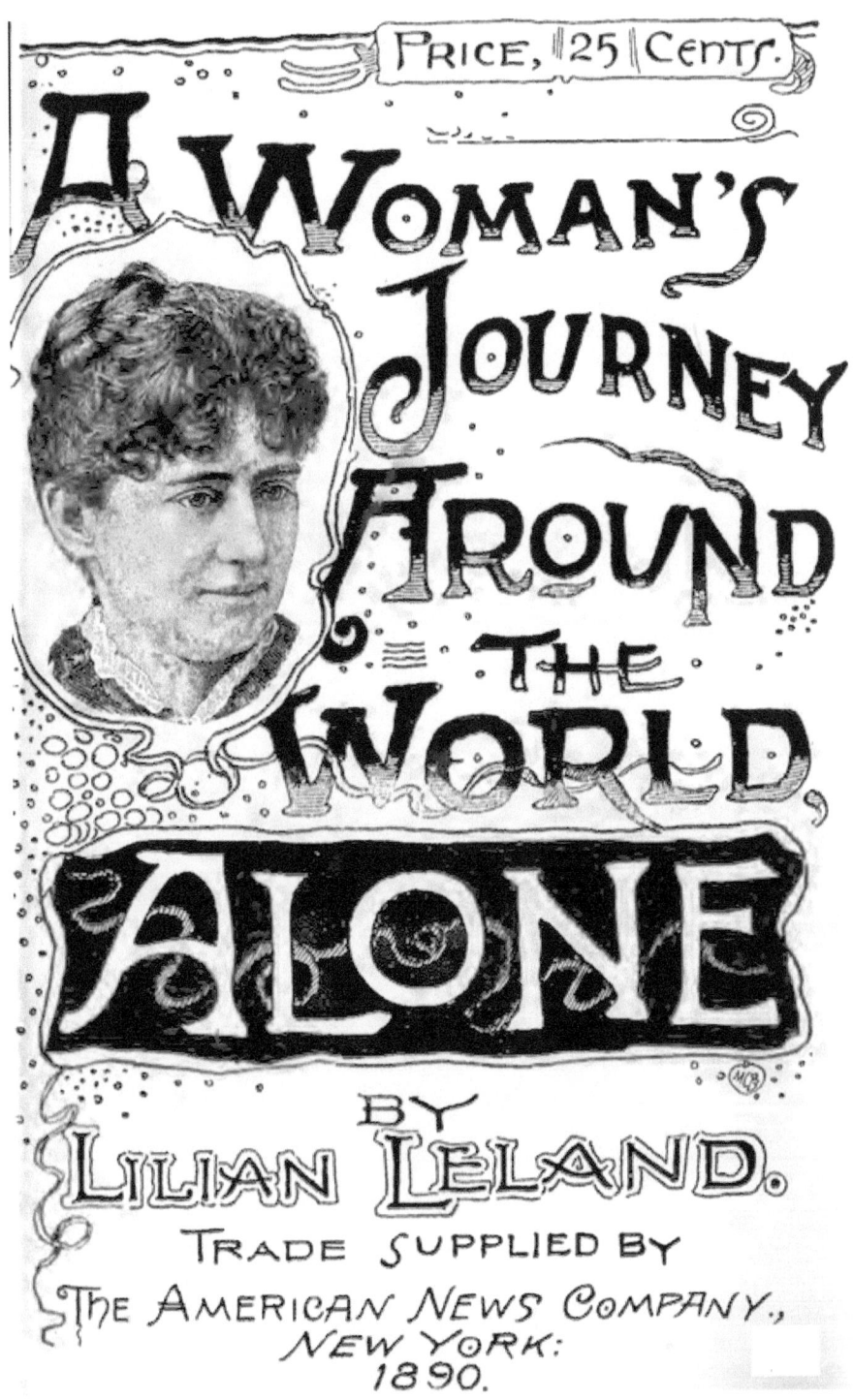

TRAVELING ALONE.

A WOMAN'S JOURNEY

AROUND THE WORLD.

BY

LILIAN LELAND.

FROM THE
PRESS OF JOHN POLHEMUS,
102 NASSAU STREET.

TRADE SUPPLIED BY
THE AMERICAN NEWS COMPANY.

NEW YORK:

Dedication.

TO THOSE WHO HAVE BEEN KIND TO ME

IN EVERY LAND

AND

ON EVERY SEA,

THIS SIMPLE RECORD OF MY TRAVELS

IS

GRATEFULLY INSCRIBED.

LILIAN LELAND.

REFERENCE TO CONTENTS.

	PAGE
INTRODUCTION,	vii
HOW I CAME TO GO,	1
OFF FOR CAPE HORN. Straits of Magellan—A Hurricane—Valparaiso,	3
CALIFORNIA. San Francisco—Chinatown—Big Trees—Southern California,	14
A STAGE RIDE,	23
YOSEMITE,	26
GEYSERS,	33
SANDWICH ISLANDS. Honolulu—Cannibals—Lepers,	35
HO, FOR JAPAN! Yokohama—Dancing Girls—Tokio,	45
A JAPANESE JOURNEY. Tea Houses—Human Horses—Nikko—An Earthquake—Kobe—Kioto—Japanese Theatres—The Inland Sea—Nagasaki,	58
CHINA. Shanghai—Hong Kong,	83
SINGAPORE,	92
JAVA. Batavia—Buitenzorg—Bandong,	99
CEYLON. Kandy,	110
INDIA. Pondicherry—Madras—Calcutta—The Himalaya Mountains—The Sacred Ganges—The Pearl Mosque—Delhi—Jeypore—Bombay—Towers of Silence—Caves of Elephanta,	114
BOMBAY TO CAIRO. Aden—Suez—Pyramids and Sphinx—The Nile—Alexandria—Waterspouts,	146
THE HOLY LAND. Jaffa—Jerusalem—Temple of Solomon—Bethlehem—Beirut—Smyrna,	156
CONSTANTINOPLE. Whirling Dervishes—The Black Sea—Mosque of St. Sophia—Turkish Women—The Sultan,	164

	PAGE
GREECE. Athens—Acropolis and Parthenon—Corfu,	170
ITALY. Naples—Pompeii—Vesuvius,	175
ROME. The Vatican—St. Peter's—The Old Masters—Palaces and Churches—Forum and Colosseum—Florence, San Marco and Uffizzi,	184
VENICE. Doge's Palace—St. Mark's—Tomb of Canova—Milan—Italian Lakes,	206
SWITZERLAND. The Alps—Lucerne,	219
GERMANY. Strasbourg—Dresden—Berlin—The Rhine—Cologne,	223
HOLLAND. Amsterdam—Hague,	237
BRUSSELS,	240
PARIS,	242
LAND OF THE MIDNIGHT SUN. Denmark—Norway—Arctic Circle—North Cape,	251
RUSSIA. St. Petersburg—Peterhof—Moscow—Warsaw,	269
ENGLAND. London—Hampton Court—Windsor—Stratford-on-Avon—Kenilworth—Warwick Castle,	280
SCOTLAND. Edinburgh—Abbottsford—Holyrood—The Trossachs,	290
IRELAND. Giant's Causeway—Dublin—Killarney—Blarney Castle—Queenstown,	294
HOMEWARD,	299
THE UNITED STATES. Rocky Mountains—Colorado Springs—Garden of the Gods—Grand Cañon of the Arkansas—Salt Lake City—Lake Tahoe—Sierra Nevadas,	302
YOSEMITE—SECOND VISIT,	318
THE COLUMBIA RIVER,	331
YELLOWSTONE PARK,	336
THE RETURN TO NEW YORK. Minnehaha—Farm Life—Niagara—The Hudson River—Home,	349
IN CONCLUSION,	356

INTRODUCTION.

The successful accomplishment of a journey of nearly sixty thousand miles, made by a young woman, traveling alone, is calculated to excite wonder and admiration; and when the record of that journey is replete with original thought, the emanations of a bright intellect, it possesses a special interest.

LILIAN LELAND, at the age of twenty-five, without premeditation or preparation, started upon a voyage which, unexpectedly, became the commencement of a journey which carried her around the world, to many lands and on many seas, from Cape Horn to the North Cape and from the Rocky Mountains to the Himalayas; but little less than sixty thousand miles in distance and covering a period of about two years.

She traveled without escort or protection except chance acquaintances met on the way.

No woman has ever traveled so far alone, with the single exception of Ida Pfeiffer who went twice around the world. Next to Lilian Leland is Isabella Bird, whose admirable books have earned for her a well deserved fame.

The ease and comfort with which Lilian Leland accomplished her remarkable journey, and the enjoyment she found in it, were doubtless greatly due to the fact that she possesses qualities specially adapted to such an experience. Although so fragile and petite that at twenty-five she had the physical appearance, as well as the diffidence and timidity of a girl of seventeen, she possessed an amount of nervous energy and a power of endurance seldom found in a woman.

Retiring and reserved in manner, she was, nevertheless, capable of facing the greatest possible danger without flinching, or the most aggravating difficulty without annoyance. With a highly nervous organization which renders her keenly alive to everything calculated to excite fear or irritability, she has a self control which enables her to meet every emergency with perfect composure.

Charming in person and manner, she conceals beneath an attractive exterior a perfect self-reliance and an indomitable will.

She never complains, never finds fault, is always smiling and cheerful in appearance, no matter what she feels or thinks.

Always anxious to oblige others, she is never willing that others should discommode themselves for her.

That such a woman should make such a journey, and be everywhere the recipient of kind, respectful and courteous treatment, is not strange.

This story of her travels is composed of letters, partly in diary form, written for the entertainment of the family circle who watched her progress with affectionate interest. The pleasure the family and friends who received them found in reading these letters suggested the idea of publishing them.

They are a record of personal experiences, interspersed with observations and thoughts of the writer, rather than an account of the places or the people the traveler saw. She cares nothing for dates or dimensions, and statistics have no fascination for her—but she sees the beauties of nature and has a ready appreciation of all that is human, while her descriptions are vivid and full of charm.

The writer of this introduction having had these letters placed in his hands for editorial revision has not made an attempt to adapt them to any standard of literary criticism, nor to deprive them of the freedom and informality of style permissible and enjoyable in a private letter. Excepting, therefore, that they are put into the form of a continuous narrative, the editor has been content to be little more than a proof reader, believing that any effort at alteration or condensation would deprive them of the interest they now derive from the personality of the writer.

It is proper to say that Lilian Leland is at the time of this publication, several thousand miles distant from New York and will not see this story of her travels in type until after it is published. The editor, therefore, assumes entire responsibility for whatever shortcomings or defects there may be.

EDITOR.

NEW YORK, *January* 15, 1890.

A Woman's Journey

Around the World, Alone.

HOW I CAME TO GO.

If there was any one particular thing that I had always had a horror of, it was traveling, and especially traveling alone. The fatigue and deprivations of travel—the attention to baggage, tickets, changes, et cetera, required in traveling alone—were appalling to think of. Any enjoyment which involved an hour's ride on the cars, or the finding of a new locality, even in the familiar city of New York, I considered not worth the trouble. On the other hand, I had talked, since I had been "knee high to a grasshopper," of the widely extended travels I wished to make, and for some time past, being out of health, I had yearned openly for the sea, and wished, in piteous accents, that I might be permitted to go to California, via Panama, or to Europe, or somewhere—anywhere.

Between the gentle reader and myself, confidentially, I was a fraud of the most deceitful type. In my secret soul I didn't want to do anything of the kind; but it amused me to say I did. Fancy my horror, then, one day, when the head of my house walked in and said, "Here is a fine opportunity for you; the beautiful new steamship Santa Rosa is to be sent around the Horn to San Francisco in a few days, so if you really wish to take a long sea voyage I will secure a passage for you on her." Now I happen to have another strong characteristic besides this one of expressing desires to do all kinds of things that I would really rather not do except in imagination, and that is an utter inability to take back anything, or to show any weakening of determination; therefore, when the steamer was found for me to go on, there was nothing left for me to do but to go. So I went; steadfastly ignoring all loopholes of escape offered me by my anxious friends.

I am not possessed of much real courage, I fear, but I have plenty of bravado, and a large stock of determination, known to my friends as mulishness, which, backing bravado, makes that base imitation outcourage courage. Therefore, after a week's scramble and hurry and bustle, I found myself looking across a rapidly widening gulf of water at the aforesaid head of my house as he was being taken back to New York by the little tug that accompanied us down to Sandy Hook, while I was being carried out to sea by the Santa Rosa—a saucy laugh still on my face, but terror and desolation in my heart. Two months at sea without possible communication with home or friends; two months with all the possibilities of disaster, illness and death to those I had left, and I not to know or be on hand to avert or console. Two months of sea with all the horrors of possible storm and shipwreck. All this whirled through my head at once, till I was dizzy with the terror of it which I had fought successfully up to this moment. Now I strove with a mighty impulse to stretch out my arms and call to him before it was too late forever, to take me back to my home and family and not let me go on this dreadful journey. I conquered. I swallowed both terror and tears, smiled coquettishly at the passing Captain, and flung him a saucy remark to hide the trouble that possessed me. I sat apart and looked at the sea for hours, turning my thoughts by degrees from what I was leaving behind to future enterprises, successes, joys; until at last, when I went below to supper, my emotions were buried deep as ever under a bravado gaiety, and I was put down by my fellow passengers as a most heartless and unfeeling woman.

OFF FOR CAPE HORN.

On Sunday, February 24th, 1884, brightest and coldest morning of the year, the fine new steamer Santa Rosa was laboriously hauled out of the mud of the East River wharf, at the foot of Ninth street; a difficult operation, in which the strained staccato voice of the pilot played the most important part, and proceeded slowly down the river under the Brooklyn Bridge, on down the bay, past Governor's and Bedloe's Islands, through the Narrows to Sandy Hook, in the teeth of a wind so bitter cold that the passengers were utterly unable to face it for more than a few moments at a time. So cold it was that the steam which condensed upon the smokestack froze there even under the rays of the bright midday sun. At Sandy Hook the compasses were adjusted, the pilot put off on a tug, and the Santa Rosa got under way and soon left the land far behind.

As we got out to sea the temperature moderated a little. The next morning rose cloudy and by afternoon the wind had risen to a gale, which increased to something like, if not quite, a hurricane. We struggled out on deck that night in spite of the wind to take a look at the brilliant phosphorescent sea that was rolling and tumbling from beneath the stern of the vessel; but after the briefest of glances we were glad to scramble breathlessly back to the comfortable social hall, where we tried to tell stories and be sociable and maintain a decorous appearance, while the vessel rolled and pitched and creaked in every timber. At last we gave up the struggle with laws of gravitation and retired to our several cabins, there to be shaken and pitched and rolled about like so many dice in so many boxes until we were heartily tired of it and yearned for a moment's rest on solid earth again.

All that night, and the next day and night, the gale continued to blow. The sea ran very high, the waves coming down with a crash overhead that was rather terrifying. Indeed, they broke the shutters of some of the upper staterooms near me. What with the roar and whistle of the wind, the noise of waves dashing overhead, creaking woodwork, crash of lamps and crockery, flying chairs and cuspidors and trunks, we got very little sleep. My trunk slid up and down my stateroom the whole of the first night, with a bang at each roll that threatened to knock out the sides of the cabin, and we passengers were obliged to maintain a tight hold on berths and sofas to keep on them at all.

Two days more of rough and gloomy weather and then the winds and waves subsided, and we found ourselves enjoying the most delightful, balmy days, as we sailed through the acres of gulf weed with which the sea was strewn for miles and miles, for we were still crossing the Gulf Stream. We fell to basking in the sunshine on the forward deck in broad hats and Summer attire, while the steamer assumed the aspect of a floating laundry as the wet carpets, curtains and bedding were hung out to dry.

About this time we found a stowaway on board. He was a poor, miserable, seasick, half starved, half suffocated and wholly villainous looking creature. He appeared very much as if he might be an escaped convict. The captain set him at work. The sailors called him "Sweet Violets," and he answered to that name throughout the voyage.

The Santa Rosa is magnificent in her appointments. She has accommodations for three hundred persons in the cabins; but a literary man, who is an invalid, and his wife, with myself, completed the passenger list. With the captain, purser and a young gentleman going out as shipping clerk, we made six at table. Perhaps six more uncongenial people were never got together before; for, of the six, one was distinctly good, one naughty and one intellectual; another was very sedate and quiet, another frivolous; and the last eminently practical; but we were all on our good behavior, bent on being agreeable and jolly, and so got on finely.

Now we had beautiful weather, growing warmer and brighter daily, culminating at the equator in one intensely hot day, when the passengers and officers bloomed out suddenly in pink and white muslins, or white flannel shirts with silken cords of brilliant color; and then cooling off by degrees as we approached the Straits of Magellan until we got back to ulsters and fur shoes, and deserted the hammock swinging at the stern and the cool, starlit, upper deck, for the cosy social hall.

On our approach to the equator the gentlemanly purser, who had been the first to appear in white flannel and red silk trim-mings, causing us to remark the very "heavy swell" that morning, concluded that "discretion was the better part of valor" and shaved off his beard to avoid undergoing that operation at the hands of old Neptune, who is supposed to arise from the sea to attend to the shaving of those unhappy individuals who are crossing the line for the first time. Actuated by the same prudent motives he forsook his cosy little stateroom and occupied each night a different one of the hundred or more beautifully fitted up, but vacant cabins, until the equator was well passed.

Those ten days on the tropical ocean were as lazy and happy as they were bright. Perhaps we appreciated them more for the sudden relief from the piercing cold of New York; and although the days passed so lazily there was no lack of interest. In the morning we must take a turn on deck for a breath of fresh air and a glance at the weather, which brought us down to the breakfast table with appetites that approved of everything set before us. There were no dyspeptic murmurs of discontent; we were all hungry and everything tasted good.

After breakfast we adjourned to the deck, where we watched the sea, noting the daily diminution of the waves from foam-capped mountains to the tiniest ripple; and the varying color, now green, shading from the palest tint back to the darkest and dreariest as the waves broke; now gray, now blue, the brightest, most brilliant beautiful indigo blue imaginable; and then the snowy foam that capped the waves melted to the palest blue before it was swept up into indigo hills again. We woke one morning, the fifteenth from New York, to find ourselves in shallow water of pale green, with the Abrholos Rocks close at hand. There was nothing to be seen but a narrow sand strip with a lighthouse and a couple of frame buildings on it.

Besides the sea itself we had flying fish to look at, as they shot out from the ship's approaching bow, flying straight as a dart clear above the waves for long distances before dropping back into the sea. Occasionally one flew on board, but was dead by the time it was picked up. Then there were the Nautili, the prettiest things imaginable, looking like tiny ships of fairy pattern, with rainbow sails; and they rode the waves bravely. Now and then one careened over on its side, dipped its lavender tinted sails and was completely wrecked by the next wave; but usually they kept themselves steadily upon their course.

When one is tired of these, there is the hammock in which to take a nap, and from which you are probably awakened to look at a distant sail; or perhaps we speak a vessel; or a school of porpoises is passing, jumping violently out of the water till they give the impression of so many half-submerged revolving wheels of fish, so perfect a half circle do they describe at each leap. Or perhaps a sudden shower rises, the furious raindrops beating down the waves and then departing, leaving a delightful freshness in the air. Or whales are to be seen spouting in the distance.

Once we stopped the engines in midocean to "key up," and lay all day, rolling, as it seemed to us, to the verge of upsetting, while the quiet that resulted from the cessation of machinery was only broken by the creaking of woodwork as we rocked from side to side on the long smooth ocean swell.

In the evening there was that interesting constellation, the Southern Cross, and as we approach the Straits, that mysterious group, formed of two bits of white fluff and one tiny black one known as the Magellan clouds, though of course they can't be clouds, or they would have been blown away by a Cape Horn hurricane long ago instead of remaining fixed up there, as they do, keeping watch over the Straits from which they take their name. These interest us until it becomes too cold and stormy to enjoy the deck, and then the social hall seems very inviting, and stories of the sea are exchanged, punctuated sometimes by a general slide of the company from starboard to port as the winds and waves increase.

Entering the Straits of Magellan on the 18th of March, we find low, sandy, barren, deserted banks on either side of us. It would appear that the water is shallow, for a man is kept "heaving the lead" until we come to anchor for the night in Possession Bay.

We find the scenery improves as we advance, growing greener and higher, until we arrive at Sandy Point early the following afternoon, though it is still sandy enough at that place to make its name highly appropriate. We again cast our anchor and proceed to investigate the place and people with an interest born of twenty-three days' complete isolation from the world of land and folks.

Point d'Arrenos, or Sandy Point, is a small Chilian settlement. An officer came out in a boat and took the captain and myself, the purser, and the shipping clerk ashore. We went to the Governor's headquarters and had a walk all over the place ; it takes only fifteen minutes to do it. The gentlemen bought a quantity of the most beautiful skins, at very low prices. Being the only lady in the party, I came in for the presents ; a very beautiful bouquet was gathered for me while the furs were being purchased, and, returning to the boat, the boatman presented me with two live, red, crusty and curious looking crabs. Whatever I shall do with them I don't know. The people, Chilenos, as children, are very pretty, with their beautiful large black eyes. Three Indian women, wrapped in blankets of fur, came into the store where I was and regarded me with as much curiosity as I did them.

We got under way again early next morning, passing Elizabeth Island and Whale Sound, where we saw any quantity of seals and several whales. Indeed, one great whale came uncomfortably close to us, for there was no telling what mischief she might do us if she happened to take offence at our presence and should try to chastise us with a gentle flip of her tail or to bite off the screw.

We never left the bridge these days, although it was very cold, because there was so much to see. The scenery grew grander steadily, the banks had come to be magnificent palisades now. Great glaciers were to be seen on either side of us, stretching blue and icy from the top of the cliffs down to the water, while far beyond were glittering peaks of snow from which we caught an icy breeze. These peaks of snow were so high that we frequently thought them. white clouds at the first glance. We were three days passing through the Straits. The last night we anchored in Borgia Bay, a lovely little place, uninhabited, with the exception of a single Indian hut.

We presently saw a canoe start from the shore and come for us. There were four Indians in it, and a fire. They carry fire in the bottom of their canoe, always transferring it from boat to hut and hut to boat. As soon as they were within shouting distance, all four set up a chorus of shouts for whisky. They simply remarked "whisky" ensemble. After a few minutes they made a slight variation to tobacco, from that it was an easy gradation to pipe, and one, coming on board, ventured the highly appropriate remark "pantaloon," a remark which won an immediate response from the tender hearted crew in the shape of divers coats, trousers and caps. This was cold weather; I was wearing fur shoes and an ulster, the tops of the mountains all about were covered with snow, and these people were out on the water rowing about, with nothing in the world on them but a piece of skin over the shoulders. They flew into the pantaloons, however, with a haste and skill that bespoke a previous acquaintance with this desirable piece of furniture. Two men came on board, leaving in the canoe two women, one with a tiny pappoose in her lap, the other a young girl, quite pretty and pleasing. Even she did not disdain to "seek the seclusion" which a pair of trousers "grants," and with the addition of a cutaway coat and hat she was transformed into a dude, much to her own glee. The women kept up a constant chatter for "carita" or charity. The woman with the baby, who seemed to boss the whole tribe and do the family talking, requested "carita" for the "pickaninny." The men were given pipes and tobacco. The Chief Engineer offered one of them his segar for a light, which was gravely taken by the Indian, who jammed it into his pipe where he left it and proceeded to smoke it. Having given them food and complied with all their demands but the first—whisky—they were sent away and returned to their hut rejoicing in their good clothes and apparently cherishing the most amiable feelings towards us.

We remained at anchor that night, taking water from a mountain cataract. Sailed again at an early hour, seeing beautiful glaciers all along both sides of us, and mountains that seemed to be solid rock. Reached Cape Pillar at 1 P. M., and made our first acquaintance with the Pacific Ocean, but we didn't find it a bit pacific. We soon lost our appetites again and grew very sad. We took to our berths early, not to reappear for twenty-four hours, and then only momentarily did we gaze into each other's wan and haggard faces, and crept sadly and discouragedly back to our berths again, expressing ourselves feelingly on the subject of high seas. All night long and the next day till night it blew a hurricane, and oh, how sick we were! Even the invalid—so called, I began to think, from his superior health—"caved." He was seasick all night; so was I. Oh, how sick! The only one who bore up bravely was Mrs. H.——, who is always a little seasick in fair weather or foul. She resisted. I could not raise my head without a wild and uncontrollable desire to turn a double somersault out of my bunk, or turn myself wrongside out. I must confess that after fifteen hours of that sort of thing I began to doubt—to hesitate over, as it were—the wisdom of taking another sea voyage to Japan or Honolulu, or anywhere, as I had contemplated doing soon after my arrival at San Francisco. But I wouldn't have missed this storm for anything. I had no idea how serious it was at the time and was too sick and miserable to care. Now I'm mad because I didn't have spirit enough to go out on deck at the risk of being blown away. The wind blew so hard it took the ball off the mast head, and the barometer insisted upon going down to hurricane weather. But I had such sublime faith in the captain and officers and in my everlasting luck, and such beatific ignorance of the difference between a storm and a hurricane, or how much of waves and wind a ship can stand, that I didn't realize my good fortune in coming through it. The sea washed fifty feet of railing off our port side, broke the glass in the pilot house, carried a stateroom away—cleaned it out entirely, swept a cask of water from the forward deck and jammed it in between the mast and the pilot house, and lifted the great iron anchors. Below everything was confusion. Mr. H——'s hat came across the way from his room to mine and stayed. I remained awake all night momentarily expecting his trunk to follow. I should not have been surprised even if he had come himself, the tendency my way was so strong. I had my trunks secured, but every few minutes I would hear some small article, like a soap dish or cologne bottle, which I had fondly believed to be secure, pop out on the floor where it would roll from one side to the other for the rest of the night. It was more than my life was worth to attempt to get out of my berth, not to mention my absolute want of interest in anything. The stewardess was nice, and the captain paid me cheering little calls at intervals, giving me sympathy and consolation and belladonna, and eventually assisting me to the deck, when it was safe, where I revived. Oh, we had a delightful time! During the storm there were no candidates for dinner. The purser said he went into the dining saloon once but did not consider his dinner a success. He said it was tiresome dodging things. The racks, or, as we call them commonly, "fiddles" were on the table; oh yes, but "fiddles" were not equal to the occasion.

The stewardess concluded that the floor of the saloon was the safest place to dine, as it was surrounded by walls; at least she couldn't fall off of it, that is, she thought she couldn't. She took up a position in a corner on the lee side, with her plate in her lap; but she was barely settled comfortably when the meat departed from her plate, the plate followed the meat, and she slid after both; but none of them seemed to be satisfied, for they immediately drifted back again. But the dinner had got the start of the stewardess, so, as she couldn't catch up with it, she concluded to postpone it, as they do picnics, "on account of the weather."

After twenty-four hours the hurricane subsided, though the waves continued to roll mountain high for another day or so, and then we sighted land again, the dim outline of the Andes being visible. On the 26th of March we dropped anchor in the snug little harbor of Valparaiso. Valparaiso looked very pretty from the deck of the Santa Rosa, rising abruptly from the bay in mountains that form, nearly, if not quite, a half circle. It is a picture in yellow and gray tints, the hills being bare of vegetation.

Immediately after landing, one begins to climb. The streets in the city are all steep, some of them laid in stairs. The horse cars, like those I afterward saw in Europe, have an upper deck that quite took my nautical fancy. They have female conductors, not old or bad looking women either. This novelty also met my approval. We took a horseback ride up over the mountains whence we got a beautiful view of the city of Valparaiso, the bay, and the Pacific Ocean.

Climbing up these mountains we encountered a train of heavily laden donkeys. These donkeys exhibited a degree of intelligence that made me wonder how the term "donkey" ever came to be used as an opprobrious epithet for stupid, blundering people. Instead of stupidly lagging behind and getting beaten, or foolishly rebelling against their hard lot, they would hurry on ahead of their driver and so gain a moment's rest, or time for a bite of succulent cactus, before that relentless task master came up. Riding on, we encountered one little beast that had outstripped the train and was lying by the roadside peacefully enjoying a hard earned siesta.

The ladies of Chili do not wear bonnets as a rule. Their street garment is a black shawl, which they wear over the head, giving it a close twist about the throat that converts it into a hood with a long cape. The ladies have beautiful dark eyes. It is supposed they have olive skins beneath the powder. It is said that the ladies of Chili never wash their faces; they merely add a fresh coat of powder. Many of those I saw were very beautiful. We remained at Valparaiso five days taking coal. Meanwhile our magnificent new steamship was on exhibition, numbers of people coming on board to see her. I began to feel as if I were on exhibition too, for these Spanish people did stare in the most distressing manner. The two other passengers went to a hotel during our stay, but I was too truly fond of the sea for that, and as the captain and officers were ashore a large part of the time, I had the ship to myself a good deal and began to take quite a proprietary interest in her. So when the American Consul brought his two pretty daughters on board, I took them off the captain's hands and monopolized them, leaving our handsome young purser quite out in the cold.

Meantime there was the U. S. naval ship Wachusetts in the harbor, and a group of dashing young officers with whom we exchanged compliments. One of them took a party of us to Vina del Mar, the Coney Island of Chili. It was a pretty, quiet, village-like place, with tree-shaded streets. On the cars we passed some native villages that looked like squares of dry goods boxes, so small and low and uniform were the houses, while the streets were the merest passageways.

On the first of April we sailed again, taking with us about thirty Spanish passengers. We three established passengers had our doubts about the sudden advent of a crowd of chattering people, and certainly the confusion of the night we sailed was a violent change from the serenity and quiet we had enjoyed up to this time. The new people were seasick and they occupied all of our favorite corners in the social hall. And the place was crowded with people and babies and things. To Mr. and Mrs. H——, who had occupied the saloon more than I, this was a serious matter. I lived on the upper deck principally. And then, too, the babies cried at night; but I was used to babies and loved them anyway, so that didn't trouble me either. And then it grew hotter every day as we approached the equator. But I liked hot weather. And then there was some painting done on the steamer. But really and truly I *do love* the smell of fresh paint. All these things, however, combined to make the other people miserable, and I wonder now that they didn't crush me with my aggravating fondness for everything they considered so unpleasant. But they didn't! They quarrelled among themselves finally, and I sat at table surrounded by people who were at drawn swords with each other, while they were all on good terms with me. As they wouldn't speak to each other I had to bear the brunt of the general conversation. There was a tiny bit of a boy on board, the son of a captain, who talked learnedly of the "foksle" and nautical things generally in a baby prattle that was very fascinating.

I found French very useful as a medium of communication with the Spanish ladies. Five days of intense heat taught me two Spanish words—"Mucha calor." I don't know how to spell them, but that is the way they sound, and when spoken in accents of suffering and despair the phrase is quite as expressive as our "very hot." It was hot! Red hot! Everything was hot. The saloon was hot, the deck was hot, the passengers were hot; their tempers were likewise.

One day we came across a number of huge turtles floating about in the ocean. A long-legged bird stood on one of these big creatures on one foot in a pensive manner and seemed to be enjoying the sail. He may have taken the turtle for a small island. Some of our sailors went out in a boat and caught several of the turtles while the engines were stopped to "key up." We had turtle soup without any mockery from there on.

Through all the hot weather I accumulated avoirdupois, until the idea that I was traveling for my health became palpably absurd. I caught many incredulous glances in response to my plea of invalidism and was obliged to bolster up my word with sundry and various oaths and much impressive solemnity. The weather cooled gradually as we approached California, and while the other people rejoiced at our speedy arrival at San Francisco, I, with my usual contrariness, objected to arriving anywhere. To tell the truth, I had a relapse into my old shyness about investigating new places. It was all very well talking about taking care of myself when my arrival in a strange city was not to take place for two months. But now that it was imminent, I began to tremble in my boots and wish myself safe at home again. I tried to persuade the captain to turn the ship around and go back, and, failing in that, I asked him if he thought I could rent my stateroom by the year, as I had become attached to the sea. And so when we broke our "eccentric" three days before our arrival, and had to stop the engines for the day, and all the rest of the passengers were in dismay thereat, I rejoiced with my customary wickedness. But alas, all voyages, however pleasant, must have an end. And so, on a breezy cold night, we sailed through the Golden Gate and up the bay to the company's dock, where, after a good deal of hurry and confusion, and many hoarse orders from the bridge, and equally hoarse responses from the wharf, we found ourselves, at midnight, on the 18th of April, at the end of our journey.

CALIFORNIA.

Having made the much dreaded transfer from steamer to hotel successfully, my spirits rose again. At first I missed the motion and noise of the steamer, and felt totally lost in the vastness and solitude of a whole room after having lived fifty-four days in a luxurious but tiny cabin, and heartily wished myself back aboard ship among my friends and at sea. However, I ventured out on a voyage of discovery; my end in view, the Post Office ; my ambition, letters. I walked home, and on my way I encountered a whole troupe of little Chinese children in green and red and purple and red dresses, and curious thick-soled embroidered and tip-tilted shoes, and neatly braided pig-tails.

San Francisco is a city of hills, and very steep hills at that. Indeed some of the streets are so steep, in some parts of the city, that they have been laid in stairs. Glorious hills for coasting these would be if snow and ice were part of a Winter's programme here, which they are not. In San Francisco flowers bloom in the gardens the year round, and strawberries are always in season. The small boys are not to be done out of their coasting entirely, however, and for sleds they substitute carts, consisting of four wheels and a flat board, on which they dash down the hills to the imminent risk of life and limb.

From the bay the city rises in a succession of terraces formed by the cross streets, the blocks of buildings appearing like so many steps to the top. From these terraces the houses overlook each other and the bay, which presents a bright and changeful picture with its ponderous men-of-war, stately ships, fast steamers, hurrying ferryboats, restless, fleet, and self assertive little tugs and white winged sailboats, and many other craft, ever present and active. Across the bay one sees an undulating line of hills, and in the middle distance Angel Island, with the Island of Alcatraz directly in front of it, from whose fortress and earthworks cannons command the bay and often fire salutes to foreign visitors as they come and go.

In San Francisco the sun shines with unvarying brightness every day, from May till October. During this time not a drop of rain falls; the mornings are often ushered in with fog, which lifts by nine o'clock, leaving the day warm and bright until noon, when a strong wind blows in from the sea, bringing with it a good deal of sand from the shore thereof. The gripmen on the cable roads bound toward the beach find it necessary to cover their faces with double veils to protect their eyes from this sand; and the householders wage eternal war with the dust, with the aid of a garden hose, carefully washing windows, doors, steps and walks, every morning regularly, which the wind as regularly recovers with sand and dust. About the first of October it comes on to rain for a day or two, which lays the dust, hardens the roads, and freshens things up generally, followed by the pleasantest, brightest, warmest season of the year, for the winds cease for a time. The next hard blow that comes on is likely to be a norther. It comes in mid December, ushering in what is called the rainy season, which means it will rain hard for two or three days, then rain or shine alternately two or three more days, then rain nights and shine brightly several more days, perhaps clear entirely for a few days, and then commence with a norther again, going through much the same programme, introducing by way of variety a cold spell, perhaps a hail storm and several frosty nights, through all of which the hills about array themselves in the green attire of Spring and the roses bloom with undiscouraged luxuriance in the yards and gardens. By March the weather settles into its customary brightness, only ruffled by an occasional shower, or perhaps a day or two of rain, in April or May. There is hardly a morning in the year when a fire is not desirable, and hardly a day in the year that a fire is necessary all day. A small apartment is sufficiently heated almost any evening in the year by the gas used in lighting it. The houses are knobby with bay windows, and the sunshine is courted in every way possible, it being always warm in the sun and always cold in the shade.

It is really the most absurd climate that ever was in the world. When you go out for a walk you always have to take a fur cloak and a lace parasol. You go along the street with the sun shining, and you think "What a beautiful Summer day it is, almost too warm." You turn a corner, and, whew! an icy January wind strikes you. You shut up your parasol and put on your fur cloak, only to take it off again at the next corner.

It is perfectly ridiculous. Soft coal is burnt here, which fills the air with black smoke and dust. You never know, when you are walking along the street, whether your face is clean or not. Nine times out of ten it has a black smudge on it. The city abounds in big hotels, one of which, the Palace, is the largest in the world.

An old Californian, who had been a shipmate of mine, turned up in a few days and told me of the places in and about San Francisco that were desirable to see. There were the Cliff House, Oakland, Chinatown, some big trees close by, besides those on the way to the Yosemite Valley, and some geysers. I commenced with a moonlight drive to the Cliff House, a most delightful and, I was told, a very improper sort of an excursion; one that no lady will miss if she can possibly help it, or confess to except under bonds of strict secrecy. I confess I failed to discover the slightest impropriety in a very pleasant drive, on a bright night, to the sea, finished by a seat on the public balcony of a hotel with the broad ocean bathed in moonlight below.

The Cliff House surmounts a steep palisade. Below it in the sea are a few large pointed rocks, and on the rocks are scores and scores of seals that keep up an incessant barking and growling and splashing in and out of the water. Being anxious to see the seals and the sea by daylight, I found on inquiry that it was quite the correct thing to go there in the morning, and that there was nothing necessarily immoral about a trip out there alone on a cable car. Riding on the front seat of a cable car is almost as good as riding on the cowcatcher of a locomotive. There is nothing before you to cut off the view; there are no tired, sharp-cornered horses to distract your attention from the scenery. You get the full benefit of the blustering wind as you ride along, and an unbroken vista of the road that is gliding up to you and beneath you rapidly and smoothly. At the terminus of the cable road you take a steam car, which, after winding around among some mammoth sand hills for fifteen minutes, brings you out at last to the beach. The Pacific Ocean lies before you, glistening in the sunlight, or perhaps heaving gray and ominously under a lead-colored sky, while an insignificant black bit of iron, that you know to be an immense steamer with several blocks of staterooms on it and folks enough aboard to make a city, is rolling and tossing in the most lonesome and helpless looking manner. Under these circumstances one is apt to have a picture in one's mind of the unhappy seasick passengers and a vivid realization of the vastness and power of the ocean, while at the same time a sudden admiration is awakened for the skill and ingenuity of man, who builds and manipulates a vessel that is a mere atom tossing on the ocean, and yet goes steadily on its designated course with little reference to wind or waves.

One day I went, about two hours by train, to see some very large trees, which, with the help of some trees not as large, form a grove that is utilized as a picnic ground. One is not impressed at first sight with the immensity of these forest giants because the surrounding trees, while of varying size, are all very large so that the proportions are maintained. At a little distance you seem only to have some good-sized trees before you among some saplings. Coming to examine one of these saplings closely you discover, very much to your surprise, that it is considerably larger than an ordinary tree. Then what you had taken to be an ordinary tree turns out to be a giant. You find an opening at the root of a tree that you had at first set down as pretty large, as trees go, and then you discover you can walk into this tree through the opening without bending. Inside you find that when you stand in the center you can only just touch the walls on either side of you with a cane held at arm's length. Then you say that it is a large tree and no mistake. You are conducted to the largest tree of the grove, which you are still inclined to look at with unappreciative eyes, but after measuring it by yourself and taking a walk around it, which you feel would do for a stroll before breakfast, you admit that it is certainly a very large tree, and walk on through the grove with your sense of measurement thoroughly mystified and an utter loss of confidence in your own eyesight, which causes you to forbear to speak of any tree you see as large or small until you have positive statements of other people regarding its dimensions.

From the grove one strolls naturally down to the river, over which one finds a bridge, composed of single narrow planks laid end to end, and supported on sticks stuck sawhorse fashion in the bed of the river. There is no hand rail, and altogether it is a giddy looking structure. On a tree near by I found posted up "The Rules and Regulations of the Bridge," which I copied:

RULES AND REGULATIONS FOR POVERTY FLAT BRIDGE.

I.—Any lady crossing this bridge faster than a walk will be fined five dollars.

II.—The builders of this bridge will not be liable for any accident that may result from two or more people attempting to cross this bridge at the same time from opposite directions.

III.—Persons found criticising the architecture and construction of this bridge are notified to wade.

IV.—Not more than five people allowed to cross from both ends of this bridge at the same time.

V.—It is positively prohibited for any person to drive more than one horse across this bridge at one time.

VI.—It is strictly forbidden to allow children under six months of age to walk across this bridge unaccompanied by their parents or guardians.

N. B.—Any one wishing to construct a bridge like this can find plans and specifications at Poverty Flat Bar.

I went through the Chinese quarter of San Francisco under the escort of an old Californian, reinforced by an officer in citizen's clothes. I must confess I was not particularly anxious to visit Chinatown, having heard much about the smells and dirt, but as I had been told that it was one of the most interesting features of the city, I went without demur, and was well paid for it, for I was very much interested by what I saw.

Arriving at Chinatown, we found the streets thronged with Chinamen, here and there a Chinese woman, and frequently Chinese children—Chinese children who acted very much like white children, who cried and screamed and scolded and stamped their little feet when they were interfered with. Presently we went to a large building which was literally a human hive, for it was honeycombed with almost air-tight boxes in which whole families lived. Truly, I think the Chinese have found out to a dot the smallest amount of space, food and air necessary to sustain human life. One subterranean apartment contained a very old man and woman and several cats and dogs. This room was too small for us three people to get in all at once, although the woman was on the bed and the man was squeezed in a corner and the animals under foot. So the Californian remained outside the door and peeped in. He expressed himself as entirely satisfied, however, with the whiff he got of the atmosphere from the door he was standing in, it being the only opening into the room. They have no chimneys; their fires are made in a kettle over which they cook, the smoke therefrom making its escape from the room the best way it can, or remaining in it, usually the latter, I fancy. We did not stop to consider the question, but hastened to the comparatively fresh air of the courtyard above. The said courtyard was lined with the fire kettles of the inhabitants of the building.

After this we went out of one dirty, ill-smelling and dark alleyway into another, our guide making ineffectual efforts to light our way with a candle. Our next visit is to an opium den, where we watch the operations of burning and preparing the drug for smoking, and eventually the smoking itself, which takes less time than is spent in getting it ready. The drug must needs be very fascinating, for the place is anything but attractive or savory. There were five of its votaries in this place. One had not begun, or had finished his siesta, for he sat up and eyed us. Two others were on a sort of bed together enjoying a social pipe. Another was sleeping the sleep of the just to all appearance, while the last one, whom we were watching, was taking solid comfort out of his careful preparation of the drug, and three whiffs, and more preparation followed by three more whiffs, which seems to be all the opium smoking amounts to. They lie on hard shelves, with a quilt over them and a block of wood for a pillow, in seemingly cramped attitudes.

We left them in their paradise and went to a high-toned restaurant where Chinese family dinner parties were given. A dinner was in progress at the time, the men dining and the women and children forming an outside circle around them, through which the waiters had to break their way to serve the dinner. The women and children were laughing and chatting merrily. One pretty little Chinese maiden of about eight years was playing "bean porridge hot" in choice Chinese with a

Chinese lady, with evident enthusiasm. A very pretty Chinese lady was in the outer room when we entered, looking in the glass and primping quite in the American style, until, being apparently satisfied with her personal appearance, she returned to the dining room. From here, having inspected a Chinese drum and fiddle and tom-tom, the melodious strains of which had lured us from the street, we went up another alleyway into a room where a really pretty, finely featured Chinese girl was making cigarettes. We were introduced to her, as well as to another really pretty and altogether charming young girl, who laid herself out to be sociable and entertaining, and began by telling me I looked very nice, which compliment I returned with sincerity. I quite fell in love with this charming little lady, and would like to have had time to cultivate her, she seemed so bright and sociable and sweet. From there we went to a josshouse and observed the "gods," ending with Confucius, all surrounded with tinsel and paper flowers, and each being supplied with a bowl of tea in case they got thirsty in the night, and each having a glass with a burning wick floating in oil, suspended above him.

From the josshouse we went to the theatre. To get there we had to go up winding stairs, and around corners, and through intricate passages until finally coming out *via* the common dressing room or green room (which reminded me forcibly of that picture on the drop curtain of a theatre in New York of the Roman Colisseum, with the actors preparing themselves and going out into the arena to act), onto the stage, where we sat at one side and watched the performance. The play was apparently of a dime novel type, that is, "blood and thunder." But it reminded me decidedly of the "Merchant of Venice," being a long-drawn court room scene, the judge therein mercilessly ordering off to dungeons and finally sentencing to immediate death an unfortunate being who turns out to be his own son, a fact which seemed to grieve him very much when his attention was drawn to it. They talked very emphatically and grimace very energetically, and when any action occurs they go through it very deliberately. Men play the female parts, though they have one woman actress among them whom I saw behind the scenes. When they want to make some changes in dress they don't leave the stage; three or four "supes" come and stand in a line in front of them while they go through a very deliberate transformation scene. This being done, the supes retire and the play continues. They paint very heavily and grotesquely, and when wearing false beards fasten the moustache to the lowest edge of the upper lip, which has a very peculiar effect. They sang part of the play, and when they were talking the tom-tom put a period to every paragraph. Chinese music, while it is undoubtedly crude, is not half as bad as it is said to be. So far from being driven away by it I rather liked it; it is rather pleasing; but what else could be expected of an unregenerate creature like me, who has the bad taste to like hand organs? In short, Chinese music is better than no music at all. The floor of the auditorium of the theatre was packed to the doors with Chinamen. A corner of the balcony was reserved for the ladies. All seemed intensely interested in the play, though no applause or laughter or demonstration of any kind came from the audience. We tore ourselves away from the melodious cadences of the mellifluous tom-tom, took a peep at the rooms of a secret society, saw some beautiful carving, and bade good-bye to Chinatown.

With the idea of seeing something of southern California, I re-engaged my old stateroom on the Santa Rosa, which has taken its place in the P. C. S. S. Company's line, and leaves the city every ten days for San Diego and intermediate ports.

It seemed at once homelike and strange to me to get back to the familiar deck and cabin where I had lived through fifty-four happy, changeful days; strange, because the once roomy decks and saloons are now swarming with passengers. The quiet that once reigned is now broken by the hasty chatter of parting friends and the buzz of the donkey engine as it slings aboard heavy cargo, while the porters keep a stream of smaller boxes sliding down a gangway. With a final burst of exertion and profanity, mingled with the clanging of the gong that warns the visitors ashore, the hatches are closed, the gangways removed, and the finest steamer on the coast moves slowly away from the wharf. While the crowd on the decks wave their handkerchiefs to the crowd on the wharf, the vessel swings out into the stream and takes her way around Telegraph Hill, past the Island of Alcatraz, out through the picturesque fort commanded Golden Gate, past the Cliff House and the Seal Rocks, across the harbor bar, where the seasickly inclined conclude to retire, and on down the coast.

We reach Santa Barbara early the following evening. Here I desert the ship and betake myself to the Arlington Hotel, said to be the finest in the West. Santa Barbara is a resort for invalids. It is as much like an eastern aristocratic village as anything they have in California. In a drive about one sees many beautiful residences set in prettily laid out grounds.

Coming unheralded and alone as I do, I am the object of the largest amount of curiosity. Every one asks, "Who is she?" "Where did she come from?" and "What is she doing here?" As the people these questions are put to know almost as much about me as the questioner, there is a good deal of dissatisfaction floating around. An old Californian and sea captain here drove me about to see the place, including a big hog ranch and the Santa Barbara Mission Church. This old building is a relic of the early days when only the Spanish monks had their homes here and made some effort to reclaim the savages from heathenism. The monks still keep the Mission and exhibit some very old and correspondingly vile pictures and relics. I am afraid the clean little pink-and-white piglings, running around in the bright California sunshine in the broad fields, interested me more than the cold, dark, musty church, with its hideous pictures of the judgment day, where the horned devils and imps were hastening the doomed sinners into the yawning pit and sea of fire with pitchforks. Such pictures were well suited to the savages' taste for burning and torturing their enemies, but are too crude and brutal for these times.

Acting under an old resident's advice, I go to the stage office and secure the box seat on the stage which leaves at half past six to-morrow morning for the other side of the mountains that form a background for Santa Barbara.

A STAGE RIDE.

Los Alamos, *May* 28*th*.—Ye gods! Sixty miles on the box seat of a stage coach at one sitting. Eleven hours for one drive was pretty steep—so were the mountains. We flew around winding roads, mountains straight up on one side, valley straight down on the other, curves both abrupt and steep. "Yuba Bill" said there was room for two coaches to pass each other most of the way, but it didn't look so, and I shouldn't care to try it. Oh, what a glorious ride. Four horses and a good hard road, with such a view from the mountain top. On one hand, beyond the long slope to the sea, Santa Barbara and the glancing ocean itself; on the other, such rich, green hillsides and valleys! A day brilliant and beautiful beyond description, thermometer at the exact degree of heat most desirable, and no wind.

The driver introduced me to one of the passengers, whom he graciously permitted to sit beside me part of the way, there being room enough for three where there was easy driving. This passenger whiled the hours of ascent by imparting to me some information about the country. He went back into the coach on the down grade very reluctantly, and even my earnest sympathy failed to console him for the loss of that outside seat. We took up one woman on the way who talked in a shrill satirical voice from the moment she struck the coach until we dropped her at a convenient post office. We changed horses three times, and took a simple but neat and delicious lunch at a place in the mountains. A post office and a hotel of the most primitive kind make a city back in the mountains. A double team is equivalent to a town.

I dazzled the other passengers with my chatter, and then, having dropped them one by one in various stages of bewilderment along the way, my spirits rising with each deposit, I devoted my whole soul to reducing "Yuba Bill" to a chaotic mass of admiration. All my funniest stories and the latest New York slang were trotted out for his amusement. Consequence, the last two hours, the "tiredest" part of the drive flew by like minutes, as we came clattering through the valley, laughing and talking like two old comrades. "Yuba Bill" isn't a "Yuba Bill." He's more of a "Jeff Briggs," pleasant and modest.

This is a lovely country for farming. Think of twenty-nine thousand acres in one farm. Then take breath and think of sixty thousand acres in one farm. Take more breath and think of thirty miles in one farm. And what a beautiful, beautiful, beautiful country!

I'm most dead to-night from the jar and jolting. I think probably to-morrow will finish me. I am the only woman in this hotel. The landlord received me from the box seat and whisked me out of sight of the curious spectators into a tolerably comfortable room. There he left me to remove the dust of travel, returning for me shortly to take me down to supper, where he made himself as entertaining as possible. He took me to the parlor afterwards, and after lighting the lamp and opening the organ, left me to my own devices. I played and sang until I thought I heard the other boarders making preparations for flight, and then went to my room and to bed, entirely satisfied with my day's work, and was soothed to sleep by the singing of Moody and Sankey hymns somewhere in the immediate neighborhood. Was called in the morning by the polite landlord, escorted to breakfast and bestowed carefully on the box seat at half-past six, for my return journey.

May 29th.—Back again sixty miles, one hundred and twenty miles in two days. On the return trip I admired in detail the beauty of the country that I could only take in in general at the first sight. It was raining until ten o'clock ; that is, I called it rain, but the driver said it was only fog. This time we had two men, a woman, a perfect shrew, and three children for inside passengers. The woman divided her time between recounting her sufferings from an injured limb and its treatments in the key of x, and saying "shut up" to her children in the key of y sharp. Arriving at our lunching place, she gave me several sharp, vixenish looks of curiosity, but failing to elicit any responsive interest from me, gave me up. Winding up through the mountains the sun was bright and it was dry again, but we could see the fog drifting through between the mountains into the valley from the sea. Blown by the wind, it very much resembled smoke, and was a pretty sight. All the way along were brilliant wild flowers, and we saw squirrels and lizards constantly.

The driver, who by the way turned out to be "Bill," just Bill, "plain, simple, ordinary Bill," picked flowers for me as they came within his reach, and took his turn at story telling. He came here from Boston, a sailor around the Horn, twenty-nine years ago, has driven stages ever since. He is the first natural man that I have seen since I've been in Santa Barbara County, excepting the retired sea captain who advised this trip. There is so much affectation and effort to be entertaining and funny here. He is good looking, with a contagious laugh. His face would make his fortune on the theatrical stage, with its mixture of expressions of stubborn independence, contempt for snobbery, and natural good humor. The general effect, taken with the twinkle of his eyes, was comic in the extreme. Nearing the end of my return journey, he confided to me how he had "been sold" on me. He had been told a lady had engaged the front seat. Had expressed himself more forcibly than elegantly on the subject of being talked to death by some "old hen." Had driven up to the "Arlington" with the determination to be as dumb as an oyster the whole way. Had been "sort of struck by lightning" when he saw me come out, but hated to give in. I had noticed that he wore a very severe air when the coach drove up, and my spirits fell a trifle. But he thawed out in about ten minutes, and before the end of the journey he voted me the jolliest kind of a girl. The end of the second day he suggested that since I liked staging I should go back again the next day.

As far as slang and humor and originality go, I am very much afraid that California is deteriorating. I never saw such a gossipy, correct, well behaved, precisely speaking lot of people in all my life. Even "Bill" spoke the best Massachusetts English. I, a New Yorker, am striking California "cold" with my originality, independence, and slang. I am a heroine in this house for having taken that trip across the mountains. Am complimented on my daring by the gentlemen. The ladies are shocked into a state of admiration. They say they "would like to take that trip, but it would kill" them. And they don't see how I "dare" travel alone, and they "never saw any one like" me in all their lives. The idea of my taking a sixty mile stage ride for my health is greeted with ridicule and scorn.

YOSEMITE.

I left San Francisco at 3:30 P. M. June 10th, arriving at Stockton by rail the same evening. Part of the way was through water-covered meadows, reminding me of that story called "Afloat in the Forest," for there were trees growing right up out of vast sheets of water. The rest of the way was through freshly plowed ground, covered with rabbits that took flight as we came along. For quite a distance you could see a line of skurrying rabbits, with an occasional one, less nervous than the rest, sitting bolt upright and listening with its heart in its ears; but as we came along, it too would succumb to terror and outleap all the rest in its frantic efforts to escape the imagined pursuer.

I arrived at 8:30 with a carriage load of ladies and babies, one of whom, a mite of a girl of three or four years, informed me, after apologizing for crowding me, that it was "hard" on her to be up so late, as she was accustomed to going to bed at half-past seven; and that she was very much fatigued; and that she had a doll that was not at all fatigued, in her grandmama's trunk.

In the morning a train took me on to Milton, where at about ten o'clock A. M. a stage took me to Copperopolis, where, again, another stage took possession of me and carried me on toward the mountains. As I was the only passenger on these stages, there was no one to dispute possession with me of the high box seat. The latest driver being a strikingly handsome man with an angelic smile, my satisfaction is complete. For a time the road lies over level ground, but later begins to rise at a gentle slope. We pass Table Mountain, which plays an important part in one of Bret Harte's stories, and the Tuolumne and Stanislaus rivers, made familiar by many allusions in the works of that popular author, as well as by Mark Twain.

At "Chinese Camp" we take up a party of four, en route for the Yosemite, who have just made a detour to "Murphy's" to see the big trees of the Tuolumne grove.

Immediately after leaving "Chinese Camp" we begin to ascend the mountains in earnest. The bright morning has departed, and after a slow clouding up and an ominous sprinkle or so it sets in to rain with a will. This raining in the middle of June is in defiance of all the protestations and assurances that have been made by Californians, that "It never rains in California, at least not at this season of the year." I am forced, after a little, to vacate my high and unprotected seat and climb into the interior of the coach, where, with curtains down, I and the four new passengers sit and chat and make every effort to keep ourselves dry and jolly.

It transpires that it has been raining steadily back here for four weeks, and the roads are something terrible ; the horses sink above their knees in the mud at every step, and this, added to the long steep hills, makes our progress slow. The road winds up the mountain, a deep gorge dropping suddenly at our side, down which the Stanislaus river rushes turbulently.

Our stage is drawn by six fine horses, and we change them frequently. We reach "Priest's" just before dark, where we find a warm fire, good supper and comfortable accommodations for the night.

An outcoming party arrives at about nine P. M., half frozen and wholly drenched, whose painfully vivid description of snow and mud blocked roads and cold, rainy weather in the valley, so discourages the party with me that they decide to remain at Priest's until the weather is better.

I woke up at four in the morning ; the coach was to start at five. The rain was coming down in torrents. I was warm and comfortable and sleepy. I said I would not go on to-day. Rubbers I have not, my waterproof reposeth peacefully in the bottom of my trunk in San Francisco, and I am not fond of wading in snow. I listened pensively. The rain stopped abruptly ; then I heard a little bird singing. I said to myself : "It will clear off," bounced out of bed, flung on my clothes, flew out to the coach, ordered a five-story trunk to be taken off of *my* front seat, paid for the drinks, and, having half persuaded driver and landlady and interested bystanders that it really was going to clear off and that the rest of the passengers were doomed to unbounded chagrin at the beautiful day on which they had given up their journey, departed defiant and triumphant. At the next halfway house, however, we took up a party of three pretty girls, their father and little brother, all as determined as I to push on to the valley.

The rain continued to pour down in torrents, but I clung to the box seat in spite of it, for it had a kind of hood which protected me and the driver a little. This driver was very nice and kind, and covered me up to the chin with blankets and canvass coats to keep me dry.

After several long drawn and desperate struggles with mud and the laws of gravitation, oh! glorious climb it of California! we reached the summit twelve thousand feet above the level of the sea. We found the summit covered with, I am afraid to say how many feet of snow. We were now obliged to leave the coach and pile into a big sled. We rode three miles in this coverless sled in a driving sleet, and I had brought my duster and a straw hat. The snow rose in white walls on either side above the heads of the men standing upon the sled. The road was a succession of sharp apexes and deep cuts. After toiling wearisomely to the top of a short hill, getting stuck often and having to be dug out, we would come like lightning down the other side, bringing up with such a thump at the bottom that people and cushions and robes fell violently with one accord off the seats. Fancy, sleighriding on the 12th of June.

When we reached the end of the snow we took to a stage again, and as it was raining hard and I was drenched and numb with cold, I meekly yielded up that choice box seat, I had clung to so far and so tenaciously, and climbed into the very center of the coach, a piece of weakness I shall regret forever and forever, for presently it brightened a little and we began our grand but terrific descent into this beautiful valley, set in the heart of the mountains.

The Yosemite is beyond anything any one can imagine in beauty and grandeur. That is all one can say. We come upon the Valley very suddenly, and the coach drew up for a moment on the ledge of the road at "Inspiration Point" for us to take a general observation.

Thousands of feet below us lies a green and placid valley, eight miles long and three broad, while around it rise abrupt walls of gray granite, varying from one to four thousand feet in height, and surmounted by lofty snow-crowned peaks and domes. The verdure of the valley, richer and greener for the continuous rain, climbs half way up the palisade, and then the gray walls tower naked toward the sky. As we drive briskly down the grade, which is a narrow road winding along the face of the palisade, so narrow indeed that the coach seems perilously near the precipice that yawns at its side, while from the other side rises abruptly the granite wall, the driver points out and names the most prominent features. The graceful spreading waterfall across the valley, with the white mist rising up about it, is the Bridal Veil. And this white, thread-like fall on this side is called "White Horse Tail." The three cone-shaped cliff points rising one above the other are the "Three Sisters," and those delicate, castle-like formations are known as "Cathedral Spires;" while away yonder, looming high above the palisades at the other end of the valley, is the great "Half Dome," a snow-crowned, sharply-cut mass of stone; and before us rises a majestic palisade of granite, rising sheer three thousand feet, the most imposing in the valley, "El Capitan."

Our six horses are taking us at a rattling pace down the narrow, precipitous zigzag ledge. The leaders skirt the very edge of this terrific chasm as we turn sharp corners in a manner that is at once delightful and terrifying. If a leader should miss his footing or a break occur, trivial under other circumstances, we should be hurled over this frightful precipice to a fearful death. Both driver and horses are familiar with their business, however, and nothing occurs to mar the sublimity and grandeur of the scene. We reach the placid green valley through which the Merced River runs, a peaceful stream, while the rain drenched foliage is glittering under the last rays of the sun so lately emerged from the storm clouds.

With the morning dawns the first fair day that has been seen in the valley for four straight weeks, and having rather enjoyed my severe experiences with mud and snow, on the whole, I am very glad I hastened on. I go to see the sun rise on Mirror Lake, in fact several sunrises, for as fast as the sun climbs above the palisades one has only to move closer to the shadowing wall to hide it again from sight, and then wait again for it to rise.

The reflection in the lake, of hill and sun and sky and forest, is very perfect and clear. A venerable Indian brings a cornet and executes some fearful notes that are echoed with excruciating fidelity to the original agony, and we return to the hotel to prepare for another excursion.

A PERILOUS CLIMB.

We find a train of donkeys and small climbing horses waiting saddled for the party, for, once in the valley, I go with the troops of people that are going here and there. A guide is engaged to lead a detachment of tourists hither and thither, each one pays his two or three dollars and joins the excursion. If there are ladies alone the guide places them in line next himself where he can lead their horses if they are timid or goad the animals if they prove lazy.

The party starts off with a gallop to the foot of the cliffs, and then climbs a winding horseback trail, a ledge varying from two to three feet in width. The view of the valley is exquisite. As you go up you hardly dare look back or down, but if you do have the courage, the beauty of the scene is something never to be forgotten. I found it lovely beyond description, though serious doubts about ever getting down again, as we climb higher and higher up this dizzy trail, would obtrude themselves on my mind.

Half way up a halt was called, and all dismounted to look from an overhanging ledge on the scene below, while the horses were ungirthed and allowed a breathing spell. When we resumed our saddles we continued upward in steeper, narrower, and shorter zigzags, until we reached the top, where we got a good lunch, warmed ourselves at a good fire, and climbed a path that led out to the jutting cliff known as Glacier Point, and, after a brief rest on a veranda that overlooked a part of the valley commanding a fine view of the Vernal Falls, got into our saddles again and commenced the descent.

Once more we look from giddy heights on the beautiful scene; once more we note the points of interest in this exquisite picture, Cloud's Rest, Half Dome, Cathedral Spires and El Capitan rise in lofty majesty before our eyes true to their names in stature and in form. Two seasons are before one's eyes at the valley. Winter reigns cold and bleak on the frowning, snow-clad granite, while below the luxuriant foliage is bathed in the sunshine of Summer.

Going up is a dizzy operation, but coming down—oh, my! What delicious sensations run down your spine when your horse ambles calmly down an abrupt declivity to the edge of a precipice and gazes pensively, perhaps admiringly, down a few thousand feet into the valley below; or when he trots contentedly along on the outside edge of the ledge and you hear the gravel from his hoofs clattering over the edge and down, until the clinking sound is lost in the distance. The horses are very gentle and sure-footed and decline to be guided; the safest way is not to try to guide them. They walk as near the edge as possible, to frighten you, I think, into getting off and walking, which many people do. I can outmule any horse I ever saw, so I declined to get down. I went up to have my blood run cold, and it did. But I couldn't help being amused at the other people. There was a woman who was frightened to death because her horse kept so close to the edge. She exclaimed and fretted all the time in this vein :

"Oh, I am so frightened! Oh, my horse is turning his tail around to the edge. Oh, dear, how shall I ever get down again? Guide, did you ever see any one so foolish as I am? I make so much fuss I know. I am very foolish."

"Oh no, ma'am, you don't make much fuss. You're only a little nervous."

"I know I make a great deal of fuss, but I can't help it. Oh, guide, he's turning his tail around!"

There was one man with terra cotta hair and mustache and gloves, on a while mule. The horses that carried fat women up groaned all the way. Mine sighed plaintively. On the way it snowed and rained and shone brightly by turns. Still, I could spend several weeks in this valley, or all Summer, with a great deal of pleasure.

With many a backward glance on the valley and its picturesque walls, we climb the winding road once more, and plunging at once into the forest, resume our struggle with mud and gravitation.

Up to Priest's the roads were something frightful. Many times it seemed as if we were surely going over, the ruts were so deep. The horses were in mud half way above their knees. We reached Priest's again after a pleasant day's journey only getting stuck once in the snow and walking a little way.

On the return we left Chinese Camp in a carriage at four o'clock in the morning with the overflow from the stage which was ambitiously trying to carry the consolidated passengers of three stages. At Copperopolis we had breakfast, after which we, with the passengers of still another stage, were all crammed into and onto one stage. Eleven on top and nine inside. My driver looked after me nicely; made me a nice bed of mail bags in the center on top, which was the easiest place on the coach. I reclined comfortably at my ease and enjoyed the agony and efforts to hang on of the people who had seats, for though this was the best part of the road it was jolty enough. We finally reached Milton in various stages of demoralization, where I took the train; stopping at Stockton for lunch, in brilliant spirits, well pleased with my trip, as I ought to be, for I was taken excellent care of from one end of the journey to the other by agents, hotel keepers, fellow travelers and drivers, as it seems to be my fate to be wherever I go. And so ends my delightful trip to the Valley of the Yosemite.

THE GEYSERS.

There is a short ride on the railroad from San Francisco and then a stage ride to reach the Geysers. Instead of the stage we took a team and drove over just ahead of the stage, a three hours' drive. The road is very narrow and winds in and out of the mountains, turning the sharpest corners on the edge of the steepest precipices. These corners are so sharp and so frequent that you come "slap" onto another team before you can see it, and you usually meet a team just in the very worst place for turning out on the road. This we managed to do twice that day; once in going and once in coming back. We were driving along as nicely as could be when we whipped around the corner and there was the return stage. Well, we paused and considered, and there was an eloquent flow of language for five or ten minutes; then we got out and "clum" a perpendicular bank, while the carriage was hauled and squeezed around the outside edge of that stage; then we drove on and left the two opposing stages to get around each other and exhort their horses and "cuss" the road and the man who made it and his family at large.

Reaching the Geyser Hotel, we shed our dusters and overcoats and start for a walk among the Geysers, stopping at the gate to select a stick for a cane. And you need a cane, for after going down a little hill you begin to climb, and from that on you climb up and climb down steep declivities, rocky paths, steps of board and earth and rock, all equally steep, difficult, slippery and dangerous; for they lead you in and around and among holes in the ground where a hot steam comes hissing out, and you get a number of involuntary steam and sulphur baths before your walk is finished. The ground is mostly sulphur in spots, and soda in other spots, and I don't know what else, but it's white and yellow and green, and all the while you hear the steam hissing out of the holes and hear the water bubbling below; and here and there is a large open hole with water in it boiling away in the most violent manner, and scattering drops of boiling water out and making a great fuss about it all the time. Sometimes the path leads you across an open well of boiling water, on a plank, and one part of your walk takes you right through the hot sulphurous steam that is escaping with a great deal of fuss from the bank at one side of the narrow ledge, while on the other side you can look down a steep declivity into the boiling brook below. It is hot about there and reminds one somewhat forcibly of the "seething gates of hell," or words to that effect. You feel very much as if you were walking on the lid of a boiling cauldron, and that is just about what you are doing. In many places the ground, or rather the sulphur and soda and ashes, you walk on is hot, sometimes wet with boiling water. After this walk one is inclined to sit down and rest and reflect on the peculiarities of this world we live on.

Returning to the hotel, we dine and rest a little, and afterwards interview a monkey who is chained in a small inclosure. A gentleman held out his hand and the monkey shook hands with him; then I held out my hand and his monkeyship took a finger in both paws and proceeded to bite it, and seemed to be quite offended, chattering at me resentfully, when I snatched it away. Fortunately I had my glove on, so the teeth did not penetrate the skin, but the little animal left a mark which is sore and swollen for a day or two.

We start back without waiting for the afternoon stage, as they tell us it will be an hour or more before it gets in, but we meet the incoming stage in the very first and worst bad place on the road. We try to squeeze past and get jammed together, and plenty of objurgation follows; everybody but myself gets out and considers the situation. Remarks are made about what ought to have been done; and the character and antecedents of the man who told us the stage wouldn't be along for an hour are discussed with much freedom and emphasis; and finally by lifting the carriage a little and driving up a step and studying the situation, and lifting and driving up another step, and unfastening this and that, and fastening up again, and bringing much science and energy, and all the "cuss words" in the language to bear, we squeeze by and all is plain sailing for the rest of the trip. These mountain roads are very pretty and interesting and exciting, and after them ordinary driving seems rather tame.

THE SANDWICH ISLANDS.

It seemed very strange to be setting out upon so long a voyage without a friend to see me off, but so it happened. My former shipmates were all absent from the city, and my stays in San Francisco had been so intermittent and fleeting, and so occupied by preparations for further excursions, that I had not got much acquainted with any of the residents. I was rather glad, on the whole, that it was so, for now I was forced to attend to the details of tickets and embarking myself, and to find out how I should really get on quite alone. I found this easier, and pleasanter, perhaps, than it would be in New York or Boston, for although San Francisco is an active and enterprising city, its business men are not yet too overwhelmingly busy to be very polite to a lady, or to make some extra effort to be helpful to her. The clerk in the O. S. S. Co.'s office took me to look at the vessel I wished to sail in, showed me my proposed stateroom, bespoke for me every attention from the stewards, and was generally very kind.

At last, on July 15th, I stood on the deck of the Alameda, as she moved out into the stream, alone and an utter stranger to the many people around me, each of whom had been surrounded by friends who were now waving encouraging handkerchiefs to them from the dock. Amid all the hubbub attendant on a departing steamer, the solitude of a desert reigned in my heart. I placed my camp chair in a sheltered corner by the wheel house, and looked at the people walking in couples up and down the deck and at the sights of the bay, now grown somewhat familiar to me. I kept my seat on deck until long after we had passed out of the Golden Gate and the vessel was heaving in a way that threatened seasickness to some of us.

I was placed at the purser's table, and was introduced by that agreeable officer to the people sitting next me, and was sufficiently amused by the chatter of those around me. As I became acquainted I found the captain dignifiedly jovial, the purser amiably talkative, and the chief engineer genial and handsome.

The Alameda is a very well arranged vessel. The dining saloon is large and well lighted, the staterooms very comfortable and commodious, and the decks broad. The dining saloon and social hall are just amidships, the engine away aft, while the staterooms are forward of the saloons, thus being free from smell or noise of machinery.

After a day of seasickness people began to come out of their cabins and be sociable. I think the sea rather arouses one's social qualities. I found another young lady on board, who, like me, was going alone to Honolulu, and we presently fraternized. We spent most of the time on deck, for the sea was smooth and the weather fine and growing warmer daily.

My old friends, the flying fish, were again to be seen skimming from beneath the vessel's bow as we sped on, and schools of porpoises floundered and flopped out of the water in their haste to get along, while whales spouted in the distance, showing now and then a glistening acre or so of back, as they rose to the surface.

Nothing can be lazier or more care free than this life at mid-ocean. No wonder that sea voyages are recommended to restore health to invalids from overworked brains. The fresh air, the sunshine, and the enforced indolence are at once restful and stimulating. At night the foam, cresting the waves as we cut swiftly through the water, turned to a bright phosphorescent glow. And we were hushed to sleep by the sound of the water washing the steamer's sides, a soft breeze humming through the latticed door, and a distant muffled thud of machinery. The officer's regular tread on the bridge and the half hourly ringing of the bells chime well with the other sounds, and withal one sleeps like a top and wakes in the morning light of heart and hungry.

When one gets tired of doing nothing and has no soul for the beauty and grandeur of the great ocean, one can turn to the ship's library, make up a card party or listen to the musicians at the piano, of which there are usually plenty, good and bad.

It grows warmer daily until, on the seventh morning at sea, we wake to swelter in a sultry heat, and to see a long low strip of land fringed by cocoanut trees with fluffy tops, all bent in one direction by the vociferous "trader"; a sharply cut peak rising in the background; and presently we are made fast at the wharf of Honolulu.

I bade good-bye to my compagnons de voyage, surrendered my trunks and keys to an expressman, was confided to a carriage by the ship's doctor, and so reached the hotel without any of the anticipated difficulties. I went to bed and to sleep, from which I was awakened from time to time by the arrival of my trunks, next my keys, and finally the housemaid, solicitous for my welfare; then I was permitted to sleep, which I did in a most emphatic manner till it was time to dress for dinner. Went to bed at half-past nine, waking up this morning at seven, after a solid night's sleep, as sleepy as ever. I suppose it is the effect of the climate. The weather is hot but there is a strong breeze blowing constantly, which keeps it comfortable. The hotel is situated pleasantly in a kind of grove of banana, orange, mango, and other varieties of trees. My window, or rather door, opens on a porch that faces the mountains, 6,000 feet high. Beside the front porch there are two banana trees, each with an immense bunch of green bananas growing on it. Only one bunch of bananas grows on a tree, and then they cut it and another grows.

Carriage hire here is ten cents by law; drivers ask from a dollar and a half to four or five dollars, and you pay twenty-five cents. It is said that if you offer them the legal ten cents, they return it with the considerate suggestion that you might need it. From the observatory on the top of the hotel you get a fine view of the city, the surrounding country, the sea and the king's palace, which is close by.

I had fancied that in going to the Sandwich Islands, I was going to an uncivilized, heathen place. Imagine then my disappointment at finding an ordinary looking city, with pavements and electric lights and telephones all over the place. Actually, I have not since found a place where the telephone was in such general use. People telephoned invitations to visit or ride, and telephoned when they were ready, when about to start; and when they arrived, they telephoned home to that effect, and so on.

The natives are very dark, and of a large, fleshy build. The women are even more inclined to fleshiness than the men, and magnificent creatures they look, in their flowing "holokus."

The "holoku" is the native dress for the women, and is in point of fact a simple Mother Hubbard gown. Usually this gown forms the entire toilet, but as it completely envelopes them from head to heels, and the climate is warm, it is both proper in appearance and comfortable in effect, as well as becoming. The natives are a very genial, happy, affectionate people. I see boys of all ages conducting themselves toward each other in the affectionate manner peculiar to school girls, and in driving one meets along the street occasionally a man and a woman walking with arms about each other, school-girl fashion. Perhaps the most significant commentary on the peaceful and affectionate character of the Hawaiians is the common greeting that is used in place of our "How do you do?"

In meeting and in parting, or in passing on the street these people say "Aloha," which means simply "love" or "love to you."

I've seen some real live cannibals walking along the street, that eat folks now, when they get a chance. They are brought here from some other island to work. Not long ago they got into a quarrel among themselves, and one man getting killed, they ate him rather than waste him. So it is said.

There are plenty of mosquitos at Honolulu, and the cockroaches are as large as mice, and disposed to lunch, I am informed, on the hard, protective surfaces of the human pedal extremities.

This climate is probably the loveliest in the world. It is pretty hot for two or three hours in the morning, but not red-hot like New York; at noon a breeze springs up and blows quite violently until seven or eight next morning, making it just pleasantly cool. So boisterously does the wind blow, rattling windows, slamming doors, swaying trees, and howling and whistling around corners, that it makes one think of March and imagine it must be cold outside in that blustering gale, which is, however, not the case. If you open a window or door it will sweep through and slam and blow everything about, but for all its howling and bluster, it is a warm wind that fans your cheek so rudely, and has but recently left the region of the equator. It rains, off and on, all day in a mild drizzle, but the sun shines all the time and no one notices the rain. You can see it raining through the sun on the mountains most of the time, with sometimes five or six rainbows in full bloom.

It is not so easy to travel alone as one might think, in fact, it is nearly, if not quite, impossible, for there are so many other travelers that you are necessarily in company most of the time, and then fellow passengers, ship's officers, hotel managers vie with each other in giving all the information and aid possible to a lady. I am everywhere assisted by kindly people, in spite of all resolutions on my part to act for myself and bother no one. Perhaps the pleasantest part of it all is in feeling that this kindness is not thought a bother by these pleasant people, but is done with all the evidences of sincere pleasure in extending such politeness to a fellow creature. My experience here is only a sample of the kindness very generally shown me.

Having slept through nearly forty-eight hours, I am finally seized with an energetic fit and array myself preparatory to starting out on a voyage of discovery. First, I consult the gentlemanly clerk. Does he know where the O. S. S. Co.'s office is? And if so, will he kindly point out the direction for me to start out? He knows, and with my permission he will walk that way with me. I say "That will be very nice if I am not interfering with business." He: "On the contrary," etc. It is very hot, had we not better ride? No, I should be sorry to have him sustain a sunstroke on my account, but I have been asleep for two days and am in search of exercise, so we walk to the O. S. S. Co.'s office. I secure my stateroom and am promised impressively by the gentlemanly clerk in charge that if it is a possible thing I shall have my stateroom all to myself. He will hold this stateroom for me and seize any opportunity to make a change for the better. I need not pay until they have finally done the best they can for me. We depart happy and triumphant.

Now that I am thoroughly rested, my friends, the officers of the Alameda and the kind people to whom I have letters of introduction came forward, and in a series of drives, dinners and visits contrive to show me the place and make my stay a very pleasant one. We drive about the city into a lovely valley, where I see rice and taro growing, which latter is the principal of the native dish poi, the "night-blooming cereus" and other plants, and get an idea of the country lying back in the island;

and then to Waikiki, the Coney Island of Honolulu, seeing
banana orchards on the way and cocoanut trees when we get
there; and then we drive to the race track where we saw all the
world of Honolulu; and then to a baseball match.

Another drive several miles back in the island takes me up a
mountain to a narrow pass, where the wind draws through
with such force it is almost impossible to make any headway
against it. The gap in the mountains winds a little, and after
rounding a certain difficult point, where the wind blows one
back as fast as one walks, one can stand with back to the mountain wall and look across a chasm that descends from your feet
and is guarded by an iron rail, quite across the island to the
sea on the other side. The return is comparatively easy, as the
wind carries you around the corner and half way down the
hill in the twinkling of an eye. It lifted me fairly off my feet
and I came down on the rocks as lightly as a feather all in a
heap, a step or so ahead of the wind.

I was taken by the doctor who has charge of it, to see the
Leper Hospital here. He had been ordered to pick out the
worst cases among the lepers to be sent to Molaikai, another
island, where all the hopeless cases are sent as the hospital becomes overcrowded. A dreadful place, they say, aside from
the misery of being parted from friends. He was in despair
over this order, as he could not make up his mind to consign
any of his patients to that terrible place. His humane treatment and sympathy for his patients was attested by their attitude toward him. The children, girls of eight and nine years,
were aching for a romp with him, running out of reach with
screams of laughter when he made passes at them. The older
people, smiling and pleasant, say some welcoming word. With
those who were just grieving over some recent development in
the progress of their disease he had a pleasant, hearty, reassuring
air and was very apt to leave them laughing. One woman
gave him a piece of bone an inch long which had fallen out of
the end of her finger. She was inclined to weep over it; he wrapped it carefully in a piece of paper and told her it was a love-gift, and left her smiling and half consoled.

I believe much has been said against the arrangements of the
hospital. Personally, I should not like to live there. But to
these natives who live in huts and hovels and are accustomed

to dirt, confinement in narrow quarters, hardship and primitive life, the hospital must appear palatial. It contains no pier glasses or statuary or Eastlake furniture, to be sure, or any of the luxuries civilization has made a necessity to many people, but it is nevertheless as comfortable a place for them as any place would be with their affliction and the separation from their friends. They have comfortable beds, with plenty of bed clothes, of which they don't need many in that climate, and their customary diet of poi and fish. Their rooms are open and airy, the helpless ones lie quiet, while those who are not disabled run around in the grounds and help take care of the rest. All are overlooked by the Sisters of Mercy in charge, to whom great credit is due for the patience and self sacrifice exhibited in devoting themselves to such a life. I went there quite an unexpected visitor and was received and taken through without delay or excuse, so am satisfied I saw the hospital as it is. The doctor seems to be thought much of by the natives. All the children along the streets saluting him as we passed and apparently anxious to have a romp with him.

A native band plays once a week in the public square at Honolulu, and once a week in the grounds in front of the hotel, and on the wharf whenever a steamer is departing. It is a large band with all the modern instruments, and they play all of our best music, classic, operatic and popular, and their execution is exceedingly good. The native music is very beautiful and has a character of its own which is most pleasing. While performing native airs, the band often sing a bar or so with great effect, their voices being very soft and sympathetic. One of the peculiarities of the native music was the commencing of a phrase with a long note and finishing with a short one.

On the day of sailing all Honolulu came down to the wharf to see the steamer off. And I, ten days before, an entire stranger in the city, had a circle of friends to bid me goodbye and bring me flowers and fruit.

I was introduced to King Kalakua, who, with Princess Likelike, was on board seeing off friends. When I was introduced to him I began to chatter like the blackbirds "when the pie was opened." I ran on with my usual audacious frivolity, when suddenly it occurred to me that I had not heard him speak to any one of the many people he had been introduced to.

I was horrified and silent, therefore, for an instant which gave him time to recover from the dazed condition my audacity had thrown him into, and he condescended to talk to me a little, until I, fearful of committing some worse breach of etiquette, detached myself. I watched him afterwards and saw he merely shook hands with the people to whom he was introduced. He is more like an Englishman than a native in his dress, gravity and personal appearance, apart from color. As for the Princess Likelike, she is a Parisienne, barring only skin, in black jersey and flounced silk skirt, walking length, small neat bonnet with peacock-blue wing around it, booted and gloved and carrying parasol and wearing stays, presenting just such an appearance as ladies generally do on Broadway.

At last we sailed, and I was once more at my old place, as far forward on deck as one can get and stay on board, and threatened with general and complete disintegration by the wind, which was dead ahead. Various gentlemen have tried to sit it out with me in that favorite spot, but they are invariably driven back to the cabin by the wind and the peculiar lunging motion in that part of the ship, and I alone remain, the admiration of sailors and passengers. But pride, they say, must have a fall, and mine was about to take a little "tumble." The sea was high and the ports, therefore, all closed; my little stateroom was consequently insufferably hot; I could not eat in the warm close saloon. I fled to the deck, where I "ate" a good supper, and after a jolly evening in the wind and spray, which was washing the deck fore and aft, I went down to my oven at half-past ten with much reluctance. Was not sick as I expected to be, but could not sleep in that stifling atmosphere. The moment it was light I struggled into my clothes and flew, with a seasick gasp, on deck, where I remained all day unkempt and damp. I didn't venture down into the dining saloon again till night, and then I beat a hasty retreat. Heat and motion combined were too much for me. I was disgusted and ashamed of myself, after sailing from New York to San Francisco and never missing a meal for anything short of a hurricane, to be demoralized by a miserable little sea like this! They call it heavy weather on this side, but there is a big difference between Pacific heavy weather and Atlantic heavy weather. I had one comfort in my ignominious qualm. The captain was seasick for half an hour and the first mate was seasick all night, and the doctor isn't well yet. If these old tars "caved in" to the malady in their well ventilated upper deck staterooms, I don't think I need grieve over my collapse in an oven.

I was the only woman on deck the third day, and received many compliments for my seamanship, for I was as "chipper" as usual. One gentleman said he watched me while I was talking to two gentlemen together, and kept count, and he said I talked forty-five minutes out of an hour, and the two gentlemen only fifteen minutes between them.

This hot stateroom business is a foretaste of what I shall encounter, I suppose, on my way around the world, but I'm a pretty fair sailor, even under such adverse circumstances, and am willing to take my chances. The fourth day being pleasant, the seasick ones slowly emerged from their dens; few remain on deck, however, and all are very much demoralized.

Among the passengers was a woman with six children ranging from an infant up. All six were on deck that first day, spread out in a row on the benches, in various stages of seasickness. The last to come out was a little girl of four years, and instead of taking the position at the end of the line she wedged herself in between two of her prostrate brothers, with a "misery-loves-company" air that was pathetic to see.

There is a learned judge on board who is trying to sum me up and finds me the hardest case he ever tried, combining frivolity and evident enjoyment of life with a readiness for death, shipwreck or disaster; frank sociability, and open enjoyment of "taffy," with, at the same time, an impervious reserve.

Really, I don't know what the rest of the passengers would have done for amusement without me. I talked one day from breakfast to lunch with the Judge, and he was taken with gout and didn't put in an appearance until the next day, and of course they made the most of that. The Judge was very interesting. When he was not cross-examining me, he repeated yards of Shakespeare and Byron, or gave way to the expression of his own odd sort of cynicism. I lent him "The Rubaiyat of Omar Khayyam," which was just in his way, and he liked it very much.

I find an enjoyment in traveling alone that I should not get if I had any one to take care of me. My peculiarity is in getting fun out of things that everybody else considers the nuisances of traveling, like going through the Custom House and Health Officers' hands, attending to my own baggage transfers, buying my tickets, and selecting my staterooms and bargaining with hack drivers.

Really, it is curious what friends I make. Friends who are anxious to insure my future comfort and safety. One might think that with my frankness and frivolity I should sometimes be misunderstood, but I never seem to be. I get all kinds of advice and offers of assistance in case of need, and assurances of friendship and interest in my success. And in being handed over from one captain to another, I get first class recommendation, like this: "First rate sailor, always jolly, takes things as they come, and never growls." I am very proud of my friends on this ship, because I came on board without acquaintance or recommendation.

I have made the acquaintance of a very singular man—a man who adores the wife he has lived with, without break or separation for twelve years. All this in direct defiance of the laws of science, philosophy, and human nature in general and particular. He regretted the head winds that delayed us, he regretted the loss of an hour of the precious time he was to spend with his wife. All this after twelve years of steady married life. I am amazed! And more than that, he was not ashamed of it. Will wonders never cease? Strange as it may seem, I have always believed, and all the arguments and experiences of a lifetime have failed to entirely annihilate my theory, that somewhere in the world such a man existed, and here I have really found him. Now I am satisfied. I feel that I have not lived in vain. I can now return to New York happy in the consciousness of the existence of one loyal husband whose love has stood the test of marriage and of years.

Arrived at San Francisco we were detained off quarantine an hour, and just escaped being quarantined ten days on a supposed case of leprosy on board. I quite enjoy going through the Custom House. Think I am going to have lots of fun that way in Europe. I shan't mind being quarantined, either, if I ever come to that. I'm always sorry to leave the ship.

HO, FOR JAPAN!

ON BOARD STEAMER CITY OF TOKIO, *Sept.* 13*th*, 1884.—Once more at sea! And how I like it! But oh, what a rush and tug it was to get off. I was up this morning at six, was seasick at eight, heartsick at nine, and a complete wreck of despair at ten. At eleven I had got my spirits up again and tackled those trunks, and got them full and half shut in short metre. I engaged a girl to come and sit on one of them while I took breath, and then I closed them and locked them. Among my other well known talents I possess a genius for closing trunks. No one can beat me at it. Sometimes if I don't feel energetic I get a boy to try it, but it usually ends in my closing it while he looks on and is immensely instructed. At twelve I sat down to recover my little traveling cushion with the most brilliant red satin to be had, then I strap it up with my rug and shawl, put on my hat and wrap, seize my ulster, grab my parasol, pick up my satchel, reach for my shawl strap, cast a wistful eye on my two chairs and two trunks, and lo! I am ready to depart. The hackman having successfully manipulated my trunks and chairs, the carriage waits, and I—after a friendly farewell to the natives of the hotel—am stowed with my several belongings, within it, and off I go.

I reach the Tokio in good time, and the agent of the Pacific Mail S. S. Co. introduces me to the Steward and invokes the kind attentions of the servitors generally in my behalf; then presents me to the Captain and is otherwise kind and attentive. I have received a Godspeed by telegram that almost reduces me to tears. Presently we move slowly away from the wharf and down the bay past the wharves of the Alameda and the Santa Rosa, out through the Golden Gate to the sea, where we take aim with our bowsprit at Japan, and go it.

A former traveling companion came to see me off. With a frivolous desire to make a good impression on my future fellow passengers, I had put on a new dress to go aboard ship in, a dress that proves to have a particularly fractious pocket. My friend seeing me disburse sums of money at intervals for fees and telegrams, has ample opportunity to note the difficulty I have in getting anything out of that pocket. "That's just like a woman," he says laughing over one of my prolonged struggles with it, "never can get anything out of her pocket." When all the good-byes have been said and we are moving away from the wharf and people are waving handkerchiefs, my friend gets out his to wave at me. I have put my hand into my pocket and searched around but I can't get at my handkerchief, it is way at the bottom of the pocket with sundry keys, cardcases, pocketbooks, pencils, knives and goodness knows what, on top of it, all wedged in so tightly I can't get near the desired article. Still I make an effort, twisting and groping around in the pocket while the steamer is moving off and the friend on the dock, divining my intentions and difficulty, is convulsed. He alternately waves his handkerchief and doubles himself up with laughter at my expense. I divide my time between laughing immoderately, stamping my feet with impatience, and wrestling with the pocket, but all is of no avail, the handkerchief rests peacefully at the bottom of it until we are out of sight of the dock. It has served a purpose, however, for I have left my native shores in a gale of laughter instead of a shower of tears.

On leaving the docks the Chinese steerage passengers, of which there were a large number, threw overboard a quantity of bright colored bits of paper, prayers to their gods for good fortune and safety. It was a variegated shower; a very unique and pretty sight.

Our Commander is a Commodore; I sit at his left, and I have the very nicest young man on board ship at my left. He is a naval officer, the paymaster of an American naval ship on the China station, and is going out to his vessel. The passengers on board are an Englishman, a genial bore, going to remain in Japan, I think; a learned German gentleman, going over my route; a diplomat going to take his place in the English legation at China, and the handsome American paymaster. Of course, with true patriotism, I like the latter best. These gentlemen provide me with extra cushions and rugs till "I can't rest." There are also two other ladies, traveling alone together, who are young and good looking, and two more ladies with their husbands.

Seated on deck with a group of intelligent, cultivated, traveled gentlemen, representing several nationalities, making a semicircle around me, discussing literature, governments, countries and peoples, and varying from the frivolous to the scientific, I am enjoying myself as much as ever. We have quite a charming circle. The young Diplomat proves to be a very nice fellow indeed. I very much like his views of our country, which are at once critical and friendly, quite thoughtful and entirely sincere. The Commodore is a man of intelligence and ability, and is pleasant, but is very despotic, narrow and cynical in his views. It is curious to notice how every one accepts his statements without demur. Nobody contradicts the Commodore. He is a very strict disciplinarian, and all the machinery of the ship's service runs like clockwork. The entire crew and saloon service is made up of Chinese. At one stroke of the bell the waiters all stand behind the guests at table, at another they turn, at another they go to a side table and take up their especial dish, at another they return to their places and wait for another stroke to place them on the table. The premature placing of a dish brings a severe rebuke from the Commodore.

Who says a sea voyage is stupid? I am kept occupied all the time. I am engaged to walk with one, to talk with another, to play chess with another, to play whist with several more, quoits with others, and all unite in kindly attentions to me. I am singularly successful in playing games. In all games my side wins. I played quoits for the first time. This is a dangerous game for people standing behind me, as that is where my quoits eventually fetch up. We have been having delightful games of whist. I prove to be a fair player and a singularly lucky one. I have changed partners until I have got the poorest player and the other two are very scientific players, but my luck is invincible. We have an English missionary minister on board, and my opinion of missionaries has risen to a very flattering standard on the observance of this reverend gentleman's interest in his wife and three children. It affords me the sincerest pleasure to see him put his baby to sleep, carry it around and nurse it most of the time. He plays whist too.

Everybody is surprised, amused at, and interested in my voyage. They tell me that they never saw or heard of such a thing before as a young woman of my quiet inoffensive type starting out on such an enterprise; at the same time they say I shall find no difficulty about it, and encourage me in every way. I am gathering all the information possible from my fellow-travelers as regards Europe, as well as Japan, and India. After a week at sea one feels very much at home on board ship. We play games, read, and lounge, regardless of motion or surroundings, and feel as safe rolling in the center of this vast bowl of sea as we should at home in our own parlors—at least, I do.

September 26th.—According to custom, we have dropped a day in midocean. We went calmly to sleep last night, Wednesday, and woke up this morning to find it Friday instead of Thursday. I shouldn't have minded the loss of one day if it hadn't happened to be "duff" day. I feel that I have been swindled out of my duff. Social amenities being fairly established, we sing in the evenings before and after whist, the singing being of the most primitive kind. I have a fair standing as a *prima donna.* A young naval officer's wife plays nicely. We dance, too, and when it comes to waltzing I have my hands full. I am aware that the egotism displayed in my letters is becoming something terrific, but I am afraid you will have to bear it until I reach Japan and can write about the country. This voyage is supposed to be the safest in the world. It is out of the line of other steamers so no collision is possible. On the other hand, no help is near in case of accident by fire or breaking machinery. We haven't seen a sail since we left San Francisco and don't expect to see any before reaching Yokohama. The fallacy about never taking cold at sea is exploded; several of us have dreadful colds. I am enjoying mine now.

September 29th.—Well, we've had a gale. It came on to blow three days ago. It rained too, and we were driven inside by the rain and the frequent arrival of waves on deck. The ship rolled fearfully, causing people standing to take seats with more haste than grace, and in any place convenient, regardless of proprieties or consequences. The prevailing mode of descending the stairs was to pitch headlong halfway down, make a carom on the banisters, and shoot off at right angles the other halfway. People who left their cabin ports open were rather dissatisfied on going to their staterooms at finding their personal effects floating about in a heavy sea that had come in. All ports being closed, it was very close below, so I deserted my stateroom and took my cushion and my ulster, and slept upstairs in the social hall, which was well ventilated ; that is I slept when the weather permitted. We had a terrific sea on, though not so bad as I experienced at Cape Pillar, and the crash and clatter was not encouraging to sleep. Walking or standing or eating—all were attended with uncertainty, many of the passengers taking their soup and coffee, via sleeves or shirt fronts; indeed, eating was quite an art and only to be acquired with long practice. It requires some dexterity to keep a plate of soup from overflowing first one side and then another, and to eat it, and at the same time keep an eye on a cup of chocolate so as to catch it and bring it to a level at each successive roll. To-day is smoother, and we think our storms are over.

I have enjoyed our gale with all its attendant discomforts immensely. The rest of the people have their own opinion of a person who enjoys rough seas. We still play whist, and I still win. Usually I play quite well enough to please my antagonist, but there is no satisfying my partner. He is very hard to please ; I think he is unreasonable. Winning for him is not enough ; he requires that I should play scientifically. He says I play by intuition, and that there are certain well defined rules of the game which I ignore. I say he is altogether too exegetical. I think when I win by the audacity and originality of my play, he ought to admire it, at least as long as I don't trump his aces. So then we have a long discussion about it and other things, in which it appears that he criticises me because he takes an interest in me, and wants to improve me, which is very kind of him, but not exactly complimentary and thereafter he questions me and cross-examines me and badgers me, and "improves" me, until I say, "Well, this is quite refreshing. I haven't had such a quarrel since I was a child and tried to manage my brother," and he gives me up as a hopeless case of intentional perversity quite beyond his comprehension. "Improve" me, indeed ! I've seen several people who have wanted to improve me before, and the improving process has quite lost both its novelty and its charm. Besides, I think I am quite good enough already. All the same he is very nice, gentlemanly, intelligent and sincere, and I like him immensely—though I think it is a mistake to play a trivial game as if it were a matter of life and death. The Diplomat, whom, although he is an Englishman by education,

I consider the next nicest gentleman on board, listens and joins in and enjoys our wrangles, and rather sympathizes, in the way of understanding and approving of me and my ground. When the Paymaster gets quite puzzled over my incomprehensibility he turns me over to the Diplomat, saying, "She says so-and-so; can you understand that?" and the Diplomat quite disappoints him by comprehending at once. They twain are good friends, as they should be.

I place the Diplomat second only because he is an Englishman and tinged, though ever so lightly, with English notions regarding women. It is really nothing but a remnant left of inborn prejudice. I notice that he enjoys discussing with women and has a respect for their opinions, and that at the same time he is quite delightfully frank in disagreeing with them, two points in which he differs from the ordinary Englishman. The Paymaster says, after a discussion in which I have expressed myself rather doubtfully, assenting to most things with a "perhaps" or "that is comparatively true," "You are a very negative person; you seem not to be positive of anything. Is there anything of which you are positively certain?" And I reply, "Yes, I am perfectly certain of the uncertainty of everything." He calls that a "paradox" and a "glittering generality" and asserts his belief that it doesn't mean anything. I calmly say, "Perhaps not," and he consigns me to the Diplomat, who understands perfectly and thinks up another "glittering generality" that matches it.

October 3d, 10 A. M.—We expect to reach Yokohama about five o'clock to-day. We have had our last concert; played our last games of whist and of chess, finished and returned our borrowed books, have taken our last moonlight promenade on board the Tokio, and now, having packed our trunks, we all adjourn to the deck to watch for the first sight of land. We are coming to the end of a very pleasant voyage, which has been marked by the general prevalence of fine weather and pleasant companionship. All have remained good friends to the last and all agree that the time has slipped away with amazing rapidity, a dull hour being a thing unknown on board the City of Tokio.

October 4th.—So much that is entirely new and novel has been passing before my eyes since yesterday morning that I hardly know where to begin to describe it, and truly it is indescribable. I think I shall begin at this end of events and say that I am supposed to have the pleasantest room in Yokohama, overlooking the Japanese harbor, the Bay of Yesso, there being only a roadway between the hotel and the bay ; and that at this moment a "sampan" (boat) is passing my window with several men in it. One of them, standing up in the center of it rowing, is attired in a loin cloth and a black coat, which latter garment flaps picturesquely in the wind.

Coming up the bay yesterday the scenery from the time we first saw land until we reached Yokohama was very pretty. Unlike the Californian coast, which is barren and uninteresting, here it is green and apparently under cultivation. The effect of a hill all laid out in terraces is charming, and we saw many of them. We saw many small and large boats, and they too seemed odd, all the sails being square. The "water scape" is dotted with squares of canvas, and presently a Japanese junk drifts slowly by us and we have a good opportunity to observe its construction. It appears to be going backward, the stern being so much higher than the bow ; and its great square sail instead of being smooth is "shirred," to speak in dress language.

We have long before this seen the famous mountain Fugiama and have observed that it looks as grand and majestic and "calm" as our "genial bore" had described it, to which finale of a lengthly flight we had flippantly responded that. if there was one thing more becoming to a mountain than another we should think it was "calmness." Coming to anchor, the scenery really beggars description. We are the objective point for which innumerable "sampans" and four or five steam launches are making. They come alongside and vie with each other for places. The steam launches are from the various hotels. The sampans are for general hire. Other boats, fishing boats, are drifting by. Of all the different varieties of dress the Japanese have the widest range, and each variety seemed to be represented in that conclave of boats. There were boatmen clothed in a long gown, a cross between a dressing gown and an ulster, leaving the chest bare. Others, by way of contrast, had absolutely nothing on but a loin cloth, and very well dressed they looked, too, in their golden-brown skins. I admired them immensely. What they lacked by way of clothing on their bodies they made up for by that of their heads, which were tied up in cloth, usually white but often colored. Another dress consisted of a pair of blue-black suspenders, crossed on the back, and blue-black sleeves fitting closely and reaching from the wrists up to above the elbow. I was so taken up with this curious way the people had of clothing themselves in the most unnecessary places that I didn't remember to observe whether they had anything else on or not. I think they wore a skirt with that costume. Another costume consists of blue-black trousers, which are almost close fitting enough to be tights, and blue-black close-fitting blouse shirt. I rather admire this close fitting costume. The hotel boys wear it, and they go about so quietly and so lightly. They are little undersized men, but they look neat and trim in this dress, which is finished off by black or blue-black cloth shoes. These shoes I should call foot mittens because they have a separate apartment for the big toe.

Having been advised by the captain and the purser of the Tokio to come to the Windsor, I concluded to do so, although the Grand Hotel, which is next door, is supposed to be the most fashionable. Failing to find any other reason for going to it, and finding that one insufficient, I let the purser place me in charge of the Windsor Hotel keeper, and presently, after many farewells, I and my baggage and several fellow travelers who were brave enough to prefer quiet comfort to ostentatious fashion, and the Paymaster who, I think, had it on his conscience to look after a certain lone feminine creature, were all stowed into the Windsor House steam launch and were making for the shore. Arrived there, we walked along the "bund" to the hotel, a distance of a block or so, and for once in my life I went along the street with my eyes wide open, for this at last was Japan. And here were curious looking, curiously dressed people; and here were odd looking little children carrying still littler and still odder looking children on their backs; and here were the much talked of jinrickshas. Reaching the hotel I was taken to this charming room, where I received my trunks and keys presently, and dressed for dinner. The proprietor's wife, an American, called on me and was pleasant. My room faces the bay, and opens at each side on a veranda also looking out on the bay. The Paymaster found a friend of his, a Lord Dundreary, and brought him here to dine with me and to tell me about Japan. He is to supply me with a passport for the interior.

Everything seems very safe about here. I have an all pervading sense of security. The Japanese disposition is friendly and polite; indeed, their politeness overpowers me. I had two native guides call on me to-day, and could not prevail on either of them to sit down while I read their many letters of recommendation, and they bowed very low in responding to every question I put. I have engaged one sent me by a gentleman, cashier of the firm of Walsh, Hall & Co., and shall set out with him for Nikko in a day or two. I started out by myself this morning, being put in a jinricksha by the proprietor of the hotel, who ordered the man to take me to the P. M. S. S. Co.'s office and Walsh, Hall & Co.'s bank, which he did. A jinricksha is very comfortable on the whole, though one is apt to consider every pound one weighs when a fellow creature is in the shafts. Thank goodness I weigh only 101 pounds; I lost five pounds at Honolulu and haven't recovered them yet.

Walsh, Hall & Co. were very polite and friendly, particularly the Co., who got me the guide and tried to find "Ito," Miss Bird's guide, for me. Mr. Centre, of the P. M. S. S. Co., was not in, but called on me afterwards and put his services, along with those of almost all the other people I have met, at my disposal. I have to request my fellow travelers whose time is shorter than mine, not to waste it in waiting on me. I have received so many kindly attentions—better yet, such thoroughly gentlemanly attentions—from them that I believe they consider me a sort of protegé of theirs in general and in particular.

The walls of my room are decorated with a combination of fans and Japanese photographs, and panel pictures, and biblical pictures, and San Francisco advertising placques (just fancy) otherwise it is comfortably American in its furniture, with the exception of an inlaid or mosaic work-table, which it is going to break my heart to part with. So much for my first twenty-four hours in Japan.

October 8th.—Well, I've done it! I've been and indulged in the most disreputable "racket." Now I feel better. I went with a gentleman to a first-class Japanese restaurant and dined Japanese fashion; drank saki, was entertained by Japanese singing and dancing girls. Nobody in Japan must ever know it, because it would ruin the young man forever, he occupying an official position, and for the same reason he can't tell on me, though I don't care. He said it was not disreputable, only singular. However, it was just what I wanted; it brought me in direct contact with Japanese girls. Now to give an account.

First, we dismissed our jinrickshas; then we walked down a little narrow Japanese street and turned into a restaurant through a square doorway and not very light passage. We were stopped at the foot of a short flight of very smooth polished stairs, where we remove our shoes. Thence we go up into a square, low ceiled room, opening on one side by sliding doors upon a balcony of flowers that looks into a garden. The room is carpeted with matting and absolutely bare of furniture with the exception of a solid block of wood as high as an ottoman, marked something like a chess board, on which they play "go-bang," two thin cushions and a tall candle. We each take a cushion and kneel on it; a girl comes in at the door, creeping on her hands and knees, and prostrates herself still lower before us.

We give our order, viz.: the names of the dancing girls we want. After sending for half a dozen we get three, and while we are waiting supper is brought; soup in the nicest little lacquer bowls with covers to them to keep it hot, fish in various shapes, sausage and baked chestnuts of a very large kind. The first course, though, is apple blossom tea; that is, a tiny cup of hot water with a single blossom in it and a little salt. Next came rice cakes, very nice, thin and delicate, and then the soup, fish and sausage and chestnuts and little cups of tea, about twice the size of a thimble, and tiny bowls of saki.

I thought of "Omar Kahyyam" all the evening. A bowl of water and a bottle of saki stands between our two trays, and we have paper napkins. The bowl of water is for us to dip our saki bowls in and hand them to each other to drink saki from by way of compliment. We exchange compliments with the singer of the first rank in the same way. The dancing girl was a slip of a thing, only thirteen or so, I imagine. She danced or rather performed and sang in a weak, unmusical voice. The prettiest and brightest girl played on a samisen, an instrument similar to a guitar, while the other danced. There were two additional girls as waiters. The dancing is rather a posturing by way of illustrating the song that is sung. Between whiles we drank saki and talked to the girls, and I and the girls examined each other's wearing apparel and trinkets and then played "gobang," the girls giving me my first lesson in that noble game and beating me every time to their own infinite amusement. They would not let my escort tell me or even look at the board. In fact, the entertainment was conducted quite entirely for my amusement.

After that more song and dance, and then they played a song and dance game which is something like "beans porridge hot." The game is between two, and a wrong gesture is paid for by an article of dress. This game, if carried on to any extent, would be attended with startling results; but the Japanese girls are particularly averse to anything like exposure, I'm told, so the game is seldom carried beyond the loss of hairpins and handkerchiefs and small articles that may well be spared without any serious disarrangement of dress. It was a very exciting game, however, and we had a perfectly hilarious time over it. It is very rapidly played and there is a very abrupt climax where a mistake is made; and confusion on one side and screams of laughter on the other always follow. I am told that the Japanese have little or no idea of privacy, the sexes bathing together and going about half naked, sometimes entirely so; but that is a matter of custom. Exposure for the sake of exposure is as objectionable with Japanese women as it is with us.

At half-past nine, after a jolly evening, we broke up. The girls were quite delighted with me and came down the stairs and helped me on with my shoes, which they admired; and after a warm good-bye, which was quite affectionate toward me, we left them looking after us on the doorstep. That has been the pleasantest and most instructive part of my visit. I'm more interested in the women and children of the different countries than I am in men, gods or temples. I foresee that I shall be very tired of temples before I get to Europe. At this Japanese tea all the waiting on us was done on hands and knees. Some came in on their knees; the others dropped down the moment they entered, and none of the girls stood up in the room except to dance. On the other hand, my guides bow very low and very frequently, but nothing will induce them to sit in my presence. I had the pleasure of dining with chopsticks, much to the amusement of the girls over my awkwardness. There's nothing like converting your shortcomings and trials into a source of amusement, a habit worth cultivating when traveling.

Yesterday I went up to Tokio and called on our American Minister, Mr. Bingham. I told the Paymaster I was going alone, and he telegraphed his friend, the Lord Dundreary, to whom he introduced me and who had very kindly offered to show me around, to meet me at the depot, which he did; and I was not permitted to go to the cars alone. The proprietor of the hotel, Mr. Wolf, took me to the depot with the aid of the tiniest and most ridiculously built Japanese pony you ever saw. Lord Dundreary met me at Tokio and took me to Mr. Bingham, who received me kindly and introduced me to his wife and daughter and ordered his secretary to make out my passport for Europe, and was exceedingly courteous generally, promising to call on me in Yokohama.

Lord Dundreary took me to the temples of Sheba, all very wonderful, very brilliant, very curious, and so forth. I was much amused by the perfunctory air with which a priest led around the devotees and had them kneel, and knelt himself and went through his performances of praying, and yet kept one eye on me, the curious foreigner. We went into one temple, removing our shoes for the purpose, and knelt, which it is quite necessary to do to get the proportions, the ceiling being low. We went up a high hill, where we got a lovely view of Tokio and the bay, and were regaled with apple blossom and hot water, and we admired the pretty Japanese girls who waited on us rather more, I fear, than we did the temples. We went up and down this hill by way of a long, unbroken flight of one hundred and one steep stairs. At the foot a sort of fair was going on, and there were numerous tents with various performances within. We went into one and witnesssed a horrible representation of an execution with imitation blood and making of ugly faces. I was more interested in the people than anything else. The women and small girls go about with babies on their backs, most of the latter awake and contented and grave; here and there one has fallen asleep, and its poor little unfortunate head dangles about in the ambitious attempt to rest it on its own back, to the imminent peril of its neck. As we ride along through the crowded streets our jinricksha men shout at the people to get out of the way.

There is a continual bombardment of visiting cards. I don't have much time to do anything but receive calls. The interest these people manifest is very kind, to say the least. I went to my banker's to-day to get some money changed, and asked about a guide incidentally. In an hour or two the cashier called and offered his services; in an hour or two more he sent me a note and a guide. Next Mr. Centre called and offered his services, and in the evening the head of the bank called on me, loaded me up with advice, and ended by sending me pillows and linen for my trip. When I got back yesterday I found a number of cards and notes. To-day the "Genial Bore" of the Tokio called, also an English lady and gentleman in the house. Mr. Gay, the silent partner of Walsh, Hall & Co., followed suit and is extremely anxious to be of use. The Diplomat succeeded him, and then Lord Dundreary. I invited the Diplomat to dine with me, and it ended in my going to dine with him at the Grand, which is the best hotel for dining purposes. He came back with me and we have spent the evening in a last discussion. We go in opposite directions on the morrow, and the probabilities are against our ever meeting again. Everybody takes care of me. The Paymaster left me a letter of introduction to his brother at Nagasaki, after having done everything he could to further my interests here.

A JAPANESE JOURNEY.

October 9th.—Tea house on the road to Nikko. Noon. So far so good. Up at half-past five this morning, off in a jinricksha alone to the train for Tokio. At Tokio my guide, Také, meets me, he having gone there in advance last night to engage jinrickshas, which we get into at once, and off we go at a rattling gait. Just fancy men running in the shafts, hour after hour, with a steady unvarying trot that a horse might envy!

For a long distance we kept in the city. There is a lot of Tokio, and even here it is rather thickly settled and village like. I have to keep my eyes open all the time, and can't begin to take note of all that passes before them. I am myself an object of interest all the way along. I like to see the little four-year-olds come flying out to join some playmate, and fetch up on the sidewalk with a jerk that makes that topknot of hair stand out "several ways for Sunday" at the sight of me. Children are children all the world over, and I recognize the same surprised look in these little dark skinned, curiously dressed creature's eyes that one notes in the eyes of white children when they see anything as strange as I am here. They seldom cry, it seems; and almost as soon as they can walk the next baby is strapped upon their backs and they play around, carrying this load with very little reference to it. There are advantages and disadvantages in this mode of carrying children. On one side, it leaves one freer and better able to attend to other things; but, on the other side, it makes all but impossible that attention to an infant's face which is requisite to the attractiveness of its personal appearance. I see little mites of four with a big six or eight months' old baby on their small backs, and little two-year-olds with dolls strapped to their backs as a preliminary measure.

This is just the place for a small boy that I am acquainted with to come and live, to whom dressing is a long and tedious proceeding. He wouldn't have to dress here at all. I see little children all along the street playing and running about without anything on whatever, and nice and brown and fat they look, too. I am writing this piecemeal, scratching a word or two at stopping places. We have got to a tea house at Nakade, where we dine and shall spend the night. It is four o'clock and Také is preparing my dinner. I have got into a quarter where I am still more of a novelty; the children catching sight of me run alongside a little way, until I smile at them, and then they are suddenly stricken with shyness. We have just crossed a little river, jinrickshas and all, in a flat boat which was poled across. It being but a few steps to the tea house, we walked, little children rushing from all quarters to look at me. I sought seclusion within. Two or three little ones belonging here came and looked at me, but a few smiles, judiciously distributed, dispersed them.

These tea houses are very nice. Rough it, indeed! If we had anything half so neat in America we should do well. The rooms are all but bare, sometimes entirely so; but really I should hate to "eat off the floors" for fear of soiling them. I have to remove my shoes before entering a tea house. The room I'm in now is on the ground floor, just a step or two from the ground. The whole sides, which are made of innumerable panes of paper, slide open, revealing a little garden almost as clean as the room. The floors of the rooms are covered with matting and they all open into each other by means of thin sliding panels of wood, or heavy paper, or a large sash glazed with small panes of thin white paper; but everything about them is scrupulously clean, wooden posts and roof and all; and, being open so much, the air is fresh; there is no odor of cooking, no close, fusty, dusty smell of carpets and furniture.

This house is quite a stylish one. It has a picture on the wall of an impossible Japanese gentleman reading an improbable scroll, and an æsthetic earthen placque, evidently very ancient, and an inscription in Japanese that looks very much as if translated, it would read, "God bless our home," or words to that effect; besides a jug of flowers and some mineral specimens. One room has a large round window, and in it stands a tiny goldfish globe on a rack. The gardens are pretty, and I don't object at all to the dwarfing or rather curious training of the trees. Sometimes it is pretty, as, for instance, over the bank of the moat, as we pass out of the gates of Tokio; the trees growing near the edge were trained to spread out like a roof away beyond the edge, and sometimes down the bank. In another place a tree is trained to spread all in one way, like a comet's tail, making a nice awning for a seat. I saw one tree trained in the shape of a boat with a full sail. I could hardly believe it was all one tree.

Whenever I leave a tea house, every one about it bows low and says "sianella" and "arigato," or, "good-bye" and "thanks." They are very polite, and not intrusive; on the contrary, even in the street the children behave toward strangers better than our street "arabs" do if they see anything as unusual to them. Instead of being annoyed by their curiosity, when we stop I encourage them to come in and see me when they come peeping. At the last place I told my guide to tell them they could stay in my room, and I had three or four women and two little children to entertain me. They are very inoffensive, not a bit presuming or aggressive. They showed me pictures and books and finally one girl, the sister of the master of the establishment, gave me a picture of the dancing girl I saw the other night. In return I gave her a bit of red ribbon, and sprinkled them all with cologne, to their infinite delight. I played "gobang" with them, and cultivated them and the children to the extreme limit of my Japanese.

Japan could certainly give America several points in cleanliness and safety. I slept at Nakade last night in a house that opens all over with sliding panels, and was innocent of even the mildest form of lock. And I slept, too, with a sense of perfect security. When I wanted to go to bed I told Také, and he told the girls, and they said good-bye and retired. This morning I was awakened by the mingled sounds of a creaking well-sweep, which was kept in active operation, and the sliding open of panels on three sides of my room. I rose, therefore, and arrayed myself behind the screen that had been placed before my bed last night. I clapped my hands, feeling very oriental in the act, and Také appeared with water in a copper basin the size and shape of an ordinary sieve. Presently he brought my breakfast of eggs, toast, chocolate and rice, which I keep forgetting to attend to in the counter interest in the girl who gives me a morning call and who is taking a lesson in English. She brings a little book, and writes down in Japanese "sugar," "salt," "water," "chocolate," and "teapot."

After breakfast I depart, carrying with me the blessings of the establishment and the earnest invitation to come again. I brought with me three jars of Leibig's extract of beef, a can of condensed milk, ditto sweet corn, ditto apricots, ditto corned beef and some candles and bread, salt, pepper, sheets, pillow-case, towels, napkins, teaspoon, knife and fork, one bottle of claret (I am positively forbidden to drink water), my rug shawl, pillow and waterproof, can of chocolate and paper of chocolate.

UTSONOMIA, *Oct. 9th.*—Oh, dear! Is there no escaping civilization? I've got a Brussels carpet on my floor! In a few years Japan will be ruined if this thing keeps on. I don't suppose its half as uncivilized now as it was when Miss Bird was here. I haven't been troubled with fleas at all. San Francisco can give Japan a few points on fleas.

When I say a room in a tea house is absolutely bare of furniture, I mean absolutely bare; I don't mean it has a table, chair, bed, bureau and washstand. When I come to the room it contains *nothing*—except that this one has a carpet. When I arrive they produce a chair and set it ostentatiously in the middle of the floor, and put my pillow on it, under the impression, apparently, that that is the American style. Then they rummage around and get a table, of unpainted pine, and spotlessly white. In all my travels I have never met with such matchless cleanliness; everything seems to be in a perpetual state of newness. The bamboo fence, the outer slides of the house, the wooden bucket—everything is glitteringly new. One might think these were new houses; perhaps they are, but I notice, as I ride through the towns and cities, that no matter what the business of the stores may be, fish market, grocer, or manufacturer, you can see right through the house from front to back, and all is conspicuously clean. The streets have no sidewalks; there is a two-foot board walk, sometimes, along the sides; but they are occupied by goods for sale, and by the shoes or clogs of the occupant, visitors and purchasers. As I have said, I have to take off my shoes every time I enter a teahouse; that is, step up onto the platform that divided the room from the passage way, which said passage way is about two feet below the platform or floor of the room. The floor of the passage is earth, and all shoes must be left upon it.

The sliding panels separating the rooms are all thrown open in the morning, exposing the entire internal economy to the gaze of the general public. Passing along the street in the morning, I come across whole families in a state of absolute nudity, taking a morning bath in the front room. I've no doubt whatever that they consider it a very laudable performance and worthy of an audience. I see many people along the road, woodcutters and field laborers, with only a loin cloth on of the most primitive kind, and plenty of children up to nine years whose only adornment consists of a circular tuft of hair bearing a striking resemblance to a penwiper, on the crown of the head. The only apparent use for clothes on a Japanese child is to make a pocket on the back for a baby, the babies being put inside the kimona (ulster), which is then wrapped tightly around the large child and tied around the waist and at the back just above the baby's knees. When a baby has lost its first youth it is fastened only by a band around its legs, if fastened at all, and is expected to hang on with its hands without further support.

I can't say as much for the cleanliness of the children as I can for the houses; they are dirty little creatures at best, and many of them are afflicted with sore heads and faces, brought on, perhaps, from dirt and neglect. However, they look very cunning to me, with their brown skins and black hair, whether in their kimonas and wooden clogs or in a state of nature. The style of wearing the hair seems to be quite a matter of taste, and is as varied as the dress. Many wear the penwiper tuft, large or small, the rest of the head being shaven, some leaving a wisp of hair over each ear and in the back of the neck. Others have one or two or all of these wisps, minus the penwiper; others have the penwiper tied tightly and stuck stiffly together and trained like a little stick of wood toward the top of the head; others shave a round spot in the center of the penwiper, and others add another fringe of penwiper over the forehead. Others still are shaven, or, as we would say, sand-papered all over, the hair sometimes being partly grown like that of our own young Americans. The kimona is a cross between an ulster and a dressing gown, and has sleeves reaching to the bottom, or nearly so, of the garment, which are made use of as pockets. The children seem to arrange their own toilets according to their own personal fancy or temperature, as I see them getting in or out of their kimonas at all times and places.

Near the houses I see large quantities of thin white rice cakes laid out in the sun to dry. They are afterwards taken in and ironed instead of being baked or toasted. They are ironed with a hot round flatiron to brown them, first on one side and then on the other. The stoves are a high bank of earth, topped with round metal-raised rims or holes with covers upon them. I see cotton in various stages of conversion to clothes, from raw cotton to cloth coming from the looms worked by women. I see in stores everywhere boxes marked " Devoe's Brilliant Oil, Improved Cans"—another distressing mark of approaching civilization. I've got a tin kerosene lamp nearly a yard high and as slender as a cane.

My jinricksha men interest me very much. I catch myself watching the play of their muscles as they trot along with perfect regularity of motion. They run entirely with the legs and with as little movement of the body as possible and show a fine development of muscle. They wear trousers just long enough to bear the name, and jackets of dark-blue cotton. They are forbidden by law to go naked, but they would be much more comfortable without the jacket. Doing a horse's work they ought to be permitted something like a horse's freedom.

NIKKO, *October 10th*, 8 P. M.—Have just been besieged by a lot of Japanese curio sellers. I made a small purchase of the first one that came and after supper he returned to the attack with his brothers in trade. They seemed to be quite friendly, and instead of resenting each other's presence, were disposed to give each other a chance. I kept shaking my head at them— " No, no, no," saying " No can buy;" "Arigato" (thanks), and "Sinon" (good-bye), while they turned out their carved ivory, brocaded silk and lacquer work for my inspection and pointed out the extreme " Ichi ban " (first class) quality of their goods. I amused them very much in my struggle with the Japanese vernacular, and having seen all their things, I, by way of response, showed them my manifolding book and how it worked. They were delighted with the several copies, and we parted with mutual satisfaction, although I made no purchases.

We arrived here at three this afternoon. I am glad I came. It is much prettier than I supposed it was. The temple grounds form a sort of park on the side of the hills. Nikko is high up and close to the foot of the mountains. It is very picturesque, and there is a rushing river with many waterfalls that roar in my ears all the time. To get to the temples we cross the river on a pretty bridge. Another bridge spans the river only a few rods above this one, which is painted a brilliant red and is opened only once a year. Saw some temples to-day and shall see more to-morrow on my way to some springs, which are somewhere or other, and to which I am going in a kango. I particularly enjoy going to places that I don't know anything about, even their names. The road here is fine as to scenery and most abominable for traveling purposes, being in process of reconstruction and covered with broken stone. When I can no longer stand the jolting and anxiety for my human horses, I insist on walking, though, apparently, they are far from expecting such a thing. The sides of the road for miles and miles are lined with a thickset row of pine trees, very large and very old, three hundred years old, I am told. They are as large as any but the largest of the pines in California. They form a beautiful vista of long shaded avenue.

I am beyond any communication with any one I know, alone in a strange, uncivilized country, traveling along with five men, only one of whom can understand a word I say. He (my guide) fancies, I presume, that he speaks English fluently; which is far from the case, however.

October 11th.—I have been to-day away up into the mountains to Chiu-zen-ji, situated on the banks of a lake of that name, beyond which as " Satow " says " rises the sacred mountain of Nan-tai-zan." All this I have found out since my return. I went there this morning without the remotest idea as to what my destination was. Také called it the geysers, but I failed entirely to observe anything of a geyser character. He probably meant falls. I saw some very fine ones. Také evidently considered them worth seeing, so I went. I think it is quite fortunate I was so ignorant of the sort of journey I was to take, for had I had the remotest idea of what I was to go through before reaching my destination, I should most certainly not have undertaken it, and should have lost thereby a most interesting jaunt. It was a clear case of "where ignorance is bliss 'tis folly," et cetera, and this morning I was literally " not climbing any mountains until I came to them," so I started out as lively as a cricket to go somewhere, and the conveyance was a kang or kango. A kango reminds me of nothing so much as a turtle, the rider figures as the creature while he reclines on the under shell and is sheltered by the upper. The head and tail are represented by the bar of wood sticking out at each end, by which it is supported. After some consideration and a general discussion in choice Japanese as to the best way of getting into a kango, I backed into it. I discovered at once that the kango had been built without the slightest reference to my hat. So after a short effort to reconcile my hat to the roof of the kango, I settled the difficulty by taking it off and going bareheaded.

We went gaily along, I in the kango, two men carrying me by means of a pole, running over my head, from which depended the basket I was in, with a third man to relieve the others at intervals and my guide on foot. He told me it was seven miles, and you may get some slight conception of the quality of those seven miles when I tell you that we were from eight A. M. to six P. M. making the round trip. We went gaily along until presently we came to the mountains and proceeded to climb. The kango ceased to be of service and became an extra burden, for there was nothing but a mountain foot-path, and that of the most perpendicular description, varied occasionally by a flight of stone stairs or logs at intervals to break the slant. Then we came down a hill or two. One hill being exceptionally steep and sandy I found it more rapid and convenient to slide down on my back. At another place we descended the side of the mountain by means of a ladder of limbs of trees, double runged, so you couldn't fall through. Finally we reached a level, and my spirits were beginning to rise when more stairs appeared. Fancy walking up several miles of stairs. I might have been carried up, but I couldn't think of requiring so much of human beings.

At one place, being thoroughly exhausted, I consented to be carried up a couple of flights with the idea that the worst was over, but more and steeper and equally interminable flights hove in sight, and I got out again. My guide told me the bearers were accustomed to carrying the people up the stairs and all, and that they were very much amused at my ability to climb; they had never seen a woman who could climb so much before.

, think they thoroughly appreciated my consideration in not adding my weight to the kango up those horrible stairs, for they showed it in the care for my belongings, the comfortable arrangement of my rug and wraps, and by bringing me water when I was too exhausted to ask for it or know what I wanted (which was quite out of their province, superseding the guide, whose business it was to attend to me) when we arrived at a tea house. I think the working class of Japanese render their service, as a rule, in a more cheerful, willing, even generous, manner than any other class of servants I have met with. But I am always well treated.

Having arrived at Chiu-zen-ji I saw the lake, the mountains, and some temples. The place is a Japanese Summer resort, with numbers of buildings, all closed, it being out of season now. October here is the October of our Eastern States. The place is really very pretty, reminding one slightly of the Yosemite, being in the heart of the mountains, but not nearly so grand. No perpendicular granite heights. The return was much easier, though I still had a little climbing and a great deal of rough descent where the kango could not go in its normal position. And having returned I am glad I accomplished it. Though very tired and expecting to be more so to-morrow, I enjoyed myself very much. Most of our way was along the course of a rushing mountain river. Mountain streams reaching the villages are made to run in a two-foot wide, deep, stone gutter through the center of the streets.

HOKONE, *October 12th*.—I started out with my guide early this morning to finish the temples, but in reality they finished me. Very curious, very unique, very wonderful, but—terrible confession to make—I am afraid I don't appreciate temples. My tastes are perhaps a trifle æsthetic as regards combinations of color, and I don't admire ugly figures, whether they be saints or idols. Otherwise there are many pretty things to be seen. For instance, the polished black wood, and the hanging curtains of bamboo so constructed that you can see through them as if they were gauze. But the prettiest things of all were a couple of flights of stone stairs. One contains 180 steps in sections leading up the hill to the tomb of some gods, with a high stone wall on each side of the stairs, and all, stairs, wall and landing covered with rich green moss and lichen. The slope is on one side level with the top of the wall, and the hill and wall are covered with masses of creeping vine, while outside the wall beautiful large trees are growing. I had to stop at each landing and turn on the stairs and look forward and back in sheer admiration of the richness and shading of color. There are some lovely pictures here to be caught by an artist some day and put on canvas.

I was quite thrown into a state of excitement last night over the arrival of a Frenchman and his wife at the hotel at Nikko. I had been happy in the idea that I was the only European or Caucasian within two days' journey of Nikko. I left there at one P. M. to-day. A jinricksha having only two wheels, and the seat being directly over the axle, with no springs to soften the jar, one's emotions can be better imagined than described after half a day's journey over alternate stretches of broken stone road and hard mud ruts. Having had pleasant weather all the way to Nikko and over the mountains, it has gradually turned to rain. Fortunately I brought my waterproof, and anyway the rain, as I used to be told in my childhood, "will make me grow." The hotel at Nikko was what Také described as "alle same European hotel." The European part consisted of an extra chair, a table with leaves and a phenomenally imperfect looking glass. Don't ask me the names of the hotels I stop at here. My always imperfect memory for names has been hopelessly wrecked in the encounter with these vocal gymnastics.

YOKOHAMA, *October 15th.*—I've got back to Yokohama, and a nice entertainment was given for my reception. But I am not going to tell about that until I've finished the history of my Nikko trip. I left off at Hokone. The next night I was again at Nakade, which was really the best, cleanest, quietest stopping place I had found.

My first and last tea house nights were spent at the same house. The family were nicer than the average, and they welcomed me back with effusion. With all the sisters and cousins and aunts they dropped in to see me until a large party was assembled. I played gobang again, with signal misfortune, with the mistress of the house, and then sent for Také to act as interpreter, and we had a very jolly social time. The little eight-year-old girl danced and sang for us while the mistress played a Japanese banjo. The little one played the banjo too.

They told Také that I was different from Europeans they had seen before, as I was not proud.

As I rattled through the villages, the children would all cry out something as they pointed to me—sometimes running with us a little way—which Také said meant "Look at the European," but which I afterward discovered was a mild translation of the words signifying literally " red-headed devil." European women are very rarely seen in the country and in some places where I was, I was told a white woman had never been before, though men are quite frequently seen. After a very merry evening with my Japanese friends, I went to bed, to commence in the morning my last day's journey. At the tea house where I took lunch the family came in and sat down in a semi-circle on the floor and watched with deepest interest the rearrangement of my hair. I could send them away easily enough by appealing to Také, but as they were very polite and kept their distance and as I was curious about them, I didn't see any reason why I shouldn't gratify their curiosity about me.

Reaching Tokio, Také paid and dismissed the jinricksha men, giving them each an extra fee from me, for they were quite deserving, whereat they all four came into the depot waiting room in a body and prostrated themselves before me on the floor with many "arigatos" and "sianellas" and Japanese blessings and good wishes. All through the journey, even on the last day, it was an unfailing source of amusement to them when I responded "arigato" to any small service they rendered me, or spoke any single Japanese word that I knew. And they were very careful of me, careful to tuck my dress in away from wheels, brush dust off from me, hand me anything, tie my shoes if they came undone and see that I had all my baggage with me, and never asked to be relieved of the burden of drawing or carrying me no matter how bad the road was. I had four jinricksha men, two for my jinricksha and two for my guide's, which also contained my provisions and bedding. When the road was very bad my guide walked and his extra man turned in to help mine. Sometimes I walked too. With fewer men I should have been obliged to walk more than I was able. The condition of the road was so bad, a great part of the way, that it was as much as three men could do to pull and push me over it. The two men run tandem. My trip of six full days, made in style as well as comfort, I fancy, with the expense of myself and guide —everything included—has cost me a little more than half, perhaps two-thirds what the Yosemite trip, five days and a quarter, cost me, without guide, with less style and less comfort. My guide was valet and cook as well, and I fared better under his charge than I did at the hotels on the way to the Yosemite.

The last two days of my trip were excessively hot and after I got back we had a thunderstorm. I was received by the clerk of the hotel with effusion. I found the San Pablo had arrived on the 13th and brought me only a telegram, which was not intensely satisfactory after not having heard a word from home for more than a month.

And now for the celebration of my return. I had gone to bed and to sleep. I awoke in the morning about half-past four and lay wondering what I had waked up for at that hour of the night. Presently I found out why. First I heard a distant rumbling noise like thunder, which came nearer and nearer, and grew louder, until it shook the house, until I thought it would fall, like a house of cards. It rocked me in my bed as though in a cradle, cracked the walls, stopped the clocks, and set all the bric-a-brac in the room a-jingle. This was the celebration. It was the "mild and balmy earthquake."

I thought about all the things people did when earthquakes took place; running into the street for instance; but it occurred to me that the street would be as bad a place as any, for bricks and stone would fall on me, or the earth would open and swallow me, and I felt as if the soft, comfortable bed was about as safe a place as any other; and anyway I didn't care; I shouldn't get up. So I lay still and held my breath, and waited for the ceiling to fall in on me, and quaked a little on my own account, till presently the shock had reached its climax and begun to diminish. It died away, and then another came. Before the loose things had got through jingling they were given a fresh impetus. This was not so bad, however, and was soon over, and all was quiet but for a trembling and quivering of the earth generally. Then I heard voices all about, as if a conclave was being held on the subject. But I didn't get up. I had quite lost confidence in everything by this time, so I kept still and fell into a scientific reverie as to the mechanism of earthquakes, in which I concluded that they were the result of the effort of the gases to escape, or of electricity generated by the heat, in the bowels of the earth, "or words to that effect."

And then while I was waiting for more quake I fell asleep and dreamed that the best place to be when an earthquake was under way was at sea, and that I experienced several very fine ones under those circumstances, to my entire satisfaction. This morning I was told by residents that this was the worst earthquake Yokohama has had for years. They had a similar one about four years ago. The one last night threw down some chimneys. One man in the hotel raised himself up and, reaching for matches, was thrown out of bed by the motion. While the quaking was going on the fancy came to me that it was a laugh rippling over Mother Earth. To-day, being gloomy, it seems more like a sigh heaving her bosom. This is not my first earthquake. I felt a slight one the day before going to Tokio, but it was so slight I would not have noticed it if my attention had not been called to it. They say the more you see of earthquakes the less you like them. I think I like them less.

October 16th.—It blew very hard last night; there was a young typhoon going on somewhere, I think; and as I live right on the water's edge, I heard the sea thrashing about all night. It is quite cold and windy to-day. We had another earthquake last night, a little one. I woke up just in time to feel the earth heaving with one gentle sigh at about four in the morning. On the whole, I have concluded I don't mind earthquakes. If there is another to-night I shall propably not wake up to observe it. They are amused at me because I didn't get up the night before as everybody else did. I think I was wise to lie still. I didn't suffer as much from the shock as some others, though I felt very queerly for half an hour or more afterwards.

MIYA-NO-SHITA, FUJI-YA HOTEL, *October 17th.*—I blush for my country. Away up here, a day's journey into the mountain fastnesses, where wagons cannot come, I find a hotel that is as far superior to the comfortless accommodations afforded the hapless traveler at the Yosemite Valley as Delmonico's is to a Third Avenue oyster saloon. This place is like the Yosemite, a sight-seeing Summer resort—quite as fashionable, with as good a class of visitors, but fewer. At the Yosemite, at the best hotel, they put you in a room like a square wooden box, the ceiling of which is no higher than the top of the door. The room contains only a hard, cold, comfortless bed, a wooden washstand, chair, small lookingglass and a fraction of candle; and the cuisine is wretched. This hotel is managed by a Japanese man and his wife, who speak English. The servants speak only Japanese. The cuisine is excellent; the rooms are large, high and light. I have a luxurious bed, a delightful reclining chair, two clean white pine tables, a good kerosene lamp, and a whole new candle, besides washstand, lookingglass, two straight chairs, pretty, bright wallpaper, straw matting on the floor, and a convenient and delightful bath. How is that for the interior of a country to which we send missionaries?

The Japanese bathe a great deal. I used to hear my jinricksha men bathing half the night at the tea houses, and they bathed pretty thoroughly at every stopping place on the road, that is, about six times a day. But, nevertheless, the children's faces are simply disgusting. The pride of the Japanese heart is the floor. Their children, their clothing, food, streets may reek with dirt, but their floors are always spotlessly clean.

I left Yokohama this morning at eight o'clock in a carriage which brought me along a road they call the Tokaido, to within four or five miles of this place, the remaining miles being made in a kango. This time I travel quite alone without guide or acquaintance. As I think I have said before, the people who are of the most use to me are the people I should expect the least of—the casual acquaintances of travel. My letters of introduction serve to fix my standing with these acquaintances after they have formed their opinion of me personally; otherwise they result simply in formal calls and an interchange of cards.

The manager of the Windsor Hotel has been of great service to me and very kind indeed; he sent me up here with a card to the proprietor which insured me the warmest reception and his personal attention; and fancy my surprise at receiving a note here, immediately on my arrival, from the Diplomat who is now on the way to Pekin, containing a letter of introduction to the Governor of Hong Kong. He writes that he has spoken about me to the Governor and that he is a very kind man. It seems that the Diplomat, like the Paymaster, spent his last few moments in Yokohama in an effort to smooth my path of travel as I go. I think it is so good of them to think of me at all.

October 18th.—I went to-day on a long tour over a mountain trail to Lake Hakone. A boat carried me across the lake to the town of Hakone, where I took lunch. On this trip I had no guide, but got on nicely with my three Japanese kango bearers, one of whom knew a word or two of English. I was waited on at the tea house by Japanese girls, as usual, who spread out the lunch my bearers had brought for me from the hotel, adding tea and rice to it and looking at me curiously the while.

From the tea house a very fine view of Fugiama's symmetrical cone was obtained as it rose against the sunny sky across the bay. It certainly does look "calm" with its gentle, regular slopes, pale tints and snowy crown. We take to the boat again, and go the length of the lake to the sulphur baths. One large bath is a square tank, into which a natural spring flows, surrounded by a square building. Descending a short flight of stone steps I observe several Japanese are enjoying a bath there at that moment, and I retreat.

From the baths I am carried in the kango a long distance up a very steep, winding and muddy path, and finally we reach the geysers and I must walk. The geysers are very similar to those I saw in California, only these are much more extended. They occupy the whole side of a mountain, and the whole place is overhung with a cloud of steam as dense as a fog, that rises from the innumerable boiling springs. The place seems to be all boiling water underneath, and all yellow and green sulphur, burnt rocks, and lava on the surface. I think it is a very dangerous place to travel over, but at last we got across it, after a very slow tedious climb, picking our way laboriously over the rough surface, between springs and burnt pits and hollow crusts. This difficult place once passed, we descended a very steep but short path, and then I was requested to return to the kango ; and in a couple of hours my bearers had carried me safely back to the hotel.

October 19th.—To-day I took a long walk under the guidance of Mr. Yamaguchi, proprietor of this hotel. The first thing that attracted my attention especially was the appearance of little crabs promenading the mountain paths. I thought crabs belonged to the water and was quite unaware of their apparent predilection for climbing mountains. The scenery up here among the mountains is beautiful. There are many charming views worthy of a painter. One in particular struck me as very fine. You stand on a narrow dividing ridge and look into two mountain-enclosed, horseshoe-shaped valleys, one on either hand, each containing waterfalls and a winding stream. Indeed, waterfalls are all over the place; the sound of falling water is ever in one's ears. I am lulled to sleep by it at night and wakened by it in the morning.

There is another sound, however, that is always in my ears, and that is the sound of squabbling and fretfulness in the next room to me, occupied by a young clergyman and his wife and baby. He is a tease and she is a shrew—two dispositions admirably adapted for making things uncomfortable for each other, not to mention their next door neighbors. The other people stopping here are three English tourists, who are engaged in a perfectly hopeless struggle with the vernacular and who are getting a great deal of fun out of it. Occasionally they make some remark about Americans, while dining, that amuses me. We are a good deal interested in each other, but we conceal the interest; in fact, we ignore each others existance. At least I ignore theirs, while they always get tangled up in a sentence with distracted attention when I enter or leave the dining room. They are wondering who I am, and what I mean by being up here alone.

I left Miya-no-shita, as I arrived, in a kango; but my bearers carried me down the seven miles much more quickly than they had brought me up. The loveliness of the scenery about Miya-no-shita and its approach compensates for the difficulty of access, however. I found a coach from Yokohama waiting for me at the foot of the hills, but as the driver was a Japanese who did not speak any English, instead of the colored man who drove me hither, I was obliged to make my wants known without an interpreter at the tea house where I stopped for lunch. But I got along nicely, and secured all the rice and salt and tea I wanted. I got over the dificuly of finding out the amount of my bill by offering several pieces of money and letting the girl take her choice. She selected the one of the smallest denomination, and gave me in return eight oblong pieces of copper, about three inches long by two wide and an eighth of an inch thick, with a square hole in the center. I weighed them in my hand, and, keeping a couple of them as souvenirs, handed the rest back to the girls, intimating that my pockets and strength were unequal to the task of hauling copper in such large quantities.

I reached Yokohama before night, and was welcomed back by my very kind and helpful friends there. The gentlemanly manager of the hotel took me shopping, and displayed a fine taste in delicate Japanese silks and embroidery. These beautiful fabrics seemed strangely cheap considering their fine texture, purity of quality, and the elaborate work upon them. One is sorely tempted by the dainty crepes of most delicate tints, the brilliant embroidered screens, and the comfortable embroidered silk dressing gowns, wadded and quilted, with trains, and yet so light that nothing can be quite so warm and cosy and at the same time not at all burdensome to wear. The embroidery upon them is coarse silk and very elaborate.

Another industry that produces very beautiful and artistic results is that of making vases of cloisinee. These vases have for their foundation copper, on which a fine copper wire is laid twisted into forms or figures of leaves, flowers, butterflies, birds, or whatever design is chosen. The spaces formed by the wire are then filled with a paste, colored according to the flowers or figure represented, the groundwork being usually a deep china blue. The whole is then polished, leaving a very rich and elaborate picture outlined by the fine threads of copper wire.

We are all more or less familiar with the lacquer-work of Japan, but here we find it in profusion and ranging from wood floors to the most delicate card cases of gold lacquer, the lightest, most dainty little receptacle for cards in the world. Very large and beautiful cabinets can be seen of lacquer inlaid with pearl. Satsuma ware is another fascinating industry in Japan, and many beautiful bowls and plates were shown me most artistically decorated. But the shops of Japan would form an endless chapter if I began to do them justice. I will only say they are very attractive and rich in beautiful and artistic work.

I have been once more to Tokio, where Lord Dundreary met me and took me to the Japanese theatre, of which I shall write later.

I announced my intention to proceed on my way towards China, which horrified my friends very much. I had not half seen Japan, they said, and I was promised such sights and experiences if I would only stay one more week. But my mind was made up to go, and go I would. The manager of the hotel found me a special opportunity in the shape of "Walsh & Hall's" own steamer to go to Kobe in. He introduced me to the captain, got for me the owner's own room, a palatial apartment with desk and chair and every convenience, wrote to Mr. Walsh and secured the passage and told him what day I wanted to go, and was hard at work in my behalf generally until I was off; finally taking me on board himself in the steam launch and extending the same courtesy to Mr. Walsh as a measure in my behalf. He also gave me a letter of introduction to probably one of the loveliest captains in the world, whom I saw at the Windsor when I first arrived, and whom I am hoping to overtake at Shanghai. The Kamchatka is a vessel that takes a yearly voyage to Siberia for furs for Walsh, Hall & Co. Mr. Walsh was the only other passenger.

The steamer sails at five. An easy chair is elevated to the bridge, and I take up my position in it, wrapped in my rug, and only leave it for eating and sleeping purposes. One lovely, bright day—in which I disgrace myself by being seasick for half an hour with positively no provocation except a choppy sea and the screw, directly over which I was trying to dine—and two lovely moonlight nights, and we reach Kobe on the second lovely morning. Mr. Walsh arranges that my trunks shall be transferred direct to the "Mhitsu-Bitsu" steamer when she arrives, takes me ashore, introduces me to his brother, takes me to the Walsh & Hall office, introduces me to Mr. Hall. Mr. Walsh says "This lady wants a room secured for her on the Yokohama Maru. This lady also wants a guide to take her to Kioto, and lastly this lady wants some lunch." Mr. Hall immediately proceeds to achieve for me all of these desires.

Mr. Walsh takes me to the Hotel des Colonies for lunch, where I dine table d'hote and air my French. Mr. Hall comes after me, producing not only a guide but a guide book "Satows" (I have them "fired" at me from every quarter). Mr. Hall takes me to the depot, Mr. Walsh meets me there, likewise the guide; all three combine to get my ticket. I am introduced to three Europeans who are going further than Kioto, and so, after saying good-bye to Messrs. Walsh and Hall I have company still all the way, and arrive at Kioto at five o'clock loaded to the muzzle with valuable information. Here my guide takes charge of me, and after half an hour in a jinricksha I arrived at the "Ya-Ami" Hotel.

YA-AMI HOTEL, KIOTO, *October 28th.*—Kioto is the neatest of all Japanese cities. In Kioto the streets are almost as clean as the floors. I noticed in riding through the city no ashes, no mud, no garbage, no dust, and even about the fish markets not a scrap of refuse or dirt in the gutters. I never saw a street in America to compare with these streets of Kioto. Tokio doesn't compare with it. In proportion to the houses, which are as low as we would build a one story house but have, many of them, two stories compressed in that compass, the streets seem wide. The apology for a sidewalk, and a fourth of the street on either side, are occupied with goods, curios and everything, spread out on the ground. Having gone to the theatre last evening, I rode through the streets at an early and a late hour. Going, the streets were alive with people and wares and paper lanterns; coming back, everything was taken in, shutter slides closing the fronts of the houses; no windows, nothing left but miles of clear, clean street and paper lanterns on the front of houses, an occasional watchman and plenty of hurrying jinrickshas with people going, like me, home from the theatre at midnight.

The Japanese are far in advance of the Chinese as actors. I was glad I did not go to the theatre until after I had been about Japan a little and become acquainted with their ways, for I appreciated the extreme naturalness of their acting more than I should otherwise have done. On the stage the Japanese appeared and acted and spoke as I had seen them in the tea houses. In Tokio their scenery was very good; the play was of a very murderous, superstitious order, while their mode of expression was true to nature. The story was easy, in part, to understand. It appeared to be the old tale of a drunken, reprobate husband, a poverty-stricken home, lonely, despairing wife, crying baby, and faithful servant. In the first act the brutal husband comes home drunk, demands money, and takes the mosquito net that shields the baby to sell it. The wife fights for this protection for her child until she has been seriously hurt; after which she kills herself and the servant is killed by the husband, who then gets them out of sight, while a new and wealthy wife is waiting with her servants and goods at the gate. A sort of Bluebeard story; and all this mischief is worked by a cat, who goes about bewitching the dramatis personæ and driving them to dreadful deeds. They excel in the art of depicting the ghastly, as in the running of a sword through a man's body and giving it an additional thrust and twist before taking it out again. The unfortunate man's seemingly involuntary physical contortion was in perfect keeping with the movement of that sword. I admired the art if I could not appreciate the taste of the performance.

The next act was a water scene, very pretty, natural and artistic, with the exception of a hole in the water cloth in the center, which the audience was expected to kindly overlook, which was intended for the reception of the people who were to be drowned in the course of the evening, and afterwards fished for. I think ultimately these unfortunates arose from the water and haunted and destroyed their murderers, but I did not wait to see. In the course of the play, one man had his fingers broken one by one, with an accompanying snap and agony for each finger, and another had been run through the body with a sword several times; two people had been decapitated and two or three others drowned, for the edification of the audience.

The stage was round, and to change the scene they simply turned it about like any turn table. The scene shifters and supes seem to be hovering around the performers a good deal of the time. They have their heads covered with a black hood and are supposed to be invisible, as is also the case with the men who carry lighted candles on the ends of very long limber sticks, which they hold under the noses of the performers so that you can see the expression, a performance that really defeats its own object, as you can really distinguish less behind the flickering bobbing candle than in a steady semi-light. The orchestra or parquet of the theatre is like a checker board set on a slant, with the squares sunk in, forming so many square wooden boxes. Each box holds four people and a pot of hot ashes to light pipes by, and the people walk on the narrow partitions to get to their respective boxes. The two aisles are on a level with the stage and the top edge of the partitions; the artists making their exits and their entrances by them stopping and carrying on their dialogue and performance on them midway between the balcony and the stage. When an actor enters he is followed or led by a supe poking the candle, fastened on the end of the long rod in front of him all the way to the stage, where, if he sits down, the candle, long stick and all, are placed on the floor before him. The curtain is a rag and a very thin rag at that. There is a single row of balcony boxes on either side of the theatre, and they are the best seats. The lighting is done by candles and kerosene lamps suspended from bars by cords at different heights.

At the Kioto theatre the acting, stage and arrangements were not so good; there they had four or five tall pieces of black metal, convex in shape, behind and within which candles were placed as footlights, but they interfered sadly with one's view of the stage. There I saw three plays in one evening. One was apparently a comedy. Their comedy, while good and natural, is of rather a buffoon type but very well done. One actor was extremely good in the varying expression of his face—on receiving a fee wrapped in paper, as they give them here among themselves—from the look of pleased expectation to one of disappointment and disgust and rage at finding the paper empty. These changes of expression were repeated in various forms and the business was exceedingly good, natural and amusing. After this came an old tragedy, which answered to our legitimate play and is correspondingly uninteresting. The recitative was done in an unnatural, sing-song tone and was very lugubrious. After that came a comedy drama, nothing more nor less than a Japanese "Pygmalion and Galatea," during which they had a comedy laughing and crying scene that was exceedingly well done. It appeared that a man put a crying powder in one man's tea and laughing powders in the tea of two others. The results were extremely natural and effective.

While the methods of Japanese acting are exceedingly clever and natural, the plots are distinctly supernatural. Between the acts one can have dinner brought into the boxes, and the children run up and down on the platform aisles and try to act, and be funny, and dodge in and out from under the flimsy rag of a curtain that hangs between the stage and the audience. I went to another little theatre which corresponded to our dime museums, where the performers gave us a wonderful exhibition in the way of manipulating barrels and ladders, with small boys on them, on their feet, while a man lauded their merits in emphatic Japanese to slow music.

An interesting and picturesque trip was suggested to me as a very dangerous undertaking, as it involved shooting some rapids and I should run the risk of getting drowned in that perilous operation. As I am in search of adventure, and this excursion seemed to offer some promise of "hair-breadth escapes" and so forth, I immediately resolved to invite my own destruction at once by taking the trip.

I started out in the morning with my guide, the neatest, most dapper, kid-gloved Japanese dandy, in jinrickshas, racing merrily through the streets of Kioto and across a very long bridge that spans a river whose waters are half concealed with the immense leaves of the lotus that grows luxuriantly here. We then plunged into the country, and climbed up high among the mountains, until we came to the stream we meant to descend in a boat. Here we found boats and men awaiting us. The boats were large, flat-bottomed, shallow affairs, constructed of thin, flexible wood that bent and undulated with the pressure of rocks underneath as they passed over them. They were large enough to receive me in my jinricksha so I did not have to alight, but was lifted on board by my bearers and sat in my carriage throughout the trip with the shafts propped up to keep me from being spilled. The boatmen then pushed off the slenderly built boat, guiding it into the current, and down the stream we sped, carried along by the force of the rushing water.

I was rather disappointed at finding the water was hardly deep enough to drown a person anywhere. The rapids were not so very rapid, the descent being quite gradual, but there were a good many of them. I thought them rather tame rapids at first, but on the whole found it quite exciting to be swept over rocks with a rush of water and down the hurrying stream between the high and verdure clad mountains through which the river winds. Now and then we got caught among the jutting rocks and were pushed off laboriously by the boatmen with long poles, while the pliable floor of the boat yielded and bent above the stones below. The boatmen were very skillful in their management of the boat, dextrously avoiding the big rocks that jutted up from the river bed on every side, pushing off with their long poles from a threatening collision with one great granite boulder only to encounter another. The river is sometimes quite wide but usually narrow and always rocky, sometimes descending miniature falls, over which we glide with an exciting rush. Altogether I am charmed with the beauty of the scene and the novelty of the situation, though my ardent desire for something thrillingly adventurous was not gratified.

Having passed all the rapids I and my jinricksha were taken out of the boat, and we got lunch at a tea house that was perched up among the rocks on the hillside overlooking the river. As usual, I cultivated the girls to the extent of my Japanese. They examined my hat, and feathers, and dress, and the buttons on my ulster, minutely. They were surprised when I opened my bracelet, and delighted when I took it off and fastened it on their wrists each in turn. After lunch I got in my jinricksha again, and my boys started off with me at a brisk trot that never slackened until they had carried me to Kioto and through its. long, narrow, dainty and interesting streets to the Ya-ami hotel.

After having exchanged a perfect fusilade of visiting cards both here and in Yokohama with an American lady who resides in Japan, we at last succeeded in meeting each other to-night, and spent a pleasant evening together.

ON BOARD S. S. YOKOHAMA MARU, KOBE, JAPAN, *October 29th.*—Good fortune, good fortune, good fortune wherever I go, whatever I do. Everything turns to my advantage and all the people I meet are so kind to me. Arrived at Kobe I go direct to Walsh & Hall's office; they settle my accounts with my guide, produce my ticket, send to the Kamchatka for my baggage, trot me around in search of a new stylus for my book and crystal for my watch, as I've broken the one and lost the other, and finally bring me off in the Kamchatka's boat, with her captain and Mr. Walsh, to this steamer, where I am introduced to Purser and Captain and am received right royally, refreshed with tea and cake, and made generally comfortable and happy; and then, having invoked the kindness and protection of the Captain in my behalf, my two friends bid me a very kindly farewell.

This is a new steamer. It is her second voyage. The Captain is a jolly Englishman; I sit next to him at table. I've an upper deck stateroom, and I am to live on the bridge. There is only one other lady passenger, and the stewardess is a Chinese woman.

October 30th.—The weather proves fine, as I had foretold, spite of all the signs to the contrary and the prophecies of the weatherwise. I find the scenery of the famous Inland Sea of Japan very pretty, though I have read and heard such glowing eulogies of its beauties that I am perhaps not as enthusiastic in my admiration of it as I might otherwise be. There are bright skies, clear waters, abrupt banks, and green islands that combine to make very charming pictures as we thread our way around curves and through narrow passes, under the shadow of miniature cliffs and out upon open reaches of clear sea. It is, in fact, like nearly all of Japanese scenery—beauty on a miniature scale. My scepticism is rather awakened by the frequency with which I am told that the most beautiful points were passed while I was at breakfast, or at four o'clock in the morning, or at any time at which I have not been on deck, though I have made it my business to be there not only all day but up till a very late hour at night if any of these finest points were expected to be passed. I think these announcements of beauties passed at unseemly and unexpected seasons are very suspicious. I have, however, enjoyed all that I have seen and every hour spent on the Yokohama Maru. By moonlight the whole scene is most charming. The shimmering light on the water and the shadows thrown by the jutting promontories and islands, the irregular outlines of hills and cliffs upon the evening sky, enhance the beauty seen by the more practical light of day. We reach Nagasaki at 4 A. M. October 31st.

Before noon I went ashore to lunch and then to make the tour of Nagasaki. I saw all that was to be seen there, scenery and tortoise shell and porcelain work. The fanciful creations in tortoise shell interested me most, so dainty were they in construction, so rich and clear in the polish of the material itself. I was especially attracted by the miniature jinricksha made of tortoise shell.

In driving through the streets we saw a fencing match, which was literally one of the jousts which used to take place between the knights of the middle ages, except that this was performed on foot instead of on horseback. Each man wore a helmet on his head with bars across the face, and fought with a long wooden spear. Occasionally the contestants sat down on the ground to rest.

Having finished Nagasaki, I returned on board the Yokohama Maru and sailed at eight P. M. for China.

CHINA.

ASTOR HOUSE, SHANGHAI, *November 2d.*—Coming across to Shanghai we had lovely weather and a smooth sea. When I awoke this morning we were already on the reddish-yellow waters of the Yangtsekiang, and before noon we had reached Shanghai. The hospitable Captain commands two or three of us to stay on board to lunch, after which he takes me to this hotel, and after that out riding on the "bubbling well" road to see the famous bubbling well.

Shanghai is very pretty at the bund, but it is grievously lacking in the way of drives or surrounding scenery. The whole country about is one promiscuous graveyard. Irregular mounds and uncovered coffins are to be seen in every direction. In flower gardens or grain fields the cultivation often extends to the very base of the grave, and even the grave itself is a mound of ripening grain. The jinricksha is in vogue here, and another vehicle, which is a wheelbarrow with a board seat set lengthwise in the center, one person sitting on each side of it. I have seen several of the small-footed women with feet literally of the size of a baby's. I have been inside the walls of the city of Shanghai; but a few rods within the gates was an ample sufficiency for me, for the narrow streets were one moving mass of Chinamen and one solid smell, unlimited in quantity and disagreeable in quality. I miss the politeness and good nature of the Japanese, but observe no hostility towards us.

The only indication of war in the country is the live look of the forts, as we enter the harbor, which are swarming with soldiers. Indeed, the nearer we get to the seat of war the denser the ignorance and the scarcer the news of it becomes. In New York they know all about the Chinese war; in San Francisco a good deal, in Japan a little, but in China they know nothing at all about it. The Captain invites me to go and dine on board ship again, afterwards takes me for a walk about the city, and then returns me to the hotel. So ends my first day in China.

November 4th.—To-day is election day in America, I suppose, and you are all at a white heat of excitement over it. I never took any interest in politics at home, but here in China I do. I talk politics with gentlemen until they call me a politician.

I have been out again to-day in search of purchases and mementoes of travel to send home. The part of Shanghai outside the walls is quite different from either the Chinatown of San Francisco or the Chinese city here within the walls. It has broad streets, and the shops are well ordered and comparatively clean. I don't see as many children here as in Japan. The Chinese waiters wear a long blue cotton gown over their dress, which creates quite a breeze as they stride around in the dining room.

I fail to see the reason for fearing the Chinese in America. The idea that they can ever permanently throw out American labor seems to me a mistaken one. Working cheaply and doing precisely as they are told without making the mistake of thinking for themselves seems to me to be their only virtue. On the other hand, they are dirty in their habits, slovenly in their work and stupid. The Japanese are far brighter, more polite and more agreeable people to have about. Look, for instance, in America at the sort of washing done by the Chinese. It is all gloss and no cleanliness. In San Francisco I pined for a good Irish washerwoman. I am certain I should never employ a Chinaman to wash for me if I could get an Irish, Dutch or American woman to do it. I think I have the very stupidest of all the Chinese waiters to wait on me at this house.

STEAMER VERONA, OFF WOOSONG, CHINA, *November 5th.*— Singapore is now my objective point. I only take Hong Kong by the way. I came down here this morning, being brought on board by my friend the Captain of the Yokohama Maru, in a tender. The rest of the passengers are to come down to-night at one o'clock. The company sent me word yesterday that the tender would come out to the Verona this morning at half past eleven; consequently the hotel runner and all the Chinese servants were hurrying me off under the mistaken notion she was going at ten. I convinced them of their error, and having been scared into being ready to start an hour too early, I waited only for the Captain and then started in search of a new stylus. On this excuse I got him into a store where I had purchased a lovely little musical box at a very small price, whose virtues I had been singing to him for two days, and made him listen to all the tunes of all the music boxes in the shop before going on board the tender.

I had been looking on myself as a sort of supernatural idiot for going on board at eleven in the morning in order to come down here and lie off all day, when I might be seeing more of Shanghai and then get off without haste at eleven to-night. But when I saw the arrangement I was to come off in I congratulated myself on my intuition and judgment, for the ten minutes I spent in reaching the steamer gave me quite a sufficient acquaintance with the tender. To-night I should have had to stand up in her in the cold and wet and dirt for an hour and a half, she being nothing but a bare black piece of machinery without so much as a rail to sit on. The name of this beautiful craft does not rise to the situation. It is quite inadequate to the occasion. Her name is Minnie. To get on board of her I had to climb up and around and over another craft of her own sort, only larger. Having got on board the Verona the Captain sees the Verona's Captain, who is sick in bed, but who promises to get well and get up to-morrow and pay me every attention. I am then confided to the tender mercies of the Chief officer, and having done everything that the most anxious friend could think of for my comfort, the Captain of the Yokohama Maru bids me good bye and wishes me success, and departs to look after his own steamer, which sails a few hours later than this. And so I am still the highly recommended passenger to whom all honor is to be shown.

On board the Verona I find myself practically in England. This is an English line (Peninsula and Oriental), and officers and cabin servants are all English. I am the only lady passenger, and there are but few gentlemen. They come down to-night at 1 A. M. and we sail soon after. The Doctor and Chief officer are very nice Englishmen. I think I'm to have a pleasant voyage. We shall reach Singapore in about fifteen days.

I am a good deal interested in Pigeon English. The Chinamen announce a lady visitor as "one piecee lady."

November 8th.—We are approaching Hong Kong. For two whole days it rained incessantly, and on this steamer they have no upper deck saloon at all; in fact, no place for the passengers but their staterooms and the long, dark "subterranean" dining saloon in wet weather. Everybody felt very uncertain on the score of breakfast, but no one confessed it but me. Everybody looked very rigid and severe. My expression of entire loss of confidence in digestive apparatus found a sympathetic echo in every heart. My neighbor at table proved to be a young Englishman, for whom the proprietor of the hotel was scouring Shanghai, in order to introduce him to me. We recognized each other as the much talked of, long looked for, and have been all but inseparable for two days. I leave this young gentleman in Hong Kong, but expect to see him again in Calcutta. We have a Chinese merchant on board as first class passenger, who has his own opinion of America. He speaks very good English and reads it as well. He seems to be afflicted with egotism.

HONG KONG, *November 8th.*—To begin with it has one of the prettiest harbors in the world, and secondly Hong Kong itself is very pretty and pleasant. All the way along, whenever I have mentioned Hong Kong to other people, it has been disposed of in the one expressive word, "hot." I confess to its having been rather warm the day of my arrival, but after that was pleasantly cool. The first morning, Sunday, we went to the summit of the Island of Kong Kong, which appears to be nothing but a mountain thrown up out of the sea. From the summit—and in fact all the way up the road—is to be seen one of the loveliest views of sea and land conceivable. The harbor is truly a beautiful one. The journey up was represented to me as extremely fatiguing and there were serious doubts expressed about my being able to go all the way, but as a matter of fact it turned out to be a ridiculously smooth, well kept, level road, considering it led to the top of a rather abrupt mountain. After my mountain travels in Japan I laughed its difficulties to scorn. We were carried up in chairs by Chinese coolies, of whom it takes four to carry one person in China and only three in Japan. The Chinese are larger than the Japanese, but more angular and far less pleasing, and for sheer stupidity commend me to the Chinamen. At the hotel we had to give our orders to half a dozen waiters before we could finally get what we wanted.

The American Consul, John R. Mosby, called on me. He came direct from the Governor of Hong Kong, to whom I had sent my letter of introduction, with an invitation to tea at the

Government House, which I accepted, and we went at once; was received by the Governor cordially and introduced to more Consuls. Our Consul was broken hearted over the announcement of the election of Cleveland. I had a pleasant chat with these people, a walk around the gardens, and some tea, after which I was sent home with an immense bouquet.

The English gentleman proved very nice. We went together to the hotel, dined and breakfasted and "tiffined" together; and when he was not trotting around with me, he was looking up something for me. We did not get to Canton. I could have gone up and returned just in time to catch my steamer, but should have been able to see so little, and been so hurried, that I did not try it. In the present state of affairs one can only be hurried through the streets with a government guard; one can't stop a moment for fear of creating a disturbance. I thought it not worth while. With all my acquaintance with China I saw but one pretty girl.' She was a little thing of seven, with a band of long black fringe fastened around her head, that was very effective. Finally, after "trapsing" the city over looking at musical boxes and carved ivory in a vain search for a certain kind of card box and wooden figures my young English friend took me aboard the Verona, which soon sailed, leaving him desolee at Hong Kong, with twelve tiresome days on his hands before his particular steamer sails. I expect to meet him again at Singapore and again at Calcutta, for which I am glad, for although very young he has been a very agreeable traveling companion.

It is now November 13th, and we have been two nights at sea, one pretty rough one, and my berth being crosswise I slid up and down it all night, a la cellar door. And now a change comes over the spirit of my travels. There are no gentlemen on board except the Captain and Chief officer with whom I wish to be acquainted. I therefore ignore them all, wilfully and persistently, until they are fain to accept the bann that is put on them and sleep and smoke and read the tiresome days away. The Captain I have at last seen. He is very pleasant, but is still confined to his room with gout. The Chief officer has, therefore, to do double duty, but such time as he has he gives to me. The rest of the time I am very glad to retire within myself and contemplate my virtues. For recreation I have made a young lady, who is traveling alone, and who suffers dreadfully with seasickness, my charge. I doctor her and sympathize with her and amuse her by turns. She doesn't expect to be well until we reach Singapore on the 16th, and has been sick at sea for six weeks at a time.

There is one more lady on board, traveling with her husband. She, too, is seasick and they, and all the passengers indeed, look on me running about the deck and coming ravenously down to the dining saloon four times a day, with mixed feelings of envy and admiration. This lady and gentleman, Mr. and Mrs. Few, are a curious pair. They have been taking a more extensive tour than mine and are going to Java. I expect we shall be fellow travelers as far as Calcutta. They are ancient, gray haired, bald, chipper, and inseparable. They twitter venerable affection at each other all over the ship. To me the sight of two devoted elderly people is both pleasant and refreshing.

It is hot, red hot, blazing hot, and they promise that it shall be hotter at Singapore and hottest at Java. So be it. It is very nice loafing under the awning on deck. Of course at the last I begin to get acquainted a little with some of the gentlemen on board ship. Women are always very much in the minority on the steamers, so on arriving on board I find a dozen or more gentlemen all more or less bent on forming my acquaintance. I am immediately bent on not having my acquaintance formed, to which end I try to look as forbidding as possible. I ignore their presence at dinner or on deck. I pass them as if they did not exist. I promenade the deck amongst them, but alone and wrapped in an armor of ice. I sit a little apart, gazing on space, but evidently absorbed in my own reflections. In a day or two they are the most unobtrusive and thoroughly tamed set of gentlemen you ever saw. Then I may relax a little the severity of my demeanor. Having frozen my fellow passengers to veritable icebergs I proceed to thaw, and oh! most inconsistent of feminine creatures, five minutes after the ice is broken I am talking to one of my ci-devant frozen up would be acquaintances as if I had known him all my life. I have to stop talking to laugh at myself, but the favored man is too surprised with the sudden burst of sunshine to criticise and the rest are consumed with envy. The amenities fairly established, they tell me they would never have dared to address me directly those first two or three frosty days. Sometimes the efforts to break the icy barriers are amusing. Once in starting to go below a gentleman in the companion way remarked "good-night" in a voice replete with determination not to be ignored. The good-night was shot at me like a bullet, with an inexpressibly defiant air. Sometimes three or four gentlemen will spring to my assistance while I am struggling with a refractory chair or cushion.

I am not necessarily ill-natured; it comes natural to me to smile and answer if people address me, but I manage still to impress my desire to be let alone, and truly I am quite right in being reserved. The people who would get acquainted with me at once are the people who would bore me the most, and who would be most likely to treat me to some familiarity. By biding my time I can form some idea of the characters about me and make a better choice of acquaintances, gaining usually firm friends, instead of getting myself insulted and defamed for my amiability. Most of the people I meet are English. To get along comfortably and safely with the average Englishman you must first impress him with your complete and entire respectability and fixed determination not to have any sentimental nonsense. When you have frozen that into him you may indulge in sociable friendliness in comparative safety. I like to be left to my own thoughts a great deal, and I should never have a minute to myself if I did not discipline them as I do; they would bore me to death for they are so many and ladies are so few. And so I keep the ice unbroken as long as I can with very satisfactory results, and much to their amusement and mine, for the situation becomes supremely ridiculous to me and we have many a good laugh over it when once the ice is broken and we become really good friends.

I went forward one day and inspected the steerage passengers and a very unhappy looking lot they were. They were all Chinese and as seasick and miserable as could be. They have no berths but are strewn about the forward deck in various stages of wretchedness, with their household goods around them, quite exposed to the sun but for their umbrellas or matting and with an occasional cow or other piece of live stock among them.

SCENE ON BOARD P. & O. S. S. VERONA.

English Lady: "Do they have nice steamers in America?"

English Gentleman: "There are no American steamers."

Two American Ladies (hitherto limp and seasick, sitting up very straight, in chorus): "What?"

E. G.: Repeats.

1st A. L.: "Well, I have traveled fifteen thousand miles on one American steamer and six thousand on another to my certain knowledge. Steamers built at Chester, Pennsylvania."

2d A. L.: "Did you never hear of a man by the name of John Roach?"

E. G.: "No river steamers I mean."

1st A. L.: "You have been to America. Did you go up the Hudson on the C. Vibbard, the St. John or the Drew?"

E. G. (meekly): "I did, they are very handsome."

2d A. L.: "Have you any handsomer in England?"

E. G.: "We have no rivers in England."

1st A. L.: "How do they compare with those widely known disgraces to civilization that ply between France and England?"

E. G. (apologetically): "Oh, those are very bad."

1st A. L.: "I suppose you have very handsome steamers. This is the first English steamer I ever saw."

E. G. (unsuspectingly): "Oh, this is a very good sample."

1st A. L. (sarcastically): "Then all I have to say is that it is by long odds the very worst, most villainously arranged, badly cuisined, inefficiently managed, comfortless old hulk it was ever my misfortune to travel on." (Trampling on a fallen foe.) "Where is your comfortable smoking room, with card tables? Where is your elegantly fitted upper-deck social hall? Where are your electric lights?"

No answer.

1st A. L. (cruelly): "Look at your miserable dining saloon, a long dark alley immediately over the screw, the only place for the passengers in wet weather, without an opening to look out of. Look at that miserable little glass coop with the sign upon the wall, 'Passengers are forbidden to stand in the companion.' Look at that disobliging bar, from which a seasick woman cannot get a glass of lemonade until after eleven o'clock A. M. Look at that scandalous pretense of a fire drill, in which one by one your men come shuffling up in various stages of uncertainty as to what they have come for, and having come are whispered to confidentially that they have mistaken the order in which they should stand and are dismissed. Compare all this with the luxuriousness of our Hudson River or Long Island Sound steamers, with their grand saloons; the elegance of the Santa Rosa, with her gorgeous silk and plush fittings and electric lights; the comfort of the Alameda, with her large airy staterooms in which the comfort of her passengers is not sacrificed to the ideas of the shipbuilder as to space and arrangement; with her perfect fire drill, where the men are at their various stations pumping water through the hose in so many seconds after the alarm is given. Think of all these things and blush for your country This old thing would be burnt to the water before your men found their proper places. No American steamers, indeed!"

E. G. hopelessly crushed.

1st A. L. (sings sarcastically): "For he is an Englishman, for he himself hath said it, and it's greatly to his credit, that he is an Englishman." Ignominious surrender of the British. Belligerent attitude and insufferable egotism of the American ladies for the rest of the day.

The Yokohama Maru was, however, a very nice, comfortable little English steamer, well managed, beautifully decorated and comfortably fitted.

SINGAPORE.

HOTEL D'EUROPE, SINGAPORE, *November 16th, 2 P. M.*—It requires a stretch of the imagination to believe it is in fact November, for the temperature here is suggestive of ovens. There is a beautiful chromo in my room representing a snow and ice scene in the country that cools the air visibly; it refreshes me to look at it. My room is a whitewashed box; the bed is a mosquito-net box, with nothing but sheets and pillows and is suggestive of hot nights.

I have just arrived. The first thing we saw was a lot of very brown bare boys in primitive canoes half full of water. These boys were divers. The passengers throw pieces of money in the water and the boys dive after them. They catch them under the water and come to the surface with them in their mouths. They are exceedingly anxious to dive for you, and keep up an incessant chatter of "Hab adibe, sir?" and "Yes, sir," and "All right, sir." Two of them dove clear under our steamer, coming up on the other side with the money in their mouths.

I said good bye to the Captain, who was toddling around on that gouty limb, and departed; the Doctor and Chief officer procuring me a carriage by their united efforts, getting my luggage aboard of it, and bidding me good bye. The vehicle is a little shuttered box drawn by a most unhappy pony, whose dinner of grass is fastened on to one of my trunks at the back, in case he falls by the way. A drive of three miles brings me to the hotel. We go through country and villages by turns. Sometimes the villages are built on piles and every tide sweeps under the houses. You see all the shades of brown people, Chinese, Malay, Singalese and gracious knows what else, but the scene is not as varied or as interesting as in Japan. I haven't observed any sociable cobras or boa constrictors in my room yet, but, as the Irishman said, "I have great hopes."

Dear me, what a dreadful thing it is to be a woman and to travel alone! I have thrown the hotel quite into a commotion. The unhappy clerk is in a pitiable state. He comes to my room and closes a shutter of my window that somebody in an adjacent room might possibly look through by partially dislocating his neck, and explains apologetically that there is so much curiosity and they ask him so many questions. He also inquires doubtfully what my business is and I reply by way of reassuring him that I travel for my heath, and write. The table is at the time strewn with my manuscript, so the reply is eminently satisfactory. He thinks that I ought to feel strange and frightened at being alone in a hotel, so he escorts me upstairs and downstairs to the table and back again, as the unfortunate gentleman who had charge of the hotel at Los Alamas, Cal., did when I swooped down on that wretched place. What a shocking sinful thing a woman is, to be whisked away and tucked into a back room, out of sight. I ought evidently to blush for my womanhood. But I don't. On the contrary, I glory in it. I have come so far in comfort and safety, and I feel every day more confidence in myself and the innate goodness of human nature.

My principal and favorite friend and companion and escort here is a little English lady of seven years, who resides in the same part of the hotel that I do with her parents and "ayah," and whose childish heart I have won by the exhibition of the musical box. She is a diminutive specimen of British prudence and formality, with a predisposition for caste and scandal, but is bright and pretty. She takes me to curio shops and teaches me how to dicker and bargain with the natives therein, and I must say it sounds curious to hear this infant disparage the article she set her heart on, affect indifference to its purchase, and leave the store ostentatiously to go to another when her demands are not complied with. She speaks Malay and tells me what to say and where I ought to go and what is going on that I ought to see, and what ladies I should refuse to see if they should call upon me. Fancy! I am going to take her with me to hear the band at the Botanical Gardens to-morrow. Her mother seems quite willing to have her go about with me, and she is a valuable little guide and my most ardent admirer.

Mr. and Mrs. Few and I are to go to Java together and back, and on as far as Ceylon, perhaps Calcutta. They are very pleasant, jolly, enterprising Americans.

There are people of many countries here. There appear to be Clings and Singalese and Siamese and Japanese and Chinese and Malay. I admire the Clings most, they are very black, with upright bearing and handsome faces and bright black eyes. The men of this race wear a striped cloth called a sarong, wrapped around them like a skirt, and a jacket. A piece of cloth or handkerchief tied around the head completes the toilet. They wear the hair hanging down to the shoulders or tied up in a sort of tail in the back, changing from one mode to the other at all times and places during the day. The Clings are natives of Ceylon. They look a very fine race. They are almost as black as ebony; are tall and slender and as straight as it is possible to be. They have an especially graceful, dignified, even majestic carriage. They are Caucasian in type and have very bright and intelligent looking faces. They form a decided contrast to the Siamese, who are broader, more dumpy, fatter as a rule. The Clings are invariably slim and straight, and their black skins have a perfectly clean dry shine as of polished wood. I am admiring them immensely. I believe every nation under the sun is represented here but Africa. The Cling women wear ornaments in their noses and have, literally, rings on their toes. The Cling children are as beautiful as possible. There is a clean, delicate cut of face and figure, which, added to fine large black eyes and intelligent expressions, makes them really beautiful people. I am in love with the race; they are far superior to the Chinese, who are a cunning, insolent and at the same time groveling set. The Clings are stately, dignified and proud, as their whole bearing testifies.

November 20th.—It is hot, but not so frightfully hot as I had been led to expect. The thermometer varies from 80 to 90 degrees during the day, but the air is always cooler at evening and very comfortably cool during the night. I've suffered more with heat in New York, and when New York is hot it stays so night and day. I am stranded here until the 25th of November, as no suitable vessel sails for Java until then. As I like the place and climate here very much I don't mind that particularly. This is popularly supposed to be the worst hotel in the world; the "very worst" is at Batavia, they say. I am glad I have no husband or brother, or masculine companion of any sort, along with me to make it more uncomfortable by grumbling. I am getting along very comfortably myself. In the absence of other palatable food I am laying up unweighed pounds of avoirdupois on rice and curry. I am feeling exceedingly well and energetic, particularly at meal times. I take five meals a day now according to the custom of the country, and I may say parenthetically that my appetite keeps pace with that custom remarkably well. I go down to the hotel table d'hote three times a day and fill myself to repletion with rice and curry. Twice a day I have bread and tea served in my apartment. The water all through the East is unfit to drink, so I take tea and coffee and claret in turns.

Apropos de café, the nearer you get to the home of that pleasing drink the worse the quality of it gets. I am afraid it is the old story of skim milk, knotty apples, mean potatoes and seedy waste scraps of berries of the country farm house. This is a tropical country, supposed to abound in luscious fruits. By bringing his whole mind to bear on it, Mr. Few has succeeded in finding some pineapples that are good. At the table d'hote they provide bananas that a New York grocer would blush to give away, so little and flavorless are they. These dwarf specimens of the banana are called plantains here. The only other fruit they offer is a sort of combination of orange, tomato and apple, the name of which I do not know, and the taste of which is not attractive. The table waiters are ex-jinricksha men, and a nice stupid lot they are too. Newcomers waste their tissues this hot weather by swearing at them; the regular boarders are long past swearing. I listen to Mr. Few raging and think how my brothers and cousins and uncles would suffer, and am glad none of them are along. Mrs. Few and I sit calmly munching our rice, and merely remark "bread" or "curry" or "ice" to some boy as he flies by, and possess our souls in patience until we get it. There is really no use in swearing at a Chinese waiter except for the comfort or relief you yourself may derive from a classic flow of language, for the "boy" as he is called here, is invariably worse. It is as much as he can do to comprehend a single English word, without going into the intricacies of the large and select assortment of profanity thrown at him.

They wait on you to death in the East. They begin in the morning at half past six by bringing you tea or coffee or bread and butter. It is of no use to shut your ears and pretend you are asleep. If you have locked your door the Chinaman taps insinuatingly at it until you let him in. He does not care whether you are dressed or not, or whether you want him to come in or not; his business is to come in and place the tray on the table and gather up all the shoes and slippers he can find and depart, and he does so. You may rest a little while then, but presently another man comes, with whom it is perfectly useless to expostulate. He doesn't know what you say, and cares less perhaps. He wants to empty your wash bowl and refill your pitcher. Another comes and insists on having one at least of your towels before you are through with them; then the first one comes back to take away the tea tray and return your shoes; another follows to see if you have got any soiled linen for the wash. By this time you have perhaps got dressed, so no more boys come. You may then think of something you want and may call "boy" out of your door or window until you are black in the face, but no boy will appear. He has attended to his routine duty in your room and has gone to the dining room to be ready to wait at table.

They say the beauty of a Chinaman as a servant, or, worker of any kind, is that he never thinks. This charcteristic has its disadvantages at times. The ex-jinricksha men who wait on us at the table d'hote are exasperating to the extent of being funny. In the first place they understand little or no English, and in the second place they are not systematically trained, and lastly they are ineffably stupid. Mr. Few has got a great deal of rage and I a great deal of fun out of the effort to secure hard boiled eggs. The boys go about helter-skelter offering people food. As they have no allotted places, they are usually all waiting on one or two people at once, while the rest of the people are gnashing their teeth between frantic efforts to stop a boy as he flies by. When you do get waited on, you are offered the same dish by several consecutive boys in turn if you decline the first one. We can't tell one boy from the other, there are so many attending to us; so when we tell one boy we want hard boiled eggs, and he has been absent for ten or fifteen minutes and we are offered eggs we take them, find them nearly raw, send them away with the demand for hard ones; and presently another boy comes and offers us eggs, which we try with the same result. After waiting twenty minutes and breaking half a dozen eggs each, we succeed in getting some still a long way from being hard, but sufficiently cooked to be eatable. We laugh, of course, every time we crack an egg or try to "lasso" a boy, and even the prim, staid English people who board here regularly are fain to relax a little their solemnity over our troubles.

English people are very subdued and stupid over their dinners, or anywhere, I fancy. They say it is considered bad form to show any animation or pleasure in any thing. Even the little seven-year-old girl was averse to going at all early, to hear the music. She was quite shocked at the idea of getting there before it commenced, and said she never went to the theatre until it was nearly over. One little English lady who has stared me out of countenance ever since I have been here, and has been surprised into smiling at our jokes at table, has concluded to know me and smiles and speaks to me whenever she can catch my attention. English people seem to look with especial disfavor on people who want to know them. The more independent one is of them, the more sufficient to yourself you are, the better they like you.

I took the little girl to drive with me one morning, to the waterworks, where they have a pretty park. Our coachman apparently did not know the way and took us to some other place. Miss Kitty exhausted her knowledge of Malay on him to no purpose. Finally, after he had made a good many inquiries along the road, a pretty half-caste woman in European dress got out of her carriage and came and asked us where we wanted to go, and directed the driver. After we got there Miss Kitty asked a Malay boy for a drink. He brought two glasses of water on a tray, for which politeness I paid him a few coppers, apparently an immense fee, for he invited us up to see the bungalow, threw it open for us to rest where it was cool, picked some flowers for Kitty and gave us liberty of the place, all out of gratitude ; and that brings me to another notion of mine.

All through China and Japan one is told constantly by the English and Americans that you must speak harshly and sharply to the natives, or they will not respect your orders. One would say these people have lived among them and ought to know, but I think they are wrong ; I think they say that just as the old slaveholders used to assert, that you must whip a negro to keep him well behaved. I found the Japanese particularly susceptible to mere amiability and very grateful for the least kindness, taking pleasure in giving you something, or doing something extra for you, after they had been paid. Even the Chinese who are surly, usually quite melt under kindness. An English gentleman seeing me pay a Chinaman, said he never had heard a Chinaman say "Thank you" before.

They have jinrickshas here too, but a more popular mode of travel is by the pony-shutter-wagons called "gharries." I took Kitty in one of them up to the Botanical Gardens to hear the music, played by a brass band, which started off with the Beggar Student, much to my delight. European music was very refreshing after two months of tom-tom. Kitty, having recovered from the shock of so.early an arrival, was very entertaining.

JAVA.

HOTEL BELLEVUE, BUITENZORG, JAVA, *Nov. 27th.*—I have now reached the scene of that interesting book "The Prison of Weltevreden," the reading of which gave me my first desire to travel. That desire was planted in my imagination when I was seven years old. Now, at twenty-six I have just fulfilled my childish ambition. I passed through Weltevreden to-day. It is a suburb of Batavia and the railway station is situated there.

Coming here on the steamship Godavery there was besides Mr. and Mrs. Few and myself only one native English speaking person on board the steamer, and he was disagreeable. I was, of course, next the Captain at table. I'm a fixture there it would seem. Next me were two very agreeable young men, Holland Dutch by birth, both highly educated, traveled gentlemen, owning property in Java. They speak twelve languages and adore music and dancing. One of them, Mr. Van, had been told about me by my bankers, and both have laid themselves out to be of all the use to Mr. and Mrs. Few and myself possible. The voyage down was smooth and pleasant, and although we crossed the equator, it was not so hot as to make life unendurable; indeed to me it was quite comfortably cool. Being on a French steamer, in France as it were, I had to bring all my French to the fore both for myself and my temporary traveling companions. We reached Batavia anchorage at half past five, were taken on board a steam launch, up an artificial channel, from a quarter to half a mile long, to Batavia. On each side of this channel was shallow water, in which sharks and alligators and native men and women disported in equal pleasure and comfort and entire confidence in each other.

Arrived at Batavia, with the aid of Mr. Van we got through their strict Custom House without the least trouble, put ourselves in the hands of the Des Indes hotel runner and with all our luggage were driven rapidly to that hotel. Then to our bankers, and then to the train, which brought us to Biutenzorg. Mr. Van took me to the depot in his carriage, assisted us to get our tickets, attend to our luggage, fee our porters properly, get on the right car and then, with many misgivings about us and good wishes for us and the promise to come up the day after tomorrow and look after us, bade us good bye as the train moved out of the depot. We arrived here in the course of an hour and a half, got into a Bellevue Hotel carriage, and after quite a drive reached the hotel and cast ourselves on the tender mercies of the proprietor. Both at Batavia and here we are disappointed in the hotels, they are so much better than we had been led to expect.

English is a scarce language hereabouts. Dutch and Malay and Singhalese are the prevailing tongues. These are Dutch possessions, Dutch towns, Dutch hotels. You have two courses at lunch, the first being rice and curry, of which you take a large plate and put everything else that is offered you upon the rice—fish, fowls, meats, sausages—and chop all these edibles together and eat them. After that they give you beefsteak and fried potatoes, then fruit and coffee. This is the principal meal of the day and is called the rice meal. The hotel was clean, comfortable and well served. We had the pleasure of tasting the "dorian" to-day—a fruit of most delicious flavor, a combination of hickory nuts, onions and cream in taste, but with a smell compared with which Limburger cheese is attar of roses, and which is enough to make Stilton cheese turn green with envy. We were importuned at the Des Indes by Malays who wanted to sell us sarongs and slippers for fabulous prices at the commencement, and, failing that, begged us to take their goods at our own price. I hear the sound of a waterfall and see lizards crawling on my bedroom wall, and I shiver.

November 28th.—Here as in Singapore the time to rise is before six. Six is the hour for coffee or tea. No one who knows me could possibly imagine me getting out of bed at that hour, drinking a cup of the weakest imaginable tea and eating some bread and going for a drive before breakfast, but that is what I do in this country. I have two rooms here. My bedroom is entered from a courtyard and opens into a sitting room that opens in turn on a veranda, which overlooks a steep bluff at the foot of which is a river that appears, as I sit, to run under my room, but which in reality it turns off with a short curve to the right. A little way up the river, where it narrows, a bridge half concealed by puppiia trees crosses the river, and in the water are natives of all sizes, colors and sex, playing, swimming and alternately washing their clothes, themselves, and their household utensils. Beyond the river rises a mountain, whose top is in the clouds.

Coming through the country last night in the cars, and to-day in our drive, we saw what a rich, beautiful country this is. "The garden spot of the earth" they call it, but then there are so *many* "garden spots of the earth." Japan rejoices in the same flattering reputation, so also do the Sandwich Islands, likewise Ceylon; and you don't have to go more than a mile toward the inner consciousness of a Californian to find that he cherishes a fond and inexpugnable belief that California is the original and only "garden spot of the earth."

I find all places interesting—California for its genial, sterling men and magnificent scenery; Hawaii for its dreamy, languorous quiet and fresh breezes; Japan for its polite and interesting people; Singapore for its innumerable nationalities, and Java for its luxuriant vegetation. We drove this morning through a park where tigers come at night and carry off the deer that roam about in large numbers. The owner of a plantation here says, however, that he has only seen a tiger once, and then it is a question which was the most scared, he or the tiger. He says he and the ferocious beast went off with simultaneous bounds in opposite directions. This gentleman grows indigo and india rubber on his plantation for market and coffee and tobacco for personal use. Besides banana, cocoanut, pineapple, puppiia, dorian and innumerable varieties of palm trees, Java grows the banyan tree, whose branches reach down and take root in the earth until one tree forms quite a respectable forest all by itself. I also saw this morning quantities of lotus flowers in bloom. The park is the Governor's grounds and is exceedingly pretty.

This is a country of earthquakes. We confidently expect several shakings-up before we leave Java six days from now. It was here in the Straits of Sunda, which divide Java from Sumatra, that the terrible earthquake occurred some years ago that killed so many people, sunk some islands and threw some others up out of the sea to such an extent that the straits and sea about had to be resurveyed. Snakes are plenty here, but they don't sleep in the hotel beds as a regular business. The lizards are more sociable. You can see them four inches long on your walls any time of the day. They eat flies and ants and mosquitos.

November 29th.—Mr. and Mrs. Few and myself went driving again this morning in this beautiful tropical country. It is more lovely than can be described; the population is dense, but it is not made apparent by ugly rows of houses, as in Japan. The native houses, built of plaited bamboo, are scattered about amongst the trees, so that you can look over a vast and much populated valley and see only a tropical forest with but an occasional glimpse of a roof peeping through the cocoanut and palm trees. The natives are neither pretty nor ugly, except the little children under six years, who are quite pretty. I notice a great deal of human affection for their little ones is displayed by the natives. I saw a Malay boy of eight or nine years bring a pretty little crying sister of three or four years out of the house, sitting down on a log and taking her on his lap so she could see us Americans without being scared, all with an affectionate care that might be copied by many American boys with much benefit to them. And some innate sense of delicacy seems to have suggested to the uncivilized Malay that it is impolite to point at strangers, for I saw a Malay woman put her baby's little pointing arm down every time it was raised, but with much more gentleness than I had seen the same thing done in America. I find most little brown children are as frightened at white people as white babies are at brown folks.

We got a boy to go up a cocoanut tree and pick us a green cocoanut. It was cut open for us on the spot, and we each had a drink of the milk from it. The white part had not hardened yet so we ate it with a spoon. Men, women and children all wear the sarong, which is more like a pillow case with both ends open than anything else. The men usually wear it fastened around the waist; when they wear trousers the sarong is reduced to a broad sash and arranged according to the taste of the wearer, sometimes jauntily hanging longer over one leg than over the other. The women and little girls wear it most frequently fastened just under the arms. The fastening part is a mystery; they simply wrap it tightly around them at the top and tuck in the edge and there it stays. They wear it into the water while washing, and when they take it off to bathe themselves and put it on again, or if they don a clean one, they do so while they are all wet and standing in the water, taking another duck or so to wet it thoroughly. If they have put on a clean one they proceed to wash the one just taken off. To wash clothes they first find a sharp stone, and then give their whole minds to an ambitious effort to drive it through to the other side of the earth, using the article of clothing as a club. From my balcony I can hear them a long distance off pounding the rocks with linen in the river below me. There is much invention displayed in the mode of arranging brightly colored handkerchiefs on the head. Every man wears one, and each in a different and most intricate fashion.

This is the rainy season here; it rains every afternoon and is delightfully cool. It is beautifully bright all the morning, getting comfortably hot by noon. Buitenzorg is the place where Java people come to re-invigorate their health, because it is high and cool. I am always satisfied with the weather. My balcony looks right up the mountain and into the lava guttered side of an extinct crater, about which fog and clouds are drifting all the afternoon. I must speak of the curious luncheon again, or "tiffin," as it is called. You have a soup dish, in which you lay a solid foundation of rice; on that you put curry, sausage, pork, chicken, salad of hard boiled eggs and lettuce, cucumbers, omelet, pickled beets, fish, beef and a dozen kinds of spices, all of which you chop up with fork and soup spoon and eat. As I am a vegetarian and most of these things are meats, fish and fowl, you can imagine my head wagging from one side to the other in frantic negatives as I am offered each one of these dishes two and three times over. And we have rice and curry only once a day—I shall starve.

HOTEL HOMAN, BANDONG, *November 30th.*—Our guardian angel, commonly known as Mr. Van, came up to Buitenzorg to look after his little flock of "Innocents," who were, indeed, very much "Abroad." We received him with gratifying enthusiasm. He went right to work to map out our future course to us, took us to the depot, overseeing the purchase of our tickets, and finally left us, reluctantly returning to Batavia himself, while we came on in the opposite direction to this place, where we arrived at three P. M., simply said Hotel Homan to a Malay, were stowed in a carriage and driven here. We were received by Malay servants and shown rooms at once, without a word being spoken. Tea was brought us soon, and then we rested and waited for dinner. We waited a good while. At half past seven we began to get anxious; at five minutes of eight we concluded we were not to have any supper that night. We saw no one but Malays and tried in vain to find the landlord to extort information from him, though we had been told he spoke no English. We managed to inquire of one of the native servants, who were sitting on the floor in spots, motionless as statues, when we were to have dinner, and he replied, by fingers, nine o'clock. Presently, when we were on the point of going dinnerless to bed, a bell struck, lights were lit in the dining room, and the clatter of dishes proclaimed the long waited for event of the day had arrived.

We took our seats at table. A Dutchman and his wife and his daughter sat opposite; next them a couple of Dutchmen; at the head of the table a Dutchwoman, the landlady, and next to me an East Indian, who bore a striking resemblance to Othello, only he was darker than Othello usually appears. We struggled along a little; but, woe is me! everything seemed to be cooked in oil, cocoanut oil at that. Just as I was on the verge of distraction, finding that the curry I had put on my rice was also oil, a voice said "Can I be of any assistance to you?" in unexceptionable English. It was like a thunderbolt out of a clear sky, or rather a flash of lightning out of a black cloud, for it was Othello, next me, who spoke. Tableau. We came very near rising in a body and embracing him on the spot. We all began to talk at once, and our troubles were over from that moment. By the end of dinner I discovered that the hostess spoke French, and in the morning it appeared that she spoke a little English, though she seemed to have concealed the fact from the world hitherto.

But I have got over into the next day, and am writing this on December 1st at Sindunglaya, a sanitarium. Othello, it appeared, was coming down to Tjianjoer on the same train that we were, this morning, on his way to Batavia, and is going on the same steamer as ourselves from here to Ceylon, on his way to Europe. We took a little roundabout drive to the depot at Bandong, got another excellent lunch of rice and curry at Tjianjoer, where we lunched on the way up to Bandong, and, with Othello's aid, secured a couple of little native covered carts, each drawn by three horses. Mrs. Few and I got into one and Mr. Few and the baggage in the other, and off we go for a drive of twelve miles to this place.

Here we were received by the landlord, who speaks English. It appears by a placard on the wall that this is "Gezonheid's Establissement, Sindunglaya." It is situated at the foot of an active volcano (nice soothing place for invalids). Our drive over here was bright and pretty. Bandong is a hundred and fifty miles back into the interior of Java. Did any one ever suppose they had railroads most all over Java ? It is ridiculous ; it is absurd. I am beginning to doubt if there is such a thing to be seen in the world now as a savage, uncivilized, land. We travel, as everybody else does in Java, second class by train, because it is better than first class. There is a great deal of energy and art and ingenuity expended here on whistling and snapping whips ; the engine whistles about half the time, and of all shrill, unearthly, earsplitting whistles commend me to these. They whistle one long steady shriek until everybody is on the verge of insanity, then drop into a key lower for a little while, and when you are tired of that stop with a defiant snort upward to the original note.

The drivers of carriages snap their whips in a like irritating manner. These little Javanese ponies are very fractious and the drivers are very inefficient. When their horses balk or cut capers or show a disposition to go in the direction opposite to the one desired the drivers get down and lead them or turn them right. Consequently, your advancement depends largely on the whims of your horses.

The native salutation here to acquaintances or to strangers is to squat down on the ground. It is funny, as we drive by, to see people squatting at the roadside. The men and women in Java are always pretty well clothed, but the children still run about in brown nakedness. Sometimes one sees a little nude seven-year-old reclining against a door post in an attitude of unconscious grace. I saw one pretty little girl wearing a gauze veil on her head, "only this and nothing more." Some wear bracelets simply, by way of wearing apparel, around either their wrists or ankles. Rings about the toes are considered distingué for children and adults both here and in Singapore. I have seen several very pretty little girls whose only garment, if I may call it so, was a necklace. Too much cannot be said in reference to the humane, affectionate treatment of the little children among these uncivilized people. The most natural thing for a Christian child to do when a smaller one cries after it from fright at strangers is to shake the little nuisance. I have never seen here or in Japan the slightest exhibition of annoyance or impatience towards the little children. The older child always drops its play or curiosity to soothe the fears of the smaller one. I see so many pretty little maidens of four years or so, sometimes clothed, as Mark Twain says, in "sunshine," at other times wearing a little sarong and sometimes a jacket. I would like to buy one of these pretty little tots and bring it home with me. The women are good looking while young, but only that.

HOTEL BELLEVUE, BUITENZORG, *December 2d.*—We had supper, or dinner, or whatever they call the meal, last night at Sindunglaya, at 8 P. M., and then to bed. We were up this morning at six and off soon after seven, in our little native carts, drawn each by three ponies, harnessed side by side. We travelled upward about fifteen hundred feet and then through a mountain pass between four thousand and five thousand feet above the level of the sea, which sea, by the way, could be seen from the piazza of the hotel we had just left. Then we came down at a rattling gait to Buitenzorg, having made thirty miles in three and a half hours, and getting here before lunch. The roads were very good all the way. In passing through a forest we saw a flock of flying foxes, immense bats, hanging from the topmost branches of trees. They looked in the distance like so many bunches of overripe bananas, as they hung by the feet, head downward on the limbs.

ON BOARD S. S. GODAVERY, *December 5th*, BOUND FOR SINGAPORE.—Mr. Van came to Buitenzorg, according to promise, at five. He was the guest of the Governor there. He met us the next morning at the depot with two immense bouquets of roses from the Governor's gardens, for Mrs. Few and myself, and we parted with mutual regret and admiration.

At Batavia we went to the museum and saw a collection of Japanese and Sumatra-ese work, clothing, houses, implements, etc.; then to the Botanical Gardens, where we saw a pair of orang-outangs that perfectly fascinated me with their hideousness and mixture of intelligence and animalism. From the museum we went to a photograph gallery, where we purchased some very unsatisfactory photographs of natives. Then to supper and to bed, to rise at five in the morning, drive down to the steam launch which was to bring us off to the Godavery, growling all the way along about the outrageousness of being called up at five in the morning and hustled off without any time for breakfast, to catch a steamer that was not to sail until nine, and at a distance that an hour's time would more than cover. We criticised and commented upon the annoyance with a great deal of warmth and freedom, and asked all the officers and employés to elucidate the why, but did not succeed in getting any satisfactory explanation.

Once more aboard ship, we find ourselves amongst the suave Frenchmen again. The captain welcomes us back. Our Othello is there and glad to see us. He turns out to be the richest planter in Java. Another passenger is a young Dutchman taking his little half-caste girl home to Europe to his sister, the little one's native mother being dead; and another, a young Dutch captain going home to bring out a new steamer. It is very funny to note the excitability of the French people. The movements of the officers and the crew on this ship seem to be so undisciplined and ineffective. There is more excitement over the pulling of a rope, more chattering and gesticulation attendant on some trivial occurrence than you would see on an English ship if a man fell overboard. Several times we have been betrayed by the general excitement and chatter and gesticulation into rising from our comfortable seats and rushing to the side of the vessel expecting to see nothing less than a shark eating a sailor, or a waterspout coming for us, only to find the most trivial occasion for the disturbance. A rope needed pulling in an inch tighter, perhaps, or some one saw a twig in the water. I cultivate the little half-caste girl as well as I can with only one Malay word at my command. It is delightfully cool and pleasant on deck. I have to keep up a running conversation in French and English at one and the same time. I have promised to come back to Java with the Dutch captain on his new steamer if he will go around the Cape of Good Hope. The rounding of the Cape of Good Hope is my latest ambition.

And now for a few notes on traveling alone. I have made this trip with Mr. and Mrs. Few, and therefore, taking advantage of my sex in a measure, shifted the burthen of baggage and tickets upon Mr. Few's shoulders, but I don't see that I got along the least bit better for being taken charge of; indeed, I am guilty of a private opinion that I could manage better by myself. I did the talking usually, understood our route, names of places, hotels, ways of travel, better than he did, and at all times require less assistance, explanation and coaching than he does. They were excited and anxious because they could not get an English speaking servant to go with us. I was perfectly satisfied that we should get along all right without, as we did. I am sometimes taken by strangers to be Mrs. Few's daughter.

Mrs. Few tells me blood curdling stories of insult to young ladies traveling in Japan, with their husbands and a party of friends to protect them, from jinricksha coolies. I don't understand it. I went alone into the interior of Japan and nothing happened to me that could be distorted by the most active imagination into disrespect. I have a theory as to the reason in part. It is this: Many women, even of the most thoroughly respectable, moral and religious kind, are given to a but half concealed vulgarity. Traveling with each other and their husbands, they exhibit this in whispered innuendoes, in suggestive glances and meaningful giggles. The nudeness and natural habits of the people of these countries afford abundant opportunity for this vulgar amusement. The Japanese understand this readily enough and also the fear they excite, and lay themselves out to at once amuse and frighten them. Even Mrs. Few, highly moral Quakeress though she is, jogs me with her elbow and grimaces when we come across some glaring impropriety and comments upon it in an undertone. I go along as if I were as much accustomed to seeing people in a state of nature as they are accustomed to being so, and seemingly unconscious of anything improper in appearance or action. I am not afraid to trust myself in the hands of the natives and they don't try to frighten me.

HOTEL DE L'EUROPE, SINGAPORE, *December 9th.*—We had to bid only the captain of the Godavery good bye; we passengers will still be fellow travelers as far as Ceylon. I am welcomed back to the hotel by the English ladies residing here. Slow, austere, cliquey as they are, having duly considered me, they have concluded to like me and cultivate me. They smile at me graciously at table, offer me books to read on the veranda, and invite me in to tea with their families; all with many exclamations of wonder at my daring in traveling alone. They observe that I act very quietly and independently, but they conclude that I am a desirable acquaintance, and make up to me accordingly.

Caste rages here, however, to such an extent that a merchant captain's wife, being the only lady of that standard, has no one to speak to. The Naval Captain's wife is almost as badly off, but will not descend to companionship with the first lady. The idea of class distinctions between the three of four people who "pig," I may say, in this fifteenth rate hotel is simply absurd anyway. I sail to-day for Colombo at four P. M. on the M. M. Irouaddy.

CEYLON.

MESSAGERIE MARITIMES S. S. IROUADDY, INDIAN OCEAN, *December* 12*th.*—The usual success attended my advent on board this ship. I commenced my acquaintance with the officers by a piece of unheard of audacity, *i. e.*, refused the seat of honor, between the Captain and a French Admiral—newly created such for gallant conduct in the Chinese war—and went by preference to the very foot of the table where my friends had been assigned seats. The place had been made especially for me over all the previous passengers because I was a lady and alone. I now sit opposite the Purser, who presents me with a camelia every morning at breakfast. As these keep nicely I simply pin another one on to my left shoulder, so my corsage boquet increases in size daily. Yesterday I was asked to join in the pool on the boats progress; I did so, and won ten rupees thereby. Of course I must give the others a chance of winning a rupee back, so I played again to-day and won again. They say that when we reach Colombo I will be covered with camelias and loaded with rupees. The Purser tells me that the agent told him to take particular care of me. He extended special privileges to me in the way of through passage to Calcutta, or not, at my convenience, after reaching Colombo. These last few days I have been sailing along just under, or over, New York State, on the opposite side of the globe.

December 14*th.*—OFF THE COAST OF CEYLON.—We expect to reach Colombo to-night. To-day an inspection of the ship and entire service was held. The Captain came out resplendent in epaulettes and medals.

I have been in a bad temper for three days. These annals would not be perfect without a chapter of growls, so I will write one. I have had a cold with my usual irritated state of lungs, and "the politest nation in the world" permits smoking in every part of the ship. I have observed several mythical legends in various places relating to "limit de fumeurs," but they are apparently intended only for ornament, for everybody smokes everywhere, while I sit and cough or wander about in search of a pure atmosphere, and snub ferociously every creature who dares approach me with a cigar in hand or mouth. Even the Americans, I am ashamed to say, have laid aside the respect and consideration the American gentleman usually shows a lady and add their volume of smoke to the general cloud. I suspect that if I could produce a strict enforcement of the smoking rules it would turn all the present friendliness toward me to bitterest hatred. I hate a man who smokes when it makes him beastly selfish. So much for growling.

QUEENS HOTEL, KANDY, CEYLON, *December 15th.*—Our last two days at sea were stormy. Having been promised lovely weather, the passengers protested. The Captain explained that they were not responsible for *irregular* monsoons; this was a southeast one, I think, when, according to time honored custom, it should have been northwest. Anyway it was tolerably rough, and it rained torrents, and all the ports were closed, and this is a hot climate, and these steamers have no upper saloon. I leave the rest to your imaginations.

Yesterday we expected to reach Colombo at 9 P. M. We, a number of us passengers, all "globe trotters" and bound in the same direction, had just concluded to remain on board all night, when it was announced that all the ports would be closed during the night while taking in coal; that settled it; we would go ashore at any cost. So we sat up and waited to get in. Accustomed to rise very early, we were all tired, and we watched our approach to land and fell asleep by turns. It seemed as if we were bent on passing Colombo instead of stopping there, for we sailed straight on long after we saw the harbor lights. Finally we stopped and waited for the pilot. We had been signaled and telegraphed at Point de Galle in the morning, but the pilot had evidently got tired and gone to bed, for no pilot appeared for some time. While we waited and watched the shore anxiously we nodded in our chairs by turns, anathematising the pilot between nods.

At last he came and took us in behind the big red light we had been sailing around all night; then we engaged one of the few boatmen who came out, got ashore, walked up the narrow pier between lines of sleeping Singhalese lying on the floor on either side, piled the baggage with Mrs. Few and myself on a carriage, and drove up the streets after midnight, through a strange sleeping city, to the hotel.

I have been told I must see Kandy, and with that purpose I left Mr. and Mrs. Few to-day somewhat unceremoniously and started out by myself with a fresh burst of enthusiasm at traveling alone again. The Fews are good people enough, but good people have so many detestable faults. They are so exceedingly good and moral and affectionate and tender in their own family circle, and so irritatingly selfish, unjust, and wanting in natural human sympathy toward humanity at large. I get along much better and much happier alone. Good, Christian Mrs. Few's worldliness and want of feeling for her own sex distresses me always, and Mr. Few's efforts to help me were only a bother. I am more practical, more accurate, more independent than he, at least I think so.

To come up here takes four hours; it is seven miles from Colombo. I have the whole of the ladies' first-class car to myself. This place is high up in the mountains; some of these mountains the train went around and some it went through, and some of them it "clum." I could feel the wheels digging their metaphorical finger nails and toe nails into the rails to keep from sliding back. I never went up such steep grades in cars before. The scenery was beautiful as we wound around the mountains and looked down into the valleys far below. The irrigated, terraced farms reach way up on the mountains like so many irregular steps.

Ceylon is the native place of the people whose stately bearing and light, free, graceful walk I admired so much in Singapore —the tall, slim, Clings or Singhalese. Coming through the country by train is a good way to see the people. I saw a boy of fifteen whose face and figure were the perfection of beauty and grace. Instead of little brown and yellow naked children, I now see little ones of ebony, sometimes with silver bracelets, sometimes with a silver girdle like a piece of telegraph wire around the hips; I wish I could get some pictures of the children I see. The faces here are very pretty. There is a large field all through this country for the artist and caricaturist. The Singhalese shave the fore part of the head and let the rest of their hair hang in a long tuft or tie it up something as we do horses tails. White is much worn in an artistic drapery, though the whiteness is sometimes open to criticism. The men here wear round combs in their hair, just like little American girls, made of tortoise shell.

Ceylon is one vast grove of cocoanut trees. They have very tall ones and a short kind, and they are all over and everywhere. Here grows the breadfruit tree and cinnamon tree, besides all the other tropical fruit trees.

A Singhalese boy about the hotel took our party in charge and finally took me exclusively under his wing to my entire satisfaction and his. They don't ask you if you want a boy, or at least not until amenities are fairly established; they simply join you, show you where you want to go, tell you how much to pay, drive away beggars and dissatisfied servitors, and make themselves so indispensable to your comfort and happiness that you are fain to beg them to go along with you as a special favor. My boy saw to the transfer of my baggage, after having taken me about town to and from depots, and finally brought me aboard ship. I don't know how I got him; the first that I remember he was sitting on the back seat of my carriage pointing out objects of interest; I thought he belonged to the carriage.

INDIA.

ON BOARD THE M. M. S. S. TIBRE, BOUND FOR CALCUTTA, *December 22d.*—This is the most sociable set of passengers I have encountered yet, also the most musical. Half of them are French and half English. We are very jolly at table and amuse ourselves the rest of the days and evenings with chess, music, and sleight of hand performances. I have protested violently against having my cabin port closed, so now I am permitted to sleep comfortably in as many inches of water as I see fit.

When we arrived off Pondichery the offing was in possession of a cyclone, and we modestly and obligingly waited for it to take its departure before attempting to come up to anchor. We had not long to wait. After we anchored some boat loads of very wet and very nude Indians came out to us and aboard our ship, and then the excitement and chatter ran very high. They fought over the few wretched passengers who wished to embark here. Eventually those unhappy beings were swung out in a chair "à la derrick," and dumped unceremoniously and damply into the boat, receiving as they passed under the awning, an accumulated shower down the backs of their necks. The principal passengers leaving here are an abbé and half a dozen padres and three unfortunate nuns of the Sacred Heart. It is alleged to be owing to the presence on board of these pious personages that we are having such bad weather.

It was curious to see any number of black men spring over the rail on board our ship, entirely nude with the exception of the most primitive string around the loin, and proceed to array themselves in a skirt which they seemed to evolve from their inner consciousnesses. It afterward appeared they had converted their turbans into sarongs. Thus in a few minutes we found ourselves surrounded by a crowd of very well clothed Indian gentlemen. Meanwhile a sailor created a temporary diversion by falling into the sea and getting fished out between the boats.

I deferred going ashore until the next day which proved fine. At breakfast I had the agent of the M. M. next me on one side, and Vicompte De Something or other, who had been educated at West Point, America, and knew Stonewall Jackson and General Lee well and adores America, on the other. The Vicompte placed his horses and carriages at my disposal for the day, but I had already several invitations to see the town, and had managed adroitly to combine the authors of them into one party

We were let down into the bobbing boat by means of the chair derrick, I going first to give the other ladies confidence. Having tumbled into our respective places, we started for the shore, the natives leading off with an American hurrah which deteriorated by degrees into an Indian singsong sort of chorus. Our boat being swept ashore by the surf, natives came out to the boat with a chair on their shoulders, into which we sat in turn and were carried to the beach, where, being all safely landed, we secured a push-push for each two people and started gaily off to see the town. A push-push is, as its name suggests, pushed from behind by two or three natives, the occupants of the vehicle guiding the carriage by means of a handle like a rudder. The straightness of your course is therefore determined by the steadiness of the hand of your escort or yourself. My escort was new to the push-push, so we ricochetted along the street, making a carom on every other unfortunate vehicle that came in our way, until I took matters in my own hands and did the guiding myself, while my escort objurgated the pushers. Between our zigzag course and their inefficiency we were rapidly being left far in the rear.

Reaching the Bazaar, or market place, we alighted and walked through it; and here was the prettiest thing I saw in Pondichery, a tiny Indian maiden with a tangle of black curly hair falling over two black eyes and a pretty, shy, dark face, sitting on the ground—a little bronze statuette she was—with a bowl of bright yellow flowers before her. We saw here numbers of dealers of all kinds, asking unheard of prices for their wares. We went then to the prison, like other prisons an unhappy place. In the yard we encountered another little Indian girl covered with rings and bracelets and anklets and lying on the ground. I ought to have brought a photographic instrument with me so that I could take some of the pretty pictures I see. At a fountain we saw women and girls getting jars of water, which they proceeded to carry off on their heads. The women seem to be a good deal dressed in this part of the country. They wear a great deal of drapery, and jewelry. The ears are pierced all around the rims and covered with rings and bars of gold and silver; they also wear a little tightfitting jacket that reaches just below the bust and has short sleeves, and fits them like the skin itself.

Having viewed Pondichery to our entire satisfaction, seeing two churches and the best hotel, we returned to the boat; this time walking down a long wharf and descending a very rickety stair and jumping into the tossing boat. There was another boat between ours and the stairway, and the natives in it declined to get out of the way ; we got into it expecting to step from it into our own ; but the natives manning the first boat had other views. Two of the officers succeeded in getting across, but just as I was about to cross, a free fight took place over me between the twenty-five or thirty natives manning the two boats, during which I must confess I felt very much in the way.

The difficulty was settled by our resigning ourselves to going to the Tibre in the stranger boat we were in. The rest having tumbled, with more or less personal injuries, into the boat we proceeded on our way. Arrived at the Tibre we found she had turned with the tide, and the chair derrick was on the rough seaward side of the boat. A gentleman or so went up the rope ladder; the rest of us in deference to the terrors of a timid English lady, were rowed around to the other side with much difficulty and danger and hoisted on deck, the last and heaviest of the passengers breaking the rope and falling a few inches to the deck, hurting his feelings seriously. He expatiated on the accident for the rest of the day, to my infinite disgust.

There had been a severe storm at Pondichery destroying telegraph lines and railway to Madras, therefore our unfortunate abbé, priests and sisters were obliged to come back to us to go to Madras. We reached Madras early the next morning, but alas! it was Sunday. I learned that my banker's office was closed and that the banker resided too far out of town to be reached before the steamer sailed again. I sent a note asking him to forward my mail to Bombay, and continued on my way rather the reverse of rejoicing. I was told there was little worth stopping at Madras to see and I did not attempt to go ashore. I watched the others getting off at the imminent risk of life and limb, boats bobbing up and down and natives fighting over every passenger, and concluded to stay on board. Jugglers come and amuse us, and merchants who ask fabulous prices and accepting infinitesimal ones for their goods. One juggler performs impossible tricks, frightens us with scorpions and cobras, and disgusts and mystifies us with the production of any quantity of stones and big iron nails from the inmost recesses of his being. He seems, in fact, to have a hardware shop concealed in his stomach.

GREAT EASTERN HOTEL, CALCUTTA, *December 25th.*—We spent Christmas eve on board the Tibre, having our usual jolly concert. We were by this time very jolly good friends, and managed to get a great deal of amusement out of our musical shortcomings and struggles to make ourselves understood, for one-half of the party spoke from little to no English and the other half was situated the same regarding French. Even the most ignorant of us though had mastered such simple and useful phrases as "Que est ce que sait" and "Je ne sais pas" and rung the changes on them. Indeed, it is astonishing how much information can be asked and given through half a dozen well-worn words. Anyway we left the Tibre feeling very highly accomplished linguistically.

Last night we reached and entered the river Hoogly, a continuation of the "sacred Ganges." We were obliged to anchor for the night, however, some eighteen miles below Calcutta, the channel being very dangerous and difficult of navigation even by daylight. We anchored between a few quicksands, and the officers cheered us by pointing out uncomfortably near spots where ships had been caught and had disappeared in ten minutes, never to be seen again. I asked if the officers were going ashore, but the Commissaire said "No, it is very dangerous." I said, "Why? Are there tigers here?" and he replied "No, something more terrible." I ask "What?" and he answers "Widows." It seems the "suttee" has been interfered with and the widows instead of being burnt are now sent to a lonely spot down the river into seclusion, and we had anchored opposite that spot. Be it understood I am looking for a place where tigers will come and sit under my window and serenade me.

I don't get that sympathy with my tastes that I plainly should. When I tell people that I am tired of Botanical Gardens and that I have registered a solemn vow never to go to another museum, they look at me incredulously and say, "Oh, but these are very fine ones. You must really go and see these." My remark that I am on my way home from San Francisco to New York is looked upon as a huge joke. I suspect that I am leaving the reputation of a practical humorist behind me.

Having bidden good bye to the French Captain and Commissaire, I was taken in hand by the river pilot, an English gentleman who is so valuable a man that he is carried all the way to Ceylon and back for the sake of retaining his services coming up the Hoogly, who is a sort of king in his way, and who fetched me up to the hotel and consigned me to the tender mercies of the manager.

And here my woes begin. The moment I've put foot into my room a servant presents himself for engagement. I say I am only going to stay a day and don't want a servant; he goes off and brings the manager, who tells me I had better take this servant if I am going to remain or go up country. I tell him I am only going to stay a day or two, am not sure where I am going first, and propose to communicate with friends here before taking a servant or anything else. The manager then engages the man for me at the hotel expense, until I know what I am going to do. My servant then proceeds to "putter" about until I am on the verge of insanity. When he does leave the room it is only as far as the outside of the curtained doorway, from which retreat he rushes in if I rustle a paper or walk across the floor, until I am fain to offer him double wages to go away and leave me alone. I have been told before that I must have a servant, and I asked:

"What will my servant do? Will he find out depots for me and what time my train is to go?"

"No," is the reply; "he doesn't know anything about trains, and if you take him with you he won't be allowed to be of any use to you in the next place you stop at."

"Will he engage carriages for me, carry messages? Can he take me to the theatre? Will he look after my baggage?"

"No."

"What will he do?"

"Oh, he will pack your trunks for you."

"Never;" I rejoin. "The servant isn't born who could pack my trunks with the science they require. The only man who ever shut my trunk was a hotel clerk with a head for mathematical calculation, and he performed the feat under my personal directions. I said, shut the lid as far as it will go. He did so. Now give the tray a slight kick at this end—so. Now do the same at the other end—so. Now close the lid completely —so. Sit on this corner a minute and shut the clasp; now sit on the other end and do the same. That's it. Now sit immediately over the lock—so. Push in the hasp, lift yourself and give the lid just a little jolt till the hasp catches, and then turn the key. There! And it was done to the infinite and open admiration and amusement of an interested audience of custom officers and natives. But excuse the diversion. What else will my servant do—if I let him?"

"Well, he will bring you your tea in the morning."

"Goodness gracious, not if I can prevent it. I've lost all my chances of heaven now, thinking "cuss" words when the stewardess calls me up at half-past six to know if I want tea. I don't see the use of a servant who won't or can't do anything you want him to do and will do what you don't want him to do."

Answer: "Oh, but you *must* have a servant in India."

However, this servant promises to take care of my luggage and take me to see all the sights, if I will take him up country with me. He has been to Darjeeling and Bombay before. Perhaps I'd better take him. Meantime my reason "totters on its throne" under the enforced waiting on.

I was told it was cold in Calcutta. Indian ideas of temperature and mine differ materially. Fancy a man walking the street in Summer attire wiping the prespiration from his brow on Christmas Day! And as for the sacred waters, of all the dirty, abominable rivers, the Hoogly is the most horrible. The yellow Yangtsekiang is purity itself in comparison. It makes one ill to look at the waters of the Hoogly, and it does not need the sight of a corpse floating down its turbid bosom to complete one's disgust. I have my own private and unflattering opinion of the English people whose residences are in the course of construction along its banks.

I am in a chronic state of "big, big D—" to-day. Why? Because this is Christmas, "Merry Christmas," and the bank is closed; I can't get my letters to-day nor to-morrow, perhaps not until Monday, and this is Thursday. Oh, why, oh, why, did I have my letters sent to a bank? I think this growling is a very good thing for a change. My notes were getting monotonously amiable and self congratulatory. I'm in a bad humor. I hate India, and abhor Calcutta, and abominate this great marble-floored hotel, with its yard-long bill of fare of poor meats and its army of restless servants.

December 27th.—I am in the deepest, darkest depths of dismal despair; because I am going to a fête, or ball to-night, where I shall meet some friends and have a most delightful time. Such a good time as I am going to have dancing! And oh! it is such hard work—having a good time—the hardest work I know. The prospect of the fun I'm to have fairly appals me; besides, there is a bit of a lark in it. Indeed, my whole journey is a sort of lark of the perpetual order.

Yesterday I started off in search of my letters. The bank was closed, not to be opened until Monday; meanwhile I want some money to travel around with. I get the address of the president, drive five or six miles into the country and present myself, my letter of credit and my woes, to the president in the bosom of his family. I am received most courteously. The president himself drives to the bank for money from his safe, and brings it to me in person, at the same time giving me advice about my trip to Darjeeling and begging to be called upon or telegraphed to, in any emergency or for any service. He is the gravest, most courteous of gentlemen. Unfortunately, a wretched cashier has locked up my letters and gone to some inaccessible place with the key in his pocket, so no letters for me until my return from Darjeeling. I tell a friend or so that I have been to see my banker, and they say no English lady would dare do such a thing; she would be afraid of getting snubbed, so I suppose it was an outrageous thing to do.

I have seen Cook's agent here and am going to get my tickets from him through India. He sends word to the hotel people to look out for me. I think I shall take a native servant with me to Darjeeling, and then I can judge whether I shall be able to cross India without him. They tell me I shall be swindled either way, that everybody is, and that I may as well be resigned to it. The man I've got here was very anxious to go with me; when I told him finally that I would take him you should have seen the smile that lit his expressive features. He was thinking how much he should make out of me. He began laying his plans this morning; he said he would not go if he were to be paid by Cook's agent—I must pay him myself. I said, "All right; I don't want you. Cook's agent will get me a better man." I had expected to pay him myself, but his stipulation suggested that he did not think I would know enough to inquire into the correctness of his accounts. I shall not pay anything for myself if I can help it.

I went to the opera last night and saw Miss Emilie Melville play "Girofle-Girofla." It was a "swell" night; the Viceroy was there, so we all had to rise when he came in, while the orchestra played "God save the Queen." I find myself in a nest of friends in Calcutta. Mr. Cool, whom I went about with in Hong Kong, is waiting for me to come back from Darjeeling to take me to see some sights. To-night I shall meet all the French officers of the Tibre at the ball, which is given by the French Consul. Mr. King, who was a fellow passenger on the Tibre, took me to the opera last night. Mr. and Mrs. Few and another batch of fellow travelers will arrive to-day and be here when I return, and everybody offers some form of amusement. It's a clear case of "ambarras de riches." I am dreading the long trip across India awfully. I shall have no end of good time though.

WOODLAND HOTEL, DARJEELING, BENGAL, IN THE HIMALAYA MOUNTAINS, *December 20th.*—Hurrah! American independence once more rampant and victorious! Now I just adore myself. Now I am happy. Custom, prediction, advice to the contrary. Here I am, at Darjeeling, and here I have come alone, to climb the Himalayas absolutely alone, not a vestige of a boy or guardian of any description, twenty-five hours journey, and several changes from cars to steamers and *vice versa.*

This is the biggest feather in my cap yet, for I understand it has never been done before. One lady came here once alone with a boy to wait on her and go about with her. But from what I can find out I am the first woman to make this trip entirely alone. And this is how I managed. My servant in Calcutta did not suit me, so I threw him over. Cook's agent could not supply me with one that they could specially recommend at such short notice. The agent, Mr. Higgins, observing my spirit and experience, thought I could manage alone, and I determined to do so. His native conductor took me to the train and told the English conductor I was alone; the conductor transferred me to the steamer on the Ganges River. I got a waiter on the steamer to carry my shawl-strapped rug, etc., to the train. Changing cars, a dozen boys are at the door of the car before it is unlocked, ready to grab your baggage. It is only necessary to let one take it and follow him, and having received it in your next car pay him two "annas" (about five cents). The cars are very comfortable. Ladies and gentlemen have separate compartments. Being the only first-class lady passenger, I had a compartment for four all to myself. And the officials don't disturb one or call one up for tickets or to change cars during the night.

I had a very nice supper on the steamer crossing the Ganges last night, a good breakfast when I changed cars this morning, and a correspondingly good lunch at the half-way house up the mountains. After I had made all my changes, a fellow passenger of the Tibre got on the open car that I was traveling in, which ascends the mountains. He got off the station before me, so he could not rob me of one particle of my glory of traveling alone, but he gave me an opportunity in the way of chatter, an opportunity which I embraced.

This was the last stage of my journey, the dangerous part as well, for we climb up and around and through mountains in a ramshakly sort of train, most of the time in a succession of great scallops along the edge of the precipice of hundreds of feet, the banks of which are frequently giving way. The road is often blocked with landslides. We passed many places where the road has broken away close to the rails. The mountains seem to be composed of a very loose sandy quality of earth. The railroad is very intricate; it crosses and recrosses itself. You go under an arch, and the next thing you know you go over that self-same arch. Looking back at it, the road lies below you like a piece of tangled string. Sometimes the train goes backwards and forwards on a zigzag, like a shuttle, going forward up one slant and backing up the next, until the desired height is reached.

Winding around and up these mountains, the scenery is grand. On one side of us rise the mountains, about which we are describing great arcs as we follow these curves, while a great valley yawns at the other side—a valley of jungle, of tropical forest and 'of irrigated tracts of land. Beyond, the mountains rise again to great heights. The scene is in soft tints of delicate greens and pale yellows. Higher and higher we climb, while we look back and below us on four or five scallops, around which we have just circled.

At last I arrived at Darjeeling, 7,500 feet above the sea. I had asked Mr. Higgins to telegraph for a room here and for a man to meet me at the station, which man presented himself after I had secured a boy and started off by myself to the hotel. I was then put into a sort of cart, with my back to the pony that drew it, and was driven up here. The hotel is about an eighth of a mile from the depot, and almost directly above it. One has to travel fully a mile by cart to get to it. Darjeeling is an exceedingly pretty place, unlike anything I have seen before. It is laid in terraces on the side of the mountain. Looking down from the hotel, the streets form an interlaced and zigzag pattern. I should never know how to get to any given house in this place. It is like one of those labyrinth puzzles that you try to get to the center of without crossing a line. The safest way is to do as Alice did in the "Looking-Glass House," turn your back to a place, and presently you find yourself walking in at the front door.

I was told it was bitter cold up here. It is like our early October nights, no frost, yet people here think it is fearfully cold. They say they sometimes have two feet of snow, in a tone that implies that that is hardly believable but true. The natives here are of another sort; several sorts, in fact. One kind are called Boutiliers; they look like Patagonian Indians and they wear boots of wool-and-patchwork make and material. They speak an entirely different language from the Calcutta people. I find a servant from Calcutta would, therefore, be quite useless to me here.

After supper the guests of the hotel, two in number, stepped with me into the gardens to look at the eternal snows of the

Kinchinjunga range of mountains by moonlight. The sombre silence of the night, with the pale light of the moon, impresses me deeply with the remoteness and grandeur of those towering heights whose snow-crowned jagged peaks are outlined in glittering white against the darkening sky.

After ordering a horse to be in readiness for me at five in the morning, I went to bed, where, in spite of the open fire in the room, and my rug, which I put on the bed, and my shawl, in which I had wrapped my feet, I shivered through the night, only napping now and then. It was not really cold, but the room had the damp chill of a subterranean dungeon. I was glad to leave my inhospitable bed at four o'clock, dress by the light of a lamp, and after a cup of warm tea, go out into the yard where my horse and a native servant called a "Syce" waited my pleasure. I mounted and started off, the Syce, who spoke not a word of English, accompanying me on foot.

We followed a very good road that wound still higher up the mountains for about five miles, and then, dwindling to a mere trail, it struck suddenly up through the forest and tangled undergrowth over a very steep hill. My Syce literally dragged my horse up this precipitous path, while I clung to my saddle as best I might. Sometimes we encountered great boulders and ledges, up which my Syce climbed first, and then, tugging at my rein, persuaded my horse to rear up and make a great spring after him. It was the very hardest climbing I ever saw a horse do. At last we reached the top and found a plateau, and at its furthest edge a mound with a flagstaff. Bent on performing his whole duty, my Syce dragged my horse and me to the top of this mound, and with a comprehensive wave of his hand round about left me to rest and admire.

I have no words to paint the grandeur and beauty of the scene about me. I stand upon a jutting pinnacle, and at my feet sinks a tremendous valley which sweeps up in the distance to the vast mountains that tower grandly among the clouds. The highest mountains in the world are before me, and the magnificent scale on which the whole scene is drawn is overpoweringly impressive. The picture is in pale tints; the valley is pale green, the mountain sides yellow, and the snowy crowns of the majestic peaks dazzlingly white under the rays of the morning sun. The highest mountain in the world, Mount Everest, is hardly to be distinguished from the white clouds, so high, so distant, so pale is its snowy peak, but the ragged edges of the Kinchinjunga range, lonesome and icy, are clearly cut against the pale blue sky. A white cloudy mist rises from the valley, floating hither and thither, now muffling the mountains in a fairy mantle, now framing their beauty in fleecy wreaths, now revealing, now concealing their beauties, and ever ringing kaleidoscopic changes on the lovely picture.

At last I dismount, and we commence to descend the impossible trail I have been dragged up. My Syce leads the horse, and I gather up my skirts and follow in their footsteps, jumping from one muddy boulder to another, conscious that I am passing through the haunts of ferocious wild beasts and poisonous reptiles. I am told that the beautiful mist I have just been admiring encompassed a party a few days ago on "Tiger Hill," as the flagstaff mound I've just left is suggestively called; and when it lifted a horse left standing by the flagstaff was found killed and partially devoured by a tiger. This story, told me at the hotel, increases materially my enjoyment of the trip.

At the foot of Tiger Hill we traverse the edge of a long plateau that reviews the glorious scene I've just been admiring from above, and after many pauses at points of vantage for fresh views of the incomparable picture, I set off on a canter for the hotel, leaving my Syce behind me.

By dint of asking an English girl here and a soldier there, and finally a boy, and by dropping the rein on my horse's neck at doubtful turns, I manage to thread the labyrinth of roads and eventually find myself looking down on the hotel from a road above it; and the proprietor thereof calls to me to go on a quarter of a mile further and I will find a road that will bring me to the house, where I presently arrive jubilant and hungry.

I get some breakfast and proceed to the depot, accompanied by an elderly gentleman who kindly sees me safely stowed in my car, and I am off for Calcutta. As the train carries me away, I look back and up at Darjeeling, perched on the side of the mountains, and think what a pretty place it is, and how nice it is for the people who live with such a beautiful view of mountains and valley ever before my eyes. I like India better for having seen Darjeeling.

I take the same course down the mountain, admiring all the way along. The winding road of the railway produces an ever-changing picture of valleys and mountains. I am told that in this jungle below the track, and above, there are plenty of tigers, but that they never come up on the track. I find the railway restaurants are better than the Great Eastern Hotel at Calcutta.

I have one fault to find with the railroad management; they never tell you anything; the traveling public is left to find out for itself where it changes cars and where it takes "tiffin." The trains are constantly sliding off onto sidings and waiting for heaven knows what; sometimes for another train to pass, sometimes for recent slides to be removed, sometimes for dining. If the latter, the railroad employés simply depart; the passengers one after another step out to stretch their limbs and see what is going on, and eventually discover that they are within an eighth of a mile of the restaurant, and walk up to it. The inert, incurious ones like myself stay on the cars and think they ought to be near the tiffin depot; and presently the car glides up to the depot and the bell rings for the passengers to get aboard; and most of them having just arrived, are obliged to leave their dinners before having commenced them. Your through ticket, which takes you on three railroads, says simply, on each coupon, "To Darjeeling," indicating no termini. If you ask the guard a question, he looks dazed; and even a close cross-examination elicits only the most equivocal information. The idea of any one not knowing that you change cars at Siligura, and that this is or is not Siligura, is beyond their comprehension. They know when and where they take tiffin perfectly well.

Coming back, I had a car to myself again all night, and managed to sleep well, although I caught a severe cold. Had breakfast on board the boat crossing the horrid Ganges again. On the next train a lady was in the car with me, a lady who had made up her mind to talk. I fended a little but finally gave in. Her husband wanted to lunch with her, and of course I agreed to his coming in; he proved to be one of the owners of the Ganges boats, and between them they imparted loads of information. He finished by taking us both to ride on the engine, where I distinguished myself by starting and stopping the train. They put on full speed for our benefit, and I just enjoyed flying down the track that was stretching before us. It made the other lady seasick, but I should like to have ridden there to Calcutta.

No. 10 MIDDLETON ROW, CALCUTTA, *January 3d*, 1885.—Got back to find the "Great Eastern" crammed full. Rushed to Cook's and their man, who had just brought me from the depot, rode with me from place to place until I found a " where to lay my head," and I was ready to lay it, too, by that time. Eventually found my way to this house, which is a dozen times more comfortable and neat than the aforesaid "Great Eastern," although I am situated on the ground floor, and there is a beautiful large drain opening from the floor of my bathroom into the garden, for snakes to come in—b-r-r-r!—and none of the boys speak English. Having achieved my trip in safety and ease, and alone, my friends are all trying to rob me of my glory by thinking up ladies who have done the same thing. But I need not take back my hurrah yet; these other ladies, one or two, had lived here and understood the language perfectly, while I speak not a word, and am a "stranger in a strange land."

Since I have been back I have been besieged with servants. At half-past six A. M., they swarm at my door; I tear my hair and say: "Go away; come back at tiffin time and I'll look at your letters;" till finally one whom I have dismissed peremptorily because he doesn't speak English enough, takes possession of me, and sends away all the ones I wanted to see when I got dressed, including those that Cook's are sending me. I manage to oust him finally and go without, until Cook sends me a staid gray-bearded man that I take without further parley. It seems absolutely compulsory in Calcutta to have a servant, but, oh, how they do worry and torment one and retard one's movements! People who live here, however, get used to them and their slowness.

I am opening the eyes of Indian residents with my rapidity; they get to counting on me, and presently I am gone. People are so slow here it takes half a day to draw a check or to do any trivial thing. If a train is going at 2:20 P. M., and it takes twenty minutes to reach the depot, they say they will come for you at twelve or half past, and one o'clock is the very latest they will start. They want time to lounge around the depot and sit in the car twenty minutes or so before it goes. Getting into this nice boarding house I find two fellow passengers of the Tibre, Mr. and Mrs. Durant, installed here, and a gentleman to whom I was introduced at the ball, of which ball—later. I go to the races with my friends, meet all the "Tibre Officers" there, and witness the arrival of the Viceroy's cortege, brilliant with red-and-gold postilions and dashing horses.

Mr. Cool calls and takes me to Barrakpore, where I see my first Hindoo temple and watch a man praying to the Ganges on the steps of a ghaut, an occupation which savors strongly of an acrobatic performance. He knocks his forehead against a stone for five or ten minutes together, rises and kneels and bows and clasps his hands and prays, and touches his forehead to the ground, until we are tired of looking and go on. It is absurd sending missionaries to these people; they are far, far more religious than we are. I think that we corrupt the morals of these heathen people. It is well understood in India that the less civilized a native man is, the more honest a servant he makes.

We saw girls come down to the river and wash, first themselves then their clothes, and then their cooking apparatus; and after that fill their jars with water, and then take a drink from the river before leaving it, finally throwing a few drops of water over themselves. We took a boat and were rowed up the river a little way, looking at the residences on either side. Then we returned to our "gharry" and were driven out towards the jungle, where the government elephants reside. There are fifty of these in all. I saw about thirty, some of them just coming from the jungle, where they go and gather their own food. Each elephant has a "Mahout" or "words to that effect," who takes care of him. One of the big beasts was being fed by a little naked native boy of eight years, who would not let him have the piece of sugar cane he was fixing for him until it was arranged to his entire satisfaction. He slapped the elephant's trunk and scolded at him when he attempted to take it, and finally reached up and tucked the choice morsel into the creature's capacious mouth. The Mahouts slide up and down the elephant's trunk, and sweep off the elephant's back, and scold him while he is eating, apparently ordering him to eat properly and masticate his food sufficiently. After this we went and had some tea at a little hotel opposite the station, and then returned to Calcutta in time for dinner.

To-day, at 9 P. M., I am off for Benares, Delhi, Jeypore and Agra, Bombay being my objective point. I shall reach Bombay on the 13th of January and sail for Suez on the 16th.

And now to return to the ball which took place before my going to Darjeeling. The Commissaire escorted me and we were met by the Commandante and the other French officers I knew. The invitation was in French, and the ball was at the house of the French Consul. There I was introduced to the hostess and guests, who had been told of the "Juene Americaine" who was "Si courageuse et si joli et si amiable" they said, and were full of curiosity to see me. My dancing card was presently full, and as the evening advanced my waltzes were being divided by my partners with less favored individuals. I was being lent to this one's cousin for a turn and that one's chum, and walked assiduously up and down between dances. My waltzing was supposed to be perfection. At three A. M., I deserted, leaving seven partners, to whom I was engaged for future dances, desoleé. I went to sleep on the hardest bed, a mattress that would put the floor to blush for its hardness, and dreamt I was sleeping on the stone floor I had danced on. Up again at eight A. M., completed all my arrangements, packed my trunk, got some lunch, and off I went to Darjeeling, sleeping that night on the cars, and reaching Darjeeling the next day at four P. M., leaving again the next morning after my horseback ride at 10:45 A. M. Quick work, n'est ce pas? That just suits me.

Now I must say a word about the people I am meeting, perhaps the best class of Europeans. I am growing to have an excellent opinion of young French and English gentlemen. I am treated by them all with so much courtesy, consideration and respect. Nothing could have been more perfectly polite and respectful than the care and attention I received from the French officers in going to the ball, or than their efforts to make the evening a thoroughly enjoyable one to me. The Commandante was an elderly, genial man, with amiable brows and a serene fatherly manner. The Commissaire is quite young, but very quiet, unobtrusive and gentlemanly. Then the young Englishman, Mr. Cool, is quite young also; well bred, of the dainty, dandy order, but exceedingly sensible and practical; a very pretty young man, but not at all affected. And Mr. Cabel, also English, is altogether courteous and entertaining. They trot around with me on business or pleasure, relieve me of every difficulty, place themselves so entirely at my service in such an irresistible way, in sheer sociability and companionableness ; there is no question of romance, it is simply friendliness and good nature. They think me courageous and entertaining, and it pleases them to play the cavalier, although I am, relatively speaking, old enough to be their grandmother. Strictly speaking I am twenty-six, while they are from twenty to twenty-seven.

It seems to me that these young Englishmen from twenty to twenty-seven years of age are better informed and better bred than our young men ; they have more general knowledge and interests. Our young Americans are apt to be cubs until they are nearly thirty and then business monopolizes them. Of course I haven't got to Europe yet, but here I find Europeans entertaining, well bred and gentlemanly.

It is fortunate I did not go to Canton. Mr. Cool, who went, only just saw Canton and escaped; a friend of his came away with some shot in his legs. I ought to be sorry I didn't go. If I had nothing would have happened. I never do have any exciting adventures.

Calcutta is called the city of palaces. I've been looking for the palaces ever since I've been here. They are a myth ; so are the tigers and cobras and sights. They say to me : "Why, you haven't seen any of the sights of Calcutta." "What sights?" I ask. "Why, the Botanical Gardens." And I tear my hair and weep.

BENARES, *January 5th.*—I left Calcutta last night; was attended to the depot by one of the nice young Englishmen and Cook's man. Found I was to have one English lady in the compartment with me. She proved pleasant; like me she did not want to talk, but was exceedingly kind and obliging. I was on the cars until to-day at three, when I arrived at Mogul Serai, and was met by a guide sent from Clark's Hotel for me. We took another train, which crept along for about twenty minutes, and then we took a "gharry" and crossed the Ganges on a bridge and road for about an hour before we reached the hotel.

After eighteen hours on the cars I was still able to be about, so I started out at once to see the Monkey Temple; it was not worth seeing, but the town was. I went and inspected the reception room of a Rajah and his elephants. It was dark before we started home. The people were all in the streets; sometimes it was so crowded we could hardly drive through. My native footmen got down and ran in front to clear the way. The houses are of mud and have the appearance of having been shaped up with the hands as children shape mud houses, for the sides are not evenly flat nor the corners sharp; they are round and the bottom slopes off to the ground. Parts of many houses, and sometimes the whole house, have no roof. Fence, garden wall and house, are all of mud or clay. They have wooden doors and straw roofs. The door is often the only opening. I look, in passing, through these doors and see sometimes only a clay box of an apartment, full to the door, frequently with bed and clothes. At other times I see through an inner door and catch a glimpse of an interior garden or courtyard.

The ride through the crowded city at night is interesting. The streets seem to be a general market place and the flare of fires and lights and the multitude of people are a novelty. I am just a little frightened until we are in the heart of the city and my guide says he is at home, and with my permission he will remain there and come to me again in the morning. My spirits rise to the occasion; I say a bright "good night" and am driven on through the crowds of Indians, with only my non-English speaking coachman. I arrive at the hotel safely, however, have a good supper, inspect a lot of copper work, go to bed, to start off again in the morning at seven; through the town again by daylight, to the river.

Now this is something like! This is India, romantic, picturesque, dirty. Benares would be beautiful if it were not so gray. It has a decidedly Moorish air to me. The banks of the Ganges are extremely picturesque. They are high and surmounted with old and turreted palaces and temples. Stone stairs the length of the temples reach down to the water's edge. I took a boat and was rowed up and down the river this morning, and it was the most picturesque and novel scene I have had the pleasure of seeing yet.

On these steps, or "ghauts," are little niches and stone platforms, in which are gods and on which are priests. The priests sit with their backs to the sun, and under an immense, mushroom-like umbrella. The steps are covered with people going up and down, some carrying jars of water on their heads and shoulders; here and there are men standing or kneeling and praying. We passed one crazy man singing and shouting, on the banks of the river, at the top of his voice. The water is full of men, women, and children, washing themselves, their clothes, their brass jars, getting water, drinking water, laughing, chatting, praying.

What a scene! Here is a man bumping his forehead on the stones in prayer; here is another plastering himself with colored and white clay; here is a woman washing her baby; and here a pretty young girl of wealth, with her female attendant splashing water over her; here several old women laughing and gossiping, and here a lot of men beating clothes on stone slabs and spreading them on the ground to dry, and a vast concourse of people are ever coming and going. There is a pleasing contrast of color in the robes that brighten the picture. A beautiful, a charming scene, but oh! don't look at the water, for the "sacred Ganges" is a gutter, a ditch, a sewer, everything that is dreadful, in short. The palaces were built by Rajahs with the idea that their dying in them would insure an immediate entrance into Paradise. I see a burning ghaut or so, but not any in active operation. The boat I was in was a large rowboat with a green blind saloon. I was seated on the hurricane deck while viewing these scenes.

As I step out of the boat five or six little bronze children robed in doubtful white plant themselves before me, forming a semicircle, each holding out two small hands, with a simultaneous cry of "Backsheesh." I put a quarter of a rupee (about eight cents) into the smallest hand, with an explanatory circular movement, and they disperse instantly and hold a jubilee over what is to them a large sum on the temple steps behind me.

Leaving Benares late in the afternoon, I discover I am no longer the sole American traveling in lonely state, for a gentleman of my own country happens to be traveling my way. I had crossed his path once or twice at Benares; and after encountering him again at the ticket office, we are led about by the same official as our tickets are made up and our baggage attended to, and at last we find ourselves in neighboring carriages, so that when we put our heads out of our respective windows when the train halts at depots we exchange some civilities.

Reaching Agra on the following morning, our ways still lie side by side, and after finding ourselves near neighbors in the hotel and meeting at the table and discovering that we both mean to remain at Agra but a single day, we shake hands and agree to visit the sights in company, instead of following each other about in solitary state. We thereupon order a carriage and a guide and depart on a tour of the place.

We go first to Agra fort, which is built on an eminence close at hand and overlooks the town. The fort is built of red sandstone, and is very large and picturesque. Within the fortress grounds stands the Palace of Akbar the Strong, and the beautiful Pearl Mosque. This magnificent palace actually surpasses in richness and beauty the wonderful creations the fairy tales of our childhood have pictured. It is built principally of white marble. We saunter through the large sunny rooms of polished white marble. There are marble floors, marble ceiling, marble pillars and marble walls whose white surfaces are inlaid with precious stones and jewels, formed to represent sprigs of leaves and flowers. The sprigs are placed at regular intervals, so the walls have the appearance of being covered with a brilliantly flowered wall paper. Malachite is used for the leaves, and is so ingeniously inlaid as to show a half-turned leaf with a duller green for the under side. Lapis lazuli is very lavishly used, and mother-of-pearl is formed into beautiful blossoms, from whence delicate stamens, with turquoise, sapphires and rubies capping them, arise. Diamonds, emeralds, garnets, and every precious stone known are to be seen worked into flowers to adorn these walls, and all with a profusion only equalled by the art with which they have been so placed. The apartments are large, bright and airy, those of the Emperor and his favorite wife looking out upon Jumna.

We are shown the private gardens for the ladies of the harem, and a magnificent bath of polished marble sunk in the floor, with marble steps leading down into it. In the garden I see a great slab of black marble which was once the royal seat for

Moguls, and which took upon itself the function of splitting across and weeping blood when sat upon by an odious Rajah. I saw the crack.

We then went beneath the palace, through a dark, subterranean passage, to a dismal underground chamber, where the unfortunate wives who incurred the Imperial displeasure were once consigned to the sack and placed in a hole in the floor, whence a passage connected with the river and whence the waters carried them, cold and dead, out to the Jumna.

The life of an Emperor's wife had its drawbacks. This heathen mode of disposing of superfluous or refractory wives is, however, far preferable to the fashion of beating them to death that obtains in our own enlightened country and in those of Christian Europe.

The beautiful Motee Musjid, or Pearl Mosque, is also within the walls of the fort, and is as lovely as its name implies. It is built of snowy marble and is open across the entire front. Pillars of white marble support the roof, and three exquisitely molded domes of dazzling white marble surmount it. Across the front the marble wall is cut in a series of most perfect arches, each arch being formed of nine smaller arches, each one as perfect in outline as the other. On the ceiling, just beneath the roof, an inscription runs in black marble inlaid in the white. The figures being Hindostanee the effect is rather ornamental. The white marble floor is inlaid with black marble in such a manner as to mark off a block for each worshiper to kneel upon. At one side a lattice of carved marble screens an apartment reserved for the ladies of the harem.

We drive from the fort with its magnificent palace and Mosque to the Taj Mahal, the most beautiful structure in the world. The Taj is set in the midst of a luxuriant garden on the banks of the Jumna, and is built of milk white marble. A square marble foundation, on each corner of which rises a very tall and slender minaret, forms an elevated floor on which an octagonal building rests. Within this building are the tombs of the Emperor and the beloved wife to whom this perfect piece of architecture was raised ; and above it rises a dome so perfect in proportion and outline, so dazzling in marble whiteness, as to seem to have been created by the hand of some powerful genii rather than raised by the laborious efforts of men. The octagonal body of the building is ornamented with much elaborately carved marble lattice work. Entering the door we note that the inner walls, from the outer posts, are inlaid, like the palace, with precious stones in the same lavish profusion and with the same artistic skill. Emeralds, diamonds, sapphires, rubies, granets, turquoise, carnelian, glitter against the snowy whiteness of the walls, while malachite, lapis lazuli and pearl form supple, waving, leaves and petals to the flowers that seem to bloom upon the walls. Agate, coral, onyx, bloodstones, and chalcedony are also used in beautifying these walls. In the center of this begemmed apartment is a carved marble railing, within which are two marble sarcophagi, the tombs of the Emperor Shah Jehau and his beloved wife "Muntaz Mahal, the chosen of the palace," or "Moomtaza Zumanee, the Light of the World," or "Arjmand Banee Begum." These sarcophagi are, like the walls, profusely inlaid with precious stones. The surrounding lattice is formed by eight single slabs of marble, each slab being between six and eight feet square, and carved in patterns and scroll work until it resembles a delicate white lace.

About this beautiful tomb are lovely, park-like grounds, with trees, grass, flowers and fountains. The whole structure of snowy marble and graceful outline rises from the midst of the green, luxuriant foliage, a vision of loveliness, a very poem of form, of beauty, of purity, of grace.

This most magnificent, most beautiful and costly, creation was raised to the memory of a woman. A wife and the mother of seven children has the most superb tomb the world can show. The inscription, "To the memory of an undying love," greets one on entering and adds romantic interest to the admiration of the visitor.

Back of the Taj stands another beautiful building in white marble, with a short, thick tower at each corner, and a central dome. This is hardly less beautiful than the Taj, between which and itself lies a double walk by the sides of a long basin of water dotted with fountains. It is carved to such a degree that it looks like a building of white lace.

Fort, Palace, Mosque and Taj are truly magnificent and beautiful; they represent a past grandeur and royal luxury, and immense wealth. Nothing that I have seen before in the way of temples or palace can compare with these in richness, size, beauty or art. The palace rooms are large and light and built with some reference to ventilation and habitableness.

In Agra, as in Benares, it interests me much to drive through the streets of the native city. If Benares has a Moorish flavor Agra has a Persian air. Here there are open stores filled with goods and busy people, with balconies above veiled with bamboo curtains, through which you can dimly see women peeping. The dress varies in each place somewhat. In Calcutta they wore white hats, or yards and yards of white muslin twisted about the heads, and another arrangement of yards and yards of white muslin about their bodies. In Benares they wore a large square piece of white cotton (very doubtful white) put over the head and two corners crossed in front and tied at the back, forming a hood and cloak. In Agra the women wore white full skirts and the shawl over the head, but there are many and indescribable forms of dress in the East. In Japan, China, Java, Ceylon, and India it is either an extremely abbreviated garment, or an absurdly full and long one, or an artistic arrangement of white muslin quite beyond description and sometimes very graceful.

TRAVELLER'S BUNGALOW HOTEL, DELHI, *January 8th*.— Left Agra yesterday morning quite alone again, having said good-bye to my chance companion at the end of a day's sight-seeing together; exchanged my Cook's ticket at the depot, and attended to the weighing of my baggage myself, much to the distress of the hotel man, who was deputed to look after me, and to my own satisfaction. But I found I had an English Major and his wife and daughter for traveling companions as soon as I entered the car, so my traveling alone was of short duration. Had to change cars and wait an hour and lose my lunch at a depot, and was given the shortest of short eighteen minutes to dine at a later station; arrived at Delhi at 9 P. M., captured the hotel man, and drove here without mishap.

At the hotel I find an army of fee hunting servants coaxing a very smoky fire in my room. I drive them all out. "I don't want any tea." "Stop blowing the fire." "Don't touch that shawl strap." "Let the satchel alone." "Good night." And I fall to bolting my doors—five doors—and each bolt in worse condition than the other; but I have made up my mind to have them bolted, and they, like most difficulties, yield at last to my determination. And then I go to sleep and let the smoky fire smoke itself out, and hear a noise that is a cross between an earthquake and a hurricane thunderstorm, but don't wake up sufficiently to determine which it is, until in the morning I create a sensation by saying at breakfast, "Oh, was that a thunderstorm? I thought it was an earthquake." In fact my sedate English travelers seem to be very much amused at my remarks on sights and guides and hotels as we breakfast together. I had risen at seven, had my tea and toast and been out to drive and had seen all the temples before breakfast.

I am outdoing Cook, getting ahead of the itinerary he has made for me, a specially rapid one at my behest. I get to a place feeling quite unfatigued, go and see all the sights, and drive my guide crazy trying to think up more things for me to see. This one is really put to it to keep me busy. They drove me crazy at first, showing me English hospitals, monuments, schools, orphan asylums, churches, barracks, botanical gardens, and museums; but now I say to them: "I'll discharge you on the spot if you show me anything English." As if I had come all the way to India to see a wooden seven-by-nine English Missionary church! I am a tireless traveler and sightseer. Fatigue and nervousness are weaknesses of the past. I am drinking fairly strong tea, two and three times a day, because the water is unfit to drink, and I sleep at night, in hotels or on cars, like a top, and rise as fresh from a night on the cars as from a bed of down, and ready for a day's sightseeing. I arrive in a rush and depart in a hurry, but without the discomfort of an increased heart beat. In New York I hated sightseeing; it was the hardest work I knew. Here I go through it as calmly and peacefully and untiringly as possible.

Here in Delhi I have been over several mosques and palaces and mausoleums, as large and almost as magnificent as those at Agra, and have seen miles of ruins. The ruins are really grand and picturesque. The crumbling walls of immense forts and mosques and mausoleums give the country a very romantic look, and bring to one's mind all the stories of the early ages, "when knights were bold, and barons held their sway," as the song says, although this is not Germany. The crumbling ramparts, with faded domes and minarets rising behind them, and the deep arched gateways, are suggestive of long-sustained sieges. It is really a ruined city I drive through, and it represents an earlier power and grandeur and art that exceed anything I have seen. The palaces and tombs and temples are all on a magnificent scale, with a reference to air and light and space that I have not seen in any other country.

Having finished the sights here, I should depart to-night for Jeypore, but the trains don't keep pace with my mood.

I saw a quantity of wild monkeys climbing over garden walls in the city this morning; I see wild parrots every day, and also camels, singly and in troops, loaded and being driven along. They use donkeys and buffalo and oxen as beasts of burden, and they do, literally, guide the latter animals by twisting their tails. Where they have wells, they have a bank sloping up to it; hitch oxen to the skin-bucket chains that run over a bar, and drive the oxen down the hill to draw up the water. The native villages that I see from the car window, far from any English settlement, are groups of irregular mud walls, without roofs sometimes, looking very much as though they had been scooped up from the wide shallow ditch that runs along parallel with the railroad track. The natives bathe and wash in the puddles of muddy water at the bottom of the ditch. The people climb around in the cracks between the houses that do duty for streets in these villages. Sometimes I don't feel sure whether I am looking at a village or a group of haystacks or mud hills. For a long distance I crossed pretty barren plains, perfectly flat and only a tree or so in the distance. In the early morning I would see five or six men filing across the plains, one behind the other, in the most lonesome and dreary manner. I leave Delhi at seven in the morning for Jeypore; shall reach Bombay three days earlier than Cook's agent put me down for. The hotels are very comfortable, and I am taking my five meals a day with great satisfaction. The Great Eastern at Calcutta is the worst hotel in India. It is only equalled in badness by the Astor House of Shanghai. I wear my ulster all the time in India.

EMPRESS OF INDIA HOTEL, JEYPORE, *January 10th.*—After a long day's travel I arrived here last night in time for dinner. I left my hotel yesterday morning before it was light and drove down through dark and deserted streets to the depot, went through the weighing luggage and ticket making arrangement successfully, and eventually got off. You have to get to a depot about an hour before your train goes in order to give the officials time to make your ticket for you. They have the ticket cut to the right size, for a wonder, but that is all. They go to work and print it and stamp it and write on it with a slowness of movement that no one but an Indian could ever attain to. Weighing your baggage and making out a receipt is done in an equally deliberate manner, and if, on paying, you require any change your soul is doomed to perdition, for the most patient temper will give way under that strain. I think fondly of America, where the ticket office opens five or ten minutes before the train goes, and one man stamps and slaps down tickets and change for dozens, not to say hundreds, of people in that time.

Half of the road between Delhi and Jeypore passed through hills set on the flat plains, like so many exaggerated haystacks. These hills were surmounted most picturesquely by old forts—castles, I should call them—with walls running entirely around the brow of the hill. On the plains were little villages, and the ground apparently under an attempt at cultivation. It dosen't look very arable. Hills and plains are alike bare and burnt and sandy. These old castles attract my fancy; I should like to live in one of them, they look so romantic.

Having outstripped my "itinery," I arrive here unheralded. On getting out of the cars I ask for the "Empress of India Hotel" man, and on mentioning my name am received with effusion. Cook's agent had written of my proposed arrival to each hotel. At the hotel I am stowed into a suite of apartments which are so many refrigerators in disguise. I freeze for awhile, then dine and partially thaw, and then go to bed to finish the thawing. Take my meals to-day in solitude and state, being the only guest of the house at present.

I have spent the morning crushing my guide. I began last night. I declined to send my card to the Resident to get permission to look at the billiard room of the palace and gardens; said I was tired of palaces and gardens and temples. He began this morning by pointing out a church. I wouldn't look at it because it was English. Then he showed me a park. I declined to stop or to be driven in. Then he showed me the gas works and the water works. I said "English!" and shot him a glance that made him quake. He drove me through the outer grounds of the palace, which were not half so picturesque as the streets, and bewailed that I had not got the permission to go in. I was just enjoying myself, looking at the people as I drove past, when we drew up before a row of cages with three or four tigers in them. A man is letting down the carriage steps. I say "What is this for?" Guide (meekly), "To see the tigers." I say, "Drive on, I can see tigers every day in New York." I am enjoying myself again with the people, when we stop again. I read "Museum" on the door and say, "I'm not going to get out and see any museums. I refuse to see anything English." My guide is beginning to get discouraged. He asks if I will see the Museum of Art? "No! Good heavens, no!" "The Botanical Gardens?" There I crush him with one fearful glance, and we drive on. After that we simply drive about at random, I enjoying the ever-changing picture of the streets, my guide feeling his occupation gone.

I see many camels and donkeys carrying stones, and the donkeys' loads are as large as the camels'. The children wear a cap with a long cape to it. The women of India carry jars of water on their heads, and sometimes one jar on the top of the other. All through the East are great numbers of large black crows. These crows have a preference for roosting on animals, and I see them constantly perched on the heads and backs of standing or reclining goats and cows. Once I saw a cow roll over a little, and a crow climbing cheerfully up from her spine to her side out of harm's way. This morning I saw a crow fly down with the intention of alighting on a donkey; but the donkey, observing the intention, kicked up its heels until the crow gave up the contest. The cows are more sociable. I frequently see one eating quietly with two or three crows perched comfortably on her backbone. This reminds me of the long-legged bird I saw standing bolt upright on the back of a turtle in the Pacific Ocean.

I still find that the people who know the least about the movements of trains are the railway officials. The most reliable information is to be got from hotel guides and fellow travelers. And one must carry all dining and "change cars" depots in their heads, for no big voiced brakeman will come to the door and shout, "Change cars for Jeypore; passengers for Bombay please keep their seats;" or "Ten minutes for refreshments." People in India must travel on their own responsibility entirely. I am afraid I have led the railway officials a hard life. I've been everlastingly lassoing them as they passed my car window and bombarding them with questions, whenever I could get sight of one, for they keep themselves so very scarce. In all the railway restaurants and many of the hotels in India they have on the table, conspicuously placed, a Complaint Book—a good idea, I think. The only complaint I had was that they did not give me time to eat, much less to register my griefs.

From Jeypore on I was all alone, and could therefore see more and rest more. I saw more old forts crowning hilltops, and numerous camels, also wild monkeys standing upright as our train flew by, with a baby monkey clinging to them or flying up into the trees for safety.

At Amindabad, where I dined and changed cars, I saw more old buildings and two pairs of very tall turreted monuments most unique indeed. I have seen many places in passing that it would be pleasant to stop at a day or two and explore. The road between Amindabad and Bombay is the most horribly dusty road I ever hope to travel on. While running with the air blowing through the cars I did not mind it so much, but when we stopped the atmosphere was so thick and dusty and close and musty that I thought I should suffocate.

BOMBAY, *January 12th.*—'Tis done! The long-dreaded journey across India is accomplished. I arrived in Bombay this morning, bag and baggage, jolly and triumphant, and gleeful at the sight of the sea again. When I get on that same sea I shall rest.

From Delhi to Jeypore and Jeypore to Bombay I contrived to have a compartment of the car to myself, which was a piece of luck. I came through from Jeypore without a stop, thirty-seven hours, two nights and one day. Nevertheless, I arrived here at seven this morning as fresh and chipper as if I hadn't slept two nights in my clothes, ulster and all; been nearly frozen one night and the next choked with dust and jolted about on leathern cushions. I rushed immediately to the hotel, The

Esplanade, where I lifted my trunks down off the head of an unhappy little fourteen-year-old native boy who had carried them alone up three flights of stairs. After a bath, fresh clothes and breakfast, I thought I had never felt so bright in my life. It is a lovely day and a carriage is at the door for me. I sally forth, and oh, how warm it is! and how delightful it is to be where it is warm again. Bombay is pretty.

At my banker's I draw a few rupees to finish India with, and receive a cherished packet of letters. I go to Cook's, get more hotel coupons and make suggestions in the way of improvements on the Cook plans which are graciously received by the agent who doesn't know exactly what to do about me. I leave him dazed and bewildered. Go to P. & O. S. S. Co.'s next, where I exchange my Cook's coupon for a bona fide ticket to Suez, per Steamship Massilia, leaving Bombay January 16th; then back to hotel office, where I get permit to see the "Towers of Silence." Business is done; am now ready to leave Bombay without delay on the day of sailing. Then I read my letters, take tiffin as a sort of "entre act." Some of my letters are forwarded from Singapore and therefore date way back before the flood. Here I am very pleasantly situated, Cook's coupons call for a room on the third floor. I can go below and pay a trifle more if I like. One floor below, the lovely picture I have before me is shut out by trees. From my window I look, when I raise my eyes from this diary, down upon a beautifully arranged park, surrounded by picturesque churches and church-like buildings (no wonder they call the depot "Church Gate Street" Station), and the park is filled with brightly dressed Ayahs (nurses) and children and native soldiers or police. I have an Ayah before me, arrayed in flowing white from the top of her head down, with bars of scarlet finishing the edges and red sleeves. But oh, the tremendous turbans I've seen all through India. My last bearer in Calcutta was a regular Bluebeard, with his immense twisted cloth turban and gray beard and sardonically curling mustache.

And now I want to commence a chapter of mistakes. I have made three mistakes in my travels. The first mistake was in not going from San Francisco to Australia *via* the Sandwich Islands, and from Australia up to Hong Kong. But then I should not have met the Paymaster and the Diplomat, and had their letters of introduction, which were valuable to me. The second mistake was in not going to Canton and having a narrow escape, and going on to Singapore by the French mail, which made easy connections with the Batavia steamer. But then, again, I should not have met some of the delightful people whose acquaintance I have made. The third mistake was in not going to Calcutta *via* Rangoon and Moulmein and seeing the elephants pile lumber. But then, once more, I should not have met the charming French officers nor have gone to the ball. No, I can't truly be sorry for these three mistakes, though I do wish I had seen Canton, and more particularly the Moulmein elephants. But there is a fourth mistake which I am afraid I can't find any compensation for; that was having failed to go from Jeypore to visit the "Ancient City of Amber" on the back of an elephant. I lost my opportunity there, and I shall always regret the "Ancient City of Amber" and the elephant ride.

Here is a good place to philosophize a little. The secret of enjoying travel, I may say even the secret of happiness in life, is to like what you have, what comes to you, the existing state of things, whatever it may be; to be able to see compensating comforts for every discomfort. I fancy I hear some one say: "Take the lesson to yourself, Mrs. Gummidge." And so I will. There is hardly a tragedy in my life, from babyhood up, that I am not glad of after all—which I do not find has been really to my advantage—most of them in the way of strengthening and making self-reliant my rather weak and timorous character.

I think I hear a little feminine friend say: "Oh, yes, it's very easy to be happy when one always has one's own way." But, my dear little lady, I don't always have my own way. I've had many and many a desperate contest with wills counter to mine. All I do is to accept as mine the way I am compelled to take, and be glad of it on the whole. You, my little lady, while you think you would like to be in my place, would not like it at all; you would be lonesome and frightened and nervous; you would suffer with cold, heat, dust, insufficient or unpalatable food, or fret for absent friends, and would allow these things to worry you. I can fancy even the most philosophical fuming over the discomforts of hotels and "cussing" the natives. I am taking all the annoyances as part of the fun. Perhaps, as a rule, I am rather fortunate, too. The hand I hold in life is like my usual hand at whist: four good hearts, three good clubs, three good diamonds, three good spades, with aces, kings, queens and jacks enough to make me hold high trumps whatever turns up. If I lose the game it has been a close contest and I have enjoyed it.

I can't find out whether any other woman has crossed India alone or not. I am told that ladies have been alone to Jeypore, and ladies who have resided here for some years and understand Hindoostanee go from one place to another alone. It is convenient to have a boy with you to look after your baggage while you dine in railway depots. All you really need, though, is about half a peck of two anna bits (five cent pieces) and you can get along very comfortably.

One night at dinner here, having to wait through seven courses for something I wanted, I listened meanwhile to an English gentleman near me who was talking about Americans. He said he heard an American telling a Parsee that he thought Bombay was a "one horse town" and the Parsee was wiping the perspiration from his brow in the vain effort to comprehend. If there is one thing I enjoy more than another it is to hear English people talking to each other about America and Americans all unconscious of the presence of one of the criticised. They seem to think us very funny. After this the gentleman went on to talk about China and Japan, and I just pined to chime in and tell them all about it. A gentleman, opposite me at table to-day, was a New Yorker who was "blowing" about New York at a great rate. I was so pleased to see a "feller citizen" again that I could have flown across the table and embraced him. If he had known that I was a New Yorker too I've no doubt that I should have met with an enthusiastic reception. This is the first place I've found in a tropical country where they have any fruit fit to eat. The oranges here are good. The orange grows loose from the skin. It would rattle around in its skin if it were not for innumerable connecting threads between the two; as it is you shell out your orange like a hazel-nut, and then it comes to pieces so easily, it is quite a comfort to eat it.

A long drive up Malabar Hill brought me to the "Towers of Silence," where the Parsee dispose of their dead after a manner

peculiar to themselves. The Parsee idea is to avoid defiling
Mother Earth with the cast-off garment of flesh, and so they
have constructed these towers of granite and iron, with an iron
grating for a floor on which the dead are laid. The towers are
roofless, and vultures swarm upon the top of the walls, ready to
strip the flesh from the corpse placed within. The clean and
fleshless bones then fall through the grating into a well of water
beneath, the floor of which is laid with lime and charcoal, so
that even the water therein is purified before it reaches Mother
Earth. The vultures' work is quickly done, and nothing is left
to offend the sight or breed corruption or disease. The towers
don't tower much ; they look like whitewashed tanks that one
may see alongside of railway houses. The vultures sit on the edges
looking as innocent as you please. The gardens are pretty, and
the view, being at the summit of Malabar Hill, was fine indeed.

I got up at an unearthly hour one morning to go on a steam
launch to see the Caves of Elephanta. We sail across the bay
for an hour and then climb some stairs, and there we see the
story of the creation modeled in massive stone—a cave cut in the
granite, with large pillars of stone. On the stone walls great
bas-relief pictures are cut, representing the Bramin tale of creation, which is in many respects identical with the Christian
story. Here we have Brahma and Vishnu (Adam and Eve),
before the separation, united in one body ; and here, on the
other hand, they are separated and stand side by side, a complete man and perfect woman ; and here another picture represents a birth, which is also the result of an immaculate conception. In all the pictures there is the ever present serpent,
and the angels hovering about overhead, while below and in
corners are the devils, apparently having their own opinion of
the whole affair. At the top of each stone picture is a cross cut
into the stone and shepherds' crooks, and angels are represented
in the Christian attitude of prayer to the cross. They apparently sit on damp clouds and sing just like Christian angels, and
the whole thing dates back ages before Christ. There is also a
trio of gods like ours, Brahma and Vishnu and Siva ; Brahma,
the Creator ; Siva, the Destroyer ; and Vishnu, the Healer,
which is the best part of all.

BOMBAY TO CAIRO.

S. S. MASSILIA, ARABIAN SEA, *January* 18*th*.—I left Bombay very much pleased with the Esplanade Hotel and its managers. They gave just the gentlemanly personal attention to my wants that I think the correct thing for hotel managers to do. I came on board ship in the company of an old French gentleman and his handsome daughter, whom I have been regarding with interest at the hotel. Arrived on board, I get myself and trunks stowed comfortably into the unusually large stateroom awarded to me. I fee my porters, and drive off successfully a dozen porters who imagine they can persuade me that they have rendered me numerous invaluable services for which they should receive munificent rewards. Fatigued but triumphant, I throw myself into a corner of the saloon lounge. A group of stylish looking ladies are monopolizing an officer on the other side of the saloon. Presently the officer glances at me; I feel cross, I'm not looking at him; what does he want to look at me for? I'm only admiring the ladies. After several glances my way, to which I am to all intents perfectly oblivious, he disengages himself and moves toward me. I immediately turn my back and look out of the window; he hesitates, but concludes to persevere, walks bravely up to me and asks if I am going with the steamer. I recover my temper suddenly and respond "Yes," with a smile, and ask, in my turn abruptly, "Are you the Captain?" He is. Apparently satisfied with his inquiries, he returns to his friends. Having seen them off, he finds time to chat with me a few moments, and then, as we are ready to start, he departs for the bridge.

I have engaged to buy a chair at a fixed price to be delivered on board, and am anxiously awaiting it. Finally, as I am in despair, it arrives, but the Chinaman demands two rupees more. I have already agreed to pay them a good price, having omitted the formality of beating them down, so I decline to be victimized any further. The man thereupon picks up the chair and walks off with it; looks back at me from the gangway expectantly, but I have forgotten his existence by this time, so he descends to his boat and rows off quite a distance, looking back at me all the while; but as I make no sign, presently he returns to the ship. I see him approaching, and turn away; he struggles up the gangway again, and I immediately cross over to the other side of the vessel. He follows and puts the chair down, and otherwise expresses his willingness to accept the original terms. I hand over the money and he departs.

From China to Calcutta I have been told that rank and dress are the prevailing features of a voyage from Bombay to Suez; that the places next to the Captain at table are given to the people of the highest rank, and that much quarreling and bitterness are the results. As I am a plain American citizen, without rank, who travels with as small a wardrobe as neatness and comfort will permit, and decline to add to the fatigues of travel, any unnecessary unpacking and packing of trunks or labor of dressing, with my democratic ways and comfortable blue flannel dress, I am expecting to be relegated to the foot of the table. I come down to dinner perfectly resigned to this state of affairs, and commencing about the middle go all the way down on one side of the table and up the other, and am beginning to think that I am to have no seat at all, when the waiter points out my card at the Captain's left. I take my seat and smile to myself. I think if I am ever going to be relegated to the foot of the table it is high time I began. The idea of my having the best stateroom all to myself and the seat of honor at table, all the way around the world, is too perfectly absurd. It is high time I took a back seat. I had made up my mind I should this trip. Never mind; when I cross the Atlantic I am sure to be snubbed.

January 19th.—I have taken a fancy to the handsome Frenchwoman. I think I shall find her most agreeable socially, and true enough, when, after exchanging a few smiles, we do speak, I find she is a kindred spirit. She, too, would like to travel alone and fears nothing; her great black eyes flash and sparkle at the bare idea. She takes me up and flaunts me and my travels in her venerable parent's face. She is a widow over thirty, has a son thirteen years of age, and looks like an Italian madonna, with her great dark eyes and strong, beautiful face. Her father is thoroughly imbued with the most conservative ideas in reference to women, and keeps her very close, old as she is.

RED SEA, *January 22d.*—We arrived at Aden late last night and left early this morning. I woke up in time to hear the continuous "Yes, sir," of the diving boys, a remark which comprises their entire acquaintance with the English language, and which signifies their earnest desire to dive for coins; and to take Aden in at one comprehensive glance as it passed my port while we were swinging around preparatory to our departure. I have not seen anything of that desperately hot weather they have been promising me, but then hopes have been held out to me of extreme heat and extreme cold all the way around the world that have never been realized. I am put off in each case with the unsatisfactory explanation that this is a very unusual season. I am very much taken up at present with the woes of the French lady, whose father will not permit her to speak to any one on board. I look on at this tyranny and thank my stars that I am an American.

Although I am on board an English steamer many of the customs are Indian, which causes me to reflect that I have enjoyed India very much. India has gratified my taste for the picturesque, the romantic, the historic; and curiously so, for all this lies in its people and its architecture. Nothing could be more barren than the country itself; but somehow its barren plains and fortress-crowned sandhills and crumbling ruins are all picturesque. The temples and palaces fill one with an impression of a past grandeur and glory, with their great chambers of white marble and precious stones. The fairy tales of one's childhood assume a new significance in India. One feels transported back to the days of Bluebeard amongst these natives of ponderous headgear. Little English children in India recognize their household servants in their picture-book representations of the retainers of the "Marquis of Carabas."

We have a Parsee passenger on board. His family came to see him off at Bombay, a dozen or more of dark skinned women, and they looked as if they had just stepped out of a fairy tale, in their flowing drapery of fine white silk crepe, with an embroidered border of color, and their white silk or satin shoes, as if dressed for the stage or a ballroom, worn apparently daily, and now out to the ship in a small boat.

What amuses me a good deal is the way people drink here. Whisky and water is taken by ladies daily, and whisky and soda or water are taken by gentlemen more times a day than I should like to say. These drinks are called "pegs," under the rooted conviction that each one represents another peg in the coffin of the drinker.

SHEPHARD'S HOTEL, CAIRO, EGYPT, *January 28th.*—And now I must write a chapter of woe. As we approached Suez some of the people on board thought it necessary to warn me of the dangerous country I was coming to. My usual trepidation at arriving at a strange country was not at all soothed by the dreadful tales that were told me of people whose hands had been cut off between the steamer and the hotel for the sake of their rings, and other people who had fallen victims to the murderous wrath of some slighted native. There were but three of us going to the hotel, myself and the French lady and her father. Judging from what I had seen of the latter on board, and his vile temper, I should be far safer going ashore alone than with them, and I had made up my mind to do so, but it turned out we were all to go ashore in the boat that took the through passengers to Alexandria and to be taken on the train with them to the hotel.

Having passed the place where the children of Israel once crossed the Red Sea and come to anchor, we got off in a small steam launch. It was quite dark by the time we got ashore. The manager of the launch explained to us what we were to do on landing. I helped the French lady to understand, though she spoke pretty good English. Arrived on shore the man pointed out to me the direction we were to go. Monsieur, the father, started off wildly in the opposite direction, asking loudly and impersonally where to go. As he passed near me, asking, I said, "This way, monsieur." He pushed me roughly aside and asked me to mind my own business in choice French. I did so; going where the lights were and recognizing my own baggage as it came up and seeing it put on board the train. Madame followed me after a little, and Monsieur ultimately came up and harangued and bullied and badgered the officials out of all patience. I had taken the trouble that very day to reopen my already packed trunk and show this man some things he desired to see, at his own and his daughter's especial request. His name is Jules Radu; he is seventy-five, white haired and the author of a French encyclopedia. On board the ship I was the best friend they had. Such is life!

The dragoman of the hotel took charge of us. Having got our baggage in a car by itself, we were put in another car, Monsieur scolding and fuming and retarding the business of getting aboard and off, every step of the way. Twenty minutes brings us to the depot opposite the hotel, and we get out and go in search of our baggage, which is found after a half a dozen cars have been laboriously unlocked. A scuffle then takes place between two natives as to the possession of one of my trunks, in the course of which my trunk is thrown violently from the top of the tallest man's head, happily on no one's toes. Another man picks it up, and we leave the two clawing and gouging each other savagely.

A few steps bring us to the hotel, where another commotion ensues. The men must be feed ; in the dark they are hopelessly mixed. I start to say a word aside to Madame to try to prevent my porters being feed by them, and am taken roughly by the arm by her enraged father and thrown aside and told again to mind my own business. The dragoman, as tired of waiting for them as I, takes me on upstairs to the office. I have only just asked for a room when Monsieur comes raging upstairs, walks up to the table, and striking it with his fist says in French, "Give me two rooms." Neither the clerk nor the dragoman understands. He then demands the master. I have been told to mind my own business and he has left his daughter downstairs, afraid to stir until he commands. I stand the noise a few moments, and then desiring a room myself, and having no chance until he is settled, I venture very quietly to say to him, "The master is at dinner," and to them, "He wants two rooms, for himself and daughter." The poor old lunatic is obliged to permit me to explain to him and to show him even where to write his name. He does as I tell him but ignores me otherwise. They take him to his room, and I sign my name and am shown to mine. I go down to supper, nervous and tired. I am just enjoying my rice and curry when Madame enters, tall, dark and melancholy. She slips a bit of paper under my hand, and whispers good-bye. A clasp of her hand and a pathetic look from her dark eyes, and she is gone. Something in that beautiful tragic face of hers brings a lump in my throat and tears in my eyes. I can eat no more. I try. I dare not look at the note ; I should cry sure. No use, I can't eat. I get up and flee to my room, lock the door, and read the note and weep. The tears that I would not shed at leaving New York, and again at leaving America, came now with a rush. If anybody had asked me what I was crying about, I should have said, "G-g-g-give it up, ask me an e-e-easier one." I wept on, however, perfectly regardless of rhyme or reason. The note said: "Don't come with us; my father will be so rude" (and, by the bye, they were going my way, not I theirs); and expressed grief for the same; hoped I would meet better treatment, et cetera and good-bye. I cried it out; while I was about it I shed all my last year's tears; went to bed and arose with a severe headache in consequence; had my breakfast; met Madame on the stairs; she kissed me twice and said good-bye. My tears rose again, but I laughed defiantly and said I was going to Cairo, too; it was my route, and I could not change my plans to suit her father's tempers. A last embrace and kiss and she was gone.

I followed a little later with my dragoman who had deserted them for me, and sacrificed his brother to their interests; got my Cook's coupon changed after some little difficulty occasioned by the absence of a customary seal; got my baggage weighed and paid for, and secured a carriage for myself alone, encountering Madame and Monsieur several times, but ignoring them. The last I saw of them they were surrounded by a horde of fee hunters. I heard Monsieur scolding about his fees and calling for the police. I had my carriage to myself for half the distance. The other half I was obliged to share it with three Frenchmen and an Englishman. I gave them permission to smoke and looked my desire to be let alone. They accepted the first and respected the latter, and so we proceeded to Cairo. The road was across the plains. A strong wind rattled the windows of the car. Looking out, I could see the steamers in the canal, but I could see no water; the steamers were apparently plowing their way across the sandhills. Further on, the canal stretched like a strip of blue ribbon across the waste of yellow sand, and then it widened into a bay, and then we turned inland and lost it from sight.

Finally we reached a part of the country that was green. On the desert the villages looked like terraces of sand. In the distance I saw villages walled together like one house, with minarets and towers rising from within. At Zag-a-Zig I saw signs of civilization—a woman hanging clothes upon the roof. I reached Cairo at four; was met by an English hotel dragoman at the depot, received politely at the hotel, and am waited on at table by a dark-haired Lord Dundreary. The men here wear baggy trousers and the Turkish fez, and the women cover their faces with black, except the eyes.

I go to the Pyramids to-morrow morning, and then I flit to Alexandria to catch a steamer which connects at Port Säid with a Cook party, with whom I am to go to Jerusalem from Jaffa, and back. I then go on my way alone again to Constantinople, Athens, Naples. The party contains Americans, some being ladies, and has room for just one more. I am always hurrying forward for some advantage, an extra fine steamer, or pleasant companions. I shall be glad to get to Italy, where I shall hurry no more. Trains go every day there instead of every two weeks.

January 29th. — I've done the Pyramids. Having been warned most particularly not on any account to go to the Pyramids alone, of course that was the very thing I did. Cook's here told me it was perfectly safe and supplied me with carriage and dragoman. At seven this morning we started out, and getting out of the city drove for miles along an avenue of trees and camels and donkeys. Judging from appearances the chief products of Egypt are camels and donkeys. The difference between the size of a donkey's load and a camel's is entirely disproportionate to the difference between the size of the animals. I sometimes see two large men riding one very small donkey, the donkey being hardly distinguishable under these circumstances. There is work out here for Mr. Bergh. The poor little donkeys are often horribly chafed by excessively tight back straps.

At last, after a very cold drive, I reach the Pyramids. They can hardly be called pretty, but they are curious. I decline to climb up them. I walk all around them and back to the ancient temples and the Sphinx. The Sphinx interests me most, as she lies there half buried in the sand at the edge of this vast desert of Sahara, silent but sleepless, apparently keeping watch over this waste of sand; an emblem of eternal vigilance. The temples are covered to the top with sand, and we look down into their excavated interiors. I take a last fascinated look at the Sphinx. She is ugly and not half as big as I thought, but her expression of silent alertness fascinates one. She looks as if she held the secrets of the world within her stony brain, but would not reveal. She is typical of power and of patience, of restrained force and everlasting wakefulness. We return along the avenue of camels and donkeys, along the banks of the Nile, over the bridge that crosses that river, and back to the hotel. I am told that the soil is very rich; that when the Nile overflows its banks it covers these green plains with water up to the Pyramids, and that four crops a year are produced from this land. It's well to get a little useful information now and then.

I was told that this was a dreadful country for beggars. I find them no worse than in India or in Ceylon, where they will run after your carriage for a mile or so. I've had no trouble here from them. I like this hotel. Lord Dundreary waits on me at table, and opposite me sit two women with immense diamonds in their ears. No gold is visible. The diamonds are as large as a silver ten cent piece. I saw one larger pair on an ugly Javanese woman at a hotel in the interior of Java.

The hotel dragoman escorts me to the depot, procures my ticket for me, and leaves me in the hands of an Arab boy, who takes charge of my baggage. Presently a larger Arab boy comes along and makes every pretense of being of inestimable service to me, following the boy who carries my baggage and repeating all my orders, although the boy understands English perfectly well; approves of my fee to him and desires one for himself. I have been annoyed at his interference and I have no more small change. I mention the latter fact. He tells me it is of no consequence, is much obliged to me all the same, wishes me a pleasant voyage and bids me good-bye.

The women in Egypt look very curious with their faces covered with black. The two parts of the covering, upper and lower, are kept in place by a thick piece of bamboo on the nose. I don't see how they recognize each other. I saw several at the depot with white silk on their faces and gorgeous white or colored silks and embroidered slippers beneath the long black silk hood and cloak that covered them from head to foot.

I find myself well treated at hotels holding Cook's coupons; and Cook's agents at Cairo were courteous and obliging. Their dragomans, too, are very useful. Indeed, Messrs. Cook & Son make traveling easy.

PORT SAID, ARABIA, AUSTRIAN LLOYD STEAMSHIP, *January 31st.*—I reached Alexandria safely ; was received at the depot by Cook's dragoman at ten P. M. and taken to the hotel ; found a note from my banker to the effect that he would wait upon me in the morning, which he did, so I was enabled to arrange my financial affairs to my satisfaction at nine A. M., and was ready to leave Alexandria at ten, again under the charge of Cook's man, and in company with an Australian and his sister, also bound for Jerusalem. At Alexandria there is an export Custom House, but my baggage passed through without a glance even. I sit next the Captain as usual.

The management of this ship is polyglot—Captain, Austrian ; steward, Italian ; garcon, French ; crew, anything you like inclusive of Arabs ; passengers likewise. Dinner, Austrian bread, Italian wine, French soup, Egyptian fruit. The steward speaks Italian to me and I respond in French. He is oppressively polite, fancies I have a headache, and worries me with gesticulative sympathy.

MEDITERRANEAN SEA, QUARANTINED OFF JAFFA, *February 1st.*—This trip marks an era in my travels. First experience in crowded cabins; traveling in a party and quarantine. We are obliged to remain on board twenty-four hours, and are charged five dollars apiece for the privilege. My stateroom is all bad air and seasick women. One very fat Italian woman was brought on board at Port Säid by her friends, already seasick in anticipation, and is now nearly crazy with fright as much as seasickness. The seven Cook's tourists who came on board at Port Säid, whose party I join here, are also seasick, much to my surprise. We lie motionless upon a sea of glass, with not a ripple to disturb our quiet. The engines are still, and the hush of Sunday reigns over all, broken only by the cracked voices of some missionaries who have been holding service and singing hymns.

Being obliged to remain on board, we lie about the deck and look at the higgledy piggledy town of Jaffa, straggling up from the sea, with some treacherous-looking rocks peeping up through the water midway between us and the shore. A novelty in the way of a waterspout hardly excited our interest, so languid and sick of the ship are we.

These waterspouts are strange affairs. Two whirling peaks of water; one springing upward from a placid, sunlit sea, the other reaching downward from a blue sky, stretch toward each other until they meet, and, joining forces, form a whirling pillar that travels over the water for a while, increasing and diminishing in size, until it dwindles to a thread in the center and breaks, leaving two flapping liquid points to be drawn back to sea and sky. Sometimes the column of water will break and form again, the sky spout reaching down and drawing up the sea. We saw several waterspouts in active operation at one time.

I find the seven Americans very pleasant, and they have taken me to their hearts. They are all jolly but seasick. They decline to be very much surprised at my exploits in the way of traveling, merely remarking "That's just like an American." They take a national pride in me, however. I find we shall be companions for some time, for our routes are the same as far as Athens.

Mr. Mayfield, most stately, most placid, most amiable of men, heads the party, and I find congenial companions in his ladylike and agreeable wife and daughter. Kansas people they are, and very good folks indeed. A pair of cowboys from the Wild West, father and son, are jolly and audacious and full of good natured braggadocio, they make fine antagonists for me at chess and cards or argument, while a young man from Vermont lends youth and good nature to the party.

We see from where we lie at anchor Mount Ararat, and are reminded that these are the waters where Jonah met his adventure with the whale. The whale had no business in these waters anyway it would seem, as we are told there are none here now. Our tourists are not surprised at the whale being sick—they are. Andromeda's difficulties with the sea monsters occurred in this neighborhood. We are now in a region full of historical interest.

THE HOLY LAND.

Mediterranean Hotel, Zion's Hill, Jerusalem.—Well, I am in the Holy Land, and it has need to be holy, for a dirtier place I never saw. Cook's agent came aboard early Monday morning, took us ashore, and marched us up through the streets of Jaffa to a carriage. The streets of Jaffa are narrow and are composed of four equal parts of donkey, camel, native and mud, through which we had to walk two or three blocks to the carriages, which carriages carried us through more mud and camel, donkey and native, to the hotel. There we breakfasted and hastily overhauled trunks, and then drove out to see the sights of Jaffa; namely, house of "Simon the Tanner," an orphan school, orange groves which were all orange and very little tree, and unlimited camels, donkeys, natives and mud. Woe is me! my troubles have begun. I'm now to be put through the regulation sights, orphan schools and churches. We left Jaffa the same day at two P. M. in three fine landaus, our party of eight being augmented by three Scotchmen, two of whom are ministers. They have a guide to themselves, and are to continue on to Damascus.

Having got out of the dirty city, we drove along a good road across the plains, seeing some sights on the way, climbing an ancient tower, and arriving at Ramleh at five P. M., where we were surprised to find a good, clean and new hotel, at which we stopped for the night. We walked a little in the village, until we were discouraged by the dirt and the lepers. Off again in the morning by half-past seven, and arrived at Jerusalem, after a long ride, some fun, and a good many hills, at four P. M.

February 6th.—The first morning we were here we went to the Holy Sepulchre, which contains separate sections for various nations. Turks guard the door to keep Christians from fighting. Various Christian sects sometimes engage in a free fight over the tomb of Jesus, resulting in great loss of life. We spend the morning promenading around from altar to tomb with lighted tapers. We find here the tomb of Adam, over which Mark Twain wept; also that of St. George of Dragon fame and a lot of other tombs too numerous to mention. The church is very large, and the altars handsome and rich in jeweled pictures—pictures in which only the hands and faces of the portrait are visible, the rest being a mass of immense diamonds, rubies, emeralds, sapphires and pearls. In the afternoon we go to a convent and follow the road where Jesus walked with his cross on his back to Calvary. We are called upon to note the places where he stopped and rested the cross, the mark being left in the stone.

The next morning we go to the Mosque of Omar and Solomon's Temple, where we are escorted around by an old Turk, the master of the harem, who is uncomfortably attentive to me, I almost feel destined to become an inmate of that harem, as my friends have prophesied for me. We, as many of us as have them, have brought our slippers, and I am the "belle of the ball" in my beaded and gold-heeled Java slippers, as I step into the Mosque. This is really worth seeing. An immense dome, all of mosaic in the rich, subdued tints we see in Turkish rugs. Lovely effects are seen in windows—beautiful pale tints shining through mother-of-pearl lattice work—all lovely, gorgeous, splendid. It all covers and surrounds an immense rock, the rock on which that inhuman parent, Abraham, sacrificed, or was about to sacrifice, his son at the Lord's command. Underneath this rock are altars, and they tell you the rock is suspended in the air, unsupported from beneath.

The Temple of Solomon is close at hand ; it contains more altars and several pillars placed very near to each other, between which pillars it is supposed only the good can pass. Quite large cavities have been worn by people squeezing through. Beneath the church is supposed to have been Solomon's stable. Here we find lots of little heaps of stones piled by people who wish to get the Lord to remove illness and misfortune from their families. The lattices of the windows above are full of bits of yarn, tied there for the same purpose. We go to a convent in the afternoon, in the chapel of which we find the same picture I saw in smaller form in the Mission church at Santa Barbara, California—a picture representing the day of judgment, the good people going off on one side with harps and olive branches, and the sinners being hastened on into the flames and the lake of fire at the point of toasting forks, applied by the gleeful devils; snakes, and dragons *ad lib.*; a sweet picture to contemplate.

To all these places we had gone on foot, picking our way through the dirty streets and people, over a rough and uneven pavement of jagged stones, thickly overlaid with filth; not exactly the golden streets we had heard of. One could not see much in this way, for one was far too busy watching one's footsteps and dodging donkeys with wide reaching paniers filled with dirt, to see anything else.

Our next trip is to Bethlehem. I have looked forward to this with many pleasant anticipations. We can go as we choose, in a carriage or on horseback. I choose a horse. Cook's agent, Mr. Clark, promises an easy one. I congratulate myself when I find that the carriages are springless, not the easy landaus we came in from Jaffa, and that my horse is easily managed and a pacer. We have a lovely ride to Bethlehem, seeing various tombs and wells and getting a glimpse of the Dead Sea on the way. The coach rushes through the narrow streets of Bethlehem at a rattling pace, scattering women and children, donkeys and camels, until we reach the Church of the Nativity. Here we see a lot more tombs and altars, and pictures of the crucifixion, the tombs of the parents of Mary, the room where Jesus was born, the spot where his cradle rested, and the room occupied by St. Jerome. Some of these people appear to have tombs in several parts of Judea, a city tomb and a country tomb, and a tomb at a fashionable seaside resort. Indeed, their saintly remains are scattered about in the most promiscuous manner.

We start for Jerusalem again, and here my woes begin. My horse, a delightful pacer if he will, is in a hurry and he positively declines to pace; he will do nothing but trot or gallop in a hard, jolting fashion that threatens to reduce me to a jelly. I expostulate with him in vain. My saddle has got twisted, and the gentlemen with me assure me that it is all right, although I am hanging on the side of the horse, and of course resting too heavily on the stirrup and getting it more twisted. I reach the hotel bruised and lame. On the principle of "hair of the dog cures the bite," I start out on the following morning, so lame and sore that every movement is painful, to go donkey-riding outside the city walls. My donkey is the fastest of the lot, and my donkey boy ambitious, so I lead the cavalcade of eight, and am in a fair way to get cured of my lameness before our tour around the city of Jerusalem is finished. Our party is kept amused by the cowboy's ineffectual efforts to inspire his lazy donkey with sufficient ambition to pass all the others.

We are called upon to dismount from time to time to see the tomb of the Virgin, or to climb a tower to get a view of the Dead Sea and a glimpse of Jordan, way beyond. There are lots of beggars and lepers about, but they do not trouble one so much as I have heard. It is best not to give them anything, unless you want a whole tribe at your heels. Just entering a gateway, I am besieged by three or four little girls. Little girls always fetch me; I've got a silver coin in my pocket, and it is soon transferred to the little dirty supplicating hands. On my return from the tombs within I am met at the gate by the mother of the children and presented with a bunch of apple blossoms as a token of gratitude.

And now for a few remarks on the subject of traveling in a party. I've been with these people ten days, and find them most agreeable people—no unpleasant or quarrelsome ones in the party. We are sociable and have jolly times together. I have been told by English people everywhere that Americans abroad are rather noisy; and have also heard that Cook's tourists come to places and monopolize everything, both of which statements are entirely correct. We do arrive at places and take possession of them. Indeed, in Palestine we are frequently the sole patrons of the hotel. If there are other guests, they are too hopelessly in the minority to enter a protest. Other people sit staid and silent over their meals; we chatter and laugh from one end of the table to the other. For those traveling in a crowd, the agent sends to the hotel in advance to engage as many rooms as are required, and when we arrive we are given slips of paper with our names and room numbers on them. I get a room that is an exaggerated refrigerator of stone, with a tiny square window high above my head. I rebel, but to no purpose. We have filled the hotel, and the rooms are all allotted. I am afraid this agent is not sufficiently impressed with my necessities. If I had ordered my horse myself I should have had a better one, I know, but leaving it to him I got a wretched one. The agent is gentlemanly and suave, and promises finely to the person, but apparently he simply orders a horse for one or a room for one, without an effort to secure the best to be had.

Traveling in a party one is obliged to go over much that is stupid and tiresome and wait somewhat on the movements of the others. I have never in all my travels been so badly cared for as here, but that is probably because accommodations are worse here than in any other country. There are many advantages in being under Cook's direct care, but I fancy I can do better for myself in the matter of securing rooms and berths. Their tickets and dragomans are a great convenience, but I prefer to secure my own rooms, staterooms and horses personally.

This is the land that flowed with milk and honey. As a matter of fact it flows now chiefly with stones. The milk is a myth, or rather is represented only by that of goats, but after much demand the honey has been produced. The hills are all rock, the fields are covered with stone, and divided by wall after wall of the same material. I never saw so many stones in all my life—the chief production of the soil is stone. I have not heard the "voice of the turtle," but I have heard the voice of the donkey. A combination of donkey bray and "Home, Sweet Home," on the piano, with variations, is particularly entertaining to the listener. The camels weep when too heavily loaded, and their reputation for gentleness and meekness is a fiction. They are vicious, and they bite and kick with specially disastrous effect.

Take it all together, the Holy Land is the barest, the flattest, the dirtiest of all the countries I have seen. China is the only country that could possibly compare with it. Many of the streets here are covered over, being literally narrow stone tunnels, dark and crowded and dirty. Every one is obliged to carry a lantern when out after dark. A market is just opposite the hotel; principal article of commerce, cauliflower. Frequent squabbles over purchases occur. It is delightful and warm out of doors during the day, but always cold in the house. I have six colds now and am catching another. Wear my ulster night and day, likewise my rug and shawl. Want to go home. Lovely oranges here; am living principally upon oranges. Dogs, bells and donkeys divide the honors when it comes to noise.

The women here wear a white muslin envelope over their other clothes, covering head and all; the face is covered with a flowered gauze, through which you cannot distinguish the features. There are all kinds of people here—many Russians and Americans. In the chapel of a convent erected by the Princess d'Auvergne we saw the Lord's Prayer printed on the walls in thirty-two different languages.

As any one who knows me might guess, the ex-cowboy is my chosen companion and familiar spirit. He is an invalid, owns a cattle ranch near Cheyenne, and has with him his son, aged twenty-four, whom I call "Jack Hamlin." But all the party are pleasant, jolly people, and we get on nicely together. The American Consul and his wife reside in the hotel and have been very friendly.

JAFFA, PALESTINE, *February 9th.*—Left Jerusalem yesterday morning and arrived here at 5:15 P. M. Tried to have a chill and a sunstroke together yesterday; fair success with both. All right again this morning. Doctored and sympathized with by the combined seven. Saw lots of camels, twenty-three in a row, yesterday, and a ferocious Bedouin, one of those who attack and rob the lonely traveler. Also an infinitesimal child leading an immense camel. His camelship accommodated his steps to the infant's. Returning over the same road we went, we find the ground covered with scarlet flowers, very pretty to see. Saw a turtle who refused to "lift up his voice" and several hundred lizards, of all sizes, in one tree. Lizards sit on stones and think as we go by. Party all satisfied with the visit to the Holy Land. Were promised bad weather and had remarkably fine weather. Sail to-morrow for Beirut.

OFF BEIRUT, ARABIA, S. S. HUNGARIA, *February 10th.*—Leaving Jaffa yesterday, we passed by a departing regiment of Turkish soldiers, followed by a crowd of weeping men, women and children. Soldiers taken off in small boats to steamer. Water front thronged with despairing families waving last farewells. Soldiers hopelessly seasick before reaching the steamer; nothing like seasickness for assuaging sentimental woes. Got aboard and took sole possession of a stateroom for six. Shall suffer untold agonies daily in dread of more lady passengers arriving at the various ports we stop at to dispute possession with me. Jaffa was a lovely place for oranges; twenty cents a hundred. We laid in a stock; every stateroom full of oranges.

Sailed from Jaffa at 5 P. M. last night; arrived at Beirut at seven this morning. Cook's boatmen came aboard and took us ashore. Walked and drove all over the place. Beirut is a great commercial center. More European in character and far cleaner than Jaffa. Women, as in Jaffa and Jerusalem, wear a white muslin sheet for drapery and flower figured gauze over their faces. All through this country immense cactuses grow, great leaves as big as a stove lid and from one to two inches thick, covered with long, sharp thorns. Camels and goats eat them by the roadside, thorns and all. Have seen them do it. They apparently consider them a delicacy.

ÆGEAN SEA OR ARCHIPELAGO, OFF ISLAND OF SCIOS, *February 14th.*—Our next stop after Beirut was Cyprus, and then, after a day at sea, at Rhodes. To-day we stopped at Scios, but we did not go ashore at any of these places for several reasons. Firstly, they would not let us because of ; secondly, i. e., it was too stormy and rough to land; thirdly, it was pouring rain; fourthly, "mal de mer" had effectually quenched all active interest in sightseeing; and, fifthly, there was nothing to see of any consequence, so they said. So we looked longingly across the intervening waters at the shore, and fought seasickness, and watched the adventures of the small boats that endeavored to come out to us. This is the seasickest party I ever saw in my life. They get seasick on the smallest possible provocation. They are seasick when we lie at anchor, with machinery stopped, sea as smooth as glass and the ship motionless as the floor nearly; and they are seasick while we sail through the Archipelago with islands on both sides and the water as free from billows as the Hudson River. We have had quite a storm for two nights, and it has been pretty rough, but not enough to make me feel a qualm at all events. I am the only one of the party who comes to the table with any degree of certainty as to the results.

Upon deck, when I am just rounding off one of my most graceful remarks, my companion suddenly rises and flees with more haste than grace, and no ceremony at all, to the stern. Just as I am recovering from convulsions of laughter at his hasty departure, he returns, saying "The phosphorescence on the water is exceedingly fine to-night." Looking at it has apparently benefited him greatly.

We have on board as passengers four Arab sheiks, the sons of the principal sheik of Arabia (who is dead, I believe), going to Constantinople with presents of horses to the Sultan. They look at me with a great deal of curiosity. They cannot comprehend my traveling alone in safety. There are a number of pretty Turkish women on board; they speak a little French or German, so we manage to exchange civilities through the saloon windows. They are second class or deck passengers, and their condition through this stormy weather, ranged alongside the saloon deck, only half sheltered by canvas, has been pitiable. This is the noisiest, ramshackliest old boat you ever saw, and the weather is getting colder as we travel northward.

IN THE HARBOR OF SMYRNA, *February 15th.*—Had time to go ashore for half an hour this morning, but concluded not to do so. The place looked too European to interest me. Could see all I wanted to see from the cabin window—about as much as I could see in half an hour on shore in the rain. European built houses, green blinds, three hotels, and a dance hall; half a dozen street cars and cabs; European pedestrians carrying umbrellas, with a plentiful sprinkling of church steeples, and all at the foot of a ruined, fortress-crowned hill. Those who went ashore report dirtier streets than Jerusalem, interesting bazaars, and an officer bristling with weapons and more picturesque and terrifying than a cowboy, who demanded passports. Everybody gave this gentleman plenty of room to pass.

CONSTANTINOPLE.

Hotel D'Angleterre, Constantinople, *February 17th.*— There is no mistake about the usefulness of "Cook" when it comes to em- and de-barking. We are navigated past passport and custom officers with a majestic wave of the hand. The name of "Cook" has an "open sesame" effect. We are not badgered by porters and boatmen. We have a special boat with boatmen in red and blue shirts with "Cook's Boatmen" in bold letters on the breast. Our steamer brought a bundle of new shirts, which were distributed the moment we left the ship, and were on the men in no time, and we departed in a glory of bright red shirt.

We reached here by sailing up the Ægean Sea, stopping at Myrtilene and at Dardanelles, and seeing the place where Leander swam the Hellespont; sailing through the Hellespont up the Sea of Marmora and into the Golden Horn to Constantinople.

On the voyage I received much attention from the four Arab sheiks. They touched their foreheads to me whenever I appeared. They invited me to come and stay in Arabia two or three years, and said they would see that I had a pleasant time. Our conversations were through the medium of an American gentleman who has lived at Beirut a number of years and understands Arabic. Before we left the steamer he said he was beginning to feel the delicacy of his position. I told them, through him, that I would come and bring my family in a few years. They wrote their signatures for me in Arabic, and I wrote mine for them. They were very fearful that I should take cold without anything on my head; thought I did not dress warmly enough. They themselves were muffled up to the eyes with a broad striped cloth tied on the head with a piece of rope. Our interpreter, Mr. Hallek, was a most agreeable gentleman. We found we possessed a mutual admiration for Robert G. Ingersoll, whom he knows and whose ideas, character and family he admires immensely.

Constantinople is a pretty city, but it is a city of dogs and fires and mosques, and mud without limit. The hotel is comfortable. I've a cunning little room, with an easy chair and a marble topped stove in it. Just imagine a white crockery stove with a marble top! It is cold here, but not dreadfully so. No snow. We started out at 1 P. M. with a guide.

First we went to see the whirling dervishes. We walk through the rough, stony and muddy streets to a round building, which we enter and stand in a compartment divided from an arena by a low railing. The dervishes are just coming in. They spend a good while kneeling and bowing and touching their foreheads to the polished floor and responding to a chant that is sung by an unseen man, always with their faces toward Mecca. Here, as in Jerusalem, there is always a fluted alcove facing Mecca in the temples. After we are thoroughly tired of this a sort of march is played, and they march around the circular arena twice in single file, stopping and bowing on reaching the front of the alcove, first to the one in front of them and then stepping forward and turning around to the one behind. After this they take off the long outer cloak they wear and drop their long skirts, which had been fastened up. This skirt is full and plaited evenly around at the waist. A broad sash heads it and a short jacket comes down to meet the sash. They have bare feet and a felt hat that resembles a yellow flower pot in shape and color. Soon they proceed to whirl. They have a step which is the waltz reduced to first principles. They whirl smoothly, calmly, regularly, rapidly, their skirts standing out evenly till they look like so many revolving convex cart wheels with exaggerated hubs, or absurdly large teetotums. After some ten or fifteen minutes of this the rapidity decreases, and presently they stop as calm, as unruffled, as free from giddiness, to all appearances, as if whirling was the simplest possible motion. While whirling they hold their arms even with the head, one hand bent at the wrist and turning out from the head and the other turning in towards it. The swiftest whirler was a boy of about twelve years.

From the dervishes we went to the fire tower. Climbing this, we look out on the country we are in, and very pretty it is. On one side lies the Golden Horn, crossed by two bridges. Here to the left is the Bosphorus, and away beyond stretches the Sea of Marmora, with Princess Island in the foreground. Just across the Bosphorus lies Scutari, and scattered all about are domes and minarets of mosques. It seems this is the last day of the Carnival, and descending from the tower—where men watch for fires night and day—we encounter two men with blue painted faces and a bear which reluctantly performs an alleged dance, to the evident distress of all the dogs in the neighborhood. Then we walk to one of the bridges we saw from the tower, and thence on board a steam launch that is acting in the capacity of ferryboat and steam up the Golden Horn. We land after "coming out of the little end of the horn," as "Jack Hamlin" says, and engage rowboats (caiques) for the return trip. "Jack Hamlin" remarks that gondolas "lay way over" these boats. I suggest "Take the caique" in short, and am crushed with a look.

The caique is, in fact, the most inconvenient and dangerous kind of craft I ever saw. It is a small boat for rowing; very narrow, very light and very incommodious, with a fatal propensity to upset on the slightest pretext, and carrying but two passengers, who are exhorted to sit perfectly still and not swamp the boat. A quiet row and we are back at the bridge; a muddy walk, a ride up hill in an underground cable railroad and we reach the hotel.

February 18th.—Up bright and early this morning and out again. This time we travel in carriages. We see the Pigeon Mosque, where we count pigeons by the thousand, and the mosque of Suliman the Magnificent, some tombs of Suliman and his family, whose lives don't appear to have been of the peaceful order, the son having killed his mother and the father the son. From here we go to the Bazaars, which appear to be one immense building, with streets and shops within it. Lots of pretty things are to be seen here in the way of jewelry and gold embroidery on velvet or silk. We go to see the Mosque of St. Sophia, the handsomest mosque I have seen anywhere, with immense domes and half domes and porphyry pillars and mosaic, and carpets woven with a spot marked out for each person to kneel upon, and seven minarets. When we arrived a few children were playing about in the mosque, which I approved of at once. One or two men were mumbling prayers, while their eyes and thoughts wandered after us. We went up into the gallery and witnessed the opening of worship below—rows of people kneeling on the rows of squares and touching their foreheads to the floor. We are told a lot of legendary history about this church, all of which our guide firmly believes, even to the tale of the man who was walled in by a miracle four hundred years ago, and who is still buried in the wall and is alive yet. He knows he is alive because, when an attempt was made to open the wall and see, the hands of the workmen were paralyzed. Whenever there is any doubt about anything, the remark "The guide says so" settles it at once.

After this we go and see one of the Egyptian obelisks, and a museum, which contains antique and battered statues and two or three hideous mummies. At another place we see figures dressed in ancient costumes; and at another, an ancient underground cistern with one thousand and one pillars in it; and so we have labored through a day.

February 19th.—This morning the party disbanded for the day, each to follow their own special inclinations. It had been proposed to go up the Bosphorus to the Black Sea, but some were unwilling to take the trip. Two of the gentlemen were determined to do it, however, and I joined them, and very glad I am I did so.

We sailed up the Bosphorus on a little steamer. The banks of the Bosphorus are lined with mosques and palaces of the Sultan and the different embassies. The scenery is lovely even now, when the trees are bare and the hills gray; in summer, when all is green, it must be extremely beautiful. We leave the steamer before we reach the mouth of the Black Sea, and climb a fortress-crowned hill, and there, before us and below, lies the Black Sea—not black and stormy, as its name suggests, but smooth and bright, its tiny ripples shimmering in the sunlight as far as the eye can see. I fall to worshiping it, as I do all seas. The day is exceedingly bright and balmy. We lunch in the shadow of the ruined walls of the fortress thirteen hundred years old, which is overgrown in places with ivy. Then, with several last backward looks, we return to the Bosphorus, the view of the latter from the hill top being hardly less beautiful than the view of the Black Sea on the other side. We are rowed across the Bosphorus in caiques to catch the return steamer to Constantinople. Arrived at the hotel, we do the best we can to make the others miserable because they did not go. Truly, it ranks with some of the finest scenery I have looked upon.

The Turkish women wear white tulle covering over the face and head, only a narrow strip of the face being visible. The arrangement suggests a helmet with a partly open visor, and they look out of a crack as an oyster might out of his shell. This tulle is often very thin, particularly so if the woman who wears it is beautiful. If the woman is not pretty, the gauzy covering softens the features and conceals the ugliness to some extent. Their eyes are generally very fine.

Constantinople is a far less Eastern-looking city than I had supposed, and is much too civilized to suit me. It is quite European, in fact; any quantity of Europeans are to be seen on the street. All sorts of costumes appear—plenty of fezes, many bright Bulgarian uniforms, and occasionally a man in short white skirt, high boots with a rosette on his toes, and belt full of revolvers and knives. Beggars are plentiful, with deformities that are pitiable. Beggars have a particularly engaging smile, and will follow carriages for miles, and smile a Constantinople smile. They have sidewalks here, but people prefer the middle of the road to walk in. They have a new "wrinkle" at this hotel; they roll your nightdress up from the bottom in a ring and lay it in the open bed, so you can just catch it up and throw it over your head. The Turkish day commences at sunrise, with one o'clock, and goes to twelve, at sunset or thereabouts. They consider it unnecessary to count the hours of the night. In going out at night one must carry a lantern. Fleas and dogs are equally abundant.

We finished up Turkey with a grand sight, namely, seeing the Sultan of Turkey go to mosque. Does not sound particularly grand, does it? Only saw a man go to church. Well, when his Sultanship goes to church he doesn't want it forgotten; but I must begin at the beginning. We left our hotel with our guide and as much of an arsenal as can be carried about by one man, in close carriages. After a pretty drive of half an hour we are set down before a building among a crowd of soldiers and sightseers. We are given the best possible places in the open porch or foyer of a house that commands a view of the street and the entrance of the mosque on the opposite side of the way. Here for as much as an hour we sit and watch the arrival of regiments of soldiers, officers, and visitors of importance. The street before us is being sprinkled with fresh dry earth and is filled, now with marching soldiers, now with prancing horses, now with officers in handsome uniforms and brilliant with decorations, now with carriages containing the mother, wives and children of the Sultan. Gorgeous red and blue and gold and green trimmed officers are passing constantly before and through the landing we occupy. From time to time carriages draw up and two or three boys from ten to fifteen years, the Sultan's sons and nephews, also in uniform, come up the steps and by us into the building —pretty boys, they are, and as grave and soldierly as possible.

Everybody is here at last; two soldiers stand before us, with arms presented; a row of soldiers on the curbstone present arms likewise; officers and soldiers, cavalry and footmen are drawn up in every direction; two carriages containing the wives and mother of the Sultan stop by the mosque door and the horses have been removed. The black eunuch is gossiping with the wives. My four Arab sheiks file by and take places; carriages with gorgeously dressed ladies with tulle covered faces cease to pass by; no more glancing at officers. A little noise and confusion at the right; soldiers present arms, band begins to play, and the Sultan drives up to the mosque steps, followed closely by a lot of horsemen. The carriage he occupies is a victoria. He sits on the back seat, not specially distinguished from any of the other officers. Two officers occupy the seat in front of him; a muezzin calls the faithful to prayers, from the minaret above the mosque. One only catches a glimpse of them, when all three have descended and entered the mosque, a lot of attendants fall in and follow them closely; then all is quiet for fifteen minutes, while the Sultan is at his devotions quite alone in his compartment in the mosque. Then there is a parade of the officers, which the Sultan reviews from behind a lattice in the mosque; the horses are re-attached to the Sultan's carriage, and they are driven away; and then the Sultan reappears, enters his carriage, and is driven off, his retainers and troops falling in and following him. The sons and nephews follow in their carriages and the parade is over. And we are driven back to the hotel. What with the music and bright uniforms and general novelty, we have been very much entertained. We have just time to have our lunch, settle our bills, and off we start for the steamer.

GREECE.

Hotel D'Angleterre, Athens, *February 22d.*—Leaving Constantinople is as much of an affair as entering it.

Again we go through the Custom House, and again our passports are called into requisition. We are rowed from one wharf to another to attend to these details, and having been properly stamped and sealed, are again waylaid by Custom House boatmen out by the steamer to inspect our stamps and seals.

We arrived this morning, after being detained by fog for eight hours in the Hellespont. Coming in we saw no signs of a harbor or of the vicinity of a city, and had just concluded the steamer intended to climb the barren hill just under our bows, when we swung short around and sailed slowly into a tiny harbor, which nevertheless was full of shipping. Cook's agent or courier was soon on board and took us ashore. This time my trunks were really examined, but as I hadn't any tobacco in them they were passed through successfully.

First blood for the baggage smashers! Lock of my trunk broken, leather strap pulled out, and cover torn off one end. Fast approaching civilization! On shore we were put into a couple of comfortable carriages and driven from the landing place, Pireus, to Athens, about five miles off. Athens is warm and green. We find the hotel comfortable and facing a public square, where music is being played all the afternoon. I listen to the "Beggar Student" while I write.

February 24th.—One year ago to-day I was running along the hurricane deck of the Santa Rosa, with a great terror at my heart, hurrying to the stern to catch a last glimpse of the little tugboat that was carrying away the last home face I should see for some months. As I ran along I encountered a certain gallant captain with a long and dismal face, and regardless of his feelings and only intent on concealing my own, I swallowed the tears that were just about to gush and laughed gaily, flinging him a saucy remark, and got snubbed. So I began a long voyage and a most valued friendship. He had his own opinion of a young woman who laughed frivolously when, if she had any heart at all, she ought to weep copiously, and I hadn't any use for a gentleman who didn't smile at me when I smiled at him. And now a whole year has passed, and I have seen all the heathen countries, have finished the East, and am tired of traveling. I think, egotistically, that I have seen the most novel and interesting part of the world. I've a lingering desire to see Pompeii and Rome and Venice. I think crossing the Alps might be nice, and I suppose the Rhine is the thing to do, but I'm afraid I've lost interest in traveling and haven't that respect for antiquities which one should have to appreciate Europe. My friends who have seen Europe say, "You really don't need to see Rome after Athens; the ruins of Athens are finer, the antiquities more antique than those of Rome." The ruins at Athens date back as far as five hundred years before Christ, and goodness knows how much longer. Now I like ruins immensely as long as they are grand, picturesque walls and temples and pillars, but when they are simmered down to a headless body of mutilated stone .I must confess to an entire want of interest in its age or history.

I have enjoyed Athens very much, and we have luxuriated in clean streets. The absence of dogs and fleas, and the presence of a good band, has contributed largely to our pleasure. The ruins are delightfully massive and picturesque. We climb Mar's Hill and explore the Acropolis, the Parthenon, Temple of Minerva, and all the rest of the great old ruins with their half-effaced bas-reliefs and graceful pillars. We look down from the ruin-crowned hill upon the city and the surrounding country and see some ruined pillars of another old temple at a little distance. We observe what at first appears to be a field of white rosettes resting on tall stalks, but which on closer inspection prove to be a regiment of Greek soldiers, whose short white skirts are plaited so full that they stand out about them rosette fashion. Very picturesque they look as they move about like so many animated white roses of large size while their stacked arms glitter in the sunlight. I saw the same kind of soldiers at Constantinople and Smyrna. They are mountaineers and said to be exceedingly valiant.

Descending from Mar's Hill we see two ancient theatres, stone semi-circles, on the sides of hills, with stone chairs having Greek names upon them, and a semi-circle of steps rising to the top of the hill. The stage is a stone floor with a wall and archways at the back, behind which were ranged ancient statues in more or less bad repair, and pieces of bas-relief. I wish I could see one of their old performances. In walking through the city we discover Diogenes' lantern, a little temple in the shape of a lantern.

IONIAN SEA, OFF CORFU, *February 26th.*—The night before leaving Athens I bade good-bye to my party, as I was to leave the hotel at the cheerful hour of half-past five. Many were the regrets at my leaving. Some brave friends were for rising early and seeing me off, but I quashed that suggestion peremptorily, wishing on no account to put them to such inconvenience. So before it was light the following morning I slipped down the hotel stair, attended by a porter who bade me *bon voyage.* Then into a carriage and off through the dark streets and country. An hour's drive to Pireus—such a splendid chance for brigands! But brigands are extinct, and all the romance and adventure is rapidly departing before the advance of civilization. I'd like to know what's the use of traveling in Greece if you can't have brigands to break the monotony of a journey now and then. Of course I had Cook's courier in attendance, and he fetched me off in a small boat to the little Greek steamer and then left me. A gentleman with a fez, who was, I think, an Albanian Greek, seeing me alone, took me immediately under his wing, his little sister of fifteen was under his other wing. He could speak French, and the officers of the ship only Greek, so he was the medium through whom I communicated. The little sister spoke only Greek, but we smiled friendliness at one another. I called her the "Maid of Athens" at once.

After three hours' sail we reached the Salamis, to the joy of the seasick, and were landed in small boats and loaded on cars, which proceeded with us to the vicinity of Corinth. This is the place where they are cutting a canal *a la* Isthmus of Suez. We could not take the steamer from Corinth because the sea was too rough. So we were driven in carriages around to the other side of the little bay, where the steamer lay sheltered by the hills, and, by means of boats again, got on board—I haven't had the pleasure of walking on board ship from a wharf since I left Singapore—then we sailed away through the blue waters of the Gulf of Lepanto.

I bless my lucky stars that sent me off on a Greek steamer and alone, for now I do come into contact with the people, and I find them more than nice. I never fell into acquaintance with people more easily. I find them social, cordial and genial, very like the French, but more sincere. I am again next the captain at table, a Greek captain, and the center of a jolly social set of gentlemen, all bent on entertaining me. One or two of the Greeks speak a little English, but French is the neutral ground on which we all meet. I do not know anything of the position of women in Greece, but the family relations seem to be the loveliest. Brothers give their sisters the tenderest care, showing an affectionate solicitude for their health and comfort that is charming. Masculine cousins entertain the warmest and most affectionate friendship for each other, and friends exhibit a sincere cordiality and *bonhomie* towards each other that I have never seen equalled anywhere else. The genial good nature and readiness to laugh won my heart. They are all very fond of music, too, and the air was full of snatches of opera.

It looks rather curious to see gentlemen kissing each other, as these people do when they meet or part, and they kiss as if they meant it, too. Two gentlemen will fly into each other's arms at meeting, and exchange two or three perfectly stunning kisses full on the lips, and then look unutterable affection into each other's eyes. I enjoyed very much watching gentlemen walking up and down the deck with arms about each other's waists, blending their voices in some bit of opera, or Greek love song in the moonlight. There is no lack of dignity in the Greeks, there is no silly monkeying or hasty anger, but they look as if they respected themselves, while they conduct themselves with the easy spontaneous affection and playfulness of children. Toward me they were at once cordial, respectful and considerate—in short, gentlemanly in every sense of the word. The passengers and captain both inquired if I was satisfied with my quarters on board, and brought their influence to bear on the steward to make me entirely so. I was, as usual, made at home on the bridge, and, last but not least, while I was the recipient of all manner of delicate attentions and neatly implied compliments, I was not treated to any nonsense or asked impertinent questions about my reasons for traveling alone.

We reached the Island of Patmos last night and Corfu this morning. I go ashore and a Greek gentleman takes me to his sisters, two pretty Greek girls who receive me cordially. The girls speak French. I am entertained and chatted with, and nothing can exceed the polite cordiality and interest with which I am received and entertained. Presently I am shown the garden, and the carriage is ready. The elder sister tears herself away from some callers, and goes with me and the brother for a drive, to see the gardens of a gentleman to whom I was introduced at Athens and who has been a fellow passenger here. He is a member of the Greek Parliament, and I am informed is their leading citizen at Corfu, much loved and respected. After wandering through his gardens (the Greeks are very fond of flowers), we drive up the hill to a place called "One Gun" where there is a pretty view. My friends come on board with me and say good-bye with an interchange of cards, thanks, invitations, and farewells. So I part again with friends, the friends of yesterday to be sure, but warm and substantial friends for all that. One never knows how many real good, generous, disinterested, warm-hearted people there are in the world until one goes among strangers in strange lands, and then it does one good to find how many people there are to lend a helping hand to a traveler. Everything tends to confirm my belief in the inherent unselfishness of human nature.

I sailed out of the pretty little harbor of Corfu with the pleasantest feelings towards Greece and her people. The climate is bright and sunny, and so soft and balmy. Corfu has a most picturesque fortress as you enter the harbor.

ITALY.

HOTEL ROYALE, NAPLES, *February 28th.*—A rough night on the water, and I have crossed the Adriatic Sea. I am up in the morning before it is light, the first one on deck. The cook is asleep in the galley and the first officer in the companionway. I slip by and out on deck to see the harbor as we come in. We sail past a long spit of land, several lighthouses, and sundry buoys, into the harbor of Brindisi, close to the wharf, and I take my first view of sunny Italy with the sunny part of the contract unfulfilled. An Austrian Lloyd steamer lies near by, and a little boat flying "Cook's Tours" flag, lies at her steps. I wave my little green ticket book and the boatman comes over to me.

My trunks pass through the long dreaded Italian Custom House without trouble or fees. I get breakfast, and am put on the car for Naples. Italian is not at all difficult. The train guard asks me if I am "Sola" and I respond "Si," and I observe that "quanto" is "how much" and "questo" is "where." There is an English translation of an "Aviso" in the cars, which informs me that carrying jewelry in trunks without declaring it "is an abusive and illegal fact."

We travel a long way up, by the blue Adriatic Sea. The country reminds me of some of Bret Harte's stories of Spanish missions along the California coast. There is an almost treeless flat landscape, with almost windowless stone houses, and convents looking out on the blue sea, with here and there a monk or gray-hooded friar wending his way from one to the other. It is picturesquely bare and bright. There is a sprinkling of peasants at work in the fields, and an all-pervading brilliant sunlight. Suddenly I become conscious of another feature in the landscape. Is that conical heap of stones, with but a single aperture, supposed to be a house, a habitation for human beings? It can't be! There is a donkey peering out of the doorway of one like it. And yet, seeing a great many of them, with signs of habitation about, I conclude they are the homes of the peasantry. Well, well, they are almost as primitive as Indian houses. In India, I couldn't tell a house from a haystack;

here I can't tell a house from a pile of stones. A long ride follows through a country, all under cultivation, entirely bare but for the tender green of very youthful crops. One change of cars at a great stone depot where I get an excellent lunch and then we get into the hilly country. After dark we pass around and through some mountains.

I am just beginning to wonder if that high mountain is not Vesuvius and the place at the foot of it Naples, that I passed twenty minutes ago, when we come into a depot that is unmistakably Naples. A porter appears and takes possession of my baggage. I say "Hotel Royale," and he takes me to the bus thereof, to the conductor of which I confide my baggage receipt and follow him into the Custom House. Heavens! Is there going to be a Custom House at every city in Italy? There is nothing mean or underhand about these Custom House fellows. The officer just asks, "Got any tobacco?" "No." "Fire arms?" "No. Here are the keys." "Oh, all right," in choice Italian. My trunks are on the counter; two official porters point to the undisturbed straps, and stretch their hands across to me crying, "Largesse, Madame," and "largesse" it is. A couple of francs fall into the hands, and the trunks are tossed into other waiting hands, and into the bus.

It's a long way to the hotel, and the bus is to wait an hour longer for the Rome train, and it's now half-past nine P. M., so the conductor puts me into a cab or hack—goodness knows which, I don't—and charges me particularly to hang on to my small baggage, and away I go at a rattling pace through the partly lighted streets along the moonlit bay to the hotel. Arrived there I present my card. "You have letters for me?" "Yes." A stack is produced. "You want a room?" "Oh, yes, front, please, looking on the bay." "All full except the fourth floor." "That will do, eleventh, if you like." And then I climb the stairs. It proves to be a pretty little single room; two easy chairs, one window with a balcony looking out over the bay, only the width of the street intervening between the hotel and water. "How much?" "Seven francs a day;" six if I stay a week. "All right, send up my trunks and don't disturb me in the morning; bon soir," and I plunge into my letters.

I am pretty tired. Two days I am going to give to absolute rest and letters, then I'll start out bright and fresh, ready to see this town and do battle with the natives therein. Directly in front of my window is an island which I take to be Capri, and close by juts out a bridge with an old stone fortress at the end of it. Hand organs are everywhere here, and I wake up to the dulcet strains of an organ grinder under my window, breakfast to the music of a marching band of Italian soldiers, write while entertained by an orchestral band close by, and am lulled to sleep by singers in the street or an adjoining amusement house, or both, too sleepy to distinguish which. "Sunny Italy" is not as sunny as it might be just now. It raineth, and when it doesn't rain an air of gloom hangs over Naples. I can see Vesuvius from my balcony. Its top is enveloped in clouds of steam all day; at night it breathes fire. I think I felt a slight earthquake shock last night.

March 10th.—After a few days' rest I recovered myself sufficiently to see the sights. I went first to Pompeii. I wandered, with a guide, through the streets of that ancient city with a great deal of interest, observing the form of houses, the paintings on the walls, the decorative art generally, the deep-set streets, with wheel tracks worn deep into the stone pavement; the large high stones in the middle of the street for people to cross upon from sidewalk to sidewalk without wetting their feet; the Temples of Isis and Jupiter, the bath establishments, with their hot and cold water baths, their drying rooms, the walls built with apertures for the warm air to pass through; all this and more, but Pompeii has been seen and written of by too many people for me to attempt any description of it. The theatre was like those at Athens. There is a museum where there are casts of the unfortunates as they died flying from the eruption that destroyed the city.

I went to the museum in Naples and studied with a great deal of interest the model of Pompeii there—a most perfect representation, in every detail, of Pompeii as it is to-day.

There were lots of paintings at the museum, but, oh dear, if this is a sample of the paintings I am to see throughout Europe I don't want to see any more. What is the use of painting unless one can paint something that is beautiful to look at. If these men of art had only been moved to paint groups of beautiful women and children, representing some bit of romance or comedy, instead of battlefields, massacres, tortures, and crucifixions, how much more attractive would these galleries be to-day! What horrible places they are now—death, murder, torture, blood, agony on every side, with only here and there a Christopher Columbus by way of relief. As for color—but I must wait until I've been through the principal galleries before I criticise. In sculpture they do much better; the human form divine is the inexhaustible theme. Still the sculptors had their nightmares, the Dying Gladiators, and that horror of horrors, the "Laocoon," the pictures of which used to fill my childish sleep with frightful dreams.

Have Anthony Comstock or Henry Berg ever been abroad? They can't have been. If they had, nothing but the keenest sense of satire could have prompted the war they wage in America, of all the countries in the world, against cruelty to animals and against art. Go to Egypt, Mr. Berg; there is a large field for you there. There are thousands of wretched little donkeys, overloaded, sore, ill-fed, lifting up their voices for sympathy and consolation and—you. All through the East you will find water buffalo and camels and donkeys trying to walk on all four feet sideways to keep their tails out of reach of brutal drivers who, when they can't reach and twist that appendage, poke at them with sticks. And, Mr. Comstock, after you had locked up and destroyed all the lovely Naiads, Nymphs, Venuses, Junos, and the immoral perfections of a host of Hercules and other gods, leaving us only the horrors; after this, if you had time, you might turn your attention to the suppression of some of the habits of the residents of Naples that render many of the streets of that city a horror to every sense and the fruitful source of disease.

The street before my hotel on the banks of the Mediterranean is beautifully clean, and so is the Via Roma, ex-Toledo, but I have driven through a long street lined with the villas of the wealthy, and while I saw, through open doors, vistas of beautiful garden stretching to the sea, I was driven through an intolerable stench, all on a lovely, bright, dry day. This is the place for you, Mr. Comstock. When out driving you could catch an occasional glimpse, through an open window, of a picture of lovely women robed only in native grace. This is the country that needs you, Mr. Comstock. America is the most civilized country in the world. America could do without you.

I wished to see Vesuvius both by day and by night, and joined a party that started at about 3 P. M., having our drive and getting up to the observatory by daylight. It was a lovely clear day and we had all the benefit of the view. The party consisted of three French people, two gentlemen and a lady, the latter pretty and all "chic" and bonhomie, the proprietor of the hotel, and myself. We carried lunch along with us, and dined on the side of the mountain, beside a little Italian restaurant, meanwhile admiring the view of the country below us and watching the setting of the sun. Then we drove up a little further where we got into a car that stood at an alarming angle. When we started we felt very much as if we were going up in a balloon. We were ten minutes climbing to the top, or upper station, in this way. The French lady was very fearful, though jolly withal. She kept saying, "Quel courage!" and "Quel courage nous avons!" It was dark by this time.

As we looked below we saw the Bay of Naples marked out like a glittering horseshoe of lights, with innumerable lights radiating inland from that semicircle. Having reached the upper station and stepped out from the cars and the shed that serves the purpose of a depot, we are besieged by men with chairs and ropes who want to carry or help us up the mountain. The French lady takes a chair. I decline positively. I've been warned against it as being uncomfortable. I've also been told that if I touch a rope that's offered me by these guides I will be charged five francs a touch. We are all put on our guard about this.

We start off, the lady in the chair, two torch bearers with large firebrands, the three gentlemen and myself walking together, all followed by a lot of other guides and chairmen. The porters carrying the lady go ahead as fast as they can to tire me out so as to make me take a chair, too, and keep up an incessant warning, which my companions translate to me, as to the steepness and difficulty and inevitable resort to the chair, which will not cost any more for the whole way than for half. To all of which I turn a deaf ear, and reply "No, non, non, non," with all shades of emphasis from mild to ferocious. On we go. It's not so very far, nor yet so very steep. There is a regular track part of the way, but it is of granulated lava, into which we sink ankle deep, and slip back as we walk; and if we walk on one side, too near the edge, it is likely to give way and let us slide down the mountain. I've a gentleman on either side of me, but the guide boys get around in front and offer me ropes insinuatingly or try to force them into my hand. Then I stop and stamp my foot and look daggers, until they get discouraged for the moment. Neither will I allow either of the three gentlemen with me to afford me any assistance, save and except driving the boys away. If I am unable to climb, I'll take a chair or other assistance, and pay for it, and not impose my weakness on any one else. So I decline arms, hands, ropes, chairs, even when we leave the beaten track and fall to climbing boulders of lava and walking over places where steam of sulphur is coming up through the ground, until we come to the very last boulder, and then I am handed up the last high step, and we have reached the top.

The crater is like a basin within a basin and we stand on the outer rim. At our feet is a broad ditch, the other side of which forms the crater, only a few feet from where we stand. The volcano is at its regular business, firing up red-hot lava and stones. Fortunately the wind is blowing from our direction, so we don't get the smoke, and everything falls away from us, though sometimes a blast will send chunks of burning lava alarmingly near. When we have seen enough of this and have reflected that this is what we see every night from the hotel, and after I have received the congratulations and compliments of my comrades for my ability to climb, we desire to be taken to where we can see the lava pouring out. So we climb down from the boulder, and go down and around and up again, over boulders and steaming crevices, until we stand on another ridge and look down, but a foot or two, on an acre or so of black crust of lava, fissured all over with cracks through which fire is escaping.

Here and there burning lava has burst forth and is flowing, a river of liquid, moulten fire, down the mountain side, nearly to the foot—a red-hot mountain stream, many feet in breadth, rippling out of the earth in waves of fire. While we watch the source of one of these red rivers it closes up, and another opens in the black crust, to flow for a while and then close up, only to break forth in some new place. The brightness of the fire is intensified by the blackness of night. The contrast between the red-hot lava and the black surrounding crust of cold lava is most brilliant. It is nine o'clock at night, and there is no moon to lessen the effect, as we stand there for upwards of half an hour and watch first the fluctuations of this bed of fire beneath the cracked black coverlet, and then glance back where the volcano is hurling burning stones and lava high above us.

We give the guides coppers, and they go down upon the crust and dip them in the red boiling lava, and bring them back to us, as mementoes, imbedded in a red-hot but rapidly blackening mass of lava. While we stand there a party of three gentlemen come singing along. The first man is supported by a guide on each side of him, the other two are clinging fast to a guide apiece. This excites the special amusement of my party, and I am again complimented on my pluck. Finally we start back.

The descent is of course easier, for one slips down most of the way, except that one must watch where one walks and not go over the side or step in any steaming fissures. We pass chairs all along the way, where they have been dropped by discouraged guides. The chair of the French lady has broken down repeatedly, vindicating my wisdom in relying on my own two feet to carry me safely wherever I might desire to go. We reach the depot, fee the guides, take possession of our mementoes, and descend the mountain in the car, as we ascended, slowly and surely. The lower depot reached, the party goes into a hotel for refreshments. There my patience is put to the test, and, I fancy, so is the French lady's. We have orangeade; the gentlemen, beer and cigarettes, and there we sit for more than an hour while one gentleman smokes cigarette after cigarette, sips his beer and dispenses his insipid remarks, half an hour after we have all expressed our desire to go at once. At last we started down the mountain, a man running before us with a flaming torch to light our way until we reach the city. The road is a very good one and winds about the mountain through fields of boulders of black lava twisted into innumerable monstrous shapes.

During that long drive I learn to hate that suave Frenchman, with his selfishness, egotism and conceit. His fussy, troublesome anxiety for our comfort, all false, and springing, like everything else about him, from his own vanity, is unendurable; and my hatred is not diminished by sitting next him at dinner the next day and hearing his shallow, false, vain, tender inquiries for my health. How I should like to tell him how disgusting is his mask of sweetness, how unendurably stupid and senseless are his remarks, how thoroughly detestable he appears to any woman with a grain of sense, with his fair, insipid, untruthful face, his suave voice and false words of tenderness. Thank heaven, I am going away to-morrow.

It was nearly two o'clock when we reached the hotel that night. I awoke the next morning to find the manager of the hotel had made a heroine of me with his comments on my pluck and determination in climbing Vesuvius at night. I've done Vesuvius as I wanted to and am happy. I went with the Mayfields, who are here, for a drive to the Observatory, where we got a fine view of the city. We went into the church and museum of St. Martin, the wall of an inner courtyard of which is decorated with marble skulls. Pretty conceit that! The museum was an interesting one and contained a large picture, like a stage scene, of the birth of Christ, with peasantry and people of various nationalities engaged in various occupations, camels and waterfalls, and angels hovering over all. This church was pretty, but I can't say I admire decorations formed of pieces of the anatomy of dead and gone saints. They may have been very holy, but their crumbling bones are not pretty. From here we drove down to the city over the dog grotto and through the Chia-ya, the fashionable drive, past the former dwelling place of Garibaldi, and home. Naples has been bright and lovely during my stay. To-night it is foggy and the air is full of miasma. Out of doors there is a dreadful stench and the foul air comes half way up the stairway. My window is closed, so the bad air has not got into my room perceptibly. No wonder they have cholera and Roman fever. Thank goodness, I leave to-morrow.

Coming from Pompeii I took a cab at the depot, and seeing I was a stranger, the driver thought he would make something extra out of me. I knew there was a regular tariff and did not stop to bargain about the fare before getting in; so after we had started the driver turned around to me and said, "You give me two francs?" I said, "I'll give you your regular fare." He persisted with his "You give me two francs?" until I said, "I'm not going to pay you at all; you take me to the Hotel Royale and the porter will pay you your fare." Then he said, "You tell him to give me two francs?" I agreed to that, and he whipped up his horse and away we went at a rattling gait, the driver laughing gaily and turning around to me continually to say, "You give me two francs? He very good horse. You give me two francs? He go very fast; you give me two francs?" until we reached the hotel, when I turned him over to the porter, who ran out immediately he saw me and gave him a slight advance on his regular fare instead of the two francs. His behavior reminded me of the Arabs on the pyramids who keep saying to you as you climb, "You make me satisfied, I make you satisfied."

I don't find the European hotel system half as uncomfortable as I expected; everybody is courteous and polite. I don't know what I should do if I were a stranger in a New York hotel, we do mind our own business so severely in New York. There is a little boy waiter here who is apparently only ten or eleven years old. He looks very cunning in his dress coat. He, too, is the soul of courtesy and always greets me with, "Bon jour, Mademoiselle." The cowboy wrote an ode to me after I left the party commencing "The little one has left us, we've no one now to tease," so my friends tell me. He used to say when he was seasick, "I'm a blighted being; consider me blit." He is "blit" now, I presume.

ROME, *March 13th.*—At Naples I obtained, from Cook's, coupons which are to carry me up through Italy, across the Alps and down the Rhine, and up to Amsterdam, and down to Brussels, and then to Paris and across the Channel, landing me ultimately, at any time I like, in London, and all for about seventy-five dollars. Fancy traveling all over Europe for seventy-five dollars. I am comforted, however, by the reflection that the hotels will make it sufficiently lively for my pocketbook to even up matters. I shall lay in a supply of Cook's hotel coupons and head them off a little in that way. Cook is a blessing; there is no doubt about that. He simplifies and cheapens travel to a considerable extent. Having got loaded up with tickets, itineraries and instructions, I paid a bill about one yard and a half long at the hotel and several fees, and departed with all my goods and the blessings of the hotel.

At the depot Cook's interpreter introduced me to two American ladies, a German woman by birth, and her daughter, who had been brought up in a convent in Canada and who was pretty and young and enthusiastic and learned. I had met them once or twice in Naples before. We became friendly right off. This pretty girl interested me very much. Her enthusiasm was so serious. She knew so much about all she had seen and she adored the antique. I haven't the slightest doubt she could have told me all about the different tribes and religions in India and discussed the difference between the Indian, Japanese and Chinese architecture, which is more than I could do, although she hadn't been there. I did get to know a Hindoo and a Parsee occasionally when I saw them, but the rest of the sects in India are hopelessly mixed in my mind.

This girl speaks four languages, notwithstanding which she was accustomed to having couriers, although she had just concluded, she said, that she could get along better without. "Good gracious," I thought, "here I've been all over Naples and forgotten that I was obliged to have a courier."

After having dreaded the Italian courier all the way around the world I have forgotten and ignored him in his native lair! I was told a lot of stories of the dangers of going about in Naples. I have been told, by the people who live there, that Neapolitans are the worst and lowest class of people in the world. I was warned morning, noon and night by Cook's men, hotel men, storekeepers, to mind about my pocketbook. Well, I did "mind," and nothing happened to me in Naples.

Arrived at Rome I was the only guest for the Constanzi, so I had all the stage conductor's attention for my baggage. Got to the hotel and found it lovely. I started out immediately in search of the bank. I found the way easily enough, and, after getting and reading my letters, went out from the hotel again on a voyage of discovery. First to the bank again to get "permits" for everything in Rome, then I walked down the prettiest jewelry shop street in Rome to the Corso ; thence up the Corso until I came to a Egyptian obelisk (how many of them are there anyway ?). I walked back on the next street, which brought me out, as I expected, at the bank again. I went by the bank instead of going up some stairs, which was my way home, to an American drug store. I didn't want to walk back and climb the stairs, so I struck up the next street. Presently I came out at the Hotel de la Paix. That hotel stood just opposite my street when I came down from the bank, but somehow it had turned around, and besides, it had moved over on the other corner of the street, and there were half a dozen streets pointing right at it and not one of them looked like mine. I concluded I had gone far enough before turning, so I walked along a little way and asked a soldier, who told me I was going right, but when the street began going round I knew I was wrong. I turned up one street and walked quickly, because it was getting towards night, and turned back again down the next, and there was the Hotel de la Paix again, and right in front of me a garden that I half suspected belonged to my hotel. How to get around to it I didn't know, I knew the hotel wasn't more than a block off, but on which street I couldn't imagine. It was too late for me to go floundering around these streets until I struck the right one, and I was hopelessly lost. I, therefore, took a passing cab, and sure enough, it just whipped around the block and deposited me at the door of the Constanzi, but it was the very last street I should have looked for it on.

After all the very foreign countries I have been in, Naples and Rome are so civilized that I feel at home in them. They are both gorgeous with jewelry shops, and I feel as if I were walking on Broadway.

It was very rainy this morning, so I took a cab and drove to the Vatican Museum. I walked all through it and want to say just here, though I ought to wait until I have finished this world of art, that neither in this museum nor in the one at Naples have I seen a piece of sculpture to compare in beauty of figure, in conception, or fineness of marble, with those modern ones I saw at the Centennial Exhibition, at Philadelphia. These are larger—some of them are immense—but they are ugly and don't look like real folks, and the subjects are abominable. One word in a certain learned Professor's ear; although these statues are made with bare feet or sandals, it is perfectly evident to me that the old Romans wore tight shoes, for every one of these statues has a more or less well developed bunion. There isn't a single statue in this museum on which you can draw a straight line from the heel to the end of the big toe; on every one among them you have to go around a corner of that bunion and slant off at an angle more or less acute before you can get to the end of the big toe; and a more marked feature yet is, that they all without exception, have the little toe turned toward the foot and curled under very close. Tight shoes were evidently universally worn. I am disappointed and indignant. I didn't come to Rome to see statues with bunions. Every time I look at a Hercules or a Gladiator knotted all over with muscles, it reminds me of what the man with the terra cotta hair and gloves and mustache said about his white mule at the Yosemite: "He's full of bunions, but he's a daisy."

Museum officials are the latest victims to my unprotected youth. They show me around and explain things to me in the most dulcet tones, and after I have passed their department they leave people locked up in it while they come and gaze at me until I get nervous and flee. Once I tried to allay the interest in me with a fee, thinking probably that was the cause of the gazing; but no, the fee was delicately declined, as if the servitor were not averse to fees; but from me, "Non, Mademoiselle. Merci, c'est un plaisir," et cetera. "Good gracious!" I think, and flee.

I went to St. Peter's next, and certainly it is magnificent. I walked up and down its great isles twice and surely in bigness it exceeds everything. I looked up at the immense statues of past Popes with hands outstretched as if in benediction, with expressions of holy love on their stony faces, and with statues of women gazing adoringly up at them, and I thought: "I used to have a regular nightmare of a book called the 'Book of Martyrs,' and there's a picture I have seen of you in Naples, and in both book and painting your regular business appears to have been lighting martyr fires, plying red-hot pincers, and enjoying the agonies of the unfortunate on the rack. Oh, I've seen you before in your red gown and lace jacket and bellows hat. This great church of yours is a colossal monument to a bloody era of martyrdom." I next went to the Vatican picture gallery. I say again that, so far as I have seen, the old paintings don't compare in point of beauty and interest with some few modern paintings I have seen in America. Many of these paintings are extraordinarily large and the colors are exceedingly fine, but they are horrible in conception and unnatural in execution. I think all the faces wear the same pious expression of sublime idiocy. The picture I saw in the exhibition at Philadelphia by one of our living artists of "Aphrodite Rising from the Sea" as far exceeds anything I have seen here, in conception, in beauty, in color, in truth to nature, in everything but size, as America exceeds Italy in progress and freedom.

They say the modern artists can't paint as the old masters did. I say it is to be hoped not. These old paintings were fine, magnificent for their time, but don't try to palm them off as better than can be done to-day. The quicker the artists of to-day stop copying from the old masters the better. Melancholy Madonnas and brutal crucifixions and tortures, horrible Laocoons, and dying Gladiators are out of date; they belong to the past. Let us now have an era of beauty and happiness, freedom and light in our arts. Let lovely women and children, and flowers and sunshine, be the subjects for the future. An era of art of that style has already commenced, I think, for most modern paintings, that are not copies, are of landscapes, flowers and fruits.

Art has deteriorated in the present day, has it? We have no artists as good as Michael Angelo and Raphael, haven't we? Why, then, can one walk through these ancient galleries and museums looking for famous statues and pictures, and instead of recognising them pass them by as parts of a mass of ugly, uninteresting art? Why, then, will the same person's interest be arrested and chained by half a dozen statues and paintings in a modern gallery? Why does one stand and look at one picture for half an hour at a time, and having broken away from it return again and again to feast on its beauties? In our Centennial Exhibition, I saw a dozen pictures and statues which commanded my admiration the moment they caught my eye which held and fascinated me. I returned to them daily to take another look at them. They had no history; I did not know who made them; they were only beautiful. I have seen nothing to compare with them here. There was not a thing in the Vatican Museum or Gallery pretty enough for me to want to know what it was and who did it. I walked through the museum three times, examining everything critically.

One thing I noticed particularly; the old masters were very much at fault when it came to babies. Their babies usually had unnaturally small heads and big legs. One nursing child in marble had hips like a fully matured woman. My memory goes back again to the American Centennial Exhibition to a sweet little statue, life size, of a four-year-old girl, so natural, so pretty, so beautifully lifelike, that I went and worshiped daily at its shrine. Modern artists are good enough for me. I've seen only one of the old statues that I would give houseroom, and I'd only give houseroom to one of the copies of it. The small marble copies of the broken Venus de Milo are very pretty.

I am getting more and more sorry for the strangers who visit New York. How in the world do they get along with our inconveniently exorbitant carriage hire and expensive hotels and general disposition to mind your own business? If I get lost here, I can step into a carriage and be taken home for from ten to twenty cents, and, at any time on my arrival, there is an attentive porter at the door who prevents any trouble about fares. He puts me into a cab in the morning, tells me what places are open and where to go and instructs my driver. In a strange city this is very convenient. As to candles, I think Europe has reformed since my friends were here. I guess the Americans have bullied them out of lighting a lot of candles when one arrives as I have been told is their exasperating habit. They only light one for me, and the femme de chambre asks timorously if she may take the burnt-out socket away.

March 15th.—Two days more in Rome. Have been to the Colosseum. Submitted to having the whole thing explained to me by a guide. If guides could only tell one in a few laconic sentences all one wanted to know instead of giving one the minute history of every scrap of ruin I should like them better. If the vast amount of information didn't go out of one ear as fast as it came in at the other I should have brain fever before one guide got through with me. I have seen the Roman Forum. I have driven on the Appian Way and seen a great deal of the city.

To-day being Sunday I made a raid on the churches. I began with St. Peter's. I heard mass there this morning; took a little campstool along and took up a position in the corner of the base of a pillar. Watched people walking about the church courtesying at odd places. Some would courtesy awkwardly and hesitatingly, others quickly and mechanically, with a jaunty nod, and still others with a long, ballroom sweep, suggestive of "visiting" in the lanciers. Was rather disconcerted by having people courtesy towards or drop down on their knees and assume an attitude of prayer immediately before me; tried to get out of the way, but couldn't do it. All the corners and all the centers were before or over something sacred. Concluded I could stand it if they could. Saw one lace-jacketed priest get up from his knees and, meeting another one, laugh and shake hands in a regular "how are you, old boy?" fashion. Listened to the service. The priest was a pretty good actor. He was evidently always praying for mercy or trying to get away from the "flaming sword." Music very beautiful; soprano sung by a gray-haired man.

Mass being over I went to the Corsini Palace to see the Farnese Frescoes. Some pretty women and cherubs. Then I did some churches: St. Maria Maggiore, very big and fine; the Lateran with the holy stairs, up which a lot of people were climbing on their knees; St. Pietro in Vincoli (St. Peter in chains); with Michael Angelo's famous statue of Moses. It needs be famous, for it isn't pretty. After that St. Maria del Popolo, where I saw a lot of "Contadina" (Italian peasant girls) and Sunday School classes of children getting trained up "in the way they should go" by the priests.

On my return I drove through the grounds of the Borghese Villa, encountering the Prince of Naples. The Prince bowed to me politely. I didn't know he was the Prince and am not accustomed to returning salutations of strange gentlemen, so I only looked surprised as they drove rapidly by. Fancy having "cut" a Prince. Must I bow to princes when I meet them? This one was a young boy.

My independent soul rejoices in the fact that I am doing everything without a courier or guide. I've been taking things very easy in Rome. I'm tired yet from my previous hasty traveling. Talk about its taking two or three weeks to see Rome. I've been here nine days and out of that nine days, one day I remained at home all day and three days I merely walked and shopped and called at the bank, and of the five days that I have given to sightseeing I have only given three or four hours. I think now, knowing where places are and taking them in order, I could do Rome very completely and satisfactorily in five days. I have risen at eleven, seen sights until four, written until twelve, midnight, and slept until ten. I will line out the programme for the benefit of other travelers.

The first day I should do as I did, walk the streets, go to banker's, look at shops, get the points of the compass located. Second day, go first to Vatican Museum, then to Vatican picture gallery, and finally into St. Peter's. Third day, go first to Capitoline Museum, then gallery opposite, then down on the other side of the hill to the Roman Forum, from there to the Colosseum, then for a drive to the Villa Borghese, or out on the Appian Way until after half-past three, and to the Pantheon on the way back to the hotel. Fourth day, I would do the palaces, and then drive; commencing with the Barbarine Palace and ending with the Borghese Palace. Fifth day, I'd do the churches and any odd palaces that might be left over, and drive. Most things close at three o'clock, so one has plenty of time to drive or shop every day. There are a few other ruins to be looked at, but some of them you see on your way to and from the other places, and they are not much to see. Oh, I forgot, there are the Catacombs. I have left them out entirely. I don't want to see any bones. I couldn't be induced to go there. I have to see enough horrid, musty, mouldy relics, as it is.

I don't want to go and examine minutely all the old relics, or decipher all the ancient hieroglyphics, but I like to go and stand on the Capitoline stairs and look down on the Roman Forum, with its arches and columns, and beyond it on the walls of the Colosseum. There one gets an idea of the past greatness of Rome. There are fine arrangements of statuary everywhere through the city. A favorite fountain of mine is a gigantic sort of bas-relief against the wall of a building, with giant men holding rampant and colossal horses, with lions at their feet spouting waterfalls into a larger waterfall that tumbles between them. These great statues are blackened and blistered and not pretty, but they are picturesque.

They seem to have an unlimited supply of Egyptian obelisks in Rome. I am forever running across them; I use them as guide posts.

SOME PALACES.

Talk about "dwelling in marble halls!" I pity the people who live in these palaces. I've only seen one that I should desire to live in more than an hour, and that one I expect would carry me off with hasty consumption in a week; for they are the coldest, dampest, most comfortless places in the world. Do the titled owners of them inhabit these galleries, I wonder, on the days the public are not admitted? And do they subsist on the half francs and francs the flunkeys receive from the departing guests at the door? If I had all these pictures I wouldn't have them hung all together in a gallery, anyway, but have them distributed through all the salons of the house in various points of vantage.

At the Palazzo Corsini I only saw frescoes. At the Barbarina Palace I went looking for the two famous pictures, Raphael's Fornarina and Guido's Beatrice Cenci, and mightily disgusted I was when I saw them. I had seen in the same gallery a couple of freshly painted copies of Beatrice Cenci that I rather admired; but beauty, oh, dear! She looks like a small boy I'm acquainted with when he was teething—mournful and peaked. She has a wan-looking chin, a Jewish cast of face, and looks blue around the root of the nose, as if she suffered from chronic catarrh. Raphael's Fornarina is also a Jewess, with just that protuberant over-ripe look that Jews nearly always have. I went to the Rospigliosso Palace, where I saw Guido's famous Aurora on the ceiling. It is large and grand, and the colors are truly lovely. After admiring that I spent the rest of the time in trying to escape an abominable torture picture which captured me at last and poisoned my whole being with its atrocity. I made my escape finally and went to the Borghese Palace. Now, this is something like a palace. I wander from one pictured room to another, coming upon a great inlaid table of different colored marbles in one room and a statue of Apollo in a corner looking out into a court. Here, too, I find the famous pictures rather unsatisfactory, but I find a number of pretty ones; here is a picture of Eve that reminds me of Aphrodite. And here is a picture of a French Eve clothed in nothing but a broad brimmed plumed hat on a nicely coiffured head and the tail of a serpent around her neck. The rest of the serpent is engaged in squeezing the life out of an unhappy-looking cupid by her side, by which the artist meant to say, I suppose, that the "trail of the serpent is over us all," and "all is vanity," et cetera.

I am afraid my tastes are abominably immoral, for, of all the pictures, my fancy was most taken by the paintings of naughty Madame Potiphar and Joseph. I saw three pictures of them in all, and each one prettier than the last. The painter is unknown, but they are the most natural and lifelike, as well as the most beautiful faces and figures, I have seen. How I should like to buy them and bring them home, or copies of them ; but nobody copies them ; all the artists are diligently engaged in copying Beatrice Cenci and the Fornarina or some wretched martyr. Joseph is represented as young, handsome and boyish looking, and I wonder at his exemplary behavior when I look at Madame Potiphar, for she is as pretty as a pink. I'm in love with her myself, with her sweet, smiling face and lovely, golden hair, just escaping from a net of pearls, and beautiful feet and limbs and the gauzy white robe, half concealing, half revealing a figure that is all grace and loveliness.

I have seen one truly lovely face on a Saint Sebastian. More palaces and pictures. I am beginning to see palaces that are something like—stage palaces, with gold chairs and red cushions faded and worn, just as we have them in our theatres. Yesterday I went to the Doria Palace. It contains a very large collection of pictures, and a beautiful hall lined with statues and plate glass. This gallery was on an upper floor, and was light and pleasant. After walking through the gallery I had made a complete circuit of the house, which surrounds a court, as all the palaces and most of the hotels and houses do in Rome. In this gallery I came across two pretty things in the way of sculpture—a couple of groups of three marble baby boys, all tangled up together in a game of romps. They were happy and laughing and natural, except that their heads are too small, and they are abnormally fat. After that I was prepared for the several dozen Holy Families, and Virgin and Childs, and St. Jeromes, and St. Sebastians, all in states of holy beatitude and suffering piety. I can tell a Holy Family a mile off now ; I don't have to look at the programme to see what it is. I don't even want to know who did it ; they are all equally ugly and distressing.

Ah, here is a pretty boy's head by Vandyke. And here is Suzanne again. Whatever had that unfortunate young woman done that she never was allowed to bathe herself in peace? Why were those two graybeards everlastingly prowling around, climbing stone walls and balconies and coming on her unawares? And here is a fat, red haired Maddalena by Titian. Titian's Mother and Child would be good, but I have insuperable objections to infant Christs with abnormally small heads and deformed bodies.

Going through this gallery I have been entertained in another way. A young English lady—I should have said American, for she was very pretty, if her feet had not been so large—was walking through the gallery. She wasn't a bit interested in pictures, evidently thought it a great bore, was rather pleased at promenading through a palace, but wouldn't even look at the pictures. She stopped and looked at herself though, in a glass, for several minutes with apparently great satisfaction. She walked jauntily along, hummed a bit of opera, and sat down on a sofa to wait for her companion, an elderly gentleman who knew a Titian when he saw it and wanted her to recognize it too. While she sat she gazed with unutterable scorn on whatever was before her. Sometimes she would not reply when spoken to. She was not really cross, but she didn't want to see and she wouldn't. She reminded me very forcibly of myself.

I went to the Capitoline Gallery, and found, among the usual Holy Families and Saints, two pretty pictures. One, an angel floating over a stream, was something like my favorite Aphrodite; and another, a Venus and Adonis in the usual state of beatitude and nuditude, if I may call it so, with Cupid in the extreme foreground looking over his shoulder at you with his finger in his mouth and the most perfect expression on his cherubic face of mischief taken by surprise.

Feeling somewhat rested and my sauciness restored, I started out to deliver my dreaded letters of introduction sent me by an eminent churchman, from America. One I delivered to a gentleman at his bank and got a new supply of "permessos." The other was to a lady who is happily out of Rome, and I am relieved from the danger of being introduced, as I was told I should be, to the "best society in Rome." I at least have done my duty in presenting the letters.

Really I am enjoying Rome very much, I don't know a soul. Two ladies wanted to take possession of me at one time, but they have gone away. I sit at table as solemn and as silent as a sphinx. I am sufficiently entertained by the chatting of the people about me. An old French lady, who enjoys the most aristocratic poor health and has a bigoted English brute of a husband, whom I abhor, tries to stare me into some sign of recognition, but I am obdurate; if she wants to know me she can bow and smile and I'll respond, but as long as she stares I shall ignore her. Next to her is an English lady. The two ladies are interesting, and being English and French, I suppose they are used to masculine snubbing. The way the French woman's English husband interrupts their conversation and pooh-poohs their opinions and calls them in effect fools and idiots, makes me furious. They talk a good deal of Americans—all English people do it would seem. They say "she is an American," and they "know by her dress and her looks and her manner," and they say "a good many American girls are marrying in these countries," and they think it "a good thing for the Americans—gives them a fresh start with some old aristocratic blood." They say also that American dentists are the best in the world, and the Americans are the smartest mechanics on the globe; whereat I think patriotically, "You bet," but am outwardly calm. Then the man looks right past me at a lady behind me and says, "Why, there is a female woman at dinner all alone." Then he catches sight of me, obviously alone, as his wife says "Sh," and he is covered with confusion most dire. Whereupon I smile broadly. He tries to recover himself by qualifying his remark, and when I rise and leave the table he bows most impressively by way of apology. I barely incline my head and walk by with hauteur in every step, but mirth in my soul. I do love to catch superior Englishmen in some "betise" or other. Just wait until another Englishman tells me the Americans over here are so noisy, talk so loud at table, and are such bad form generally.

I like going through the picture galleries alone untrammeled by other people's tastes or knowledge. To-day I went first to the Colonna Palace. It was a fine palace. Before I entered the galleries I passed through several rooms hung with great tapestries. I was delighted with these; the great pictures on them were pretty and striking. I then came to a room with a single picture on the wall, the portrait, I suppose, of the last

Prince of the house. The chair beneath it was turned to the wall. The galleries beyond were very fine, with frescoed walls and choice paintings and marble floors and rows of statuary, a long vista of beauty above and below. Then another room devoted to the family portraits, though indeed they were strewn all through the rooms, in great pictures on horseback or in robes of state, standing with princely mien in coat of mail or plumed hat and Spanish ruff. Rulers and knights and dandies and cardinals, all Colonnas. The first room I entered was an audience chamber with däis and canopy complete. It takes one away back to the Middle Ages.

At the Palazzo Spada I saw the famous statue of Pompey, at whose feet Julius Cæsar fell; at least that is the way the guide book "puts it." More pictures of crucifixions, martyrs, saints, and Holy Families mingle with portraits of dead and gone Spada Cardinals. In the gallery of the Corsini Palace were more of the crucifixion, the Holy Family, Mary Magdalene, St. Jerome, St. Sebastian, between half a dozen and a dozen of each. Here again is that unfortunate Suzanne still engaged at her toilet and as usual getting caught at it. Here is a diversion in the way of Andromeda, and here are a few hideous nightmares.

O ye believers in an all powerful fiend incarnate, a monster of cruelty who has looked calmly down through all the ages of torture on weak and helpless men, women and children, being burned, racked, torn and slaughtered, and has never used that supreme power to save an infant from the knife or a woman from the rack or fire! What have you to say for your alleged "merciful" God?

I've seen two pictures of "Let him who is without sin amongst you cast the first stone." Now, I like that. Modern artists, please copy. Picture a lovely woman prisoner; a mob of angry, disconcerted men; Christ offering stone. Of all the old masters so far, I have seen one truly beautiful one—a St. Sebastian with a lovely, lovely beyond conception, face, by Guido. Apart from that, Raphaels, Guidos, Titians, Rubens. and Vandykes are all, all more or less hideous in subject. unnatural as to form and mostly dim and sombre as to color. How I do hate to hear people talking about the superior greatness of the past and deploring the degeneracy of to-day. To-day is good enough for me.

The last two days at Rome I spent in going over the same ground I had been over, taking last looks at my favorite pictures; at the Apollo Belvedere and famous reclining figure by Canova modeled after the sister of Napoleon Bonaparte; and between you and me the photographs of many I have seen are much prettier to look at. They retouch the photographs as they do those of people, and the result is the same—they flatter. I advise you folks at home to stay there and cherish the pictures of famous statues. The pictures are clear, and you get the full beauty of outline; but the statues are patched and "restored" and yellow and grimy and chipped. The Apollo Belvedere is beautiful, but I still think I have seen modern statues that excel it in beauty.

I finished the Vatican Art Gallery making special efforts to appreciate Raphael's Transfiguration and Domeinchino's masterpiece of the Last Communion of St. Jerome, and found them exceedingly fine, only I don't admire pictures of old men at the last gasp, or of a crowd of surprised and frightened people, including an idiot boy, gazing up at a man with an exasperating beatific face going up into the sky in a blaze of glory.

On the subject of color—one good reason why modern artists don't have the same colors that Raphael did is that we don't have the colors of yore in fabrics nowadays; at least, we didn't until the esthetic craze came in. Raphael paints the white-blues, the muddy reds, the dirty browns and faded greens of the coarse and imperfectly dyed cloths of long ago. I've been seeing some similar to them in the East lately. Even his white drapery is of a slaty color. The secret of which is that the clothing hadn't been washed for a year or two. I've just been there, and I've got the shade down very fine, and so has Raphael.

After taking a last look at St. Peter's I rushed to the Barbarina Palace and took a last look at pretty Madame Potiphar, whose painter is unknown to fame, and then looked at Correggio's famous "Danai" with scorn for its utter gracelessness and want of beauty. Then I hunted up an unknown Venus and Adonis, and Psyche, that were lovely, to "take the taste out of my eyes;" then I flew across Rome, past my beautiful big bas-relief fountain, past the ancient Forum and most ancient Obelisk; past the Pantheon to the Capitol, where in the picture gallery close by I stood and gazed and gazed at that beautiful St. Sebastian of Guido's. I've found out why I like it. It isn't a masterpiece; it isn't famous enough to be put in a book of the representative pictures. It's too lovely; that's what's the matter with it. The exquisite beauty of that boyish face fascinates me. It is at once a beautiful face and a lifelike one. I'd like to buy it, then I'd get some artist to paint a Roman toga on it and an apple or some flowers on a tree above his head for him to be reaching for, and have the arrows and cords all painted off. If I couldn't have them painted off I'd cut them off and leave only the head.

I stayed there until they closed the gallery, then I stood on the top of the steps and looked down on the Roman Forum and beyond at the Colosseum, and said good-bye to Rome. I was sorry to leave Rome, with her luxurious hotel and polite attendants, from the head waiter who used to stand at the end of the dining room rubbing his hands and bowing to everybody, and smiling as we came in, and whom I cordially hated, to the little boy of ten or so, who was porter when the big porter was not there. He would rush out when my carriage drove up and hand me out of it with the air of a grand seigneur. Well, I have enjoyed Rome all alone, and now good-bye.

On the train for Florence I found myself in the compartment with a very large English woman who was, like Niobe, "all tears." There were a number of people to see her off, who endeavored to console her, but the tears flowed on and she sobbed audibly. She had a little five year old boy who was leaving his parents and brothers to go with her to England to school. The little boy took matters very philosophically; put by his playthings amiably to "go and give mamma one more kiss" at the weeping chaperon's frequent request. "Mamma" did not seem to be broken hearted, at least she looked on the parting with her boy cheerfully, which was quite right. I was preparing myself to do a big business in comforting, to listening sympathetically to numerous griefs, even to shedding a pitying tear or so, if need be, myself; but lo, once the train had moved out of the depot, and we were fairly under way, the storm cleared and she suddenly became an active, practical woman, whose only thought was to make herself comfortable. Her bright, black eyes became fixed in a piercing gaze on the satchel over my head. She took off her bonnet, a monument of black crêpe and wrapped it carefully up and put it in the rack, then she took off her cloak, then she reached up after the aforesaid satchel, and opening it rummaged until she brought forth a wool shawl, then she got the satchel up over my head again and fetched down a shawl strap, took out several fuzzy shawls and rugs and shook them, covering me with long hairs of wool from them, then she arranged her hair and put the little shawl over her head and the big one around her shoulders, then she had to get down the satchel over my head again to get a pin, then she put it up again after a prolonged rummage, and leaned back and folded her hands. I took a long breath. She had so many bundles that I could not escape sitting under a few of them. She had made preparation enough for a week's journey, though I knew she would have to do all those things up again in six or seven hours to change cars.

But my long breath was premature. She reached up immediately and fetched down a big valise—also from over my head—opened it, and produced sandwiches and bottles of wine and bottles of water and immense carving knives. She might have said with Gilbert's widow in "Engaged" "Thank heaven, I can still eat." In the course of time she and the boy were comfortably stuffed, and then the young table cloths and bottles and carving knives were put away, and the black valise laboriously strapped and put up over my head again, and each time she put it up and took it down she trod on my toes and knocked my bonnet and sprinkled me with wool from her shawl. I couldn't get out of the way, because the car was full; there were three other passengers, and the rest of the place was taken up by her and her belongings. But I didn't mind; I was rather amused, and then, she always begged pardon politely, which was a great comfort. Then the other people got out some lunch. This was too much for her. It was only half an hour since she and the boy had lunched, but down came the bulky valise again, and forth came the young table cloths and the carving knives and bottles and bread and chicken, and they took another "square" meal. I envied them their appetite; I'd soon get fat at that rate. Talk about children being fussy and troublesome to travel with; that little boy was the tranquilest creature in the car except myself.

I get into a train for an all day trip, plank my valise and shawl-strap and sun umbrella up in the rack, slip my ticket in the opening at the palm of one glove and my baggage check in the palm of the other, and a few coppers and a franc or so in an outside pocket, so that I need not move more than is absolutely necessary to produce these trifles when called upon, and fling myself into a corner; and there I am for one hour or sixteen as the case may be. For amusement I look out of the window, stare at the passengers, and think unutterable things. I had a good deal to think of this time. I hadn't made up my mind which hotel to go to in Florence. I had decided to patronize Cook's, but Cook had three on his list thusly: "New York," "Hotel de l'Europe," "De Russie." I am exceedingly patriotic, but I draw the line at American hotels abroad. "I have been there." Besides, I can go to an American hotel when I get home. Hotel de Russie sounds too narrow and local too; I want something broader. Hotel de l'Europe is more general; I guess that's the happy medium for me. So, getting off the train, I resolutely resisted the blandishments of about three dozen more or less dazzling hotel busses; I walked past them all, noted the brilliancy and newness of the New York "bus," and said to myself, "I fear I've made a mistake this time," but still walked on till I came to "L'Europe."

While I was waiting in the rather faded "bus" for my baggage, the New York dashed by, resplendent in plate glass and red velvet and new varnish and lights, and I said, "Irrepressible, you are a goose—just as likley as not they don't speak anything but Italian at this place, and then what will you do?" Filled with this idea I did not attempt to speak to the porter when he opened the coach, nor yet to the manager when he received me, so I was quite taken aback when he said in plain English, "Do you wish a room?" I said "Yes," mentally adding, "How in the world did you know I spoke English?" I'm always getting put down that way. I say to the waiter at table, "St. Julien, s'il vous plait," and he responds cheerfully "Small bottle, Miss?" Whereat I laugh and fall back on my mother tongue. I have never been able to rid myself of the notion that French will be intelligible to any foreigner. It does not make any difference whether I am spoken to in Japanese, Chinese, or Hindoostanee, I respond involuntarily in French. "Vive la" intuition.

This hotel seems to have lost its equilibrium—the floors run down hill, and they are dusty and dingy, but the bedding is delightfully clean and likewise the table linen. The attendants are exceedingly polite. I was fairly lured into eating through the first three courses at dinner, delicious soup, tasty little rice croquettes, and O my prophetic soul! mashed potatoes beaten to a froth. The last courses were neglected; I had already dined. There are two prettiest of pretty black-eyed rosebuds of American girls here. Whenever you see a pretty girl in Italy you can make up your mind at once that she is an American. English girls have lovely complexions, but they dress formally, sit formally, and speak formally. Italian girls have pretty, dark skins and eyes, but are coarse and slovenly. French girls are vivacious and tasteful. But for elegant dressing, merry laughter and bright conversation, it takes the American girl.

March 28th.—More good dinner. I have not dined so well since those happy days on the Santa Rosa, when I was the first to come to the table and the last to leave it. I ought to camp here for a week or two, but I'm in a hurry, so I shall leave here reluctantly Tuesday morning. There is an unhappy priest here who can't eat anything but fish and vegetables. I am perfectly gloating over his sufferings; he is a great unsightly hog of a man, anyway; it would improve him to go without eating anything for a month. I left all the street musicians in Naples. I missed them so much in Rome that I had to get out my little pocket musical box and set it a-going.

I forgot to say that at Naples the horses or cows, or donkeys, were harnessed three abreast; the saddle of the center one rose up like the prow of a gondola, and was surmounted with bells and weather cocks. It does not matter whether there are three donkeys or one before a wagon, you can often count from twelve to twenty-four people on the wagon at a time. Nobody walks who can ride. Boys will run a mile after your carriage, offering you a bouquet of roses as big as a cabbage for half a franc. In Rome they chase your carriage with small bunches of violets. If you won't take them they throw them into your carriage and continue to chase for centissimi. If you don't want it, you fling it back, and that discourages them a little. When you are walking, little bits of boys in green velvet jackets and knee breeches, with bright colored strings around their legs and hats, looking like miniature banditti from "Fra Diavolo," will come up to you and stick bunches of violets in between your buttons or anywhere where they will lodge. A beautiful little green velvet, black-eyed bandit of five or six years attacked me in this way.

In Florence guides are as thick as huckleberries. I had five following me around one church. I declined to be guided. At the third church I succumbed. I thought I'd take one guide to drive the rest away and to see if I was benefited by it. I have concluded I know just as much about it when I look around by myself. There isn't the least bit of use in my being told what year a tomb was built in, or how much it cost, or who designed it; I forget it as fast as I'm told. When I do have a guide I drive him nearly crazy by asking repeatedly, "Who did you say designed that?" and "Oh, yes." But after I've been told three times, I know as little about it as ever. My memory is hopelessly defective as to names and dates. Indeed, I remember better if I go alone, for I can read the familiar names, and they take a stronger hold on my memory. Besides, I object to being hurried past all the pretty things because they are modern. I insist on looking longer at the despised modern and hurrying by the hideous ancient. The guide pities me sincerely for my ignorance and want of taste. I have made my trial and am satisfied to go on alone.

I go to St. Marco and see the "Last Supper"—two last suppers, in fact—and wander through the old cells of the monks. I come to the conclusion that they were well housed, far better than the people. I have been through the Uffizzi Gallery and into its inner sanctuary, the Tribune, which Hawthorne calls the richest room in all the world, and have seen there the "Venus de Medicis," the "Appollino," the "Dancing Faun" and the "Wrestlers," besides the paintings of Raphael, Titian and Correggio. And here again I see Holy Families, Mother and Child, Crucifixions, St. Sebastian, St. Jerome, St. Bartholomew, etc. And here, too, I see Joseph and Potiphar's Wife, by Raphael, a larger picture than all the others, and because it isn't as pretty I suspect it is the original from which all the others are copies, though they vary slightly from it in minor details, to their manifest improvement. And, look here, some of these old masters are scattered about as recklessly as the pieces of the "true cross" and the crowns of thorns and "kegs of crucificial nails." I saw Titian's "Maddalena" in Rome and here in Florence she turns up again fat and red headed and dejected as ever, and I am assured that Guido's St. Sebastian is in Milan, although I saw it at Rome. They surely didn't spend their time copying themselves.

And now I find Rubens, Rembrandt and Salvator Rosa. The latter I like—he had a fancy for shipping scenes. After seeing numerous pictures and statues, Venuses with restored hands and Apollos with patched shins, if I may be permitted the expression, I walk down the stairs and across the river Arno in an inclosed bridge which is lined, from the Uffizzi Gallery on one side of the river to the Pitti Palace on the other, with pictures, literally papered, from end to end with portraits of the Medici family and their friends for centuries back. A good place for an actor to study costumes. Amongst all these I am brought up suddenly by a pretty picture of a lovely woman marked "Gwynne Eleanora, Attrice Inglese"—the beautiful "Nell Gwynne." From the Pitti Palace I find my way back again through the picture tunnel and out through a square that is filled with Hercules and Sabines to my hotel. One picture that I had liked was of a Venus combing a little winged cupid's head with a fine toothed comb and conducting a minute investigation in his hair, while he has his head twisted around and looks at you expressively over his shoulder.

I am re-reading slowly and at odd times Mark Twain's "Innocents Abroad," and am filled with a deeper admiration for him than I ever had before. He has much more underlying earnest thought in his work than I ever gave him credit for. He is with me in regard to modern pictures, and his remarks on the Mother Church are so good I must quote a passage here. Looking at the Inquisition building from the dome of St. Peter's, he says :

"Some seventeen or eighteen centuries ago, the ignorant men of Rome were wont to put Christians in the arena of the Colosseum yonder and turn the wild beasts in on them for a show. It was for a lesson as well. It was to teach the people to abhor and fear the new doctrine that followers of Christ were teaching. The beasts tore the victims limb from limb and made poor mangled corpses of them in the twinkling of an eye. But when the Christians came into power, when the Holy Mother Church became mistress of the barbarians, she taught them the error of their ways by no such means. No, she put them in this pleasant Inquisition and pointed to the blessed Redeemer, who was so gentle and so merciful toward men, and then urged the barbarians to love him; and they did all they could to persuade them to love and honor him, first by twisting their thumbs out of joint with a screw, then by nipping their flesh with pincers, red hot ones, because they were the most comfortable in cold weather; then by skinning them alive a little, and finally by roasting them in public. They always convinced those barbarians. The true religion properly administered, as the good Mother Church used to administer it, is very, very soothing. It is wonderfully persuasive also. There is a great difference between feeding parties to wild beasts and stirring up their finer feelings in an Inquisition. One is the system of the degraded barbarians, the other are the ways of the enlightened civilized people."

My sentiments exactly. Talk of ignorant barbarity! The studied atrocities that the Catholics and Protestants have inflicted on each other in the past ages, in the name of a "Merciful God" exceed everything the world has ever seen in simple savage fiendishness, and an all-powerful being who has stood calmly by and permitted the torture and massacre of his own chosen children and chosen prophets, not to mention the thousands of unfortunate women and children, is—well, he is not the kind of a God that I want to worship, and I don't think either "merciful" or "just" are exactly the adjectives that should apply to him. As for those people who cry out for the past and mourn the overthrow of superstition and the advance of science and reason, I hardly think they would on the whole care to be placed in a world such as this was three or four centuries back.

March 30th.—Yesterday I went to the Academy de Belles Arts. After wandering through a gallery of the oldest kind of old pictures and wondering why, while they were about it, people did not pretend that these little Christs and Virgins with solid gilt auriole of light around their heads were the finest works of art—I caught sight of the word Moderno, on a sign over a door, I said, "Modern, that's for me!" and I entered; and oh, when have I seen such pictures, such colors that are in themselves beautiful; such figures that stand out like live men and women, and horses, and, above all, such expressions! The old masters do not compare with artists of to-day in lifelikeness and expression. I saw one immense canvas representing a battle in which every face bore an expression most distinct, most natural; they were living faces. I saw another picture representing a rescue from a flood, in which all the expressions of exhaustion, of determination, of anxiety, were depicted on the several faces with unerring skill. Another was a great picture of many faces and armed men, faces that expressed demand and determination on one side and hesitation and uncertainty and deep consideration, on the other; while the cause of it all, the young prince hidden from the others, looks the last despairing effort to make himself known to his friends as he is forced back by determined men out of the room. Another is St. John the Baptist in the presence of Herod, an old story, but painted with an effectiveness that the old masters never reached, for the old masters knew but one expression, that of pious idiocy. And another picture: a nun in an artist's chair—the artist has forgotten his work and is leaning over her with an impetuous air, and she shrinking, half frightened, half pleading, wholly beautiful. I went direct from these pictures back to the "Tribune," the "inner sanctuary of the Uffizzi Gallery," and looked again critically at the choice collection of Raphael, Correggio, and Titian, and found nothing half as pretty, half as true to nature.

I climbed to the top of the Campanile yesterday, the square tower of the Cathedral, to get the view, all alone. To-day, I started out simply to wander up one street and down another. I was looking for marble image shops; I found them, and gave myself up to feasting on modern sculpture. And here, as in painting, the modern artists are infinitely superior to the old in design, execution and expression. I would not have one of the old original Venuses in my house, but I like the statuette copies of them pretty well; they are so white and delicately cut, but oh, what wouldn't I give to possess four or five good-sized statuettes that I saw to-day, most emphatically modern! First a pretty little snubnosed girl sitting on the back of an ostrich, in

ENJOYMENT OF LONELINESS.

whitest, purest marble ; then a little girl in modern dress, with a parasol over her head, looking with delighted face at the medal she wears; next a pretty girl with robe slipping off, simply the bathing Venus, but quite modern of face and head, and therefore pretty ; then a head of Marguerite with Faust behind her; and there was a little Italian boy with a violin ; and at another shop was a little girl with a parasol which a high wind had turned inside out and torn. The wind had blown the child's hair about, and a tear was on her cheek. All of these were extremely pretty and natural, and the expressions on the faces were most excellently true. The production of beauty and truth to nature should be, I hold, the highest art.

I have enjoyed these two days promenading up one of these narrow cracks they call streets, and down another, all alone. I have been more alone since reaching Italy than ever before in my travels, and, singularly enough this month has passed the quickest of all months before, spite of my desperate homesickness. I enjoy loneliness immensely ; roaming streets, wandering through galleries, sitting silent and self-absorbed at table, with no one to interrupt my train of thought and pleasant fancy. There is no one to wait for me at breakfast, no one to detain me or to hurry me here or there. I am as happy, as serenely contented, as one can be and be so far away from home and friends, in my absolute freedom of movement. I avoid acquaintance. A gentleman next me at table the last day in Florence spoke to me in French. One word I did not understand. I said, "Je ne comprehend pas." He said, "Vous parlez le Francais." I said, "Un petit peu, mais je ne comprend pas bien." He said, "Parlez vous l'Italian?" I said, "Non." "Ni l'Espagnol?" "Non." "Ni l'Allemand?" "Non." "Ni le Deutch?" "Non." "Ni le Russe?" "Non." Silence and disgust on one side and triumphant amusement on the other. He gave me up.

The day of nice young men to trot around with and see me off at depots is past. I make no more acquaintances, but the hotel managers are always extremely polite, and the porters see to my wants.

VENICE.

The hotel manager at Florence persuaded me that it was more convenient to go from there to Venice at night, as leaving Florence in the morning involved rising at five A. M., or thereabouts, and I concluded to do so.

I sat up until nearly morning, but succumbed to sleepiness in the last hour. At the last stop before reaching Venice the guard after looking at my ticket put the curtain over the light to shield my eyes, so I could sleep, he said. While I was dropping to sleep again, as the train moved off, I thought "That is the first time in Italy that I have seen a thing done out of sheer politeness and kindness of heart; the first kind action that was palpably done without the inspiration of an expected fee." I was so surprised and touched that it waked me up for a while. I fell asleep again just before we drew up in the depot at Venice. It had been bright moonlight most of the night. We had burrowed through a good many mountains by means of tunnels and when we reappeared at short intervals we saw deep gulches with little white villages at the foot of or clinging to the mountain side. In the moonlight the effect was picturesque in the extreme.

Arriving at the depot in Venice, a porter took charge of me, secured my trunks, and, the hotel gondola-bus of the Victoria not being at hand, and I having said I wanted to go there, and being too sleepy to change my mind, or choose another hotel, he put me into an ordinary gondola, trunks and all, and presently I was gliding up one narrow street and down another, coming out once at the head of the grand canal, crossing it, and plunging into a labyrinth of winding canals again, finally shooting around a corner and stopping at what looked to be the boarded up doorway of a warehouse. We rang and a porter came and received me.

After this mysterious winding through deserted canals, by frowning marble palaces, black with age and towering up somewhere around the clouds, I was quite prepared to be shown up a winding staircase through the bridge of sighs and down into a dismal dungeon beneath the water; but no, once within the unprepossessing door, we crossed the entresol and then a pretty gardenlike court, into another foyer that looks out on one of the fissures they call streets here; upstairs and into a comfortable room. I rushed for the window, but it didn't look out on the canal, only down on one of the fissures. I could shake hands with my neighbor across the street very comfortably.

VENICE, *April 2d.*—Another childish dream realized. Since the days when I was first taught to read, when part of that instruction was done with the aid of Shakespeare, I have dreamed of seeing Venice. Venice—the City of the Sea, the city of romance and tragedy! Nor am I disappointed in the realization. Venice, as I saw it first, gliding through the narrow watery streets of the sleeping city in the gray dawn of the first day of April, the streets, the majestic houses, the water, alike still, silent and gray—Venice was mystic and grand. I did not think of Juliet or Othello or any of the ancient romances connected with the city, as people who write books or figure in novels always do, but I was very deeply impressed with the oddity, the silence and solemnity, of Venice as it is to-day. I felt very much like a leaf of modern literature between the pages of a volume of centuries ago.

What a beautiful place Venice must have been when Venice was new; when those great marble palaces, now black with age, literally black, were glitteringly white; but I am not sure but I prefer it as it is. It is a sombre picture now, at the best, with its gray waters, dark, rusty palaces, and black gondolas. Here and there a great domed and statued church shines out white in comparison with the grim houses about, but, it, too, is dark with age. The statues are blackened with exposure and years; sometimes the faces are quite obliterated by the winds and rains and dusts and rusts of time, but they are interesting and picturesque.

These are the narrowest streets I have seen anywhere except in the native Indian and Egyptian villages; there the streets are only gutters more or less deep. I haven't had the pleasure of walking in them. Here the streets are clean and dry, but no sun ever penetrates their depths; they are like so many coverless hallways. There is no real reason for their being any wider. There are no horses or cows or camels or donkeys to contest the right of way with one here.

I went in a gondola the full length of the grand canal, to a little church at the further end (can't begin too soon on the churches if I ever hope to finish them). It was a pretty little church, with beautifully painted frescoes and marble statues. I had the bad taste to admire it more than St. Peter's. St. Peter's is so large and cold! I saw people at the confessional, ladies and peasants alike, pouring their sins, or other people's, into the ear of the priest.

My gondolier speaks a little French, and he tells me of all the places as we go slowly along. Going back he is put to his trumps to know how to lengthen out the hours (I've engaged him by the hour). He doesn't know that I am quite content to drift slowly and indefinitely about the canals at ten cents an hour. He stops at a glass manufactory and wishes me to go in and see. I amiably permit myself to be managed, go in and admire the painted, fantastic wooden statues, the articles of Venetian glass and see the process of making; buy a trifle and go on. Next he fetches up at a lace manufactory. I go in, am shown the process of making Venetian lace; a dozen girls in one room, a couple of little six or seven year olds as hard at work as the older ones and as adept, with innumerable spools and threads and pins to weave the threads about. Then the showroom, where my mania for lace takes possession of me, and I buy several articles of real hand made lace at about one-fifth what they would cost in America. Having got out of this shop, I warned my gondolier guide that I had seen enough manufactories. He then rowed me to the port of Venice, the door of the sea, with a great church on either side. The church on the left, as you enter Venice from the sea is very beautiful and effective, with its profusion of graceful, nicely arranged statues, blistered and weather worn, it is true, and with black, indistinguishable faces, but far more artistic in effect than St. Peter's.

To-day I went out on the grand canal again; investigated the two churches at the Porte, glided up behind the Doge's Palace and under the Bridge of Sighs and thence forth under bridges and around corners until I reached the hotel. In the canals, floating, I see bunches of straw, from time to time, with an occasional dead rat, which causes me to wonder—do they have street cleaning commissioners in Venice, and do they, as in New York, neglect their duties? And do Venetians sometimes complain of too much straw and dead rats, and chop the commissioners' heads off? My gondolier pointed out to me yesterday the houses of Juliet, Marino Faliero and the place where Byron lived while here.

April 4th.—New sensation! I'm chaperoning a couple of English girls around Venice, I am the smallest and I suspect I am the youngest of the three, but I'm the chaperone all the same. They arrived here last night. Having been necessarily left by their brother in Rome, they are obliged to go home alone, and are trying to finish their sightseeing by themselves. Until yesterday I was here alone with a little white haired English lady, who, while she calls herself thoroughly old school, is rather pleased at the novelties of this age of advance. She is perfectly delighted with my enterprise, and asks me a great deal about my travels, and begs me to make a book of my experiences, and says she calls it "wonderful." The two girls sitting next me last night, new arrivals, she told of my exploits, and I became famous at once. The girls said they wanted to go out on the grand canal at night, and did I think it was safe? My bright little old lady opposite had told me it was perfectly safe—she had lived here for years—so I said it was; and they asked me to go with them. We went gliding over the canals for an hour and a half, while our gondolier sang for us.

This morning I took them to the Doge's Palace. We went all through it, wondering at its pictures—immense battle scenes stretching from wall to wall. These frescoes are very beautiful, but one ought to stand on one's head to see them to advantage. The other pictures are really too big to be pretty or interesting. A confused mass of heads spread over the side of a room is not beautiful in my eyes, if it was done by an old master. Paul Veronese, Titian and Tintoretto are the artists represented here. We see the council chamber, or rather several of them, for councils of ten, and councils of three, and councils of a couple of dozen or so, judging by the seats. We see the hole in the wall for the reception of secret accusations—the lion's head that used, very fittingly to cover it, is no longer there. The rooms suggest nothing now of secrecy, or conspiracy, or dread sentence of imprisonment and death. Then we go down a few steps and enter the Bridge of Sighs, having inspected which we descend to those dreadful dungeons beneath the water, where Marino Faliero and other unfortunates, conspirators or suspects, lived and were executed almost at the doors of their windowless dungeons and consigned to the sea. Having had enough of horrors, we went out on St. Mark's Place, after a successful encounter with several guides who wanted to favor us with their company at the most reasonable rate, from their point of view. We deemed a guide quite unnecessary, and went into St. Mark's, to our doom it would appear from the disappointed guide's air, alone.

Mass was going on, so we listened to the music and watched the small boys, street arabs, sliding about the tesselated marble floors with arms about each other, trying to step on only one color and playing about unrebuked ; a vast improvement I reflected on our prim services, where a child must sit up straight and be silent, its slightest movement or wandering interest being frowned upon severely. As long as a church or mosque is free to children, for a play ground it has my admiration and approval.

In St. Mark's Square I saw a quantity of beautiful shell purses of all sizes and designs. I'm going out presently to "bull the market." I don't know whether that expression is correct or not, but it sounds as if it conveyed my idea. I wonder how many shell purses I can get through the Custom House! Shell purses and lace will be my ruin yet, but somehow Custom Houses have lost their terrors for me. I've been through the American Custom House twice, Canadian four times, Sandwich Islands once and Japanese twice, Chinese, Javanese, Indian, Egyptian, Turkish once each, and finally Italian twice, and they say the one at Naples is the next worst to the New York Custom House, and that the latter is the worst in the world. So I am saving all my terrors for the New York Custom House. I've been through all the others successfully, and if I can't get through my own native port, I'll give up traveling alone. Meanwhile I shall lay in shell pocketbooks and lace, as long as my letter of credit holds out.

I've seen several pretty English girls standing up and rowing a la gondolier on the grand canal, while papa looks on admiringly. Would like to try it myself, but am too lazy. I heard a lady at table last night tell a gentleman that Mark Twain was only a river pilot on the Mississippi, and had never been abroad when he wrote the "Innocents Abroad." She said it was all imaginary. The remark irritated me so that it destroyed my appetite and made me sick for an hour.

St. Mark's Square is not far from the hotel. I found my way there and back easily enough. There seem to be two Venices, the Venice of streets and the Venice of canals. I found a band was playing in the square, where there was a crowd of men, women, and children and doves, the doves quite as much at home as anybody. I stood about and listened, and promenaded with the crowd that marches round the square while the band is playing. I saw two pretty living pictures. A little velvet-clad girl, the center of a mass of doves with glistening, vari-colored necks, at one time, and later a very small, very nervous little dog, with a tiny muzzle of leather and a harness of tinkling bells, making wild dashes at groups of toddling doves, but the bells always gave timely warning and the doves flew away unhurt from each attack.

Yesterday the officials in the Doge's Palace explained everything to me in Italian. Though I do not speak Italian, I understood perfectly well what they told me. At the hotel everybody speaks English except the femme de chambre.

April 6th.—Yesterday was Easter Sunday, and I went to mass at St. Mark's church. There was a great deal of very fine music. After it was over I waited through a two-hours' sermon in hopes of hearing more music. There are no seats worth mentioning in these churches; the most devout kneel at prayer desks or promiscuously about the floor; other religious souls stand patiently through the long service; the more restless may wander about, in and out of the throng. I availed myself of this privilege largely.

The efforts of a pretty fourteen year old girl to look becomingly devout amused me very much. She moved by with downcast head and eyes and preternaturally grave mouth; the new boots and bonnet of a passing lady caught her eye and awakened feminine admiration; she gave them a sidelong glance and then withdrew her eyes and crossed herself penitently.

Last night we had a royal personage at dinner. He was very fair, very speckless and very silent, and very bored. I imagine he could have been nothing less than Lord Garmoyle or the Prince of Wales, but this is essentially a "Cook's" hotel. Does H. R. H. travel on Cook's coupons? The peculiar feature of Cook's hotels is a well filled house and table one day and an empty establishment the next. There was a young man, a very young man, here the other day whose loss I mourn. We discussed Mark Twain and Gilbert and Sullivan and Mary Anderson. Next to gentlemen of forty who are well past the blasé egotism of thirty years give me the young man of twenty who enthuses over Mark Twain and knows all the latest light operas and has seen all the latest actresses, and brings to literature, to the drama, to travel, the fresh, unprejudiced interest of youth.

VENICE STILL, *April 12th.*—Truly the glory and fame of an unusual undertaking is mine. I am making a long stay here. People come and go every two or three days, while I stay on. I sit demurely at the head of the table looking as quiet and inoffensive as I can, but the question always comes around presently, "Have I been to France and England, and if not, how did I get here from America?" and presently I am being plied with questions and exclamations of surprise, and the attention of the guests, from half a dozen to twenty, is concentrated on me. All other topics are dropped and forgotten in the surprised curiosity about me, and when we adjourn to the parlor one lady or another takes occasion to compliment me and question me on her own account, and all unite in calling it wonderful, like my little white-haired old lady opposite, who is always drawing me out and telling newcomers what a wonderful journey I have made.

To me, having been through it, it does not seem so wonderful, everything has gone so smoothly. As I grappled with each new country I found no actual danger in it whatever; any woman could do it that chose; so I don't feel as if it were a very great thing to have done; it is the novelty of it that I enjoy, and I do look back with a great deal of gratification and happy remembrances on my vanquished countries. Each party that comes and goes parts with me reluctantly and admiringly, from the two timid English girls, the Australian boy and his grayhaired father, to the two tiny little dried-up old English maiden ladies, who are doing Italy with such exactness and prim attention to detail. I was very much amused when I was telling a girl some of my experiences on looking up to find these two prim old ladies looking at me with their wrinkled faces all aglow with amusement at my stories. They seemed to enter into the spirit of it all.

Venice is very quiet. I've been resting here thoroughly; it is quite cold and rather rainy and cloudy many days. I've seen the principal things and have done most of the churches. Most of my time has been taken up in hunting for a singularly elusive band that plays several times a week in different public squares. I begin in the morning by asking the waiters, "Does the band play to-day?" and "Where?" The first one says "No;" the second says "Yes, in St. Mark's Place at half-past two;" the third says, "At the Public Gardens at three;" then I go down to the manager and porter; they contradict each other; finally refer to a paper and say, "Yes, St. Mark's Place." I go to St. Mark's Place; no music. I return, enter a store and, making some purchases, propound my continual query to the owner. He refers to paper—"To-morrow, St. Mark's Place." On the morrow I start fresh, putting my perpetual question to everybody, finally to my gondolier. All the returns are in now, and St. Mark's Place has the whole vote. I order my gondolier to repair to St. Mark's Place. No music and no preparation. I go back to the hotel. Papers referred to again. "Music at St. Mark's Place." "Go again; must have been too early." I do go again, this time in company of aged Australian, daughter and son. No music. I say I am going to the Public Gardens to see if it's there. I notice people walking that way. My friends, the Australians, have not been there and would like to go there too. So we walk along the Riviera, I fancy, along the grand canal, and over numerous bridges, and at last we bring the fugitive band to cover in the Public Gardens.

I sit and listen; and observe a barefooted boy of eight and a grotesque arrangement of new shoes and hat, with an unknown quantity of boy, dancing together. The shoes are offensively new and so absurdly large that the portion of boy between them and the generous paternal hat he wears is ridiculously small. I admire the agility of the bare feet in keeping out of the way of the aggressive waltzing shoes. I see two other little gamins dancing in a manner that would wring envy from the soul of a variety clog dancer. Music and dancing are born in the Italian children. It is funny to hear the mites of street boys singing Italian opera instead of the "Mulligan Guards," or "Down in a Coal Mine." From my room I hear the Toreador's song from Carmen being sung with great accuracy and force. I look down on the sidewalk and see a child of four warbling away with all his might, until his sister drags him into a neighboring house, from within which I still catch the clear tenor strains of the dashing "Toreador."

For several nights we have had excessively high winds that tore through the narrow streets, threatening to disintegrate Venice and scatter her broadcast on the sea. Venice is a marvelous city. The sea air gives me an appetite again, a good thing, for I've been losing flesh for many months. I'm as thin, if not thinner than when I left New York, but I've an appetite, so I don't mind.

I leave here, Tuesday morning for Milan. I send my trunks from here to Paris direct, and go "traveling light" across the Alps. I've almost given up the idea of going to St. Petersburg. I want to get home. I feel quite self satisfied about my travels; am quite sure I could do Russia and Siberia and Persia and the North Pole and the Soudan if I chose, but have traveled enough; am tired and satisfied and homesick.

I have done a remaining church or so, and the "Rialto." Fancy a bridge of shops! That is the Rialto. I took particular pains to hunt up the church that contains the tomb of Canova, designed by himself, because Ruskin called it "Consummate in science, intolerable in affectation, ridiculous in conception, null and void to the uttermost in invention and feeling." Having seen it, words fail to express my contempt for Ruskin. I shall always go and see the things that prominent writers abuse in future. I believe the science was there, but did not observe the affectation. The conception was too great for a feeble intellect like Ruskin's to grasp. It has what the "elegant tomb of Titian" as he calls it, lacks, and all other tombs for that matter, "invention and feeling" of the most pronounced type. There is grandeur in the great conical block of marble, with door ajar and guarded by a lion with his head upon his paws, tired of watching, perhaps, for the one who had "passed the door of darkness through" and would not return "to tell us of the road which to discover, we must travel too," as Omar Khayyam hath it. There are a few broad steps upon which, on either side the door, are two figures of marble angels or muses, with trailing robes and flowers and reverential grief for the dead artist—altogether a speaking picture full of suggestion and feeling. It compelled my admiration the moment I saw it, and impressed and fascinated me. I saw Titian's tomb, but it was so unimpressive I have no recollection of its appearance.

While I was gazing at and enjoying Canova's tomb, four men entered with a guide. The guide planted himself in front of the tomb and turned himself loose. He proceeded to shovel out information to those four unhappy men. All the poetry and repose was lost in a moment. I caught the information that the tomb was not designed for himself originally but for Titian, and left the field. I went and hunted up the wretched old daub, "John Bellini in the Sacristy," which "is the most finished and delicate example of the master in Venice." I don't want to see the others. While I was looking at some fairly interesting pictures that were not old masters, the guide tore by with the four men in his wake to go into agonies of admiration and information over the John Bellini. I returned to Canova's tomb to take a last good look, and departed.

I admire the old Paul Veronese and Tintorettos for their size and the work put upon them, if I don't admire their subject— the last judgment, with its attendant devils and toasting-forks and lakes of fire and writhing victims—not agreeable pictures to me, but ones that, it is alleged, give great pleasure and satisfaction to the all-seeing eyes of a merciful God and all good people who love Him, as well as to people of cultivated artistic tastes.

I read an article the other day about an English artist, Watts, I think, by an admirer of his, saying he had no ambition to have his pictures mistaken for real life, as the recent, and, by implication, immensely inferior French artists are doing. I infer that Mr. Watts can't paint as well as that, but I will reserve my decision until I see his pictures. If they are pretty I will forgive him; if they are only abnormal productions of a horrible imagination I will give vent to my scorn. Art without either nature or beauty is not art, it is nightmare.

Another look at the Grand Canal and St. Mark's Place and church, and I am ready to leave Venice. After a hearty good-bye from the dear little old white-haired English lady and several new arrivals who have just heard that I've been around the world alone and would like to know all about it, and the impulsive femme de chambre, who kisses my hand and who would like to kiss me, so great is her admiration for me and the "love of a bonnet" I've been concocting in Venice; and to the manager who calls my three weeks' tour through Switzerland, Germany and Holland to Paris a long journey, to whom I replied it was not as long as the journey I had come, and I therefore thought I should live through it—I am put in the gondola, the manager wishes me bon voyage, I am rowed through quiet, early morning canals to the depot by two gondoliers. I take my last look at rusty, blackened, frowning palaces, with fierce lion's heads, also frowning most pronouncedly, all along their base, and statued churches, and am handed from gondolier to conductor—from conductor to porter, from porter to car.

This is the ladies' car; nevertheless it is invaded by a beautiful young man, who begins to make eyes at me before we are out of the depot, and his parents. He drops his long lashes for a moment, and then, raising them, flashes a perfectly soul-stirring pair of lovely brown eyes at me with an air of sweetness and coquetry that is irresistible. I am fain to smile back at him and otherwise encourage his advances, for he evidently admires me, and he is the most beautiful two-year-old boy I ever saw. His parents and nurse adore him, and I don't wonder at it, for he is bright and exceedingly sweet tempered, altogether a most adorable child.

GRAND HOTEL DE MILAN, MILAN, *April 15th.*—This is a very stylish hotel. I dress and go down to dinner; meet my Australian friends, father, daughter and son, and am warmly welcomed; dine well, chat and freeze a little in the chill saloon, and go to bed. No use, I can't get up early except to catch a train. I turn out at eleven, get a letter or so, and start out on a voyage of discovery. I wander around till I find the picture gallery, the Brera, and fall to enjoying it, but I am in search of the famous picture, "Marriage of Mary and Joseph," by Raphael. At last after hurrying over some fine large pictures, I come to this famous group of piety personified, and fall to anathematizing myself for my idiotic haste to see a famous picture. As if I didn't know better from sad experience.

Presently a vista of beauty bursts on my eyes—three rooms of lovely modern pictures! Here's a feast! Oh, what color! Oh, what woodland views! What lovely women! And what entrancing historical pictures! After I have nearly finished these rooms, a women with three girls comes in. I left them studying Raphael's "Sposeolizio," and other old masters minutely an hour ago. They do these three beautiful rooms in exactly five minutes to my utter disgust.

Of course I fell in love with the great Cathedral of Milan. It's vastly more impressive than St. Peter's. The tall fluted pillars and immense stained glass windows, and absence of frills, images and tinsel, make it appear larger within than St. Peter's, and without it is certainly the most beautiful thing in architecture ever seen, with its profusion of fluted and decorated steeples. I climbed up on the roof and took a walk there and saw enough steeples there for several hundred churches. Then I climbed up to the tip-top of *the* steeple, and looked out and down on Italy at large. I started to count the statues capping the steeples and stuck around everywhere indiscriminately, and most lavishingly, but gave it up as too large a contract. I admired the cathedral the more because the guide book says it is marred by incongruous styles of architecture, and I enjoyed looking at it because I was allowed to roam from topmost pinnacle to foundation stone without molestation or guide, quite alone.

The Palazzo Reale I found close at hand. Ah, here is magnificence! Here is the royal splendor I have been looking for in the land of palaces. I was shown all through it by an official, who merely stated what things were, and left me to form my own opinions. Room after room, with great gobelin tapestries, beautiful paintings, and here and there busts! Here are the bedrooms with silken couches, dressing rooms, writing rooms, little audience rooms, and big audience rooms, and ball rooms and throne rooms, all large, lofty and elegant, with the most beautiful polished floors of dark and light woods.

From here to La Scala is but a step again, and I went and took a look at the said-to-be largest theatre in the world. La Scala is large and handsome, but I think the New York Academy of Music more beautiful. I walk through the Vittorio Emanuel and admire the two broad glass-covered streets forming a cross filled with brilliant shops. It is in effect Broadway under glass with no carriages. The streets are broad and the windows gorgeous. I got a cab to take me to the Public Gardens and he included the Cemetery, which I had no desire to see, and charged it to my account. Then off I start for Como.

I reach Como in the rain, take a hotel bus and drive and drive and drive. We seem to have made pretty nearly a complete tour of the lake before we at last come to a halt, and I am shown into the foyer of a most spacious and sumptuous hotel, and up a broad, marble stairway to a fresh, cosy room. Oh dear! I think I'd like to stay here a week, a month, a year. At the same time I tell the manager that I am going on in the morning. I have a nice dinner, the house is warm and my bed is like down.

I wake up early. I think if it rains I wont go; if it is bright I must take advantage of the weather. Out comes a ray of sunshine, and I get up. Meanwhile it clouds over, and when I stand on the doorstep ready to depart it rains, but I can't afford to get up at half-past six in the morning for nothing. I get into a boat at the hotel steps, a boat that resembles a "Prairie Schooner," having a canvas covering over so many hoops and a well defined backbone, made by a pole along the top. We row out to the middle of the lake, and I find that I am to catch a steamer "on the fly." The rain pours down and the wind blows a squall, and I observe that it is a great deal harder work to stay in one place on the water than to go anywhere.

We scurry around a little in the center of the lake until the steamer comes tearing along. Her engines stop an instant, we catch hold of the steps as they sweep past and I am snatched on to that steamer, my baggage flung after me, and we are off before you can say Jack Robinson. I try to see the scenery from the saloon window, and failing that, conclude to go on deck. Who cares for the wet anyway? I go out in the driving rain wrapped and hooded in waterproof. Presently the rain abates, and in less than an hour clears for good.

I am delighted with Como, more than delighted! It is beautiful. I am glad it rains, because there is no glare of light to try my eyes, and it makes the grass and trees look so much greener and fresher. I'm afraid I've a soul that delights in the sombre and stormy element. Certainly Como, in all this rain, fills me with a perception of its beauty, more vivid than if it were bright. I get the sunshine on it later. Did some one say the Lake of Como was blue ? I haven't seen any blue about it. However, it's lovely. The green mountains that rise from it are heavily capped with snow. Here and there one sees a little red Swiss chalet among the green. At one place where we stopped there was a large wall of red brick with irregular pieces of white marble at odd intervals. On the brick were painted four windows, and painted in each window a figure, in one a girl with a blue dress; another window contained a darkey boy, another a white cat asleep on the white sill, and another a cage with some birds. Indeed, all the windows had white birds, as if formed by pieces of marble. At the top and about the windows, ivy was painted, and creeping vines with flowers. In this manner a common brick wall was transformed into an interesting picture.

At Menaggio I took a train to Porlezzo, from there a steamer on Lake Lugano to Lugano and Pontetressa ; from there a train to Luino. Lake Lugano is lovely, too, and of the same character as Como, only wilder. One's eyes are kept busy. As we go a beautiful picture is everlastingly opening up before, and closing in behind us. We came to a banked up bridge stretching right across the lake with only a space where three or four arches were left open through and beneath it. I thought we should certainly not be able to get around that obstacle. The bridge would not take on another shape and let us pass as the mountains seemed to do as we drew closer, but lo, a couple of men came up and turned a crank and the smokestack or funnel and steam pipe canted slowly down, folding from hinges at the back, till they lay straight out, and we shot under one of the arches without slacking speed or swerving a hair's breadth from our course ; straightened up again and on we went.

I'm in luck again ; have fallen in with three Americans, a lady, pretty girl, and young man, all going my way, and awfully nice.

LUCERNE, *April* 18*th*.—Why didn't somebody tell me that Switzerland was the place to go to get warm. Here I've been freezing in central Italy, while there was a tropical country up here in the Alps just waiting for me to come and thaw out.

But that's the way I'm always getting sold. I nearly froze to death in Java and India. I'd like to have a personal interview with the man who said December was the best month to be in India. Yesterday, when the steamer stopped at landings on the Lakes, it was so hot on deck I was obliged to go below. To-day, in the cars, while traveling up among the snow-crowned Alps, I nearly melted though sitting by an open window. Hereafter, whenever any one tells me it is warm anywhere I shall take a fur cloak and a pair of snowshoes there, and if they say it is cold, a linen duster and a fan. Being warm, of course, I proceed to catch a bad cold at once. It has no business to be warm, up here, anyway, with snow in sight whichever way you look. I have lost all confidence in climates forever.

The nice young man turns out to be the husband of the pretty and nice young woman, and the other lady is their mutual mother. We came on together to-day, and if the English people who have told me that Americans abroad were loud and noisy and bad form can produce a more quiet, more polite and innately genteel trio, I'd like to see them. They are good looking and charming, and a prettier pair would be hard to find anywhere.

We had a glorious day to-day, bright and beautiful, and so full of fine scenery that I am literally exhausted with looking at it. And of all the wonderful railroads, when it comes to tunnels this one (St. Gothard) exceeds everything. Nine miles and a quarter of tunnel is a good deal. After one has circulated through the interior of a mountain for twenty minutes one begins to think it is some considerable tunnel. You not only circulate through and around the mountain, but you circulate upwards spirally at the same time. While the train goes sliding along one mountain you look across the valley and see three black holes in the opposite mountain, one above the other; and very soon we are taking aim at the lowest hole and presently it swallows us. After a protracted boring into the bowels of the earth we emerge and skim along the outside of the mountain for a while, but before long we shoot into the middle hole. Another long bore and we emerge apparently on the other side of the globe; but no, there's that same gulch up there, and there is the large stream in the cañon below, and there are those same little waterfalls up there, and there—but we have slid into the third and topmost tunnel.

Expectancy is at fever heat in the car ; nobody remains seated long. We rush from one side of the car to the other to gain the glorious view, when outside of the mountains and wonder, when inside, where we are coming out next. As we shoot into a tunnel there is a universal and simultaneous banging of windows and when we emerge there is an eager opening on all sides, and it is a toss up which side of the car is to be the scenery side each time. Sometimes there is a hasty closing of windows for the briefest of tunnels and a premature opening for only a glimpse of outer day, followed by immediate night. And, oh ! the scenery ! Green gulches and valleys, rushing streams and waterfalls, a white thread of a carriage road running through the valleys and winding around the mountains—and mountains, mountains, mountains everywhere.

Alp after Alp rises up with colossal granite sides and snow-covered head, and here a snow glacier stretched down a mountain side, and there is the great land-slide of half a century ago. It looks as if a whole mountain had gone to pieces. With all the wonderfulness and beauty of the road there are no such grades here as they have in Ceylon, where you can actually feel the wheels clutching at the rails as the train climbs the mountain ; and no such chasms stretching down from under your car at dizzy heights, as there are going up the Himalayas in India. And the coach road—well, the coach road runs peacefully along the bottom of the valley most of the way. If it runs along a bank six feet high, it is carefully barricaded at the other edge with slabs and posts of rock. What the coach road does when the train goes into a tunnel I don't know, but I am told it is carefully guarded everywhere, and that safety is the great feature of travel in Switzerland. It is quite plain you can't be permitted to have your blood run cold here ; you must go to the Yosemite Valley for that. The glaciers here don't look any more startling than a snow bank ; you must go to the Straits of Magellan for glaciers. There you may see a piece of the blue ocean frozen onto the side of a mountain if you will.

Switzerland is provided with the best of railway restaurants and hotels, at which the service and cuisine are excellent. There are the most comfortable of traveling carriages on the trains and the most polite and efficient staff of public servants everywhere. The constant feeing is a nuisance, of course, but it is not half so annoying as the lack of porters to carry one's handbags and rugs, which we suffer from alike in Switzerland and America. I would rather pay ten cents for having my two trunks and small luggage transferred from car to carriage than attend to it myself. That is all the porter asks and he thanks you for it. It is a tariff in some places. A New York porter demands a quarter for lifting one trunk from the pavement to the carriage. The hotel clerk in Europe does not "slide your key to you," as Howell puts it. The hotel manager welcomes you when you arrive and bids you "bon voyage" when you depart, and he is always ready to give you information or directions, even advice, for which there is no extra charge.

I find Cook's hotels the best for dining purposes, and if you take the second on his list you will get the best rooms they have, a first-class cuisine and every attention. Vive la Cook!

Lucerne is lovely; also balmy. I stand on my balcony and gaze at beautiful Lake Lucerne circled by snow-covered mountains. Fancy sitting comfortably out of doors and looking at miles of snow while you enjoy the balmy air of Spring. I have roamed about Lucerne alone and unattended, even undirected. I've encountered German here, and signs indicating the direction to objects of interest. I wandered along the quay or promenade until I ran across one of these directions, which I accepted, and soon found myself at the "Glacier Gardens," and the "Lion of Lucerne." The "Lion" is a great bas-relief cut out of solid rock, and the Glazier Gardens are formed of rock curiously cut by the action of a glacier. I have gradually acquired a taste for churches. I enter one that has some pretty pictures. Several women and one man are kneeling on the benches and silently praying or counting their beads. I think it is rather a good idea; they come and kneel there and reflect quietly in the cool, peaceful atmosphere. There is no long sermon which they must wait through; they can stay as long as they like and go when they get ready. I observe that most of the men I meet here carry blossoms of Eidelweis about them, souvenirs of their climbings, I fancy. The nurse carries the baby in a white pique pillow case, with a frill all around the edges. A handleless parasol is over the child's face, its edges touching the pillow all around. You see nothing but pillow and parasol.

FRANKFORT-ON-THE-MAIN, *April 22d*.—I've been having an exciting time of it for a day or two. I left Lucerne at eleven A. M. Monday for Strasbourg, my trio of Americans going with me until I changed cars at Zurich. There we parted with mutual regrets, but hoping to meet again in Berlin. In spite of my large experience in traveling alone, the young man insisted on helping me into the waiting-room, getting all the information necessary for me, and charging the guard to look after me. Give me Americans, men or women, every time, for good-heartedness and helpfulness. Half an hour from Zurich I changed cars again. Twenty minutes went by and I changed cars again. Presently I became conscious of a couple of wild Western cowboys in the adjoining carriage who changed cars whenever I did. One of them seeing me struggling along with my great shawl strap and little satchel, and having heard me ask for the Strasbourg train repeatedly, took my large burden and said, "You are going to Strasbourg; so are we, and we will try to help you if we can." They did not know me to be an American; they only saw a woman with a heavy burden; and the great American heart, whether it throbs genteelly under the broadcloth of a fine gentleman or beats in the sturdy chest of the rough Western cowboy, can't reconcile its ideas of manliness to permitting women to carry heavy burdens if they can help them.

In Switzerland you can only take as much baggage on the cars as you can carry yourself; therefore there were no porters. We had left those convenient creatures far behind in Italy. The German conductors are very good natured, but they don't mind seeing women carrying heavy baggage. It's the custom in Germany for the women to do the heaviest work, so they are used to it.

After changing cars "at every gatepost," we had three straight hours without change. We were passing through the "Black Forest" and mountains—literally through them; there were more tunnels than I could keep count of. The country was a smaller Switzerland. It was night, but it was moonlight and the effect on coming out of a black tunnel and looking down a gulch with the glistening water of the Rhine at the bottom, and a village clinging to the hillsides, white and sparkling under the moon, was beautiful in the extreme. Heidelburg was a valley with mountains on all sides and a mountain rising up in the center, half covered with a climbing village and crowned by an old castle, while the Rhine sparkled at its feet. I stood up most of the time ready to rush from one side of the car to the other, whichever presented the most attractive view.

Then we got to changing cars again; at first we thought it a great nuisance, and then after a few more times we considered it monotonous, but when we came to five or ten minutes between changes we got to really enjoying it. The cowboys were in the car next mine, and we all came tumbling out of our cars together and exchanged the time of day, and expressed ourselves freely on the subject of Swiss and German railways in general and this one in particular. At one station as we met on the platform in similar conditions of dishevelment, baggage and bad language, the first cowboy said:

"Well, I've been all over Egypt and the Holy Land, but this here beats my time."

To which I responded: "And I've been all around the world and I never saw anything like it before."

A silence followed more expressive than words of surprise. The wind was all out of his sails. They were going to take care of me, but it ended in my taking care of them, for I was the first to scramble out of my car and say, "Change cars for Strasbourg," as I passed the window from which they were trying to lasso a guard. When at last we reached Strasbourg at eleven at night, while one of them carried my heaviest satchel, I assaulted the first uniformed creature I saw with, "Hotel de la Ville de Paris," and was promptly stowed within the coach of said hotel. They said, "Well, you've found our hotel for us." They were "Cook's," too.

Reaching the hotel, I was ushered into the most sumptuous apartment I've had since leaving America. It is an octagon in shape, with a soft rich carpet in Vandyke tints; a magnificent great bed of dark wood inlaid with mother of pearl, washstand and dressing table similarly ornamented, handsome crockery, marble-top stove, and luxurious sofa and chairs. The feather bed by way of coverlet is no longer a legend; it is a settled fact. I first found it at Lake Maggiore. I have slept under feather beds ever since. I went out in the morning to see Strasbourg. At the Cathedral I heard mass, after I got in. A man with an official looking cap seized me at the door, and trotted me out into the street and around the corner to a picture store, where he started out with the aid of a women to enlarge upon the beauties of the photographs of the church. I don't know now whether he was a guide or a runner for the store in disguise. I had followed him understanding him to say I must go to the side entrance to get into the church, he had barred my way so peremptorily at the main one, asking me if I wanted to see the church. I said yes, and he carried me off. When I grasped the situation, I said I didn't want to see the pictures, and left, returning to the entrance, found my way in, heard mass, admiring meanwhile the granite columns and stained glass windows, and had the wonderful clock explained to me by a priestly official; saw the little cherub strike the quarter and the child come out, and left to return again at twelve to see it go through its greatest performance. When I came back the little side-chapel was crowded with men, women and children, all watching the clock anxiously.

Presently the hand pointed to twelve; old Father Time walked past the skeleton, whose business is to strike the bell, and entered the door on the other side, while a child appeared in the door he had just vacated; the little cherub on the right turned the hour glass the other side up, and the skeleton began to strike the bell. At each stroke an apostle comes out of the right-hand door higher up, and passing before Christ in the center, bows to and is blessed by him, and enters the door on the left. When four strokes have been struck on the bell and four apostles have been checked off, a rooster up high on the left begins to swell up, and emits a very good crow, which act he repeats at the next four strokes and the next, and then the performance is over. This clock is made to run 999 years. It checks off the days of the month, the months and the years as they go by, and notes the movements of the planets.

The journey to Frankfort was rather monotonous, we only changed cars twice. Here I went to see "Dannecker's masterpiece," Ariadne in marble, and found it very pretty. The effect is heightened by a softened rosy light, and an air of mystery produced by keeping it curtained about. At a picture gallery I saw some modern pictures. Among others Daniel in the Lion's Den, Christ and the Wise and Foolish Virgins, the Prisoner of Chilon, and others all modern and fine. I went to the "Palmen Garten," where I heard some good music and watched the children. The people and children are all well dressed, though the gardens are free. I find Frankfort bright and warm, with pleasant streets.

To-morrow Dresden.

DRESDEN, *April 24th.*—And Dresden it is, though I was "away off" in my calculations when I said to-morrow. I got up bright and early yesterday morning, got to the depot and was comfortably arranged in a car, congratulating myself on the company of a couple of Americans, a young girl and a good looking man, and that I should be in Dresden at eight o'clock P. M. I thought the man looked like Bret Harte. The conductor came along, examined my ticket, read it all over forwards and then backwards, as all the conductors do; made some jawbreaking remark and departed. The American gentleman took my ticket and said, "He says this is a ticket on another line; depot at the other end of town; train goes at eleven thirty A. M.; takes you twenty-four hours to get to Dresden; change cars every other depot." I say "Oh, dear," and then laugh at my absurd misfortunes.

I drive to the other end of town. I've plenty of time—two hours to wait. There isn't anybody about who can speak English or French. All I can say is "Dresden via Schauffanburg," and the porter says eleven thirty in choice German, in response, and comes after me at that hour and puts me in a car, and I start blindly out without the remotest idea when and where and how I change cars or when I shall arrive. I should say the train stopped at all of the gateposts and some of the pickets, but, unfortunately for my simile, there are no fences of any description in this broad open country; and how one man can tell his plot of ground from the other fellow's I don't see; but the effect of the country being laid out in even squares of different shades of green and red is very pretty.

As the difficulties gathered round me my spirits rose. My trains went everywhere, nearly, but to Dresden. I ricocheted back and forth between Switzerland and the Baltic Sea all day, and every few miles I changed cars. At midnight I was nearly halfway to Dresden, and stopped long enough to get something to eat, if there had been anything to get. Beer seems to be the only article of diet in this country. I did manage to secure a glass of soda water and a roll ; I had seized a couple of oranges on the fly, at six o'clock and had kept my spirits up between change of cars by eating some candied apricots, I'd been carrying about with me for a week, much to the distress of the Custom House officers, who observed the Italian trade mark on the box. The rest of the time the guard and I were trying to come to an understanding about where I was going and what station I should change cars at again. German fetches me every time. I can't understand a word of it. Still I got along very nicely.

I had a car to myself all the way, as traveling first class is a luxury few people indulge in in Germany. I suppose it was laughable to hear me floundering around in English, French and Italian in the vain hope of striking a sympathetic chord in the bosoms of the guards. Once a passenger in the next coach was discovered who spoke a little French, but then I changed cars right away. At midnight while I was waiting in a depot where several people were sleeping around, a German woman spoke to me. I was sorry I didn't understand, for it was evidently something extremely complimentary.

Before reaching this junction I found the little paper with a few German sentences written for me by a German fellow passenger on the Tokio, in my satchel and committed one remark to memory. So when I got out of the train I said to the porter, "When does the train leave for Dresden," in choicest German. I slid it off my tongue as glibly as I could, for I had grave doubts as to my pronunciation. To my astonishment he understood me at once, and responded, "Zwelf zwanzee," or words to that effect. Although apparently so entirely alone I had hosts of friends in reality. What the guards lacked in comprehension they made up in politeness, and did the best they could to send me on in the right direction.

Coming out of the depot at 12:20, a gentleman who had a limited supply of French told me there was one special car direct to Dresden, if I could get it, otherwise I most change once more. Unfortunately the special car already contained a sleeping man ; that would not do. I concluded I didn't mind changing, but I wished I knew just when it was to happen. I managed to keep just half awake until I changed cars for the last time at two o'clock, and then, being assured in German that I should change no more and should reach Dresden at eight o'clock, all of which I understood by intuition, I went to sleep, after a fashion, and arrived at Dresden this morning at eight. Immediately after breakfast I drove to the great picture gallery that gives Dresden the name of the "German Florence."

I seem to be a good deal of a novelty traveling around here alone; I wonder if it has ever been done before by a woman who didn't understand the language. I never get guides, and I never go back to the hotel to get information or ask them any questions. I just plunge right in to the business of sightseeing and come out all right. The funniest thing about it must be the calm, easy way with which I do everything. I have been traveling so long that I take things perfectly easy. The circumstances that surround me never disconcert me in the least. I haven't the least bit of fear and am unconscious of impropriety in my movements. I get kindly treated always. The guards call me Mademoiselle or Fraulein. One thing that amuses me is hearing gentlemen say: "I had my revolver," or a cowboy remark, "I always go 'heeled,' you know." Fancy my doing what many men do not do—traveling in all sorts of strange countries alone, at all hours of the night without a defensive weapon of any kind. I feel perfectly safe always.

April 24th.—Dresden is well called the German Florence. A more beautiful collection of pictures I have never seen anywhere, save and except that modern department at Florence, and that was very much smaller. This gallery contains twenty-four hundred pictures and upwards, the guide book says. I reveled in it for several hours, till I was put out in fact at the hour for closing. This gallery has its noted Raphael, the famed Sistine Madonna. It's better than the Sposiolizo at Milan. Rubens, Vandyke, Tintoretto and Guido are all represented here, besides many other noted artists. The whole of the immense gallery is more interesting and beautiful than the average run of galleries, but the modern department was rich. There was some exquisite forest scenes.

A picture that caught my fancy was an outdoor green room of a country circus. A strip of canvas conceals the ring, but above it you see a part of the audience and a man in tights and spangles walking the tight rope. The ringmaster is just looking in to call the next performer on. There is a fire in the center, on it a kettle covered with a plate; some odd potatoes around the edges; a pretty girl in guaze and spangles on one side with a cloak around her; a boy, also in ring array, by her side. At the back of the fire the clown sits, holding a baby and feeding it with a bottle, in all his ring attire and paint; and on the other side an exceedingly pretty girl in tights, a shawl thrown over her shoulders, slightly smiling at the compliments of a gentleman with an eyeglass opposite. She is sitting on an old trunk. Clothes are thrown about in heaps; at one side is the open untidy dressing case, with powder boxes, rouge and implements of "make up," in the usual state, and on the floor are piles of unwashed dishes. It is admirably painted. Each face is a picture in itself and tells its own story. The girl's is a particularly beautiful face. The whole story of the wandering showman is told in this picture. The trials, work, poverty, slovenliness, cares; the glory, glitter, glamour, bohemianism and romance are all before you.

The old masters couldn't even paint hair that looked as if it grew on the unhappy martyr's head, much less a natural, life-like expression—Guido's St. Sebastian *always* excepted; one of its beauties is the naturalness of its hair. I like the Dutch school very well. I saw two small, roughly painted pictures in Frankfort that were excellent, though their subjects were not pleasant, both being trivial surgical operations, but the attitudes and expressions are exceedingly good, from the absorbed look of the doctor and the sympathetic interest of the woman, to the screwed up, flinching face of the victim who wants to see, too, and has jumped before he was hurt. The Dutch and German artists are exceedingly good at depicting the roughly grotesque. A peculiarity of the German picture gallery is the admixture of Saints and Bacchuses. There is a great fat knobby Bacchus or a St. Sebastian bristling with arrows wherever you look. The German lovely woman in pictures runs very largely to flesh. I should like to buy up all those horrible torture pictures and make a bonfire of them; they are perfect nightmares to me.

As I go North it gets warmer at every step, until at last the thinnest wrap for walking is too warm. I like Germany very

much, and Dresden exceedingly. I should like to live here.
The streets are broad and clean, the windows are bright. Music
and parks and gardens and pictures abound. Everything is
bright and green and clean and lovely. I've fallen in love with
Dresden.

BERLIN, *Sunday, April 26th.*—I left Dresden very reluctantly. I skimmed over that great and beautiful picture gallery
once more, and came away feeling that I wanted to stay. If
Dresden is lovely and charming, I have no words with which
to describe Berlin. Berlin "sees" Dresden and "goes her"
several points "better." There are no streets like these, no
monuments and parks like these, no galleries like these anywhere else in the world that I have seen. O, ye fashionable
tourists who swarm through Rome and Florence and Italy in
general, with her dark, dismal churches and chill subterranean
galleries of dark and gloomy palaces, why not come to Berlin,
to Germany indeed, where all is bright and beautiful? Why,
I wonder, does Italy, the home of art, arrange her treasures so
badly, in so inartistic a manner and without regard to light.
Here in Germany they do these things much better.

I went through an immense museum of sculpture to-day,
almost entirely made up of copies of those great originals I have
seen in Italy; but so beautifully are they arranged that they are
far more effective than the originals. The Germans have an
eye to harmony as well as a practical consideration for light
and fresh air. So, too, it is about their pictures; they are
arranged here in their respective schools, but hung, it seems,
with reference to each other, so that the dark shades of one
throw up the light tints of the next. I do not know exactly
how it is done, but there is harmony; when you look into a
room your eye is caught by a vista of color that is a picture in
itself, instead of being repelled by a lot of dark, square patches
of different sizes that do not "jibe" with each other—hung
"higgledy piggledy," one might say.

These galleries are beautiful; one is especially well arranged.
The building is round; you enter a rotunda, from which walls
branch off like spokes of a wheel, and on these walls the
pictures are hung. As the walls come closer together toward
the center, the pictures are turned towards the windows on the
outer wall (the tire of the wheel). There are only a few

pictures on each wall, which is a good plan. There are three floors to this gallery, and the rotunda contains some few beautiful statues most artistically placed. Many of the pictures I have seen to-day in these two beautiful galleries were modern; therefore, of course, admirable. I went also to see the panorama, and then for a drive through these beautiful streets, and eventually to the Zoological Gardens, where all the world and all the world's family had gathered to hear the band, drink beer and coffee and be sociable.

Where have I seen such a great concourse of people before, all so well dressed and all so happy! Before the music began I looked at the "Zoo," and found it admirably arranged, the different animals being scattered about in little houses or cages here and there through the park, and much more commodiously caged than ours in Central Park. I was particularly interested in a giraffe's attempts to lie down. Lying down is no small affair to a giraffe. All those long thin legs have to be folded with precision and care. This giraffe folded up one leg and considered a little; then he folded another, and trembled on the other two; finally he got the third ready to fold and commenced to bend the joints of the fourth and let himself down. When he got nearly down he began to think it was too precarious an undertaking for a giraffe, and made one little effort to recover his footing; but it was too late then, the last leg had given way, and he was fairly down. I left him wondering how he was ever going to get up again.

Driving back through the Unter den Linden, the great broad avenue of lindens that stretches from the Royal Palace to the Arch of Brandenburg, I encounter the Crown Prince. Half a dozen carriages rush by, with four or six horses apiece, and in one is the Crown Prince. I hardly had time to see which was the Prince before they were gone. In Italy, whenever a strange gentleman bowed to me, I knew he was a Prince, for an Italian Prince wears his hat in his hand mostly. German Princes are not so polite, I judge. Politeness, however, is a feature among the Germans. All soldiers and officers salute each other, as well as their superiors, with punctilious politeness. I am amused at seeing small boys raise their hats to each other and shake hands when they meet—not stiffly and formally either, but heartily and genially. I've seen the Emperor's palace and Bismarck's house; perhaps I shall see Bismarck himself. I must say that the active rulers like Bismarck and Gladstone interest me far more than the Queens and Emperors.

Getting into a big city like this puts me to my trumps to get along alone. My guide-book has failed me at Berlin—does not give the names of galleries. I am at a loss. I do not know what galleries there are, or where they are, and the city is very large. I *won't* have a guide. I conclude to take a cab by the hour, have the coachman told to take me to all the galleries and museums in the city, give them all a hasty look, and then, having got them located, I can go and take my leisure in them, strolling into them casually. This is economy, for the cab costs me less than a guide, and I go about with far more comfort.

To-morrow I am going to Potsdam, the "Versailles" of Berlin. The Portier says I must take a commissionaire at two dollars a day; he says he can supply me with a responsible man, a married man with a family. That settles it; I'll go *alone*. I haven't been around the world alone to find it necessary to travel under the protection of a staid married man a distance of fifteen miles.

April 27th.—Well, I've been to Potsdam, and I not only got along beautifully without any guide, but I saw the sights without a cabman's assistance. This is how: After half an hour in the cars, I stepped out of the depot at Potsdam. Lots of cabs there, but I did not know where to tell them to drive. I hadn't the name of a place to start with, and my German was entirely inadequate to such an order as "Drive me anywhere—everywhere." So I started out literally to "follow my nose." I saw a park and walked toward it. Passing an omnibus, I saw the sign out, "Sans souci." "Oh," I said, "I've heard that name before. I'll go to 'Sans souci.'" I got on board and gave the conductor all the change he would have, and remarked, "Sans souci." He gave me a bit of yellow paper, and presently transferred me to a horsecar. The horsecar transferred me to another one. Meanwhile I was wondering what was "Sans souci," anyway—is it a church or a picture gallery, or a palace or a lake or—but here I caught sight of an archway with a vista of park through it. I said, "Ah, Sans souci." The conductor set me down on the other side of the arch, and pointed with his finger. I followed the direction, up the street and around the corner, to the park entrance, and walked in.

I noticed a couple in front of me walking the same way. From time to time they asked people they met, park laborers, the way. I gave my nose a rest and fell to following them. In this way I wandered along until I came to a circle with a fountain in the middle and statues all around. Beyond were stairs, very broad, and many of them with immense glass greenhouses on either side. Seeing my two leaders go up those stairs I went up, and there at the top was a balustrade of marble, a plateau, and statues and groups of statues everywhere, and beyond that a palace, on which was carved "Sans souci." I walked all around it—through great semicircular double rows of pillars at the back, where I saw a ruined castle or temple-crowned hill in the distance. I looked at my leisure then, following the line of palaces and greenhouses to the end. Such a profusion of statuary everywhere! None of the palaces seem to be open to the public. At one open greenhouse I asked a guard, "Verboten der Eingang?" He said it was. I had picked up that German from the signs about. Having seen all I wished, I returned through the beautiful park to the archway I had entered by. It was very hot, and I had been chasing palaces and following the glint of white statuary through the trees for two hours and more, so I was tired.

Passing a little beer garten, I saw two women and a baby at a table drinking beer and gossiping, so I walked in and demanded "Ein bier" of the German handmaiden, and "brot" and "pretzel," a demand that met an immediate response. I let the maiden help herself to silver, and then I sat and ate pretzel and drank beer and rested, feeling more thoroughly out of the range of my own kind than ever before, and enjoyed the solitude and silence of an unknown tongue.

I then started to follow the car tracks back to the depot, but a church led me astray. I went off at a tangent after it, and then a great dome lifted up, and I went after that. Here was a great square with several large buildings. I was looking for palaces and picture galleries, but everything was closed and looked unsuggestive of pictures. Opposite the big dome was a great building with an archway leading into a court. I walk in; find guards here and there, and see a picture through an open window. I say to the first soldier I meet, "Verboten der Eingang?" He intimates not, points to a great door and presently a guard comes with keys and takes me in, and it proves to be the palace of Frederick the Great.

The guard shows me through all the royal rooms, with beautiful polished floors, and carpeted and rugged floors, and satin furniture, and agate tables and lovely pictures. Then, having feed my guide, who has explained in German very intelligibly on the whole, I depart and go around in front of the palace into a garden near the depot, and look up at the great palace I've been exploring. I sit and rest again in the park, and cultivate two German little folks and their mothers. My German is coming to me very fast. I can understand as long as they stick to such simple remarks as "Was ist das?" and "Das ist besser." Finally, I trip across the bridge to the depot, take the train and return safely to Berlin.

The "Unter den Linden," the beautiful broad street so-called from the rows of linden trees inclosing a promenade in the center of the street, though lindens are seen everywhere here, is lined with palaces; and indeed Berlin seems to be all palaces, so grand are her buildings, and so broad and fine her streets. All the palaces are guarded by soldiers; there really seem to be more soldiers than folks here. You cannot look up a street without seeing them, singly and in swarms, and you are forever stumbling on whole regiments of them.

I saw Bismarck to-day on horseback, pacing slowly up the street in dignified and solemn state, followed by a single officer.

Germany wears an air of prosperity. Not a beggar have I seen anywhere. In the cities all appear well-to-do and comfortably clothed, and the country is one vast fenceless field of smiling cultivation. How in the world do they tell their land or rented grounds apart, I wonder? There are no fences, and every inch nearly is under thriving cultivation. Nor do you see any cattle grazing in fields. Where do they keep their cattle? But all looks bright and clean and green and flourishing, the green fields being intersected only by the white roads and varied by here and there a bright yellow plot, and an occasional red earth plot of newly plowed ground.

I left Berlin bright and early on the morning of April 29th, and expected to reach Frankfort on the morning of the 30th, but there is a mistake in my tickets. Leaving Berlin at nine in the morning on a train that flew along as far as Hof, I was at 7 P. M. changed to a train that crept, stopping at every telegraph pole. I learned that I must change cars again at Bamberg at 11 P. M. Arriving at Bamberg, I found I must wait at the depot until four in the morning. I said, "Not any, I'll go to a hotel for the night." A little old German woman who had translated my doom to me, recommended a hotel, and herself put me in charge of the omnibus conductor. She had been smitten by my charms as soon as she saw me.

At the hotel, I was shown into a room big enough for a ball ground, with a great dining table in it. I found a couple of beds in an alleyway leading off from it. As soon as I could find my way out of this barrack I rushed downstairs and told the landlord I wanted a room, not a barn. So he took me through a courtyard and up a back stair, and showed me the kind of a room I like, a comfortable single room. In the morning I had time to look around a little; wandered into a church and found mass going on—exceedingly pretty music. The church was full; most of the people had just dropped in on their way from market and had their groceries with them. I reached Frankfort at five that afternoon. Next morning I started for the Rhine.

I've seen the Hudson River and the Straits of Magellan and the Yosemite Valley and the Himalayas and the Italian Lakes, and finally Switzerland. I can't gush over the Rhine. One of its most interesting features was the wash, which was hung out to dry near the villages; another feature was dead grape vines. For about an hour and a half, however, we passed through very pretty scenery—narrow river, banks high, and turns very short, and very, very pretty castles on the hills, but the Hudson River is good enough for me. And oh! the difference in accommodations. Compare this miserable little boat that hasn't a place on board to wash your hands, that loafs along this stream, to the C. Vibbard or the Albany or the Mary Powell in all their comfort and elegance, going from forty to sixty miles farther in three hours less time. However, I saw several pretty ruined castles that I wanted to buy—castles that stood on perpendicular jutting rock and whose ruined walls were overrun with green ivy. No, I don't think I shall ever be quite happy until I possess a castle.

Cologne at last, I visit the famous Cathedral. I had seen its "highest steeples in the world" looming up above the city, before we arrived. I find it vast, solemn, and impressive within, with its massive fluted brown columns and stained glass. Then I hie me to the picture gallery where I see two beautiful pictures, Queen Louisa and a creature with a star on her forehead in the woods, "Iolanthe" I call her, both very lovely; then I take the train for Amsterdam.

And now I must say that as much as I have admired Germany, the beauty and cleanliness of her cities, the art and music to be found there, I like the German people much less in their own country than I do in America. The contrast between them and the Italians is very marked. All the attention from the Italians is with a view to fees, to be sure, but then they give you politeness, attention, information and service for the expected fee. The Germans are not cordial, they are not attentive; on the contrary, they are very neglectful. They won't give you any more information than they can help, because they want to compel you to take their guides and carriages attached to the hotels, and they want to be feed just the same. At all the German hotels I found them alike, stolid, neglectful, indifferent and difficult to get information from. And then the position of women is so low there.

Women are little more than beasts of burden in Germany. Woman carries the luggage and her lord walks on before. He may beat her a little if he likes, to correct her. In Germany I saw the strangest and most disgraceful teams to be seen in this world. In India you see water buffalo teams. In Egypt you see sometimes a donkey and a camel harnessed together, but in Germany I saw a woman and a cow pulling a plow and driven by a man. You see the whole family in the field at times, the man and the woman at work, the children helping and at play, and the baby in the carriage close at hand.

The Germans do stare most outrageously. At Berlin, a couple of men would stop, seeing me at the other end of the hotel, and watch me openly the full length of a long hall and join me going down the stairs, with eyes as big as saucers all the time. At the depots they were always promenading past my window and staring in and staring around from the other car windows. The German lady said she did not wonder at their staring, she wanted to stare too, so I presume I was a novelty.

I was reminded at Amsterdam that it is the "Vulgar Venice" by the numerous canals and bridges. I saw the picture galleries there and then took a carriage for an hour's spin around the city, seeing all the great buildings and parks; but Amsterdam is mostly canals.

I am developing a high opinion of myself as a traveler. I consider that I excel most masculine travelers, for I travel in all countries without arms to protect me, without Baedecker and Bradshaw to inform me, and without boon companion or tobacco to console me.

Having been through Holland I must say I have failed to observe the vaunted Dutch cleanliness. Hague, probably the prettiest town in Holland, was intersected with canals like Amsterdam, the water in which rivaled the Ganges in filth. I always had a suspicion that the Holland cleanliness was a myth. Now I *know* it. Still, I felt at home in Holland; I recognized the race I have descended from.

I reached Hague from Amsterdam at three in the afternoon, and learning that the picture gallery was open I went to it at once. This time I was not disappointed in a famous picture. Paul Potter's "Famous Bull" is exceedingly good. Its worth lies in its extreme truth to nature. It is a lovely landscape, with a bull and cow and sheep in the foreground, and a farmer looking cautiously around from the other side of the fence and behind a tree. A little bird is flying down on the opposite side of the picture. Flies are standing on the bull's back. His ruffled hair is perfectly painted, while the eyes of both animals wear the lustre and intelligence of life. The farmer's face is a picture in itself. In this gallery I see Murillo's Madonna, and —no, I won't take it back after all—many of the paintings of the old masters *are daubs*, nothing more nor less. Rubens' and Titian's Madonnas have hands that look, positively and without exaggeration, as if they had been through machinery, so distorted and twisted are the fingers. A small painting of Rubens' looks as if the paint had been put on with a toothbrush, for it lies in swirls and streaks and knots, making Suzanne's streaked and lumpy red-and-white limbs look anything but enticing.

After the gallery I go to the "House in the Wood," the residence of the late "Queen of the Netherlands." It contains a Japanese room and a Chinese room, and has Japanese and Chinese things scattered about generally. A small boy takes me in hand, and reels off several yards of information, all of which I have happily forgotten. The rooms, however, with their embroidered Japanese tapestry, representing Japanese figures and scenery, the lacquered and inlaid screens and articles of furniture, take me back in memory to the East. The Japanese tapestry is a wonderful arrangement of silk and birds' feathers. The ballroom is very slippery as to floor, and pictured as to walls, all the pictures being representative of the State in various phases. A gallery in the center of the ceiling was designed to contain musicians. The "Wood" was very pretty.

I drove back on the most aristocratic street, and presently passed the establishment of the kind friend I met in Java, Mr. Van ——. He is the son of an ex-Prime Minister of Holland. His father, a midshipman, was, when a boy, expelled from the navy for leading a mutiny, and went to Java, where he rose to rank and wealth and returned to Holland to become Prime Minister. Of all the friends it has been my good fortune to make, no one has been more courteous than he. He is a most accomplished man. Only thirty years of age, he speaks many languages, has been around the world, to America twice, and is the author of a novel. He is still in Java, upon his plantation there, and I shall probably never meet him again; but the recollection of his kindness will always remain a pleasant memory.

I departed from Holland very much depleted in pocket, for my ancient countrymen are the worst in Europe, I believe, when it comes to fleecing the unhappy traveler. I am tired of Dutch pictures and dirty canals.

I arrived at Antwerp to find it bedecked with flags from center to circumference on account of the "Exposition," a World's Fair going on there. I went first to the "Museum." Some tremendous pictures are there. One is so big that it is hung in sections. Most of the pictures were of the crucifixion order—a regular chamber of horrors. I came out of it, sick from the sight. Happily, there were two or three pretty pieces of sculpture with which to rest my eyes—modern sculpture; one, a woman with a sleeping baby on her knees, and oh, how perfect was that little sleeping face and form, from the backward dropping head and half parted lips that almost breathed, to the little feet, held as only a baby holds its feet, with palms turning toward each other. And then there was the marble figure of a crouching girl, laughing saucily up at some one, while Cupid hid beside her knee, laughing too.

I went to the Cathedral and got bored to death by a guide who took possession of me, and thence to the Exposition, which was opened last week, but is far from ready for visitors. It is a regular carpenter's shop. Opened and unopened boxes are everywhere, and the sound of the hammer is heard throughout. The Italian section was nearly finished, and Florence had a beautiful display of statuary. I saw again much that I had seen while there. I spent a good hour looking for the United States department. Canada was there, and Brazil and Paraguay, but no United States. I was told finally that the United States had a section, but nothing had come yet for it. I did, however, see a packing box that hailed from New York. What is the matter with my country that she does not appear at this "World's Fair?"

The "Beaux Arts" building, close by, is a part of the Exposition, apparently, though detached and requiring a separate entrance fee. Here, too, everything is confusion and hammering. Nearly half the rooms are not yet opened to the public, though active preparations are audible from within. This is the picture department, all *modern*, and O my soul, what pictures. "Vive la Moderne," say I ; the beautiful landscapes of Summer and Winter, the humorous and pathetic stories told with the paint brush, the exquisite forms and faces of women and children.

But here, too, is the one great fault to me of all picture galleries, heightened by the realistic touches of the modern painter's brush—the frightful pictures of martyrdom and crucifixion. Wherever you look, the eyes and brain are seared and the soul is wrung with the painted horrors of religious history. I turn away and try not to see, for I know they will come back to me at night and haunt me with their misery and the knowledge that it has all been suffered even as it was painted. But the hideous nightmares will start up and confront me from every side till I am ready to cry aloud against the church and the religion, under whose auspices such diabolical savagery grew and flourished.

I am getting so that I fairly dread going into a picture gallery, there are so many pictures that I have to hurry by with a shiver and a sickening heart for the miseries of the past—the *past* that so many people bewail *being* past. Ah, give *me* the present, deterioration and all. I do think that the pretty pictures and the dreadful ones might be kept separate. If I had my way, I'd collect the dreadful ones and make one vast bonfire of them, or keep them apart only to show the rising generation what vile and wicked things have been done in the name of Christianity. At present the galleries are unfit for the eyes of women and children to see.

Back to the hotel. "My bill, please, and a cab, and send up for my luggage," and I am off for Brussels. It is cold and it rains. I shall give Brussels two days, and then—Paris. In Antwerp I had a pink satin lace-covered feather bed for a coverlet. I have passed through two more Custom Houses within a day or two. But Custom Houses have ceased to have any interest for me. I am saving all my terrors for New York. New York—how I pine to see it again! I *do* want to snatch a look at Russia, but oh, I am in such a hurry to get back to "my own, my native land."

BRUSSELS, *May 8th.*—Yesterday and to-day I have promenaded Brussels hour after hour, getting lost and finding myself again at regular intervals. Brussels is a very fine city. In my walks I am lured on constantly by the vision of great buildings, monuments, and parks. After rambling around through a park, I catch sight of a magnificent building at the end of the Rue Royale. I start for it, past palaces with coats of arms emblazoned on their fronts, to see this most splendid building of them all. At last I stand in awe before it—it must be the King's palace, I think.' I ask the guard who patrols before the gates if it is permitted to enter. Yes. I enter and it proves to be the new Palais de Justice, and very fine it is.

In my wanderings I have found the Museum, and seen the pictures. I might go into the palace of the Prince of Orange, but a fit of timidity seizes me. I am tired and I've seen so many palaces, and I am sick of hearing the tiresome explanations of the lackey in attendance. If they would just let me walk through and admire! I have the strongest repugnance to knowing when pictures were painted and who they were presented to, and the finest of palaces do not compare in luxurious comfort with an ordinarily well furnished New York flat. The rooms are like so many barns of polished wood, but for the pictures. There is a bed, and a gilded chair or two, and occasionally a sofa lost in the shadows of a perfect wilderness of a room. They are absolutely wanting in the ordinary comforts and conveniences.

I am lost in admiration of some of the folks at the table d'hote here. There is a pretty, fair haired, winsome, light hearted girl with a sombre, handsome young husband. I am perfectly fascinated by the melancholy beauty of his dark eyes and drooping mustache and straight, dark brows. But why doesn't he laugh when she speaks to him so laughingly?

I left Brussels in company with a Countess and her two children and two nurses. The two little ones, both babies, were as cunning and lovable as if they were of only ordinary plebeian blood—too active and joyous, in fact, for their rank. So they had to be snubbed and hushed and crushed at last into silence, their infantile joy turned to tears, by the mother and two nurses. The oldest was only two years old, and it was very charming to hear him talk French and tell his "Petit Soeur" about the "Chemin de fer," which he abbreviated into "Min de fer," which is French baby talk for steam car.

Why can't people let children alone when they are happy and quiet, I wonder. This little boy's only desire was to stand and look out of the window, perfectly silent and absorbed in the flying scenes before him. But no, he must sit down, he must eat, he must drink milk, he must go to sleep, he must "come and kiss mamma," and his "Petit Soeur," he must do anything and everything but what he wanted to do, and then when he got nervous and excited and cross from the demands on his attention, he must be punished into silence again. Good heavens! all I ever wanted of children was that they should be tranquilly interested in any quiet amusement. All this officious diversion of children is on a par with waking the baby up to be looked at and kissed by a visitor, a practice most objectionable.

I found the country very flat in Holland and Belgium. The level, open country is divided into fields by intersecting canals and ditches, and the cattle are permitted to graze at will. We passed another Custom House, but ignored it entirely, as no one insisted on my giving it any attention.

PARIS.

PARIS, *May* 14*th.*—At last we reach Paris, and after passing through the depot door, where two soldiers thrust bayonets into my shawl strap and satchel, I was confided with my baggage to a little fiacre by the customary porter, and driven rapidly through the streets to the Hotel Binda.

Paris, the long talked of, much praised and greatly sighed for Paris! And here I am at last, reaching it almost at the end of my travels instead of commencing with it, as I had always expected I should do. To how many praises of this great city have I listened with somewhat cynical ear.

I arrived here Saturday night. The next morning was cloudy, so I slept off the fatigues of thirty days' continuous, active traveling. In the afternoon I started out to find my points of the compass. My dear little guide book contains a map of Paris. I consult it, and decide to go first to the Jardin des Tuileries and walk thence to the Arc de Triomphe. The lady cashier of the hotel tells me how to find the Jardin and says there is a band playing there. I depart, and by dint of alternately following the cashier's directions and my nose, I find the Jardin and the music. Music very unsatisfactory—band plays mere snatches of valse or opera a few seconds and then stops; effect, jerky and disjointed. I wish they would play something through just once. Large crowd; seat, 20 centimes (4 cents); standing room free.

I walk up the beautiful but crowded avenue, the Champs Elysées, to the Arc de Triomphe, climb the Arc itself, and standing on its top, look down on Paris, down on the avenue I've just traveled, on the Avenue de la Grand Armée, opposite on the Bois de Bologne, black with hurrying carriages, and on the numerous roads converging like spokes of a great wheel, all pointing to the Arc de Triomphe, the "hub" on which I stand.

How many people have described Paris to me and yet failed to bring home to my mind any real idea of its beauty. I find the Tuileries to be a lovely park with groups of statues under its trees, and that the Champs Elysées is another park divided from the Tuileries by the Place de la Concorde, and with the

Avenue de Champs Elysées running through it. The Place de la Concorde is an open circle with a fountain at each side and the inevitable obelisk in the center, and the broad avenue Champs Elysées, broader than any other street in the world, save the Unter den Linden at Berlin, extends on to the Place de l'Etoile, another open circle with all the broad avenues of Paris converging to it, with the stately Arc de Triomphe in its center, looming up so tall that it can be seen not only from the opposite extremities of these streets, but from the country round about.

These broad, clean avenues are all teeming with life and as full of activity all day as our Broadway. Each avenue presents a vast concourse of carriages. There are plenty of parks in Paris and bands of music in many of them, but no park to compare with our Central Park, which is really the finest in the world.

I don't feel like shopping, but must get new dresses right away, for I am nearly in rags. A new dress, however, requires due deliberation. I don't know what I want. Here in the center of fashion I have no soul for dress. Dressmaker, staymaker and milliner, all call on me and leave their cards, usually before I am up. I go and torment Cook's about Russia and my trunks, sent from Venice by the line misnamed "Le petite Vitesse" which I translate, "the little quickness," which does *not* describe the line accurately, for my trunks were sent some thirty days ago and have not arrived yet, and Cook's agent knows as little about them as he does about Russia; and having driven him to the verge of distraction, I leave him and start out on an exhaustive chase after the "Column of July" and the site of the Bastile.

I walk the Rue de Rivoli from end to end, see the imposing Tour St. Jaques, the famous Hotel de Ville, and the renowned church, Notre Dame. The yearly Salon is in full blast, with its display of modern art. I say to myself, "You had better finish the old masters first."

Filled with the wisdom of this course, I start for the Louvre in the morning, but oh, the idea of modern pictures is too much for me! I pass by the Louvre into the Tuileries and down the Champs Elysées to the Palais de l'Industrie, and entering, find myself in the famous Salon. At first I look hopelessly down the vista of pictured walls and say, "I'll have to take several days to this," and then with the idea that I am not going to try to see it all, but only a room or two and have plenty of time, I begin and take each picture in its turn. There are no pictures to skip here.

Thank heaven, the day of crucifix and torture pictures is on the wane. In all this vast gallery I see but very few of that school, and the few are modified in their dreadfulness. When I say a vast gallery I mean *vast*. The Palais de l'Industrie is a very large building. One does not know where to begin or when to stop. These pictures beggar description, one must see such things to realize them. My pen is not equal to the occasion. I lived in an atmosphere of loves and graces and cupids, Psyches, Mary Magdalens, Houris, Angels, Nymphs, Sultanas and other lovely feminine creatures, including St. Anthony's temptress, and beautiful forest and water scenes, for five mortal hours, and then found I had just finished the Salon.

The crucified Saviour and St. Sebastian and John the Baptist appear in modified forms here and there, but the blighting horrors of St. Bartholomew and St. Agatha are not to be found, while the stories of the mythology are represented only for their beautiful figures and romance. After I have finished all the other galleries I shall go back to the Salon for a last look, for such an array of modern art I never expect to see again. I left the Salon at half-past five.

For two days I had been roaming the streets of Paris, had wandered where I listed, quite undisturbed, utterly unnoticed as far as I could see, which was something of a surprise after all the stories I had heard about the constant annoyances a lady walking alone in Parisian streets was subjected to. But my time had come. As I walked hastily through the Tuileries I became conscious of the close proximity of a gentleman. As there was plenty of room to walk and few people it occurred to me presently that he kept unnecessarily close. So I quickened my already rapid steps. The gentleman did the same, and presently addressed me in French, intimating that as I was alone he would be happy to accompany me. I turned and gave him one half surprised, half-frightened, comprehensive look, saw that he was a genteel looking, well dressed man, then gave him the best view I could of the back of my head, and quickened my pace. He raised his hat as I looked at him, and followed a few steps, in a discouraged way, and then departed. As long as I can silence impertinence with a glance I shall get along.

The next day I went to the Louvre, but I was not equal to five straight hours of the old masters. I waded through the old department, however, and shall go through it again. Some of the immense pictures were very beautiful. I wandered through acres of Rubens, Guidos and Murillos. Rubens particularly has a room lined on either side with immense canvases. I went looking for the "most beautiful human face" belonging to the Virgin in Murillo's Immaculate Conception. The Virgin's face is very lovely, but unfortunately it falls far short in human beauty of one of the Mary Magdalens by Guido in the same room, and his St. Sebastian in Rome, and indeed many faces in modern pictures. This Mary Magdalen by Guido has a similar face to the St. Sebastian, which is to me the loveliest face ever painted. Having finished the old department of the Louvre and wandered through the museum and seen the old snuff-boxes and card-cases with pictures of Marie Antoinette and Napoleon and Josephine, and the jeweled saddles and armor of the dead and gone French Kings, I departed, leaving the modern department of paintings for another day.

May 19*th.*—Writing is next to impossible. Paris swarms with sights and dressmakers and shops, and the hotel swarms with American ladies. I had a dream once of coming to Paris to learn French, but English is the current language here. The waiters decline to understand my French and insist upon my putting everything into plain English.

I have been falling in love again with a pretty woman, a woman with a sixteen-year-old boy. I never saw such a lot of women together; the hotel parlor is full of them in the evening, and what a gay social time we do have, without a man around to disturb the serenity. We all of us talk nineteen to the dozen. They tell me where to go, and go with me. We go in feminine groups and platoons to the theatre, opera, concert, wherever we like, "Café Chantant" even. I got my lovely, dark-eyed charmer and another lively little lady (who has taken me under her wing) to go with me to see Bernhardt, and, last night we, with the addition of an elderly lady, went to hear Judic. The price of seats is very high in Paris, away above New York. At these two theatres, the Port St. Martin and Des Varieties, they charge $2.60 and $2.40 for an orchestra chair or seat in the balcony. At the varieties we reduced the price to $1.60 a seat by taking a box.

I was rather disappointed in Judic, having heard a great deal about her. She is very large and passée, but has a sweet voice and face; sings in the usual tremolo style of all French singers. Our Lillian Russell surpasses any French opera-bouffe singer I ever saw, in voice, execution and beauty. When it comes to the latter charm, I would pit her against the world. Unfortunately, the play I saw Judic in was not "Nitouche," but a very ridiculous comedy. Judic introduced the songs that I have heard my French maid Maria sing many times before I left home, "Pionit" among them.

I was charmed with Bernhardt. The role of Theodora suits her to perfection. She acted here as I did not see her act in New York. I fancy she felt under some little restraint in New York; partly that, and partly the order of the play, prevented her throwing herself into her art with the abandon she displays here.

Theodora is beautifully put on and exquisitely played. All through it is a perfect harmony of scenery and action that fills one with a perception of the story, even if one doesn't understand the language it is told in. And Bernhardt! Well, Bernhardt is incomparable. Without beauty, without figure, old, worn and thin—uttermost extreme of thinness—she was the living embodiment of grace and beauty—beauty of the delicate, fragile type, with an inseparable aroma of youthfulness and purity linked with a perfectly thrilling chord of intensity and sensuousness. The glance of her eye, the tones of her voice, the swaying of that lithe figure as she stood or walked the stage, were revelations of passion and sensuous grace.

You have to buy your programme, which, however, is a programme of all the theatres in Paris, and each seat is provided with a little wooden footstool, which is an unmitigated nuisance, and which the usher, who is a woman, comes and demands sous for at the last "entre act." These women are excessively insolent up to that time, when their animosity towards you relents until they get your twenty sous. They want you to leave your cloak in their charge, and they put your ticket in their pocket and decline to show you your places if you demur, and harangue insolently about defrauding them of their perquisites. We wanted to keep our wraps because they were light and we might need them. The woman got out of all patience finally, as we did not understand readily, and gave us our seats. We noticed then that nearly everybody kept their wraps. How they got through the clutches of the shrewish usher we did not know. "France is the politest nation in the world." I am in danger of forgetting that.

My great terror here is of getting run over. There is a continual rush of carriages, drays and omnibuses through these wide boulevards and avenues. A coachman never holds up for you. On the contrary, he will whip up and drive right at you. I believe they try to run over you. You have to pay a fine of twenty-five dollars for the privilege of being run over, I am told. It is a luxury that only the rich can afford. As the result of a fearful accident some years ago, there is now at the conjunction of avenues a morsel of curbstone, by way of refuge, in the center of the streets, where you may stand when half-way across and watch your chance to complete your traverse.

Parisians know less about their immediate surroundings than any people I ever saw. You may inquire for a large establishment next door, almost, and they will be entirely ignorant of its whereabouts, even its existence. Yes, there is plenty of politeness over here, but you are expected to pay for it. How glad I shall be to get back to a country where politeness and good nature are not a marketable commodity. Look at the elegance, comfort and convenience of our theatres; the polite and efficient corps of ushers, who take your checks, turn down your seat and return your checks to you with a neatness and dispatch very much needed over here. Look at our comfortable seats and handsome curtains. Look at our beautifully decorated, well ventilated theatres, with their fine orchestras, rich colors and many means of egress. Here no orchestra plays the choicest morceau between the acts. The curtain in first class theatres is a vast advertising sheet; the seats are cramped, and you pay a fancy price for them; the air is suffocating; you must buy a programme containing little or no information; you are discouraged at every step, insulted by furious women, and you must pay sous constantly for each fresh annoyance.

Americans have the name abroad of being very patriotic. And so we are. We ladies gather in the parlor every night and hold a regular convention of patriotism. Yes, we like Paris; Paris is adorable, we could live here a year or two; but what can compare with America—American customs, American comforts, American amusements, and American people? *Nothing*, absolutely nothing. Every American heart warms to a compatriot abroad, and looks away ahead to the time when pleasure trips will be over, and we shall set foot in the dear native land once more. I would, however, like to take this beautiful "Salon" along with me.

There are many American girls and ladies traveling together, leaving the busy husbands and fathers at home. The hotel is full of such. The two or three gentlemen here are seldom seen; their wives and daughters dine alone. The most important personage of this establishment is a small boy about a dozen years old. He calls himself the groom of the house. He is the actual manager. He runs the elevator, carries packages and ice water and letters to the rooms, gives orders, receives mail and distributes letters, attends the door, runs errands and gets cabs for the ladies, is omnipresent, always happy, always polite, always attentive. He rejoices in the name of Archie and in the admiration of the ladies. Having once heard a lady's name, he never forgets it and always addresses her by it. His especial delight is to enter the salon with his hands full of letters and look all about for absent ladies, while he sees the outstretched hands and hears the pitiful "O Archie, none for me?" on all sides. He feels his importance then, and is as gentle with us as he can be. This child is *never* rude or cross, but is ready to run his little legs off for any lady in the house. We go to Archie for everything and he never fails us. His responses are always cheerful, polite, complete, and reassuring, which is more than can be said for many older people in similar positions. Our only anxiety is the fear that he will grow big and disagreeable.

Another feature of the house is the happy little married couple who act as "Boots" and "Femme de Chambre;" who perform their duties together and do their "billing and cooing" on the stairs and landings, and who are as contented and happy as it is possible to be. Then there is the lady whose husband is usually drunk and abusive, and the handsome young man with the gray haired, aged wife. Shopping and gossip are the principal features of the hotel. The salon and galleries are quite a secondary consideration. Each new comer must be stared at, criticised and canvassed.

I made the mistake of going to Versailles with a party. The excursion proved to be a scramble from car to carriage by a handful of people of diverse views and antagonistic opinions—a very unlovely lady being the evil spirit of the party. I never saw any one so gifted in the matter of being disagreeable without intending to be so. If we started to take a carriage, she had to be personally satisfied of the time and distance going, the fare, and usually thought some other way or place would be better. When we went into a restaurant she thought the one next door was better, and continued to express this view throughout the dinner. She is perfectly helpless and dependent, will not travel a step alone; but, having joined a party, wants to run it, and whisk the members about, omitting things that she has seen before.

She hurried us through the main palace at Versailles, and the officials hurried us through the others, so we got but a glimpse of the Palace, the Grand Trianon and the Petit Trianon, with their beautiful pictures and rooms filled with historical interest, the charming gardens where Louis XVI. and Marie Antoinette used to disport, and the stables where are the old carriages and sedan chairs used in the days of royalty, which are gorgeous.

Going out to Versailles we took seats on the top of the car, where we could look across the lovely country we were flying through, and see the majestic Arc de Triomphe towering grandly above Paris, miles and miles away. Returning, we got a drunken cabman, who drove us like mad through the streets, shouting hilariously, occasionally, and nearly depositing us in the street at every turn.

A trip to the "land of the midnight sun" is my latest project. I was talking in the parlor the other day about desiring to go to Norway, Sweden and Russia, and the pretty lady that I'm in love with said she wanted to go too. The "American Exchange" folks evolved some information about Russia, and finally a man rose up in the hotel parlor and said he had just been to Norway, Sweden and Russia, and gave such a glowing description that we said we must go or die, and then a lady turned up whose sister had gone way up to the Arctic Circle and seen the "midnight sun." I want to see the "midnight sun," too, so does the lovely lady. So we have agreed to go together. Our present plan is somewhat mixed. It includes Copenhagen, Christiana, Bergen, Throndgiem, and the North Cape, thence down to Stockholm and across to St. Petersburgh; thence to Moscow, Warsaw and Vienna, and back across the Alps to Paris. The trip offers the most fascinating experiences in the way of glorious scenery and drives across the country. Meantime, we see Paris and study Baedecker and maps.

LAND OF THE MIDNIGHT SUN.

COPENHAGEN, DENMARK, *June 8th.*—After much excitement, discussion, tribulation, indecision, doubt and hurry, we finally got away from Paris on the night of the 4th of June. In those last days there were dressmakers to be attended to, last sights to see, passports to get and trunks to be packed.

I have been warned all the way around the world of the necessity of passports in Russia. We received two of those articles so startlingly imperfect as to make it necessary to send them back. Then we got them "vised." We had a man, the husband of my traveling companion, to look after our tickets, a practical man of the world whom I did not care to contradict or be fussy with. And we had a courier to take charge of us to the depot. We paid very dearly for permitting this masculine interference. To please this superior, common sense creature, I agreed to go on the evening train instead of the morning. This involved a sleeping car, some other extra charges and a different train still at the last moment. I wanted to go a second time to the American Exchange, receive my tickets and have them explained to me, and then draw my money with some idea of what I should need; but being a mortal coward I consented to draw first and have my tickets sent me at the hotel and "have no trouble about it," as the superior man called it. In consequence I drew more money than I wanted, in an inconvenient shape, got our trains all mixed up, and didn't know anything about my tickets or where they took me, or how, until after I left Paris—not to mention the extra expense for sleeping car and an additional payment for the privilege of going first class, as second class tickets had been sent me. So much for the interference of the stronger sex. Having got out of reach of that influence, we shall go along easily and comfortably, and have no more mistakes.

We reached Cologne at eight in the morning. There we had to wait till one o'clock, so we went to the Cathedral and heard mass sung, then took a little drive, getting back and taking dinner before starting again. It was a blazing hot day in Cologne. We got to Hamburg at night—half-past nine.

We were charmed with Hamburg. Our hotel overlooked a lake bright with lights and dotted with boats. Hamburg is intersected with canals, like the cities of Holland. We left next morning at nine for Copenhagen, going three hours by rail to Keil and taking the steamer there for Korsor. Six hours by water and then four hours again by rail to Copenhagen, getting to the latter place at ten at night. We don't think we shall need to go much farther to reach the "midnight sun." It is daylight now from half-past three A. M. till nearly nine P. M.

We have been traveling together four days and have not quarreled yet. I am desperately afraid the lovely lady will not want to travel at my rate of speed. It was quite understood between us before starting that we both wanted to get back by a certain time. She is very amiable and pleasant, but given to wandering from the bee line to the North Pole. She lays plans for stopping a few weeks at some nice place and resting and having her husband come over to Norway. I listen and say, "yes," and "how nice that would be, and then I could leave you there with him while I went on up to the North Cape and you could return if you were tired of the trip." And then she laughs and protests her determination to keep up with me. I expect I shall be obliged to leave her one of these fine days in some pretty place she can't tear herself away from. Meanwhile, having absolutely wrenched ourselves away from Paris and rushed through Hamburg, we find ourselves stranded in Copenhagen until Wednesday afternoon, and having, therefore, plenty of time, and being naturally lazy and fond of each other's society, we stay in the house most of the time and talk.

My first experiences in traveling with any one to talk to in foreign countries is somewhat interesting. We take it for granted that no one we see traveling can understand English, because nobody we ask questions of does, so in the cars we talk on together, utterly regardless of the presence of others. Sometimes our talk should be quite confidential; sometimes we are led into making remarks about our fellow passengers, relying upon their evident German birth. It is somewhat embarrassing after you have ridden five or six hours in the car with a girl who is German from the tips of her toes to her hair, if anybody ever was German, and you have been talking recklessly about your private affairs, not to mention having shouted across the car to your companion, "Just look at that girl; did you ever see such vanity?" "She seems to admire her own hands very much." "Got some new bracelets evidently." It is quite embarrassing after having done all this, to have that girl turn round just at the end of the trip and speak to you in first-rate English. It is embarrassing, too, just when you've been telling a little experience that you don't tell everybody, to have the Dutchest of Dutch women in the other corner lean over and ask you in irreproachable English if this is the first time you've ever been in Denmark, and then have her Danish husband join in the conversation. We conclude we will hereafter ask everybody we see if they speak English before we indulge freely in conversation or comments. And we are not discouraged from this course by a gentleman's response to the question, "Do you speak English?" given unhesitatingly and with mirth in his eye, "I ought to—I'm an Englishman."

At the hotel here we were offered a bill of fare that is as intelligible as Chinese. We picked out a word that looked pronounceable, and inquired, "What is kyling?" The man did not know the English, so he flopped his arms by way of reply, by which we inferred "kyling" meant bird or chicken. It proved to be the latter. This is the hardest language I've come across yet. There is no getting one's tongue around these words. Copenhagen is spelled "Kjobenhavn." The streets here are of cobble stones. Sidewalks are the same, marked off from the street only by a narrow strip of paving stone. Copenhagen doesn't offer much in the way of sightseeing. We go to Thorwaldsen's Museum and take a long drive by the sea, which is rather pleasant. Copenhagen is built in gray stone mostly, and a red brick structure stands out with a lurid effect from the quaint and sombre houses about.

CHRISTIANA, NORWAY, *June 11th.*—We started out on this trip in a hurry and it was going to be put through in the briskest manner. All our friends begged of us at parting not to "rush so." And many were the remarks about the folly of dashing through countries and not seeing anything. Well, we tear along at a breakneck pace as far as Copenhagen, and then we calmly sit down and wait four days for a steamer.

It had been very gloomy during our stay in Copenhagen, and we sailed from there in the teeth of a gale in the ramshackliest tub of a steamer on the line. We sat on deck while it got rougher and rougher. We were not going to be seasick—oh, no, we were never seasick. One by one the passengers went below, and every now and then some rash creature rushed to the side of the vessel, and finally the force of example became too much for us. My friend became a victim. I was hopping around very gaily, laughing and chatting, but suddenly "a change came o'er the spirit of my dream." I didn't ask to be excused, I just rushed madly below, and gave way to the emotions that overcame me. I went back on deck directly. I was afraid some one would think *I* was seasick, but pride and determination availed me not. I was presently rushing for the rail and hanging limply over it without sufficient energy to get back again. My friend was torn between two emotions meanwhile; she was convulsed with laughter at me, and at the same time horribly sick herself. She says she never saw such a limp creature in all her life as I was. I hung over the rail as if I were a rag hung out to dry. She asked an English gentleman, who had been sympathizing with us, to watch me so I wouldn't fall overboard. He came and took one of my limp arms and wound it around a stanchion. Then it began to rain, and he escorted her into the saloon, and returned saying he had strict orders to bring me in at once. I didn't care about the weather just then. I'd just as soon it would rain as not. But as he persisted, I made one effort and got into the saloon, dropping into the corner of the lounge just opposite my friend; and there we spent the night.

We did not need our stateroom. It was nice and cool here, and everybody else had gone below, and our English friend advised us that it was in a horrible state down there, and so we wisely kept out of it. A woman came in the course of the night, and planked herself down at my feet, so I couldn't stretch out all night, and a man took up a similar postion at my friend's feet. Seasick? I never was so seasick in all my life. This rickety little tub of a boat, sloshing about in a choppy sea, brought me to a pass that the hurricane down at Cape Horn might envy. I couldn't raise my head. I couldn't open my eyes or speak when our kind English friend came and looked at me. I rolled off the sofa at intervals, and after the vain effort to "throw up my immortal soul," I lay flat on the floor until I could gather sufficient strength to climb back on to the lounge.

I was just able to say to my friend, "I love the sea, don't you? Never happier than when at sea; traveling by water is infinitely preferable to land, isn't it?" These had been our stock remarks for weeks. We had pined to get to sea. When we felt a little better we exchanged compliments and laughed convulsively over our difficulties. Towards morning I created a diversion by flying off my lounge across the saloon at a sudden lurch of the vessel, and dropping unceremoniously down by my friend with my head resting against her blanketed lounge, I inquired how she felt. I lay there while we both laughed ourselves into hysterics, and finally crawled back to my couch.

Coming up the Christiana Fjord we gradually recovered and our English friend called us to come and see how pretty the harbor was. We came and looked. My lovely lady could not resist a patriotic comparison to America. It spoiled his pleasure at once. He said he was disappointed dreadfully. He thought it was beautiful when he was here before. He felt quite annoyed at it for not looking as beautiful as he thought it would.

We are in love with Christiana. The streets are beautifully clean, the air is delightful. It is ten o'clock at night now, but daylight yet—no use for candles here. We sail to-morrow night for Ekersund.

LAERDALSOREN, NORWAY, *June 18th*.—We left Christiana on June 12th on the little coast steamer Lindholmen, stopping at Christiansand we went ashore and took a carriage through the village to look at a park, which proved to be pretty and to contain a lovely fountain that produces the impression of a cascade at a distance. The park was shut in from the shore by a lofty granite mountain. It was between ten and eleven o'clock at night, and it seemed very curious to see children out playing and people enjoying a woodland picnic at that hour. It was as light as we have it in Summer at 7 P. M., and it gets no darker during the night. We hang our shawls—if the curtains are not dark—over our windows to make night enough so we can go to sleep.

We passed through some very pretty scenery, sailing in behind rocky islands sometimes, and sometimes coming out on the open sea, until we reached Ekersund. Here we took a train across to Stavanger, which gave us an opportunity to see what manner of country lay behind that lofty granite coast.

There was a succession of peat beds. The soil was swampy, and where cut into ditches earth and water were perfectly black. Black bricks of peat lay out on the ground loosely and in piles, drying for fuel. And they need it, I should think, for wood seems to be a scarce article. Along the coast one sees little but granite. It is the stoniest country I ever saw. The fields remind me of Jerusalem as to stones. Jerusalem fields are worse than these, but here the granite towers on every side.

Sailing along the coast it appears very much like the Hudson River, only that river's banks are rich in verdure. Here little but moss and the most insignificant shubbery finds a foothold on the banks of solid rock.

We reach Stavanger from Ekersund in four hours, arriving at eight P.M., just in time to miss the steamer for Eide, which we meant to take. No one at the hotel could speak English, but we discovered that no other steamer was going to Eide until two days later. As this was not the sort of hotel that we cared to stop at so long we determined to return to the steamer we had so recently left, we having crossed a spit of land which it was rounding, Stavanger being its next stop. Meanwhile, we were put into a parlor with a bed in it and a piano. The lovely lady went immediately to the piano. Unfortunately it fell to pieces under her hands. A boy came in and put it together again, and reprimanded us for smashing furniture. We tried to be good then till dinner was ready. We were the only ladies among about twenty young naval officers, but we were used to that. We were the only ladies who came to the table on board ship.

We were welcomed back aboard the steamer. The next morning we were still sailing among rocks. A double row of granite mountain islands shut us in completely from the ocean. The water is perfectly smooth and undisturbed, I should imagine, by any tempests, the mountains forming a perfect barrier and protection, and making it in effect a river. The scenery grows grander and bolder as we go north.

Reaching Bergen, we fail to find it particularly attractive. Everything is fishy. You eat fish and drink fish and smell fish and breathe fish. The bill of fare is made up of it, the water tastes of it, the air is full of it. But I must say another word about the water. All through Norway the water is the softest, most delicious water for bathing. The skin grows softer and smoother under it daily. Holdt's hotel proves to be very "dirty," as we were told. Nevertheless, being tired, we are glad to get into a room again, and rest until the following day, when we depart for Vásse Vangen.

The railroad lies along the fjord (river) and the scenery is beautiful—similar to the Hudson, but finer, I think. The hills and palisades and valleys are beautifully green and fresh. Our admiration is greatly excited by the length and intricacy of the Norwegian words. We make frantic efforts to read the advertisements at depots. We find words that we cannot pronounce without taking breath between the syllables. We attempted to write down one tremendous word, but the train moved off before we could half write it. We were ready for it at the next station, though, and succeeded in getting it all down in black and white on the long side of an envelope. Here it is, "Bekjendyorelsesbolaget." We are far too wise to try to pronounce it. Norwegian "gets" us. That's just the kind of a word they perpetrate here all the time. It makes us tired to hear them.

Getting to Vásse Vangen after four hours of beautiful scenery, we find our hotel, situated in a pretty valley. We stop there over night, but don't get to sleep as quickly as we would like, owing to some large-footed, exuberant Englishwomen, who prance on the bare floor overhead and talk loud and laugh shrilly and call to friends in the adjoining room, which causes us to reflect that we have been told that Americans abroad are so "loud" and "noisy" and "bad form" generally, and we wish some of the English people who have aired this opinion and told how quiet and sedate and decorous an Englishwoman always is were here to observe.

In the morning off again for Gud Vangen. Seven hours in a cariole, a two-wheeled cart, drawn by a horse and driven by a small boy who sits behind us and drives, peering between our shoulders at the horse. Indeed, the tiny boy who is driving two gentlemen in another cariole has to stand on his toes and crane his neck to get a glimpse of his horse. Happily the horse knows the way, for our boy gives us the greater part of his attention. Through a beautiful, winding valley, green and broad, whose sides rise up around us in fresh, green hills and granite walls, we climb to the top of a mountain, where we take dinner.

Leaving our half-way house we descended the mountain by a spiral road into the loveliest of lovely valleys, with a cascade on either side, and then drove up the valley to Gud Vangen, where we took the little steamer Laerdal, and sailed up the Nero Fjord.

This fjord or arm of the sea is perhaps from half a mile to a mile wide. A solid granite wall rises up straight out of the water on each side—five, six, seven thousand feet. When I say straight, I mean it literally. There is not the smallest vestige of a ledge or bank or foothold, from the bottom of the fjord to some thousands of feet overhead. There are no trees or shrubbery, but the rocks are partially covered with beautiful, tender green moss and lichen. The water is six hundred feet deep, deeper than the North Sea, they say, in places, and as green as grass from the shadow of the moss-covered granite walls. One seems always to be within a lake without outlet or inlet. The fjord windings are so sharp that you appear to be completely walled in with granite. It is, without exception, the very finest water scenery in all this world and the grandest. The inland sea of Japan, the Rhine, the Hudson River, and the Straits of Magellan are all small compared with these magnificent heights. My companion, who is very familiar with the Rocky Mountains, and others who have seen the Colorado River, say this is infinitely more grand. The Yosemite is the most beautiful valley in the world, and stands second to the Nero Fjord in stupendous grandeur, but it extends only eight insignificant miles. The Himalayas excel in tremendous heights and vast valleys, but Norway exceeds everything in lofty heights of solid rock. It isn't merely in one place, it is everywhere. The whole seacoast is bound with it and the rivers are cased in it for miles and miles and miles, at the stately heights of from three to eight thousand feet. It even surpasses Switzerland.

Traveling in Norway is very pleasant, because of its variety. You drive along beautiful valleys skirting the foot of majestic mountains until the end of a road, then take a steamer to the end of a fjord, and then return to the cariole, and so the land and water travel supplement each other.

Returning to Gud Vangen at four A. M. in the rain, we found our small boy with the cariole waiting for us. We breakfasted, enveloped ourselves in galoshes, waterproof shawls and veils, and started back to Vasse Vangen. Four o'clock in the morning isn't as dreadful as it sounds. It is broad daylight and people are about. We have a long mountain to climb on foot, for our one pony is not equal to the occasion. As we climb, we keep looking back at the beautiful valley with the waterfalls on either side and the river coursing through the middle, until our tyrannical small boy, who can't speak a word of English and won't let either of us drive, finally permits us to get into the cariole again, while he clambers up behind and drives. It rains very hard. We stop for an hour at a half-way house, where no one deigns to come near us, and when we at last unearth some folks in the kitchen, they cannot understand a word we say. Finally the girl summons a young man from some distant place who understands us, and to whom we confide our woes and desire for hot tea. My cup of tea goes into the interior of the small boy, who is evidently deeply offended with us for keeping him waiting so long, but who recovers his cheerfulness under its benign influence, and shakes hands with us both by way of expressing his satisfaction.

Handshaking is the "thank you" in this country. When your porter is satisfied with his fee, he shakes hands with not only the feeist but every one in the party he represents—just as we say "thanks," the French "merci bien," the Italians "gracia," and the children of the East touch their foreheads to you. It is rather amusing to have the man who simply transfers your baggage from wharf to boat, hold out his hand and give you a friendly shake. I noticed, however, that he does this *after* looking at his fee. We start out again in the rain, but it clears off in an hour, and another hour brings us back, damp and rheumatic but jolly, to our hospitable hotel at Vasse Vangen at noon. We undress, get into wrappers, send our rugs and shawls to dry, have a fire, order dinner sent up to us, and fall asleep before the maid gets out of the door. We sleep sweetly ten minutes, when the maid comes with our dinner. We get up and stuff ourselves and go to sleep between bites ; call the landlord and make arrangements for next day's trip, and go to bed—sleep four or five hours, get up and eat supper, and go back to bed and to sleep again until next day at eight or nine, when we get up feeling as if we could still sleep twelve hours or so more, and depart at two o'clock in the rain again for Eide, where, after dinner, we take the steamer up the Hardanger Fjord to Odde.

The Hardanger Fjord is said to be of a warmer, softer character than those we have seen, but we find it tamer and colder. It is still beautiful, but not so grand. A glacier can be seen now and then, although it lies farther south than the Sogne Fjord. Odde lies right at the head of the fjord, and there are many walks and drives from it. We, however, think we have seen the finest of Norwegian scenery.

A curious custom here is that of charging only half price for a woman who is traveling with her husband or father, or for a young man who is traveling with his mother or father. When I want to travel with a family I shall go to Norway.

TRONDHJEM, NORWAY, *June 26th.*—We arrived here last night on the Trondhjem, the dirtiest of dirty little boats. We were pleasantly situated near the pantry, which was full of various varieties of cheese, including the fragrant "Limburger." The steward and stewardess sat at our door and brushed shoes and buttered bread. When we wanted to get out they rose hastily, clasping shoes and slices of bread to their bosoms, while we gathered our garments about us, steering clear of the blacking box on one side, only to catch the butter plate on the other, or fall foul of the dishpan full of dirty dishes and water. We did not go to our room often, once we got out of it. On this trip up the coast it rained most of the two days it took to make it.

When I left Paris my objective point was the North Cape; my ambition, the midnight sun. Through all weathers I have clung to my desire, but my comrade began to hesitate as soon as we were fairly on our way. The rough water and bad weather from Copenhagen materially diminished her love of the sea, and the long days have effectually cured her of any lingering desire to see the sun at midnight. She does not want to go to the North Cape and wishes me to give up the trip. We have had our little tiffs from time to time, and then laughed them off, reminding each other of the remark a lady at the Paris hotel had made about parties she had seen start out so joyfully and lovingly and return bitter enemies for life. Perhaps we shall share the same fate. We have just been down to see the steamer. She is lovely, clean and new. The weather prospect is fine, and the round trip takes eight days. I am delighted. I have stated my determination to go on her to the North Cape. My friend is to decide in the morning whether she will accompany me or not.

The great trouble in this country is to know when to go to bed. It is almost midnight now, and the sun is still "setting around," just below the hills; the sky is beautifully red and yellow. No use for gas or candles. I've got to hurry and get to bed before the sun rises.

June 27th.—The choice is made and the die is cast. After breathing defiance at each other for twenty-four hours, we at last went down and bought our tickets, secured our stateroom. It is as nice and elegant as possible. We have a large ladies' saloon all to ourselves, there being two ladies' saloons on board. Ours is the larger. It occupies more than half the width of the ship, with sofas on three sides and a center table. The lovely lady yields gracefully before all this comfort and elegance and the knowledge that the steamer is going to make the trip quicker and be back here sooner than the wretched little coasting steamer we expected to go on. This is an excursion steamer only. It has lots of accommodations, but only about twenty-five passengers have engaged, so we shall not be crowded. It goes to Lofoden Islands, Hammerfest, the North Cape and other places of interest; time of trip eight days; price seventy-five dollars, "everything included—except champagne."

STEAMER HAAKEN JARL, OFF TROMSO, *July 1st.*—We are now within the Arctic Circle. The Arctic Ocean is separated from us by the usual range of rocky islands. To-night the sun will stay with us all night. Last night the sun only set for half an hour. The scenery sailing through here is fine, but not as fine as the fjords. It is not very cold here—not cold at all, we find, when the steamer stops and we go ashore. Two-thirds of the mountains about us are covered with snow, but the bases and valleys are beautifully green. We stopped at Bode, day before yesterday, long enough for us tourists to go ashore and climb up and look through a natural tunnel in the mountain. We find pleasant fellow tourists on board—an English lady, and two American gentlemen. Chess and whist have come into play again. We have also on board some German and Norwegian people; a stout woman who sketches and the author of "The Land of the Midnight Sun," Paul du Chaillu.

To-day we were rowed ashore, where three of us secured horses and rode while the others walked out to see an encampment of "Laps." Laplanders are best enjoyed at a distance. Their clothes of leather are put on them as infants and added to as they grow, in pieces. We walked our horses up to the door of their cabin of earth, and looked in on the family, men and women, and a baby. Then we went to an inclosure full of reindeer. The name reindeer always sounded beautiful and romantic to me in fairy tales, so I did not recognize this drove of soiled, unhappy-looking rams, as the picturesque reindeer of my dreams. A Lap came and amused us by lassoing them. They seemed to like it (the reindeer did). Then we all sat for a picture, having to wait a good while for a reluctant Lap to be persuaded to sit before the camera. The Laps took a deep interest in the pictures of themselves that were being vended by a man and a woman. We were then rowed across to the town of Tromso and, after a short and unsavory walk, back to the ship.

The next morning we reached Hammerfest, the most northern city in the world. Hammerfest is bad smelling and fishy. It was raining hard, so I did not go ashore. From there we went on, rounding the North Cape and sailing up to the Nordkyn, where we put about ship and returned to the North Cape. It was pretty rough, so our captain, out of consideration for his tourists, went on past the North Cape, and came to anchor behind still another promontory, where the sensitives could dine undisturbed by the heavings of the "Open Polar Sea," which stretched away to the northward.

It had rained furiously all the morning and been dark and cloudy all day, so my friends who had been *rabid* for the ascent of the Cape to see the midnight sun during the whole trip, had weakened at the last; in fact, given it up entirely, and were congratulating each other on their wisdom in so doing. I, however, had come up here to see the North Cape and the midnight sun, and meant to carry out my programme to the letter. One characteristic of these wet days has been the clear, bright nights, and I saw the clearing up signs in the north, where the sun does his rising and setting, so I joined those who were going, the only woman in the party.

We landed in the ship's boat on a mass of broken rocks, a great landslide, over which we had to pick our way. Then we had a long ascent, which was as near the perpendicular as I want to try to climb. After an hour and a quarter of "tooth-and-nail" climbing, we reached the top of the grim palisade. Then came a long level walk, sometimes rocky and sometimes marshy, and then there was a glacier to cross, another little climb, and we had reached the summit of our ambition, the North Cape.

I was the first one from our vessel on the Cape. A few of the others came up soon. We sat at the foot of a little monument, erected to King Oscar a year or so ago, on this second day of July, 1885, and rested; looked at the sea, drank champagne (brought up by the sailors) and waited for the sun, which was setting behind a convenient cloud, to rise. The sun here, at its lowest point, is some fifteen or twenty minutes above the horizon. There was nothing very gorgeous about its appearance; but the whole picture was pretty. The "Open Polar Sea," as seen from the North Cape, eight hundred feet above it, the sunlight softened by a passing cloud, suggested limitless "cobwebby gray velvet, with the tender bloom like cold gravy," with just a glistening satiny finish. When the champagne was all gone, the sun rose high from behind that convenient cloud, and we retraced our steps in a happy glow of sunshine and gaiety, born of gratified ambition and a sufficiency of champagne.

We saw the moon, too, by the way, a moon that was faded and pale, a moon without a vocation, a superfluous moon in this bright land of the midnight sun; and as for the stars, well, I had forgotten there were stars, for they had all "hidden their diminished heads." We gathered up some birds' eggs, flowers, and bits of white marble as souvenirs, and returned over snow and wet ground, picking our way gingerly down the mountain side, that was so dangerously near to the absolute perpendicular. We made a quicker descent than ascent, however, and having found our way back across the landslide, got into our boat, and were soon aboard the Haaken Jarl, which got her anchor up at once, and steamed gaily out, under a brilliant three o'clock-in-the-morning sun, to sea, where we rolled violently until we passed behind the protecting granite islands on our way southward.

On the return trip, we encountered fjords and glaciers ; and a stiff gale, which caused us to wish the granite coast and islands were further off. I prefer to enjoy my gales in the open sea, where there is plenty of room to thrash around.

Our Fourth of July was celebrated gorgeously on board the Haaken Jarl. The two American gentlemen were very patriotically inclined. Out of deference to us, the ship was arrayed in flags, the Stars and Stripes flying first at the masthead, and a salute was fired from our eight guns. The French, German, and Norwegian guests paid graceful tribute to our country in speeches at a dinner where champagne flowed freely, and everybody got as near to being gloriously drunk on the "glorious Fourth" as good breeding would permit. A subscription was started for all the sailors and waiters on board, and they were also treated to beer. The little handful of Americans made as much fuss as they could in their determination to celebrate the day and give expression to their patriotism.

What attracted my attention most particularly was the marked difference between the atmosphere at dinner and supper. At dinner, all was gaiety, compliments and champagne. At supper there was a general air of fatigue and gloom. The young doctor, the leading spirit of patriotism at dinner, was now leaning his elbow on the table with his chin in his hand, the picture of sullen discontent. He refused to eat anything, and spent his time expressing his disapprobation of the world at large, and flashing fiery glances of scorn at the rest, who were wearily trying to eat. When offered food he rejected it, saying he had dyspepsia, and with another flash of his eyes, added in a tragic tone, "It was the bread." However, we sat on deck until we saw the sun, full and clear, come from behind the clouds at 11:30 P. M.; then we retired, satisfied with our "glorious Fourth."

The L. L. was not displeased with our trip to the North Cape on the whole, the steamer being so nice and comfortable, but she is a fair weather, good hotel and brilliant shopping traveler I fear. Magnificent scenery doesn't pay her for poor accommodations. It is beautiful and civilized cities, with pretty drives, grand houses and fine shops that she finds most interesting.

HELL, *July 7th.*—I've always expected to fetch up at this place sometime. I've heard a great deal about it, but I never knew its exact locality before. Nothing like traveling to improve one's mind and extend one's knowledge. Hell turns out to be in Norway, not far from Trondhjem. I have arrived by the Norway train, express, they call it here, but I should hate to travel by their way trains, if this is express. Hell proves to be a very pretty place. The scenery is very fine. There is a nice little depot where they dispense hot tea to the sinners who travel through the land. Now I have seen the place I should not mind if I did have to take up a permanent residence here. There is no observable smell of sulphur, and the inhabitants are very well bred. I am afraid the fires are low.

STEAMER CONSTANTINE, GULF OF FINLAND, *July* 10*th.*—Leaving Hell on the morning of the 7th, pursuing our way to Stockholm, we were required to change cars three times during the thirty-six hour journey. The peculiarity of the arrangement being that it was the ladies' car that was being perpetually taken off, the smoker going right through.

At the railway restaurants they have no waiters. The traveler walks in and helps himself from a bountifully supplied table, then he tells the maiden at the desk what he has had and pays accordingly, unbounded confidence being placed in the traveler's honesty. Those who want to "put on frills" take plates and knives and forks and napkins to the side tables. Then they take a plate in one hand and a fork in the other and meander around the center table, helping themselves to what they like, and take to their own table. *We* put on frills. You should have seen us start with a soup dish and a spoon for the soup tureen and then thread our way back through the crowd of people. We managed to get a small meal this way, however. Finally our train reached Upsala, where we found a real live express train to take us the rest of the way. There were no more stops. We flew along for about one hour through a lovely country and then we arrived at Stockholm.

We had but one day to give to Stockholm. This one day proved to be the Queen's birthday, so Stockholm and the ships in harbor were brilliant with flags. Stockholm is the northern Venice, and is really charming. There are broad canals intersecting it, and in view from our hotel there is an island in the canal turned into a restaurant, filled with people, dining at the water's edge under the trees. The palace was just opposite our hotel and separated by a broad canal, the harbor of the city. We were shown through a part of the palace, which was filled with Japanese, Indian and other foreign articles, including an immense pair of elephant's tusks from Siam. I renewed my acquaintance with Cloisine, Satsuma, copper and screens.

After the necessary visits to bankers and Russian Consul, we drove out to the deer park and saw as much of the city as we could in so short a time. We drove through many narrow, hilly streets, and some broader ones bright with shops. We find furs are particularly cheap and otherwise attractive here. The only drawback to our entire approval of the lovely sealskin ulsters we look at is the excessive midsummer heat.

Coming on board the steamer we again meet the Doctor and the Widower, as we call the American gentlemen who were on the steamer with us at the North Cape. Perspiration is on the Doctor's brow, but on his arm he bears a fur-lined, fur-trimmed overcoat, the wonderful cheapness of which had tempted him to buy, regardless of the weather. We found our little staterooms on the Constantine fairly comfortable, and the food good from a Russian point of view, though we experienced some slight difficulties in obtaining what we wanted through our inability to speak Swedish or Russian.

The following morning found us at Abo, where we lay some six or eight hours in the heat. A party of four young people came on board here—a very handsome, dark-eyed young man, with two sisters and a brother of twelve years. I awoke to the knowledge that the boy, who sat next me at table, could speak English, when he passed something that I was complaining about because it was out of reach. He wore a uniform and looked so intensely Russian that it had never occurred to me to ask him for anything. The L. L. followed him up on deck with the idea of asking him some questions, when the eldest sister came to the rescue and asked if she could be of service. Presently the other sister and the elder brother joined her in telling us about Abo and the church we might go to see if we liked, to which the young man would escort us, with his sisters. We gladly accepted these kind offers, and strolled off to visit the church and some royal tombs which were in it. During the stroll we became somewhat acquainted, and after our return these amiable young people continued to entertain us, showing us sketches of their home and places they had visited. Finally, the young man produced a book, in which he asked us to write our names and addresses opposite our birthdays, it being a sort of calendar-autograph-album-picture-book. Our two American fellow travelers are readily admitted to the acquaintanceship, and after our names have all been written, the young man introduces us to his sisters, the Princess Vera and Princess Olga, his brother Prince and himself, their guardian; presenting his card, Prince Nico B. M——.

Fancy our surprise and pleasure at finding we had been entertained for half a day by princely personages and didn't know it. If we had thought of meeting Princesses at all we never should have expected to find them so accessible or simply charming and unostentatious. Fancy a Prince taking up a group of travel-stained tourists and conducting them personally about town. We learn that our friends are Princes of royal blood, and that their great-grandfather was the last King of Georgia. We observe that they all have the tiniest of dainty hands and feet, for which the Georgians were famous. The elder Princess is the quiet, prudent housekeeper, the Princess of the religious novel, who dispenses bread, soup, religion and clothes to her peasantry, and looks after them generally, acting as doctor and nurse to a village full of people, over whom she rules in a small way. The other Princess is fair, bright, chatty, accomplished, and is only nineteen. All three are religious to the backbone, active, industrious, economical, amiable, polite and self-sacrificing in the extreme. Their whole education has been to do as much for their fellow creatures as they can. My republicanism is not proof against such an array of virtues. My heart has already been won by these amiable qualities, and I cannot take it back because I discover the possessors thereof are princes of royal blood.

Our royal friends continue to entertain us in the most friendly manner. The Prince paints a charming little sketch of the Abo Cathedral for me and another for the L.L., and in the morning when we arrive at their home at Helsingfors he escorts us all about the place. He takes us to the Russian church to hear the lovely musical service, to the gardens, and finally, with his sisters, to the baths. The bathing in the Baltic Sea is very fine indeed, and the younger Princess is an expert swimmer. After the baths and a short walk, we bade a reluctant good-by to the Princesses, while their brother still assisted some of our party to see the town, giving himself only an hour or so at home out of that whole day of his return, and coming back at five to spend the last hour with us and see us off. He brought a lot of photographs of family and friends to show us, among which were many of notable names of whom I have read. We left him standing on the dock, waving his handkerchief from the point of an umbrella, in one hand, and three or four letters he had volunteered to mail for us in the other. He has promised to send us his picture, and we are to send ours in return.

He was a real prince, for we have met him on his native heath. He was a prince among men, for never have I seen a sweeter, more lovable disposition. He showed us sights, wrote us programmes and directions and letters of introduction, and painted us pictures. His only regret was that he was not going to be in St. Petersburg to show us about and entertain us there. When we passed their villa on the coast and the Prince's handkerchief and letters were out of sight, the Princesses' handkerchiefs hove in view from their veranda, and there on their little wharf at the foot of the garden was the little Prince, waving his hat for dear life. The elder Prince is as handsome as a picture, neither smokes nor drinks, and is the most considerate, affectionate brother I ever saw—polite and thoughtful for everybody.

RUSSIA.

HOTEL D'EUROPE, ST. PETERSBURG, *July* 13*th*.—To begin with, we had heard much against Russia before we got here. Russia was "hot and dirty," "all Russians were vile." We were to be marched by the captain of the steamer up to the chief of police and our passports examined before we could go to a hotel; our baggage was to be unceremoniously dumped on the wharf and portions of it confiscated; therefore we trembled. But lo! none of these things came to pass. The lid of the L. L.'s trunk was lifted and a book looked at suspiciously. My baggage was treated with the usual scorn—simply chalked. I was disappointed. I had made sure my strap would be undone and my copying journal seized as seditious matter, and myself sent to Siberia. At the hotel we had to quite insist on our passports being taken to the police inspector. Finally they were taken and we got official permission to leave St. Petersburg. Permission was also got to visit the Hermitage and the Winter Palace.

The first things one remarks on arriving at St. Petersburg are the gilded domes and steeples. I've no doubt they are pretty in Winter, but on a blistering hot day you wish them in the infernal regions with their dazzling glare and glitter. It proves to be hot in Russia—hotter than Hades, in fact. With my natural fiendishness of temper I remind my suffering, groaning fellow travelers that it was only a week ago they were protesting against a cool climate and were pining, literally languishing, for a hot climate; that they had said several times a day how they hated a cold Summer and sighed for warm weather. Now that their prayers were granted, they, the hot weatherites, were the most violent in their protests against the heat. Of course I said, "I told you so."

We had a good long ride up through the town to the hotel. We endeavored to read the Greek looking signs, and exclaimed at the muffled appearance of the natives in all this heat. We rode in a drosky with unmanageable horses. The drosky driver wears a tall hat with curled brim and concave sides and a heavy wadded ulster that buttons under one arm, the long skirt of which is gathered into the waist at the back and belted around in front. We don't know whether they have anything else on or not. We hope not, for, as I said before, it is hot. The drosky drivers are all stout. The soldiers also walk along in the blazing sun with heavy overcoats depending from their shoulders, and ladies go about well wrapped up. It would seem that the Russians don't know warm weather when they feel it. Getting to the hotel we undress and order ice. Mr. and Mrs. D——, a pair of American fellow travelers recently encountered, invite us to share their guide, carriage and expenses.

We go the first evening, it being Sunday, to the "Islands" to see the sunset. But a sunset at half-past nine P. M. is too tame for us. We go to a concert garden. The concert garden is distinctly "naughty," but the chief end and aim of an American lady's ambition abroad is to see those things she would not dare see at home. At the garden we see the best trapeze performance I ever saw in my life. Then some "Hanlon, Lees, Girards" sort of people perform and a girl walks the slack wire most excellently well; curtain drops; bell rings, and another show opens on the other side of the garden. After that a band starts up in another corner. We gather ostensibly to hear the music, but really to talk loud and drink beer—evils of a party. At last, being surfeited with naughtiness, we go to the hotel at midnight, where we groan with heat in our several apartments until morning.

The following day we go to the Hermitage first, a picture gallery, museum and collection of jewels—lots of old masters; more Murillos than I've seen anywhere; several Immaculate Conceptions; some old portraits. Guide goes off with our passports and does not come back. We look at all the Murillos over again, and swear. Russian lackey explains in Russian— we swear some more. Guide turns up again with more "permissions." He explains hurriedly. Most everything belonged to and was made by order of Peter the Great. We see the beautiful and costly jewels in snuff boxes and scepters. We see some crowns, dating way back to the Greek and Roman crown of gold leaves. Then we go to the Winter Palace and walk through room after room of mirrored and polished elegance. The white room is the most unique, being what its name indicates, pure white in all its appointments. We are shown the room where a dynamite explosion occurred, and the room where the last Czar was brought to die after the bomb exploded in his carriage.

How tired we get of walking on polished floors! Nothing is more fatiguing than walking on their slippery surfaces. We consider we have done a day's work in getting through these two palaces. Nevertheless, that evening we start out and "do" another music garden. A good joke is made at our expense. Mr. D―― is protesting to the guide his desire to see something more than the night before. He says "I don't want to do as we did last night. I want to see something. Why, last night we just stood around there like a pack of fools." Guide (amiably and sympathetically), "Yes, that is so."

On the third day the L. L. and I go to the church of St. Isaac's. Here is a richness for you—a dozen columns of malachite and lapis lazuli. They looked to be from twenty to thirty feet in height, and a foot and a half or two feet thick. I've seen malachite and lapis lazuli used as jewelry, also inlaid in small pieces; at Versailles I saw a great bowl of it; but when it comes to making the pillars of a church of them I am surprised. There are many pictures in this church simply crusted with jewels, immense rubies, stunning diamonds and tremendous emeralds and sapphires. St. Isaac's appears to be the richest church in the world. It approaches the dimensions of St. Peter's at Rome. We rejoin our friends and start out to see "Peterhof." We are first driven at a desperate pace through St. Petersburg in droskies that hold two and a driver, drawn by the fastest of steeds. The drosky has no back or sides, so we hold fast to each other for dear life. We next take a small steamer and sail down the Neva for an hour; then we get a carriage and drive up into the town—first to the Commandant to get permission to visit the various palaces. We drive all about the palace grounds. They are superb. Versailles is nowhere.

In front of the palace is an avenue of fountains, culminating in a grand group of fountains and waterfalls and statuary, at the terrace before the palace doors. Besides this main avenue, fountains and waterfalls are scattered about the grounds in the utmost profusion. Wherever there are branching roads there are fountains. Sometimes a broad flight of stairs is seen with water tumbling down them. There is a great square with rows of pillars and fountains all about it, and outside of it are as many lions' heads belching water. We enter the great palace and go all through it; it is magnificent. Palaces are much alike wherever you go; they only vary in size and degrees of grandeur. They all have polished floors; silk, satin and tapestried walls; satin chairs and sofas here and there, and some fine pictures. Most of them have Japanese and Chinese rooms. Of all the palaces I have seen, Russia presents the finest and richest.

Coming out of the great palace, we encounter the lady who owns it in common with her imperial husband—the Empress of Russia herself. Only a pretty, quietly dressed lady in a basket phaeton, with a child beside her and another behind her in the footman's seat. She drives herself and has no attendants. She bows politely as she passes. She dosen't live here, but in a quiet retreat near. We take to our carriages again, and are driven to a tiny little palace the personification of cosiness and comfort, where their Imperial Majesties may retire for rural quiet; similar in purpose, but more cosy than the "Petit Trianon" at Versailles. We went also to the house from which the place takes its name of Peterhof; the house of Peter the Great, a little, low-ceiled building of very ancient type. Here there are many articles that Peter the Great used—his bedroom, bed and bedding as he left them, his kitchen with utensils and platters. The walls are of bluish, square tiles. We all pined to steal one tile as a souvenir. We are shown many pieces of Peter's own handiwork, his paintings from childhood up. Peter was a "Jack-of-all-trades," but contrary to the proverb, *good* at several. Back we go to St. Petersburg.

The next morning we start out to see the fortress church whose tall, gilded slender spire has dazzled our eyes from various parts of the city, and St. Peter and Paul, which we take to be three different churches, and groan accordingly, but which turn out to be one combined church inside the fortress. It contains the tombs of dead and gone Czars and their families —among others, the late Alexander II. (who was annihilated, as it were). At the arsenal, before admitting us, they asked us if we were English. Being told that we were Americans, we were welcomed. Here we inspected an array of ancient artillery, by which it appeared that Peter the Great had invented the

"Krupp" gun, and had it made to order, and the revolving six shooter as well. Indeed, most all of the latest inventions in implements of war are to be found here in crude and clumsy form. And everything was made at the order of—most things by—Peter the Great, personally. We go from here to a monastery and to a little church, seeing somebody's blood stained sword by the way. At a shop we saw artistically fashioned articles of malachite and lapis lazuli, some of which we bought.

Moscow.—Arrived here, we go out in the blazing sun to see the city. We are half dead with fatigue, and the glare of the sun and the heat are intolerable. Still, we are glad we came to Moscow, it is so curious. It is ancient, it is Moorish, it is Oriental.

First to a picture gallery. There are many Oriental pictures, and many fine pictures of incidents in Russian history. At St. Petersburg everything was said in praise of Peter the Great. At Moscow we get the reverse of the picture. At St. Petersburg he appeared as the inventor, the man of wisdom and justice, the industrious man and freer of slaves; but here in Moscow he is represented as an inhuman father and brother and a merciless despot. We have seen many pictures of Peter, but in this gallery are two, which are great as representations of character. Never have I seen a more expressive face than is given him by the artists in these two pictures: one representing him with the son who has conspired against his life, before him —the son whom he had imprisoned and tortured and finally had executed. The other represents him on horseback in the public square, witnessing the arrival and execution of the rebels who took part in the conspiracy against him. In the first picture he looks all the anger, indignation, outraged feeling and scorn of one who has discovered a dangerous enemy in his own child. In the latter he looks the hauteur of a powerful despot crushing his foes in triumph. The pictures are faithful likenesses of the man and are wonders in their delineation of expressions of human emotion as shown in the face. There is a picture of his sister, whom he also consigned to prison. The finest, most striking picture in the gallery, is a dreadful one—representing the fearful fate of a beautiful rival of Queen Katherine. She and Peter are represented as great rulers of Russia, though we hear a good deal about Alexander Nevsky. The churches here are Japanese like in color and Moorish in design, and very large. Their brightly colored exteriors and many domes and spires, also in vivid colors, make Moscow unlike any other city in the world. It has a fairy tale effect.

Moscow is a charming and unique picture. We go first to the new church, which is plain white on the outside, but gorgeous in great frescoes inside, and delightfully cool on this hot day. The gentlemen are admitted to the inner altar. We sinful women are not permitted to cross the threshold of this sacred place. Even the Empress may not profane this holy spot by her impure feminine presence, woman is so much viler than man—according to the Russian church. We go into a couple of smaller churches, next to the palace, that are very old. In one we see a picture supposed to have been painted by St. John. It is well he is dead, for the picture is so bad and black that one can see nothing at all until the guide points out an eye and then a nose, and then by straining the imagination *very* hard, one can conjure, out of the general gloom, a blackened head of Christ. This is a very old church, dark and with curious designs on the walls, and old gilded pictures. Across the court is another church, the church where the Czars and Czarinas undergo their coronation. Here they have a dead saint some hundreds of years old, covered with a black cloth with a round hole on the forehead, where the devout might kiss the holy skull. We omitted that ceremony.

St. Basle is the gorgeous green and yellow and purple church we had our eyes on ever since we set foot in Moscow. It is the oddest, most interesting thing we have seen yet. The interior is composed of Gothic, frescoed, corridors around the central altar, but these frescoed walls are in the most curious of ancient designs and colors, quite different from anything else in the world and quite indescribable. On the exterior it is a most picturesque pile of domes and spires, painted in all the glowing tints of the rainbow. We see the great bell of Moscow, which I have seen pictured many times, and which was broken and recast and broken again because the ladies of Moscow threw so many jewels into the molten metal that its temper was destroyed—so the guide says. The great bell is within the Kremlin walls, which, by the way, we have been running in and out of and through all the afternoon, via the sacred gate, where every passer through pulls off his hat and prays fervently. Our drivers never fail to doff their hats, and while they hold their hat and reins in one hand, cross themselves assiduously with the other. O holy, dirty Moscow! Everywhere you see shrines and dirt. Opposite the holy gate is a corner where every pious citizen turns in four different directions and crosses himself and mutters prayers to four different shrines, and kneels to each, while the busy throng, having finished their devotions, swarm by intent on business.

Russia is dirty, her people are likewise. Moscow is especially so. But it is a holy land and a pious people. There are plenty of rich churches and poor people. Religion, poverty, ignorance and dirt, go hand in hand—might be called concomitants of each other. The most ignorant and oppressed countries in the world are, I believe, also the most church ridden. America is the most radical and the most civilized country in the world. Russia, Ireland and Italy are but little in advance of heathendom, which is only a grade lower in ignorance, superstition and dirt than Christiandom, for none are so deeply religious as the heathen. In St. Petersburg, as well as Moscow, our drivers were forever taking off their hats and crossing themselves as they drove past shrines and holy places.

After seeing the great bell, we returned to the hotel and went to bed for a rest. I had been quite ill all the afternoon, but had been amused at the general fatigued air of our party. Everything was very new and interesting, but the utterly inert and listless air with which the whole party dragged themselves about was too funny. There was a solemnity about it that suggested grave reflections on the worthlessness of life. How hard people will work to enjoy themselves! Having a good time is the hardest work in the world. After a couple of hours' rest, we all dragged ourselves together again, the most forlorn, used-up looking party you ever saw, to go to dinner at a Russian restaurant, a dinner at which we all started out bravely to eat everything on the Russian bill of fare in the Russian style, but slipped up on the first course—soup—and fell to drinking apollinaris and admiring the snowy costumes of the waiters. After dinner we adjourned to a garden called the Hermitage, where an opera bouffe was being played, as well as some out-of-door performances. The style in Russia is to come out of the theatre between the acts and witness an acrobatic or trapeze performance, and then return to the next act of the opera. There was a great deal of buffoonery about the acting, but the singing was good.

Next day we saw the Royal Treasury, which contained the coronation thrones for ages past, very rich and elegant, and many beautiful jeweled sceptres and glittering crowns of the past Czars. We saw, too, many of their portraits, and below stairs the ancient coaches of royalty, large and gilded. We went to the palace, with great halls, with silk lined walls and polished floors, and then into the old palace. All here was novelty again. Like the picturesque old church, it was distinctly Moorish in design, rooms small, ceilings arched and frescoed in fanciful patterns—small-paned, stained glass windows, all sombre and fanciful and old. A stairway led up to the council hall, into which in former times the opposing parties, coming from different ways, entered by different doors, only meeting in the hall.

We drive to Sparrow Hill to see the sun set, and look at a peasant's house or two—one very small peep is enough for me. The peasants have the most rooted objections to fresh air. It is hot weather, but such windows as they have are closed. There is sure to be a bit of holy picture on the wall, though, somewhere. We had to send our passports and get official permission to leave Russia. Next morning we were off for Warsaw, thirty-six hours by train.

The journey from Moscow to Warsaw is very long and slow, and most comfortless and uninteresting. The prospect from the car windows is flat and bare; the small places we stop at now and then are poor and straggling; the people look rough and miserable. We see women roughly treated by brutal railroad officials. We find nothing but beer and poor sandwiches to eat and drink; and the road is the roughest I ever traveled over. The carriage rolls and pitches at times like a vessel at sea, only the pitching and rolling is of a jerky, jolty, violent kind. Our compartment has leather-covered seats that pull out at night and form lounges. There is no obliging colored porter at hand to pull them out though, and they are dusty. But by this time we are used to making the best of such comforts as we have, so we sociably enjoy each others' society during the day, and at night we curl up in our respective rugs and sleep in defiance of jerks and jolts.

WARSAW.—We find a most enthusiastic guide here; one who insists on our admiring everything; who calls the park here the most beautiful in the world, and tells us that General Grant called it "some Arabian Nights." It is a pretty park, and in it is a pretty little palace that looks out on the water on two sides, and contains some lovely pictures. In one of the lakes is a tiny island, and on the island a stage, surrounded on three sides by perfectly concealing foliage. The fourth side opens on a narrow neck of water that divides it from the mainland. On the mainland is a rising half circle of seats for the audience, roofless and quite open to the air. The audience looks across the water on to the stage, which boasts real trees and a canopy of leafy foliage, in lieu of the usual painted scenery. In the palace, by the way, was a lovely picture of a girl, with the most exquisitely beamful feminine face. On the way out we stop to see the Summer garden and restaurant, where musical performances take place at night. At Warsaw we had to show our passport at the hotel and write on them the Christian names of our parents.

Leaving Warsaw at night we reached Vienna the next afternoon at five and proceeded to hunt up information about trains to Switzerland. The information was so hard to get, and put Switzerland so far off, that I concluded to take the fast express that I'd heard of to Paris. We rose early the next morning and spent the day making inquiries about trains, shopping, banking, sightseeing. We had heard of Vienna being a rival of Paris, of the Hotel Metropole as the pink of hotels. We found Vienna a small city that fringed off into Shantyville, and the Hotel Metropole a house where you paid high prices and got little in return. I left Austria with feelings of utter disgust and dislike. They are a stupid, stolid, disobliging, grasping lot. There is no place in the world where you pay so high and get so little, even of common politeness, in return, as in Germany. We did the Ring Strasse, a gallery, a palace, some shopping, and left that night, parting at the depot, going our several ways. The L. L. from whom I part here, is a shopping as well as a fair weather and good hotel traveler. All the way up through Norway she pined for Stockholm, St. Petersburg and Vienna, large cities where she could investigate the shops. She hardly felt that she had seen a town unless she had investigated the shops. Her pleasure at Vienna was only marred by the necessity of so early a departure, for the shops are particularly brilliant and enticing.

I had the porter, several waiters and a courier, whom I sent to the railroad office, finding out trains for me. Nowhere else have I taken such trouble to be accurate about trains. But all my trouble was of no avail. I at last got on a train that took me wandering all over the country, sans comfort, when I might have had a through train with sleeper but for the stupidity of the people I had to deal with. I was consigned to a train without sleeper, with changes at five A. M., and other changes not down on the bill of fare, instead of carrying me directly through to Paris, as I had been assured by porter, courier and railroad agent, it would do. On the French frontier, at midnight, I was compelled to tumble out of the car with my baggage—not a porter to carry anything, and pass through a custom house. The usual thing happened to me, however, my baggage was chalked and passed on without investigation. I have a car to myself, and that is a blessing, so I wake up at five A. M. tolerably fresh, after two nights on the cars, to get off the train at Paris.

Paris is a great city, and I feel at home here. I am driven to the hotel in the early morning, behind a horse that is only just able to stand, and falls down eventually, breaking the shaft, just a block from the hotel. The driver tinkers the arrangement together, and we proceed to the hotel, where I am received with enthusiasm by the portier. I am pretty tired, but for all my tired I am filled with relief, for I am alone again.

I spent two days in Paris, visiting Pere la Chaise one day, and the Gobelin Tapestries the next. I religiously hunted up the tomb of Abelard and Heloise, though Mark Twain has partly destroyed the romance connected with these two people in "Innocents Abroad." It is a quiet, picturesque, pleasant little village on the hillside, this "City of the Dead," and there is as little of gloom and horror as may be in connection with the last resting place. I walked through its shaded avenues for quite a while, watching the people coming with wreaths of fresh flowers and watering pots, to work over and beautify the tombs.

At the Gobelins I expected to find a noisy manufactory, but I was quite mistaken. The long, cool, shaded rooms are very pleasant on this hot Summer day, and very quiet. It is interesting to watch these great pictures growing under the busy hands of men. The men are hidden behind the work, while they run their needles back and forth through the barrier of perpendicular threads. You can see the left hand gathering together and pulling apart half a dozen threads, while the right puts the needle through them, and then chops the thread securely down to place. If you like, you may look behind and see the innumerable bobbins hanging from the various colored threads, and the picture whose design is being worked out, hanging at the back, where the workers may turn and glance at it and work accordingly. Some of the frames have a design slightly marked on the threads, but many seem to follow the picture entirely. There were many rooms with different tapestries in process, some of them being worked on the right side, and then cut, making a plush-like finish.

I shall leave Paris with some trepidation, for I have all my luggage with me now, and London is the much talked of, long dreaded great city, where there are so many things one must or must not do. The terrible Channel is to cross, and a Custom House to pass with all my baggage.

ENGLAND.

RUSSELL SQUARE, LONDON, *August 7th.*—The Channel proved delightfully smooth. I went on board at Calais, and after an hour and a half of delightful sail we reached the Dover coast, and presently I make my first acquaintance with the English chimney pots. I inspected the little Channel steamer above and below, and then took up a permanent position on the bridge until, coming into port, all passengers were requested to go below. There we must unstrap our hand baggage for inspection. Then ashore; aboard the train, and in an hour and a half we were in London.

I arrived in London a stranger and alone on Sunday evening, July 26th. I had here to have my trunks, which, in the course of my peregrinations, have grown from two to three, examined. This was done in a superficial sort of fashion, and presently I was in a cab, driving up from Charing Cross to Russell Square. I have heard much about the dangers of this great city, and truly, I think I should be afraid to walk alone on this Sunday evening, on these streets so full of young roughs. The sidewalks are teeming with them, walking and standing around in knots. Such a lot of cub ruffians I never saw before. I have sent word of my coming to this boarding place and I am welcomed cordially. It is not particularly attractive, but I've been told that I will be much more comfortable, and that it is not pleasant for a lady to be alone at some hotels in London. In the morning I began by going to the American Exchange, my banker's next, and then I plunged into sightseeing.

I went to Westminster Abbey, gazed at the names renowned in history and literature and studied out the ancient inscriptions setting forth the virtues of the dead. It is the most interesting church in the world, with its buried ages of royalty and fame, birth and brains. The inventive and literary stars of Britain lie here with her Kings and Queens. I went to St. Paul's next and then to the Tower; but I could not get admittance, it having been closed since the dynamite explosion there.

I turned my attention, therefore, to the National Gallery and its fine array of pictures, the Turner collection principally. Having dispatched my letters of introduction, a response comes from one next morning. It is a reception day and will I please call? Oh, dear! I'd rather die! I thought everybody was out of town and I was quite safe. I get out my best "bib and tucker" and my Japanese card case, and, stepping into a hansom, I am off to make a ceremonious call.

These hansoms, by the way, are delightful. There is nothing in front of you but the horse. You are, to all intents and purposes, driving alone without the trouble of handling the reins or thinking where you are going. The driver is perched high up behind you. He opens a tiny door in the roof and asks the top of your head where you want to go. There are a pair of doors in front of you over which you look. It's a two wheeled vehicle and when the horse slips, which he frequently does, you are apt to fly through these doors somewhat abruptly. London streets are rather dirty and exceedingly slippery. The number of horses one sees fall down during a drive is alarming. The streets are smooth and nice to drive upon, paved with blocks of wood mostly, but the horses ought to be sharpshod. Driving along Picadilly I've seen the horses' feet slip a good foot at every step as they ran, in such a distressing manner do the horses go sprawling and sliding along. The wonder is that they do not fall oftener.

I was received by a silent English maid and ushered into a silent English house, where were several, not exactly silent, but hushed English ladies. The air of quiet that reigned was curious. It was the hush of a funeral. I managed to have a pleasant call, however, and left after having witnessed a distressingly affectionate parting between two of the ladies. Coming out I drove to the South Kensington Museum, in which I find copies in plaster of all the masterpieces of marble in Italy and France, besides many other interesting things. One thing that interested me was a great set of pictorial titles or plaques illustrating the history of King Harold. Upstairs were some paintings, among which I found David Garrick and Mrs. Siddons. It is a very large and very fine museum. Returning home, I find another letter of introduction has been responded to. I am to call Thursday. Wednesday I am determined to see the Tower.

When my intention to continue my journey around the world, alone, was announced, friends anxious to aid me, or fearful that I should meet with difficulties, sent me numerous letters of introduction. Many of these I have not used, having a dread of being "entertained" or of putting any one to trouble, besides always finding agreeable society in the chance acquaintances I made.

Among the letters sent me was one from Washington, very seldom given to any one, I am told—a letter from the Secretary of State, commending me to all the United States Ministers and Consuls in the world, and requesting their kind attentions and services in my behalf. With this letter came the assurance that it would doubtless prove valuable in smoothing away the numerous difficulties I was expected to encounter.

How easy and free from difficulties my journey has been may be judged from the fact that I have had neither occasion nor desire to present this letter since leaving Yokohama, until now.

Now, finding that I cannot see the Tower of London without the intervention of the American Consul, I present my letter to him, am graciously received and obtain a permit for the Tower. And subsequently, a card of admission to Westminster Abbey to witness the funeral ceremonies in honor of Genl. Grant, which were very impressive. The music was very fine.

On going to the Tower, I find a nice looking young man just presenting his permit, an American, too. It is one of my bold days, so I claim him as a countryman of mine, and we get acquainted right away. Our party is augmented by three Australians, and we proceed into the Tower. Of course I had thought the Tower was one single round tower, shooting up like a lighthouse, which it isn't. It's a square building with a round tower at each corner, but there seems to be an additional tower or so set around, and quite a village around that, all inclosed by the walls and moat. There is a great gateway in the river face of the wall, close before which are the stairs where all royalty were wont to land in the old days when the Thames washed these steps, and there is the old ring where they used to fasten their boats. The great "portcullis" is still in good condition, while just overhead is the place where the little Princes were imprisoned. Entering the Tower, we are shown the stairs under which the bones of the little unfortunates were found. We are then conducted upstairs to a council hall, and then to the main portion of the tower, now converted into an arsenal. The arrangement of implements of war is very artistic, railings and doors being constructed by ingenious arrangement of bayonets, guns and pistols. Here are old suits of armor, too, worn by famous men in battle, and many interesting and terrible curiosities. We are shown a dungeon cell called "Little Ease," so small that it now serves as a doorway merely, for a proportionately palatial dungeon cell, where we are told Jews were put for chipping coins to obtain silver.

Outside we see the block on which the best blood of England was spilt; here Lord John Grey was beheaded, while his wife, Lady Jane Grey, looked on from an upper window in the prison, from whence she was brought a few hours later to be executed on the same spot. We are taken, later, up into the rooms where she was confined, as were also many other prisoners at different times, who cut their names on the walls in many fanciful designs. There is an inner dungeon where prisoners were put at night sometimes, for greater safety. We look out of the same window that the unfortunate Lady Jane looked from when she witnessed the execution of her husband; and then we descend. We have already glanced at the little chapel close by. And having spent an hour in a bygone age, we retraced our steps under the great portcullis, and outside, finally, of the Tower walls, grim record of many tragedies.

Meanwhile, I had cultivated the young American. He evidently possessed a simple, sincere, earnest and genial nature. A mere chance acquaintance, I could not help comparing this rising business man, developed from a hard working boy, to some of the millionaire friends I had been recently traveling with, and they fell several pegs. But oh! how the comparison would insult them. Why is it, I wonder, that men whose money represents so much labor of their own, frequently value it so much less, except for what it buys, than those who have always had thousands at their command? This young business man would, I feel sure, be ashamed to do one of the trivial, mean things I have been seeing millionaires doing every day. A California stage driver would put them to the blush for true gentlemanliness.

I spent a day in the British Museum, with its great collections from Egypt, Athens, and every part of the world. These two museums, the British and Kensington, are the finest and most extensive in the world.

After the Museum I made another call. I found Lady H—— and her daughter very lively and chatty. Here I met the æsthetic maiden in full bloom—a young lady with a pretty face, wearing a velvet "æsthetic" hat. She had a long neck, which the low cut "Kate Greenaway" dress and limp turn-down collar exposed to the fullest advantage. The dress was shortwaisted and scant of skirt: she looked a perfect caricature.

A visit to "Madam Tussaud's" has quite a historical interest. I admired the wax figures very much. Many are modeled from ancient pictures and are very correct as to costume. Seeing the prominent people of one time grouped together, brings vividly to mind the contemporary events belonging to each reign. Henry VIII. and his wives are an interesting group—Queen Katherine and her maids of honor, Anne Boleyn among them. The life of a Queen had its perils. The "Chamber of Horrors" was not so horrible after all. I've seen more horrible things in picture galleries. I was disgusted with the "Chamber of Horrors." It did not make my blood run cold a bit. I did not linger there. Among the many models of living people, those of Irving and Ellen Terry were very good. There were a host of notabilities, ancient and modern.

I went out by rail to the Crystal Palace, and wandered around in that great glass house until I was tired. And I saw many other things in and about London too familiar to need description.

I had accepted an invitation to dinner with some hesitation, not being a "dinist." I went, however, and had a pleasant, quiet dinner with a quiet lady and her quiet children. The lady is an adept at drawing one out, so I spent the day talking. The next day my friend, the L. L., put in an appearance from Paris. We spent the day gossiping, and finished it at the theatre with the "Mikado." The next day I saw Grant's funeral service, which was very impressive; the Abbey was crowded, the address good, the music fine. Later, to the Inventories, an affair similar to our American Institute Fair, but larger, with outer grounds, and music.

After a week of lovely, bright weather the traditional gloom and fog have put in an appearance. I have met a pretty little couple here that interest me. They are variety performers, professional skaters. No more charming little pair have I seen in a long time. They are young, good looking, quiet, and English; have traveled a great deal, of course, and they like America. They say one may rise from the lowest variety stage to the first rank in the dramatic profession in America. Here that cannot be done.

I went also to see the "Private Secretary." The play is very amusing, but the audience interested me most. An English audience laughs very loud and boisterously, when amused, if they *do* consider it bad form to show amusement or emotion. An American audience expresses its pleasure in a much quieter, more refined way, however spontaneous it may be. A *loud* guffaw in an American audience always attracts the attention and amusement of the rest of the people because of its loneliness and singularity. Here the whole audience guffaws in a manner that seriously interferes with the play. Between the acts you may have cake and ices brought to you in your seat. (Saves the ladies the trouble of going out "to see a man.")

London is a great and busy city. The cab system is delightful. I like London. After getting swindled once or twice by cabmen into paying double price I found out how to manage. I had studied the little placard pasted up in front of the dashboard of the hansoms, but as I did not know where a "circle" began or left off, and can't guess with any accuracy as to miles, that did not help me much. I concluded, finally, that a shilling would cover most of my trips—you have to pay a shilling for any distance—and that if it ever called for more it could only be sixpence. When I was driven a long way and was in doubt, I would simply hand out my shilling and walk off, certain that if that was really too little the man would call me back, while, if it were right, he would believe from my confident manner that I knew all about it. The plan works beautifully. I deal out my shilling now regularly and flee with never a look behind me. I find the London cabman, under this method of treatment, a very reasonable and polite being. No "pour boire" is asked or expected apparently. The feeing is by no means as bad in England as on the Continent. I have had no disturbances with cabmen at all.

I find the English railway depots bare and comfortless. There are few officials, no attention and no information. The traveler is expected to be familiar with the country he is in. Names of stations are not conspicuously placed, and no brakeman opens the door and remarks in stentorian tone, "Nun head, c-h-a-n-g-e for Crystal Palace." On the Continent your ticket is looked at before the train starts, but in London you have no use for your ticket until you have descended from the car and want to pass out of the gate. So you have no means of knowing which station is yours. One's best and almost only source of information is the guide book. I have given up asking people for information; I refer to the "Satchel Guide to Europe" when I want any.

Yesterday I went to Hampton Court, a short distance out of London. I was charmed with the first sight of it. There was a great gate with the coat of arms above it. The walls that form an angle on each side of you are covered with ivy, and the angle is converted into a garden. This was the palace of Cardinal Woolsey, afterwards used by Henry VIII., from which Anne Boleyn went to her execution, and where Jane Seymour died. After entering the gate, you cross a court to an archway. In the archway is a staircase, up which you may go into the hall, where the walls are hung with tapestries and the stained glass windows contain the pedigree of Henry VIII. and six wives. Descending the stairs again, we enter a court with a fountain in the center. In an opposite corner we find the King's staircase, up which we go to the picture galleries. I say we, because I have been overtaken and overrun by a crowd of English girls and one man. I imagine it to be a girls' boarding school let loose. One of the girls leans affectionately on me while looking about her, for which she apologizes when she discovers I am not one of her mates. They are apparently well-to-do girls, but oh! I never saw such a dowdy lot. You never see a set of New York shop girls looking like that; a New York girl will impart style and fit to such clothes as she may happen to have.

We see some old paintings, many of them portraits of kings and queens. We pass from room to room, audience chamber, bedrooms and reception rooms, till we have seen them all, and then return through a series of closets and small apartments, and hallways that open on the courtyard. The main rooms open on a park, affording a beautiful vista of tree-lined avenues spreading in every direction. We descend, finally, by the queens' staircase, opposite the kings'. We pass under a third and last archway, and out into the beautiful park. After a circular walk, I discover an open side gate, with the legend, "To the Vinery," on it, so I walk in. I am lured from the straight and narrow path by a long arbor of trees—trees growing so closely as to form a perfect tunnel. Having explored this I return to the Vinery. It is a hothouse; you stand in a large room of glass, under a canopy formed by one vine, one hundred and twenty years old, with more than one thousand bunches of grapes depending from it at almost regular intervals. It is beautiful. I depart, taking a last admiring glance at the ivy grown walls and turrets of the palace.

London is not as clean as Paris, neither is it as dirty as Jerusalem. But it seems to be a healthy city. I believe I should get fat in London. I have already developed a tremendous appetite, by degrees. I should be fat now if I had had sense enough to go to a hotel where I could select a breakfast from a large bill of fare. When I have to evolve a menu out of my head I fare very badly. I have made the acquaintance here of the neat and trim English maid who "knows her place," and the ferocious English cook who rules the house. I spend my last days in London in the usual whirl. I stole half a day to run out to Windsor, and saw that place most thoroughly. I am dead in love with those stately old stone castles. "Stately pile," is the name for Windsor. It is a pile of turrets, the feature of the landscape for miles around.

BIRMINGHAM, *August 15th.*—I left London at 10 A. M. yesterday morning. The guard of the train looked at my ticket, and in a surprised voice asked if I was alone, and showed considerable anxiety on the subject. He had only seen the ticket to Birmingham. If he'd seen all the tickets I've got in my satchel, he'd have had a fit.

There was one lady in the car going to Oxford. She opened fire presently. She liked Americans, had been to America, and had seen several of the great women travelers, Miss Cummings and Miss Bird. I paraded my travels. She was delighted; thought I was so young and so forth. Indeed, she kept talking about the American girls in general, their prettiness and charm, to all of which I agreed you may be sure. She laughed and said: "The guard thinks you are a young girl on her first trip alone," and thereafter she was hugely amused at the guard's anxious inquiries and fatherly smile. He was a handsome, benign, gray haired, jolly faced man, the kind I always adore. At Leamington I changed cars for Warwick and Stratford. Another handsome guard had a fit of anxiety.

At Stratford-on-Avon I saw the little house where Shakespeare was born, and the corner in the fireplace where he used to sit. The old house is very interesting, with its cracked stone floors and tiny diamond panes in the windows. It contains many old relics of the bard and his time. Some old copies of his plays were as interesting as anything to me.

On my return journey to Warwick I encountered another anxious guard. "Are you alone?" is the perpetual surprised remark. He locks me securely in the car and tells me to call on him if any one says a word to me. This is at midday. He doesn't know that I've been rushing around the world at all hours of the night without anybody ever "saying a word" to me. At Warwick I am too late to see the Castle. A cabman prevails on me to hire him to drive me to Kenilworth and back at a very reasonable price. I do not regret it.

Kenilworth is only too charming. I walked around its broken walls and up and down its old stairways, out upon its dismantled ramparts, looking down on its ivied walls and green carpeted lawn. I do admire it all—this great castle where Queen Elizabeth was entertained so royally, and Amy Robsart died. I want a ruined castle. I must have a castle. I'm sure I shall never be happy until I own a ruin like Kenilworth. It's the loveliest thing in ruins I've seen. I adore ruins—"ru-uns" my fellow countrymen frequently call them.

I have seen nothing so picturesquely beautiful as Kenilworth Castle, with its stately granite walls, unroofed, decorated with ivy and perforated with lofty Gothic windows, arched gateway and great portcullis, and beautiful, grass carpeted sweep within the half inclosing walls. Hampton Court was lovely, but not so picturesque or courtly as this. Windsor Castle is a stately pile from the outside, but the interior that one sees—the state apartments—are decidedly shabby, like a second class boarding house. But Kenilworth has no tawdry furniture, no faded curtains nor strips of threadbare carpet to mar it. Nothing is left but the stately brown stone and ivy.

Leaving Kenilworth my cabman drives me through the beautiful grounds of Lord Leigh to Stoneleigh Abbey, and then on past Leamington, where I pick up my baggage, to Warwick, where he confides me to a hotel, the "Woolpack," and where I dine and sleep most comfortably, ready to be on the spot when Warwick Castle is opened in the morning.

After all, a castle in good repair is not so bad. Warwick Castle is simply beautiful, from its solid gateway up the curved road, cut apparently out of rock, the walls rising several feet high on either side, covered sometimes with ivy, up to its inner gateway, through a long stone arch to the inner grounds and portal. This inner lawn, surrounded by stone walls, tower, castle and turrets, now clearly outlined, now half hidden by the trees and climbing ivy, is the loveliest thing ever seen. We are shown the state apartments in the castle. The first room, the great reception hall, pleases me the most, with its polished stone floor, a beadstead on wheels, and the great fireplace with huge logs of wood, ready for a fire when required. This room is full of armor, some of Cromwell's and Guy of Warwick's. It also has the great punch bowl, said to hold unbelievable gallons of punch. The other rooms are filled with pictures and presents from different parts of the world, and secret doors. The view from the windows is delightful, and includes the Avon. Leaving the castle proper, I walk across the lawn and climb "Guy's Tower," look at the country, and then flee to Leamington for my train. I arrive at Birmingham, take a hansom and drive around by the hour. Cabby walks his horse so I won't miss seeing anything. I remonstrate to some purpose. I dine at a "temperance" restaurant. No beer and no vegetables. No anything but chops and steaks. England has lots of habits of ancient uncivilized days yet.

SCOTLAND.

EDINBURGH, *August* 16*th*.—I arrived here after a long and tiresome night on the train, at 7:25 this morning. We passed Melrose at 6:25, and I ought to have got out and spent a couple of hours there; but I had not been able to find out whether we stopped there or whether another train would pass to-day, or whether I could see the Abbey on Sunday. Even if I had known all this, it would have been almost impossible for me to take advantage of my knowledge by stopping over one train. I was so nearly dead with fatigue, therefore I came on. Arrived at Edinburgh I kept up long enough to get a cup of chocolate and an egg, and then went to bed, not to sleep, but to rest. I took the Satchel Guide-book, my tickets and Bradshaw to bed with me, along with various maps. After three hours' study, I had worked out my arrivals and departures up to the final departure at Queenstown, just one week from to-day, and I've got to fly. I've concluded to stay over another day here, and go back to Melrose Abbey and see this place properly; then, after doing the Trossachs, I'll simply slide through Glasgow, and across the Channel to Belfast. By noon, having my programme all clear in my mind, and an incipient Bradshaw in my note-book, I permitted myself to sleep until three.

The guide-book study was an absolute necessity. I never saw such complete and dense ignorance on railroad matters in railroad people in my life. Cook's man, whose business is studying time tables, gave me the wrong ticket to a time table that did not match. The man in the ticket office of a central depot gets out a book and studies it before telling you when a train goes or arrives, and isn't sure then, but directs you to Cook's for information. Englishmen's stories about signs being posted everywhere conveying useful knowledge, all bosh.

No information to be had for love or money in England. The unhappy tourist travels at his own risk. No signs, no brakeman of stentorian voice, only one obliging guard, trying to be ever present at a dozen carriage doors at once, and making a great failure of it. English railroad management is the worst in the world. I have my doubts of Bradshaw, even.

England is the first place where I have had to study a Bradshaw. In every other place in the world but Austria I've only had to tell the porter of the hotel where I wanted to go, and he had the time table on the tip of his tongue. America is good enough for me. I like the comfortable cars of the Continent, the cheap cabs and hansoms, the ever ready porters and the careful handling of luggage in Europe. But I yearn to see the man at the depot put his head in the door, and shout in a voice that commands attention: "W-a-y train for Tenafly, Demarest, Closter," etc., and the brakeman open the car door and yell: "Passengers for Troy, et cetera, cha-nge cars; passengers for Albany please ke-ep their seats." I want to see some of those signs set along by the cars with the names of all stations to be stopped at. Give me America for explicit information. I want to see a crowded depot once more, too.

I rose just in time for dinner, where I sat with two Californian ladies, in unbroken silence until dessert, and then the younger lady could bear it no longer; she spoke to me, after which I did considerable talking. I tell her about my travels until her eyes are as big as saucers. It begins as usual:

"What steamer did you come over on?"

"I did not come over."

"Did not come over!"

"No, never crossed the Atlantic."

"And you're an American?"

"Yes." "How did you get here then, did you fly?" and then all comes out about my travels, and I am a wonder of absorbing interest again. I make friends so quickly, I am only sorry to have to separate from them so soon.

I went back to Melrose Abbey the next day, to see the old ruin which I found very fine and beautiful as a piece of architecture, but not knowing anything about architecture, I failed to see the extreme and excessive beauty my guide-book raves over. I like Kenilworth the best. My Satchel Guide also mentioned "Abbottsford," acquaintances talked of "Abbottsford," and carriage men agreed in favor of "Abbottsford." Finally I gave in to the general cry, and went to see this wonderful "Abbottsford," and very glad I was that I had done so. Abbottsford, the home of Sir Walter Scott, proved to be a very lovely place. The writer's rooms are kept just as he used them.

They are very pleasant rooms and filled with souvenirs of renowned men, curiosities from foreign lands, pictures of, and presents from, his friends and daughters. It was more interesting than a museum.

It was not until I had got out of the depot and was driving to the hotel, that I awoke to the fact that Edinburgh is a very beautiful place. It is a curious and quaint old city, remarkably clean as to streets, and built on hills and in valleys around a central hill where looms the castle, beneath whose granite walls spread a beautiful public park, into which all the hotels in the city seem to look. I think Edinburgh is the prettiest, most picturesque and cleanest city in the world, and so deliciously quaint and antique without being decayed. What a stronghold this castle, that sits up on the hilltop, must have been in olden time! No enemy could hope to scale the precipitous granite sides of that palisade. Holyrood is an interesting place, abbey and fortress too. Many beautiful monuments adorn the city. There is one to Mary, Queen of Scots, opposite Holyrood; an Albert memorial and monuments to Sir Walter Scott, Robert Burns and Lord Nelson. In a courtyard back of a church is the grave of Thomas Knox.

At Holyrood I saw the pictures of ancient Scots, among others, Macbeth, Malcom and Duncan, Robert Bruce and Douglas, also Mary Stuart, the lovely Queen of Scots. I went through Lord Darnley's rooms, saw the secret staircase, and climbed the other stair to Queen Mary's rooms. The rooms look bare and comfortless now, and far from suitable for a Queen, but they say she had them filled with rugs and lovely things.

After looking at the ruined abbey, I repaired to the Castle, that apparently impregnable fortress which overlooks the town from the top of a hill that rises direct, with unscalable granite sides, from the center of the city. After entering several gates, we cross a bridge over a moat and enter some more gates, and finally we reach the inner courtyard of the Castle. Our guide regales us at every step with tales of the betrayal of Douglas or Bruce. Within the Castle, we find again the rooms of Mary Stuart, cramped, bare and dingy. We go into the treasury and look at one lonely crown, a broach or so, and a scepter— pitiful array, after all the richness I have seen in Russia. But

I've seen no beggars or wretched houses, or miserable people in Scotland, so I don't find fault.

At five o'clock on the morning of August 18th, I arose and departed gaily for the Trossachs. After a tedious journey we arrived at Callendar. From Callendar we went to Lock Katrine by coach, through the lake on steamer, and then by coach again to a place on Lock Lomond, and then by train to Glasgow, eight changes in one day. The drivers on the coaches indicated the points of interest, and recited selections from "The Lady of the Lake."

I was rather disappointed in the Trossachs. I had been told in England I should see the loveliest scenery in the world. One who has spent his life in London, and judges from the standpoint of Ludgate Hill and Hyde Park, might well admire it, but to me, who have seen the grandest sights the world holds, it was the least pretty of any of the famous scenery. The Trossachs are low, bare and ungainly. The setting of the lake is too tame to be very beautiful. The lakes do not compare with the Italian lakes or those in Switzerland. Most of the scenery was very ordinary; prettier than the dry cornstalk plains of Ohio and Illinois, to be sure; very pretty in spots indeed, taken by themselves, but not pretty enough to "set the world on fire." Many of the places we were called upon to admire were long, low barren hills, without abruptness to make them picturesque, height to make them grand, or verdure to give them color. There is not much beauty to me in a gray, treeless slope. However, there were some pretty bits of greenness here and there, and an occasional strip of road under the trees that was delightful.

IRELAND.

Reaching Glasgow, I flew to Cook's adjacent office for information—information not to be got with any accuracy at the depot; then I remove myself and baggage to the proper depot, get some dinner, "take a walk around the block," and then wait patiently for my 10 P. M. train, for I propose to cross the Irish Channel this night. Really it does amuse me to see myself loafing around depots at all hours, changing cars at midnight, always calm and comfortable and safe. I put the most implicit confidence in porters and they take every care of me. No one ever molests me; people look at me curiously as I go about alone, but no one disturbs me. I have never had occasion to feel uneasy. I dreaded the trip across the Channel, but found on reaching the steamer that she was clean and most comfortably fitted up. I had the ladies' saloon all to myself and woke up on the Irish coast, after a perfectly smooth passage. Got into Belfast just in time to catch my 6:10 A. M. train to Portrush, thence by electric car to Giant's Causeway.

In transit from depot to depot in Belfast I made the acquaintance of the Irish car and driver. Car-driving is novel and interesting. The imminent prospect of finding yourself lying on the roadside at every corner lends an excitement to the drive that is positively enchanting. Irishmen are worse frauds than heathens. Indians and Arabs are bad enough, but an Irishman can "see" their grasping swindles and "go them several better." A stranger must pay four prices. The importunity to make useless purchases and give serviceless fees is dreadful—worse than Egypt or the East generally. One peculiar feature of the begging is that not a word is spoken. In the East you are assailed with the everlasting cry of "Backsheesh;" in Ireland you are followed by a silent horde for miles, who only smile at you persuasively. When coaching, while changing horses, the hostlers at the horses' heads implore us not to forget them.

But to return to the Giant's Causeway. I went as far as I could toward that place on the electric car on which everybody was deeply interested in our locomotive power, and promulgating all sorts of curious theories about its action and dangers,

Finally we reached the end of the railway, and took to the car again, the original "low-backed car." I made acquaintance here with a native of the country, a young girl of the better class, but oh! all classes seem to have the brogue and heaving, sprawling walk of an Irish washerwoman I used to have. They are pleasant and social, however.

I took a guide and boat, and went rowing along the coast and into the famous caves. Looking at it from above or below, there is nothing pretty, picturesque or interesting about the Giant's Causeway. There is a palisade of very ordinary height that looks like an organ, the bluff being composed of regular pillars of uniform size and varying length. You are told these pillars are known to be hundreds of feet in length, and no one knows how much more. At one point the pillars are curved as if they had once been softened and a heavy weight had bent them.

When, however, you go ashore and walk on the ends of these pillars, you begin to be surprised. You are climbing on steps formed of the cut off ends of hundreds of granite columns, standing wedged tightly in together, yet each distinct from the other, with acute sides that fit one against the other. There are octagons and all the other kinds of 'gons, and no two alike, and yet they fit each other perfectly and are as clean cut as if made by a sculptor. They arrange themselves in groups of eight; each stone is different in size and cut. How in the world they ever came there is unknown. They are presumed to be of volcanic formation. They look like so many angular pillars of stone cut out and stacked up together, like piles in a dock, to construct innumerable Greek temples and churches with. Their height is unknown, but as they are dug out they come off in sections, the upper end of each section being always concave and the lower end convex. They say there is a similar formation on the Scotch coast opposite. It is the most curious and unaccountable natural formation in the world.

At the hotel here we are asked what we will have with useless formality, for the bill of fare has been already decided on by the cook and there is no departing from it possible. One Englishman asks for duck, but comes down gracefully to boiled beef and cabbage. Returning to the cars I get a front seat on a very much overloaded coach to the electric railway. There are some drawbacks to this electric car. It stops at the end of the electric part of the road, a quarter of a mile from the depot, and can go no farther. The more independent steam engine is at the other end. We, the passengers, want to catch a train, so we walk this intervening space in hot haste. I get on the cars and am joined at a later depot by a lady and gentleman with the prettiest kind of a little girl. A neat coachman waits upon them and addresses the man as "My Lord." Good gracious! who am I traveling with now?

I reach Belfast at five P. M. and leave again on the train for Dublin at seven the following morning. A young man from Berlin shares the railway carriage with me. He has been to New York and likes it, and is astonished at my being alone; asks if he can assist me with my luggage, and is astonished again at my traveling so "light." Says his sister couldn't travel alone any more than she could fly, and when she does travel she fills the racks with her luggage. Says he himself never travels alone; would be afraid to travel without a servant. Agrees with me, however, that the servant has to be looked after and is a nuisance generally.

I reach Dublin at last, get a car-man to drive me about Phœnix Park, see the spot where Lord Cavendish was murdered; drive to the King's Bridge depot, get some dinner and am off again on the cars for Killarney. I don't want to stay in any Irish city long. They are more unpleasant than Bergen in Norway; they are so dirty and poverty stricken. My drive to Phœnix Park was through drove after drove of cattle, a cattle market being situated near the park. On the train to Killarney I meet a fat old Irish woman who loves to travel, has been all over Europe and is delighted with my journey. I do nothing but tell my travels; everybody is curious about me, seeing me alone, and I tell my story with a good deal of frankness and pride as I am questioned. I change cars at Mallow.

While waiting on the platform I see the beautiful Irish girl. Many are the heretical remarks I have read about Dion Boucicault's lovely Irish girl; but here she is a living fact, lovely as can be, a raving beauty; black, wavy hair, great dark eyes, delicate mouth and fresh, clear skin. I can't take my eyes off her. I walk around her and take up a position against a pillar to get a better view of her sweet face as she chats with a friend. Three or four young men, fascinated like me, notice my movement and laugh and comment among themselves on the curiosity of one woman admiring another. I tear myself away from the beautiful creature and proceed on to Killarney, where I arrive at 9:30 P. M.; am taken in a hotel bus and driven some miles, it seems to me, into the country before reaching the hotel. I begin to think they mean to take me on to Glengarif when they finally draw up. Now, I've reached the stamping ground of the tourist. The house is filled; the piano is in full blast.

If I am going to sail on the Servia, I've not a day to lose. I need not sail on the lakes, for I find I can see all from the vantage point of the upper deck of a stage coach en route for Glengarif fortunately. Killarney was very pretty, and the drive to Glengarif, and Glengarif itself likewise, prettier than the Trossachs, I think, but still not a "patch" on the beautiful places I've seen. Ireland and Scotland are very tame after the Straits of Magellan, interior mountainous Japan, the Himalayas, Italian lakes, beautiful Switzerland and Norway, not to mention Ceylon and Java.

Upon the stage coach I was seated amongst a Scotch family, a girl beside me, her young brother opposite, and father and uncle alongside. And they prove to be most delightful companions. Never have I had a more intelligently interested audience. They knew something of each country as I spoke of them. They questioned me and drew me out and were delighted with my voyages. They had a keen sense of humor and were convulsed with extracts from Mark Twain, whom they have read in part and enjoyed. I entertained them all the way, and was finally sorry to part with them at the hotel, which was full.

I had to go to the next, not having taken the precaution to telegraph my arrival. The girl invited me most cordially to stay with her. They shook hands with me all around and told me to be sure and come back to them, if I could not get other accommodations. The other hotel not only took me in, but turned out to be the best. I rushed headlong into an acquaintance with a young Englishman who sat next to me, who had been to South Africa (I want to go to South Africa, too). Young man's mother hovered near protectively but pleasantly.

At half-past six in the morning the coach comes along with my Scotch friends, and I climb up to a seat beside them and we fly merrily along to Bantry, where we take the train for Cork.

We reach Cork at eleven, put our baggage in the luggage room and start off. My Scotch friends and I go to Blarney Castle in a car. It's not particularly worth the finding, but we religiously hunt up the blarney stone and then return to Cork. The ride is quite pretty. My Scotch friends are about sailing for their home, Glasgow, from Cork, their short vacation tour being just ended as my long one is. For once I am the one who stands on the wharf and waves good-by to departing friends. They rank with the nicest people I have met. I liked them, and they liked me, and a few hours together had developed a strong friendship. I discovered the girl was a step-daughter of the man, and he must be the exceptional step-father that proves the rule of bad ones, for there are few real fathers as good and uniformly genial and indulgent as this man was to the children of his dead wife who had no claim of blood relationship on him. I have a particular admiration, anyway, for a man who takes a couple of young people off on a vacation tour with him, instead of going off with some boon companions to have a good time by himself; and finds his enjoyment, too, in the innocent, harmless pleasure suited to their years and sex. I have heard a lot about Scotch thrift and closeness, but there was no closeness visible here. They were as generous and whole-souled a set as our frank-hearted, open-handed Californians—a bright, intelligent, well-informed, witty and united family. Vive la Scot!

After seeing my friends off, I find my proper depot, get my baggage transferred by a good-looking Irish boy, get something to eat at an adjacent hotel, and take the train for Queenstown. My last trip on this side of the Atlantic. I reach Queenstown, get a boy to convey my baggage to the hotel, which is close at hand, and here I spend my last night in this old country!

HOMEWARD.

I have had lovely weather in Ireland and Scotland, and now the eventful, long expected morning of the 23d of August dawns brighter and clearer than ever. The Servia is lying at anchor in the bay. I walk down to the steam launch that is to take me off. Some hundreds of passengers are just discharging themselves from her with a view to getting a glimpse of Ireland before the next and last tug goes off. And Queenstown is a very pretty place. The houses on the abrupt coast overlooking the bay appear to be built on top of one another. Presently I am on board the Servia. My stateroom proves better than I anticipated; my luggage is all on hand and in good order. Having satisfied myself on these points I return to the deck to take my last look at the "old country," which, while I have enjoyed it very much, I am only too happy to be leaving.

And now I am at sea and it is the 25th of August. I have seen my last sight, changed cars for the last time, left the last hotel, and am rapidly and surely approaching the end of this long and pleasant voyage of mine. My stateroom is comfortable, my room mate fair, fat, French, perhaps not forty, but along there, good natured and sensible. My table friends are an elderly couple who are distinctively American, bright and interesting. I have recognized among the people the three girls I encountered between Naples and Pompeii and the Englishman I sat with two days on the box seat of the stage coach coming out of the Yosemite Valley more than a year ago. The weather is fine, sea smooth, decks crowded. I am quite charmed with the friends I have made. We sit together on deck and play chess and whist in the evening, winding up the entertainment with a Welch rarebit and beer. The lady adores Bret Harte as I do, and is literary and Bohemian in her tastes. My room mate says everybody exclaims when she points me out: "Why, she is only a young girl."

We are on the "banks." The weather is excessively disagreeable, rainy and chilly. The rough shoal seas here are beginning to make a little impression on the great steamer.

Still she is the steadiest steamer I ever traveled on. She is so crowded, however, that there is no place to be comfortable in. Rows on rows of chairs on deck make walking a disjointed and hazardous undertaking. Even now, in this bad weather, there is no alternative for many of the passengers between the wet, comfortless deck and the narrow compass of their staterooms.

My heart reverts with many a pleasant recollection from this last to the first steamer voyage of my world's tour, to that beautiful "Social hall," with its lovely gray velvet cushions and brocaded curtains; with its four comfortable corners for the four passengers during that first week of storm, to the beautiful succeeding days in the tropical seas; and the jolly six at table, all bent on having a pleasant time; to the evenings on deck or in the "Social hall," where we told stories while we held on to the cushions tooth and nail, and braced ourselves for coming rolls.

AT HOME, *September 1st.*—The last day or two on board ship were at once delightful and anxious. I had no more time to write or think. My Californian acquaintance and I renewed our friendship. He introduced me to several pleasant Englishmen. An American clergyman had also become deeply interested in my singular voyage. I talked straight through the last three days. The night before we sighted America the success of the book they said I must write, and all of my future enterprises was drank in champagne by my friends. Yesterday afternoon as we neared New York, I was so absorbed in looking for familiar landmarks that I nearly missed my dinner.

Nearly at the end of our voyage, it was my turn to be anxious and in a hurry; it was my turn to look excitedly for a familiar coast and point out objects of interest to foreigners. We had passed Fire Island, Sandy Hook, Rockaway, where still loomed up the grand "Rockaway Hotel," and beyond lay Coney Island, with the Observatory traced delicately against the slowly darkening sky; and presently the lamps shone out as we approached the Narrows, and Coney Island was a glittering belt. On we came, up through the Narrows and then we dropped anchor for the night. It was too late for the health officers, and too dark to see anything but the shore lights and the Coney Island boats, brilliant with electric lights as they went by. So we calmly went below and retired for the last time into the little staterooms, to sleep, despite the noisy preparations for to-morrow's unloading.

I rose at an early hour and went on deck full of expectancy, to see that face first that I saw last when I sailed out of, instead of into, this harbor nineteen months ago; to receive the welcome home and the shock of an unexpected bereavement; to say good-bys to the many pleasant friends; to receive congratulations; to pass tediously through the last Custom House, and then to drive home, arriving there not as I had expected to do, in unalloyed joy at being home again, but in tears for the absence of the cheering welcome of the father who has passed behind the dark curtain of death, the knowledge of which has only reached me to-day.

And thus ended, though in tears, still successfully, my long, long journey around the world.

THE UNITED STATES.

After seeing many other countries, I desired to know more of my own.

While I have found so much that is comfortable, charming and interesting, in other lands, the results of my observations in this one have filled me with patriotism and pride. America is new, undeniably new. It hasn't any ruined castles, but it has some of the finest scenery in the world; and our traveling accommodations are unequaled on the globe. Charles Dickens and other English writers have criticised us severely, and their criticisms were not undeserved; but America is pre-eminently a land of progress, and the improvement of even a few years is almost marvelous. In the comfort and conveniences of living as well as of traveling we now excel every other nation.

Leaving New York early in June, skirting the banks of the majestic Hudson, rushing through the valley of the Mohawk and gliding along the shore of Lake Erie, and across the plains of southern Michigan, I reach Chicago. It is a handsome city, with fine broad avenues lined with great houses of stone and iron, looming up toward the sky. A drive discloses many beautiful residences. Most artistically laid out in drives and lawns, decorated with flowers and foliage, is Chicago's beautiful park, skirted by Lake Michigan, which lies gray and glittering under the sun, stretching out beyond the reach of the eye. Altogether, Chicago is a bright and pleasant place in which to rest before proceeding westward.

Once on the train again, there is little to lure the traveler between Chicago and Denver. If you travel from choice and not from necessity, you are as glad to be on the road again as you were to rest a day, for to the born traveler there is nothing quite so satisfactory as motion. When the train moves out of the depot, or the steamer leaves her wharf, then is such a person truly happy, whether just arranging the small baggage in the seats of the sleeper, or sniffing the fresh breeze of the sea from the vessel's deck.

On, across the broad, red, muddy Mississippi River, through Iowa, where "it is so wet that a man can't live any more than a year or two without getting web footed;" across the equally red and muddy Missouri and through Nebraska, where the "grasshoppers are so thick that they stop the cars," to Colorado, and the outline of the Rocky Mountains emerges from the horizon in the distance, looking like the puckered-up edge of pie crust bounding this broad, undulating, pie-like plain.

Travelers are frequently disappointed in the appearance of the far-famed "Rockies." Seen from across the great plains their dim outlines are not imposing. Distance and perspective reduce them to mere foothills, and it is not until near and among them that you are impressed by their height and grandeur.

From Chicago to Denver was once a territory of cornstalks and barren plains. But with the advance of immigration and civilization it has become a pretty and fertile country. Where once were endless fields of unromantic cornstalks are now green banks and pretty villages. The cornstalks have gone further West to "grow up with the country." Even the plains that were once bare and desolate are now carpeted with green and bright with wild flowers, among which plump, rabbit-like little prairie dogs disport.

Denver is pretty. The city is scattered loosely about instead of being compactly built, and therefore spreads itself over a wide expanse of territory. The streets are broad, and cost but little to keep in order, as they remain hard and smooth without paving because of a peculiar quality of the soil.

Leaving Denver in the morning, three hours brings us, via the Denver and Rio Grande Railroad, into the Rocky Mountains, passing Castle Rock and Palmer Lake, and stopping at Colorado Springs, where there are many beautiful drives and several springs to visit. The roads all about are smooth and hard, and the teams at the stables very good. Manitou is within easy driving distance, although one can go there by rail.

At Manitou are iron and soda springs. It is a strictly temperance place. There is a sign on a refreshment house there which is almost as pathetic as it is honest. It reads thus: "Barley water and bad cigars." Another sign on the outside of a canvas tent where candy is sold reads: "Ice cream Parlor," which seems to describe it rather extravagantly to say the least.

The drives leading up into the narrow cañons and through Monument Park are very fine. Monument Park is a plateau with groups of large rocks and perpendicular slabs of granite of grotesque shape standing upon it. The Garden of the Gods is similar, the great chunks of granite bearing peculiar resemblances that give them names such as the "Bear and the Seal" and the "Lady of the Cañon." Most of the rock is of a deep red and yellow sandstone.

The cañons are exceedingly beautiful. Driving into them, the walls grow higher and steeper, and you seem to have reached the end of the road constantly as the walls close in before you; but, as in the Italian lakes and the Norwegian fiords, it opens up as you approach, showing another stretch of cañon still narrower and still grander.

Leaving Colorado Springs, all one's anticipation is centered on the glorious scenery we are soon to pass through. For the Denver and Rio Grande possesses the great attraction of running directly through the finest part of the Colorado scenery. But it is still several hours off, and I have leisure to observe my fellow passengers.

In the opposite seat of my section sat the Pullman conductor—a gentle young Eastern fledgling, apparently consumptive, hoping for restored health from the bracing Colorado air. In the section opposite a bright, intelligent, handsome woman, who is going to visit a Mormon lady—a sixth wife—at Salt Lake. Opposite her is an extremely long, pale, crushed-strawberry haired young man, who is contemplating with much dissatisfaction the limits of the panels above him, which are to form the under crust of the niche he is destined to fill to overflowing this night. The next section contains an elderly woman and her daughter, a well-developed girl of exceedingly blonde complexion and brown eyes of most curious expression. Behind them a very disagreeable old man who had secured a whole section and was obliged to give part of it up to an old lady who happened to know him, of which piece of generosity he babbles endlessly. A woman and a boy are in the next section. Behind me an Englishman and his wife. He is of conspicuously sporting aspect—a pugilist, I should say. But, oh! where are those Englishmen who said Americans abroad were such "bad form?" Our deepest, wildest wilderness cannot produce anything so grotesquely glaring as this pair, their appearance and their dress. Behind them a little married couple of the purest American type. On the other side a woman with her boy, both seasick. Next a family of grown folks and children, one a tiny girl with laughing, dimpled face, and the sweetest blue eyes in the world. Besides the stationary people are a floating element of two women and a boy, who had insisted on traveling on the car, although there were no vacant berths to be allotted to them until midnight, and were growling about it. They came and occupied my section for awhile, and with something of an air of humor ran down the road and management, while the fledgling conductor sat and listened with an occasional gleam of comprehension in his dark consumptive eyes.

The fixed idea of sleeping car travelers seems to be that they all ought to be supplied with lower berths. As half of the berths obstinately insist on being upper, there is great dissatisfaction if the car is more than half full. These women particularly had the most rooted objection to upper berths, and an inexpugnable belief that the conductor ought to go through the car and see if there was a single unfortunate man in possession of a lower berth, and if so evict him at once for their benefit.

It has been my misfortune to meet some women who seem to think that a man has no kind of human right as against their selfish fancies. To me there is nothing lovelier than the generous courtesy extended by the stronger sex to, may I say, the finer? But if there is one sight to me more mortifying than another it is woman arrogating to herself such unselfish courtesy as a right. This was the kind of women these two were. After they had worn the berth question threadbare, they fell upon each other and quarreled and taunted and teased, with exterior good humor, howbeit, and only a gleam now and then of the real bad temper underneath.

One of these women was a type I have seen more than once. She had a handsome, placid face and an outer air of amiability that had earned for her the reputation of good nature and unselfishness. But beneath she was pure egotist, a selfish and uncharitable cynic. Sitting there next her, hour after hour, and hearing her cool, caustic replies to her friend and seeing her glance of utter ill-humor, I knew her to be a woman that I should hate with fierce, undying hatred should I be obliged to see much of her.

How confidential people grow after thirty-six hours in a Pullman car. And how one will be drawn into frank acquaintanceship after enjoying for twenty-four hours that solitude only to be found in a crowd. A young girl was just describing to me the exact kind of man she wanted to marry and the particular amount of affection she should require from him, when, as her tones grew obliviously loud with her intense interest in the subject, I glanced at the fragile young conductor and caught him twisting his face in an agonizing effort to crush a laugh that was struggling for utterance. He was looking the other way, and even after I said, "He has heard every word," and the girl was disowning every sentiment expressed as fast as she could, he made a brave effort to drive the laugh back. But it was no use; he broke down under my scrutiny, and laughed it out and confessed.

Way up in the mountains there we observed a curious formation of cones of clear sand, large and small. The small ones are supposed to have been made by ants, the larger ones by whirlwinds. The formations are precisely the same in appearance, only varying in size.

After circulating around the outskirts of the Rockies for a while, our train plunged directly in among them, and presently we entered the Grand Cañon of the Arkansas. And very grand we found it, this long, deep, winding crevice in the earth, whose walls of red and yellow sandstone stretch up perpendicularly 2,000 feet toward the sky, that is but a strip of blue above us. The train does not run very fast here, and they might run slower and still not displease the passengers. As it is, we try to look above, behind, before and below us all at once, in the vain effort to catch the complete picture. The Royal Gorge is the narrowest part of this cañon, but all of the long, sinuous cañon is so beautiful it is hard to distinguish one part of it as finer than another. As magnificent as the scenery is, there is nothing to make one nervous about it. As we look up to the top of those grim walls of stone we are much better pleased to be running smoothly along at their feet, beside the winding river, than to be standing up at the top there looking down. The road through here is one of the greatest triumphs of civil engineering in the world.

Later on we take to climbing. Around about and up the mountains we go, at the steepest of grades, now shooting into a snowshed for a little, then out again and around and about, higher and higher, looking below us at the track recently traversed and across the valley high above at the track we are expected to get around to presently ; and we do, gliding around the muleshoe curve and on to the top of Marshall Pass. Looking back we see four lines of roads, sections of the spiral we have just ascended.

But the finest picture of all is to come, and many are the lamentations because we are to pass the grandest part of the road, the Black Cañon, at night. It is 11 P. M. when we enter this famous cañon. The moon is full, however, and shining brightly down into the dark chasm, lending a weird charm to the scene, touching the prominent peaks with silver light and making the deep, dark corners gloomier by contrast, while the rushing Gunnison River glitters brightly under its rays as it rolls turbulently on. The cañon is very narrow, the walls looming up grandly, sometimes shelving over the train. Our way is very winding. We cross and recross the roaring river several times, dashing from one side to the other on iron trestle bridges and around curves, with an ever changing picture of solemn grandeur about us. Great walls of granite looming above us ; falls tumbling down them to the already riotous river below, and then before us rises a mighty monument of stone, a cone of solid granite pointing to the sky—the famous Curricanti Needle.

We leave the Gunnison River to go plunging down the Black Cañon, following up the Cimarron Creek which has added its waters to the Gunnison, and presently we are out of the mountains and speeding across a vast verdureless, billowy plain, hedged around with sharply cut cliffs.

Next morning we find ourselves running through the great Utah Desert, which is bounded by a range of cliffs cut sharply and ridged and guttered as if with rushing water. The sand looks baked and cracked, and is here and there swept up in ridges and hummocks and cones as if by whirlwinds. It has the appearance of having once been a sea.

We see the azure cliffs, and later, Castle Gate, as the two great sandstone pillars guarding the entrance to Price River Cañon are called, and we are in the heart of the Wahsatch Mountains. Having crossed them, we speed again across level plains, bare but for cactus, and the rest of the trip to Salt Lake is marked only by fatigue and dust.

At Salt Lake City, a young married couple and myself, strangers until then, joined forces and took an open tourist car for the beach, to bathe in the Great Salt Lake.

Of course we were on the lookout for Mormons, and eyed with suspicion any man who was accompanied by more than one woman, quite forgetful of the fact that we were two young women with one unfortunate young man between us, and therefore, by the same rule, clearly Mormons. But for the most part we saw women and children together, and a few men and young boys. Two boys behind me were telling of an acquaintance's second marriage, and how the first wife had taken it, and the progression of another courtship, and whether "she" cared anything about "him" or not. Two women and three children sat in front of me, a similar family in front of them, and again in front women and children of one family. Behind me were three women with children, and further back two seats were occupied with a large party of women and children, judging by their sociability, of two different families. There was little talk; all the light chatter and sociability that should naturally distinguish such a pleasure trip to the shore were absent. To us, who had only gone on such excursions with friends and for a social outing, there was sadness in the inertness and silence of these people.

The women were clad in calico, and their relative positions in the family scale were marked by some extra bit of finery. For instance one wore a bright new bonnet, while that of her sister wife's was shabby; another wore a faded common shawl, while the younger wife had a pretty new zephyr wrap that contrasted strangely with her coarse dress. And they were all men and women of a coarser fiber than any Caucasian people I had met outside of Utah, and apparently lower in the scale of humanity. In the women is seen the coarseness of undeveloped intelligence, of eternal drudgery, bearing the impress of writhing hearts out of which rebellion and morality had been all but crushed. Their hands were rough and hard with labor. They are not unkind to each other, these woman; there was a consideration for each other that was apparently natural and reciprocal, as of fellow sufferers under the same immutable law.

Over and over again I heard one woman say to another whose child had got mixed up with hers, "Do you want Ella with you?" And the answer being usually "yes," the child was passed over to its own mother. In this way the children were kept separate while together. Never were more pitiful sights of union and disunion, never sadder examples of crushed and broken womanhood.

I have seen poor and hard working people out for a day's pleasure in many countries; and no people perhaps enjoy their rare picnic or holiday as do the poorest and hardest worked people. But here, in Utah, was none of that boisterous and rude humor that naturally distinguishes their uncultivated ideas of pleasure. There were no heavy jokes, no clumsy chaffing, no laughter, no spontaneous conversation or pleasure in the society of one with the other; all was dead and lifeless, and overhung with the gloom of sorrow and hard work.

The whole life here is to me inconceivably sad. The families of women and children living and going about together with hearts and souls crushed and necessarily asunder; the homes with two front doors; the rows of from two to five or six, perhaps more houses together; the porches with one man and two women resting in them in the cool of the day, silent and distrait; the double house, with a woman sad and lonely on one porch, while her husband, with the other wife, is laughing and chatting on the other.

And yet, reflecting on these rows of houses, the building of each addition of which has wrung some woman's heart, I thought after all what better are we than they? This is bad enough and sad enough, and the United States certainly ought to interfere in behalf of these women as it did in behalf of those other slaves of darker skin once held and tortured in this free country.

But is Utah the only place in this great country of ours where polygamy is practiced? Is this the only spot where men maintained marriage relations with several women at one time? Is Salt Lake City the only one where women's hearts are broken? It is bad enough here, God knows, but there is a redeeming feature. There are no drunken, reckless, cast-off women, sacrificed, crushed, wholly depraved and scorned and scoffed at and despised by the fortunate few who enjoy comfort and protection, and good names. Here all names are good, and if there be any immorality, as I think, and depravity, they are all situated alike on an equal basis, and none can flout her sister women for possessing less virtue than herself.

To me it is all sad and demoralizing. The life together of many wives of one man is necessarily so. It must be the death of delicacy and of the finer emotions and sentiments. It is degrading to the women and demoralizing to the men, as any condition of master and slaves must always be, and in Utah the sex relation is reduced to that, obedience and resignation to suffering being the leading features of the religious teaching of the women.

To be sure, the situation of these women lacks that degrading monetary consideration which destroys the self-respect and reduces to the gutter our unfortunate women. In Utah every woman works hard to support herself and children and enhance her husband's means. Their symbol of the beehive is a good one, only the drones are masculine, and it is the women who work busily making honey for his kingship. Yes, I'd like to have an end put to the iniquities of Utah. I would like to have an end put to similar iniquities all over the world. "They are against the law?" Are they? Yes, but how often is the law enforced? Oh, yes, it is against the law to marry more than one woman, but a man may mislead and desert and send to death and destruction a dozen unhappy girls with impunity. The law doesn't care how many girls are ruined; all it is particular about is that a few words of legal or religious sanction shall not be said over more than one of them with the same man.

In Utah they only destroy happiness and moral perception, in our States they blight the character, and ruin the future lives as well. In Utah women have the consolation, if consolation it is, of believing that they are fulfilling the divine instruction, and while they suffer here they have hopes of a heaven hereafter. Our unfortunates not only suffer here and become outcasts, but they are doomed to eternal perdition after this life. It is a question after all which system results in the most suffering. Our social system preserves the fairest exterior, certainly, but ah, how many aching hearts are hidden beneath, and how much deeper is the degradation of our degraded. Had we not better, while we are pressing the Mormons of Utah to the wall, purge the Mormonism that exists in the "States," and which exists in the more distressing form because it is without the Mormons' religion and without their principle? I think we had.

However, we were on our way to take a bath in the Great Salt Lake, that mysterious inland sea that apparently has neither source nor outlet. Our little train ran across some sandy flats for an hour before we reached the beach, where we found bathing houses and suits. The bath fully realized our anticipations. The water was a little chilly, but so heavy with salt that one floats on the top rather too easily; it is hard work to keep under enough to swim. This makes the bathing delightful to timid people. One has not that sensation of sinking, and confidence is easy to have in a sea that insists on your remaining on the top of it. One needs to be careful not to get any water in one's eyes or mouth, for it hurts the eyes and strangles in the throat.

An hour's ride brought us back again to the hotel, where we found something to quiet the tremendous appetite the bath had awakened. In the morning we found it was a race day, and that therefore there was not a carriage to be had. We were consoled, however, when we found the Mormon Temple and Tabernacle, the Beehive and other interesting sights were within easy walking distance. Salt Lake City seems a pleasant one to live in. Even those Gentiles who are loudest in their denunciation of the Mormons speak in the highest terms of the attractiveness of their city as a place of residence. The streets are broad and bright, the climate pleasant.

The Mormon Tabernacle, a most curious oblong and squat building, is especially famous for its acoustic properties, these being so perfect a pin's fall at one end can be heard distinctly at the other extreme of the great building that holds five thousand people. We tested this to our entire satisfaction. The speaker in the pulpit can be heard perfectly in any part of the house without raising the voice above a natural conversational tone. The Tabernacle contains an organ of which they are very proud, otherwise it is a very plain and simple building. There is an allegorical picture or two painted on the walls representing the finding of the revelation by Joseph Smith, and other incidents in the history of their religious belief.

The new temple, still in process of construction, looms tall and massive beside the Tabernacle. It is not to be a hall for preaching, being divided into many chambers, where special and sacred ceremonies may be solemnized. The Endowment House is near at hand, but is closed. Rather the prettiest of the three buildings in Temple Square is the Assembly Hall, though it is not as large as the others. Its hall for preaching is cozier than the Tabernacle, and here, too, are an organ, the emblematic beehive and allegorical pictures.

From Temple Square we walk down the street, past the erstwhile residence of Brigham Young, to the great arch called the Tithing Gate, through which all produce passes and a tenth part is taken. On the top of the arch is the symbolic beehive. An eagle is standing on it and clutching it with its strong talons, which is just about what the American Eagle is up to now in sad reality. Opposite Bingham Young's we see President Taylor's residence, a fine new mansion with two front doors. The number of front doors in the houses are replete with sad suggestion to the visitor of families that live in anything but unison. And so we rove about the city, until it is time to pack up our traps and resume our journey.

Leaving Salt Lake City, we encounter the gentlemanly Pullman conductor of the Denver and Rio Grande Railroad, who kindly takes me in charge and sees us to our cars on the Central Pacific Railroad, where I am in for another long night and day. My two friends leave me in the morning, and then I fall to making new acquaintances. A bright, breezy, slangy young American starts the ball a rolling by giving me an orange. A great burly, gruff farmer seconds his motion by also giving me an orange. Another American, a "drummer," with a nose suggestive of cocktails, also gives me an orange, and still another gentleman, rather handsomer and better bred than the rest, cultivates me through the medium of a proffered orange. The drummer takes me out on the back platform, where I enjoy myself in the cool air, until I discover I am keeping the gentlemen shut in the smoking room, so delicate are they about disturbing me, when I retire. Thereafter they take turns in dropping into the seat near me for a few moments and chatting and lending me books. We were crossing barren alkali plains until near night, and I heard a great deal about the richness of this, seemingly worthless, land under irrigation.

Toward night we stopped at one little dry-goods box of a depot, about which were a few wigwams, the Indian proprietors of which came to the train and endeavored to establish themselves on a friendly footing with the passengers. The men, robed in old blue army coats and pants, with ancient black plug hats on their untidy black heads, do not suggest the dime novel brave of our childish fancy. The women look more like, with their blankets wrapped closely about them, and their pappooses strapped in approved Indian fashion on flat pieces of wood first, and then to the mother's back, where they are truly as solemn and unblinking as they have the reputation of being.

Neither men nor women had the stolid faces I had been taught to believe. Both were, on the contrary, very smiling and persuasive, not begging openly, but showing their babies and beads and volunteering information and evidently hoping to be given something in return for these courtesies. One woman did, I believe, venture a suggestion about the usefulness of ten cents. Their voices struck me as rather musical and pleasant..

There were several other ladies in the car who carried their lunch baskets, so I was the only one to go out at the dining stations, consequently I was filled with dismay when, after an early breakfast, I learned that we were not to stop for dinner until 3 P. M. (in spite of the oranges). After stopping at one place for about five minutes the slangy young man came in and shouted to another man, "That was a splendid lunch!" "Lunch!" I said with the deepest reproach, "Oh, why didn't you mention it sooner?" And then I laughed, for the sincere distress on the young man's face was too much for me. I want to say it again, and I say it boldly, the American man, be he educated or otherwise, refined or coarse, dissipated or religious, has, as a rule, the most perfectly gentlemanly manner toward women. Sometimes it would seem that the rougher and more reckless types preserve the deeper sense of respect and consideration due to ladies. Many times I have been struck by the exceeding delicacy in the courtesy of a dissolute, one might think unprincipled, man. Often I have been touched by the gentle consideration of men I had rather not come in contact with at all, much less socially.

One of the pleasant features about the politeness of American men whom one meets in traveling is its entire disinterestedness. They pay many little considerate attentions to a woman who is alone, not to open an acquaintance with her, but merely out of manly sympathy and kindliness. The entire disinterestedness is shown by the forbearance to press an acquaintance on a lady which his politeness to her would prevent her declining if she choose. It was in this kindly manner that these gentlemen did all they could to make me comfortable, and then left me to rest in peace.

At Truckee the hotel is supposed to be very bad, but to me badness in hotels, as in people, is purely relative. I've put up at worse hotels than that at Truckee and I've stopped at better ones. The best thing one can do in traveling is to carry one's comfortableness along with them in one's satchel or shawl strap, as much as they will hold, the rest in one's heart.

In the morning at seven I took the coach for Lake Tahoe, the first bit of staging for me in two years, and I was very happy when I found myself once more on the box seat with the driver. The sun was straight in my eyes all the way; but what of that? The air was fresh and the country about was green and beautiful. So rich in color after those arid deserts of cactus and alkali! Colorado is beautiful, but Colorado is not rich with luxuriant verdure as is California. Had we not all noticed the difference the night before as soon as we left the plains of Utah?

The drive from Truckee to Tahoe City is but fourteen miles, just the thing for Eastern tourists to take before going to the Yosemite as a sample of that style of travel. Short enough for women and children and invalids to bear comfortably and long enough to enjoy. The road runs along the Truckee River and is picturesque and pleasant; the rich green about us contrasting strangely with the snow on the mountain tops. The coach drops you at a pleasant hotel, directly below which is a wharf from which a little steamer will take you across the lake.

The lake itself is very beautiful, imbedded in the mountains like a sapphire, so blue is it, but they are destroying the beauty of the hills about by cutting the timber. This is a great mistake, I think. Tahoe should become the property of the State, as the Yosemite is, and be preserved as it and the big tree groves are from spoliation or defacement, for the benefit of California and her visitors. One day Tahoe should be a popular Summer resort. It could easily be made but twelve hours' journey from San Francisco, and the trip takes one through some of the finest scenery of California in crossing the Sierra Nevada range of mountains.

But one does not appreciate the special beauty of the lake until one goes out upon it. Sailing on its smooth surface one would think it is plate glass we are gliding across and not water at all. It would seem impossible that water could be so clear. But water it is, pure mountain snow water. The clearest crystal glass is the only simile possible. At a depth of over ten feet the bottom is as distinct before your eyes, with every bit of rock or moss, and every tiny fish, as if you were looking into a shallow case with a crystal cover. It is one of the things that must be seen to be appreciated. Sailing on the unruffled crystal bosom of Tahoe is one of the surprises this world holds for wonder seekers. Fishing is not very successful in the lake, although trout may be caught in adjacent mountain streams. The lake is far too clear, the fish waft themselves about and look up at you and observe all your preparations for their discomfiture. They swim around your bait idly and then smile audibly as they lazily swim away in search of safer food.

Near the shore, at a depth of six feet, I saw a small fish playing with a smaller dead fish on the bottom of the lake, very much as a cat plays with a mouse. It caught sight of it, rushed at it, bit it and shook it for a little and then swam away, investigated a piece of tin, returned with a rush and bit the fish again, swam off around a bunch of moss and returned and gave it another nip, went and buried its head in the moss and waited and returned again, and so it swam around and pretended to go or to be indifferent, or deeply absorbed in something else, but always returning to worry the little, dead fish.

As I preferred to cross the Sierras by daylight I took the early morning train for San Francisco.

It was not very long before we struck the snow sheds, of which there are forty miles. We saw Donner Lake en passant through occasional gaps in the sheds left for the tourists' benefit. Donner Lake is too beautiful a spot to be allied forever to so sad a history as that of the unfortunate Donner party who were lost in the snow here, suffering starvation and its concomitant horrors, and many of them death, before relief came.

From the open spaces one catches many a charming view, now across and now down the full length of the lake, as we circle up the mountain side. It lies there deep in the mountains placid and silent with the green and wooded slopes rising up from it, beyond which rise again other mountains, whose tops are still clad in snow. As we rise higher we see patches of snow now and then near our track. At many of the stations the snow sheds still cover us. Forty miles of snow sheds is a good deal, indeed one is heartily sick of them before one is half through, and to some people the flickering of the bright light through the cracks of the sheds is very tiresome to the eyes. The sheds are, however, a necessity out here where the snow falls so deep and so frequently.

Having fairly crossed the summit, however, we are rid of them at last, and can see all the beauties of the warm, sunny side of the Sierras as we descend. Here again the scenery is grandly beautiful, but different from the beautiful cañons of Colorado. Here it is richer and greener and more open, it would seem, for we ride at the top of it instead of at the bottom. Winding around steep mountain sides, where we can look deep down in the green valleys and across at wooded slopes, rising again toward the sky, and ever and again in the distance some peaks of snow, until at last we round "Cape Horn," the sharpest curve with the deepest and most precipitous sides on the line.

This Cape Horn is, however, far more easily rounded than that other Cape Horn that reaches down into the Antarctic Ocean, the dangers of which I encountered in making my first voyage to California. They comfort one by saying this spot was once very dangerous, but it has been improved until the delightful spice that probable and imminent annihilation gives has left it. It is as dissatisfying as would be doubling the Antarctic Cape, with the sea, ordinarily so soul-inspiringly stormy, as smooth as a mill pond. I know I should have cherished the deepest feelings of animosity toward the Santa Rosa and her amiable captain if it had not been for our luck in striking a hurricane off Cape Pillar.

As we descend valleyward it grows warmer momentarily, until at Sacramento we find the weather excessively hot. But for the luscious peaches that were handed through the car windows to us by venders at the depots we should have been more tired, hungry and thirsty than we were. We get a parlor car here, and though it is still very hot, one catches the passing air through the great open windows as we sit at ease in the comfortable revolving chairs, and by and by we catch the cool salt breeze from the coast, and then the train is taken bodily on a boat, and carried down and across the broad Sacramento River, and a little later one finds it cool enough for an extra wrap, and then after the rapid, thorough and successive dusting of the passengers the porter announces Oakland ferry, as the wind comes tearing across the bay and through the car.

Nowhere in all the world have they such luxurious ferry-boats as these. Our Eastern ones are fine and substantial, but here they add the luxury of carpets and velvet upholstered sofas, and a great plate glass rounded front to the saloon so one may look ahead from that comfortable place.

And then, San Francisco, as ridiculous in grand hotels and shabby wooden houses, broad avenues with perfectly conducted cable cars and absurd climate, as ever.

I'm sure the hotel is full of fleas just waiting to devour the unwary strangers, and yet—I love San Francisco, absurd climate, fleas and all.

It is almost two years since I sailed away from San Francisco, westward, for Japan; and now, having made the circuit of the globe, I reënter the city from the east.

YOSEMITE—SECOND VISIT.

I left San Francisco at 3 P. M., by the Southern Pacific Railroad for my second trip to the Yosemite. Before, when I took the valley trip, I was told it would be dusty; I carried my duster and it rained all the way, when it didn't snow. This time I resolved to be prepared for any emergency, so I carried my duster, my waterproof and my ulster. On this occasion, however, all the prophecies of heat and dust were fulfilled.

Next morning we had breakfast in an apartment whose walls were made of wire netting, giving us the sense of being in an exaggerated flytrap, before taking the coach for the new stage route to the Yosemite.

It was positively warm and I was really enjoying myself, melting slowly and surely but comfortably, while the rest of the passengers really suffered and averred that it was hot. This idea I rejected, however, laughing to scorn the Californian notions of heat until a thermometer was produced at one of the stations attesting to 96 degrees in the shade. That convinced me that while 90 degrees in New York is misery, here in this dry air I could support 96 degrees and a heavy cloth dress with cheerfulness. I was sorry, though, that they convinced me it was so hot, for I felt in duty bound to suffer with them for the rest of the morning. And I was sufficiently uncomfortable already on account of the dust, which did not need to be proven to me, without adding the actual degree of incontrovertible heat to my agony. What little air there was stirring was following us in such a manner as to keep us in a cloud of beautiful dust that sifted through a duster as easily as it would through a sieve, covering our hats, filling our hair until the most youthful of us appeared to be quite gray.

The morning was spent climbing over a winding road up the foothills to "Grant's." This place is kept by the man who has built the new road at his own expense, we are told, from pure love of road building and the beautiful country he lives in. As we journey it becomes evident that the road was built by an artist whose love of the beautiful was backed up by a practical knowledge of civil engineering.

Such serpentine winding and turning was never seen before in roads. Sometimes we wound around the side of the mountains in a succession of scallops similar to that erratic railroad that climbs the Himalayas, only these were smaller scallops. This kept us always on the side of the mountain where we could see into and across the valley, and so at last when we had reached the top we had a succession of views of the valley, each one broader and more comprehensive, until finally we looked, not only down in the valley, but out on the surrounding mountains that formed a horseshoe from where we rode, and clear across the yellow plains of the San Joaquin Valley to where the Coast Range rose dim and misty against the sky. Now, too, we had left the heat below us and the dust had been laid and the air freshened by a passing shower. A particularly brilliant sunset left some bright crimson clouds in the sky that deepened to magenta and purple as the sun sank lower.

Having reached the summit we plunged into a forest road shaded by great trees, though we still caught views now and then of inner valleys, sometimes under cultivation, sometimes deep forest, now thick with tangled undergrowth, now swept clear by fire that had blackened all the trees about. They say the Indians used to set the brush on fire every year in the Fall to burn the forest clear of undergrowth.

We meet some Indians now and then with tawny skins and shaggy black hair, clothed in old army suits sometimes, more often common laborer's garb, not at all suggestive of the dime novel or stage Indian. I look in vain for the stately brave with eagle eyes and long, straight hair, adorned with bright, defiant feathers. I miss the stalwart chiefs of fiction with massive chests of bronze, fringed leggins and beaded moccasins. Somehow, things never do turn out as one has fancied. The pictures never seem to agree with the originals.

At about 6 P. M. our coach drives up to Clark's, where immediately on alighting we are assaulted by the proprietor and his zealous servants with feather dusters and whisk brooms, and dusted and brushed assiduously for a few moments before we are invited into the office to register. Is there anything more satisfactory after a long day's travel than a good supper, a refreshing bath and a clean soft bed? All these one finds at Clark's. The table is fresh and neat, the dinner well cooked and well served, the baths of delicious soft mountain water of melted snow, the beds white, warm and very grateful to the tired frame, while the sleep that comes to one under all these conditions is as sweet and sound as it is refreshing.

With the dawn we are up again and off on the morning coach. While I, by the unfair use of the privileges of my sex, have secured the box seat, where I am guiltily happy in my ill-gotten point of vantage, though I disapprove with all my soul of women who exact sacrifice of men because they are women. A man has no "show" at all under such circumstances. He must either resign his just rights or be condemned as a brute by the aggressive ladies and looked down on as a boor by the gentlemen. I will do myself the justice to say that I had hesitated, declined and at last reluctantly accepted the gallant sacrifice asked for me only after a reassuring wink and sundry inviting nods and becks of the driver.

There is not so much advantage in having the front seat, for there is no cover to the coach of any kind, so all can see as well, only on the box one can see the horses and escape a good deal of the dust. We continue to wind around the mountains in scallops of the most serpentine of roads, rising higher and getting a still grander view of the valley and the Coast Range than that of the day before, but reach the summit at last and commence the descent into the valley.

Up to this point this road had been far preferable to that other road I went over two years ago, though in the Spring of the year everything is greener and fresher and therefore more beautiful, for the other road has not the magnificent views across the country that this one has. But in descending into the valley the road is safer and tamer, running behind trees and points and only giving one an occasional glimpse of the valley —a nice enough road for timid people to come in on ; but I prefer the delicious dangers of the road on the other side, that makes its whole descent on the unprotected verge of the magnificent precipice.

I think the grandeur and beauty of the valley strike one more forcibly when they appear to one suddenly after a long, tame approach, and then the continuous and unbroken view one gets of the whole as one rides down that zigzag road, the horses skirting the very edge of chasms of thousands of feet as they whirl around sharp corners. Any one who loves the breath of danger should by all means come in by that road, for it is delightfully thrilling and still safe enough. The drivers know their business and so do the horses.

Having been over both roads, I should advise people to come into the valley via Milton, seeing the Calaveras big trees and passing through the Tuolumne grove, making the grand descent; and leave it by the other road that terminates at Raymond, getting the magnificent view of the country out to the coast as you ride toward it, and taking in the Mariposa grove of big trees. This plan would give the traveler the greatest amount of enjoyment, robbing the trip of the monotony of repetition.

I have already written of the Yosemite Valley and the trail up to Glacier Point. I can only say that, seeing it for the second time, it loses none of the admiration its sublime grandeur and beauty commands at the first impression. El Capitan rises majestic in its 3,300 feet of solid granite before us; beyond the Half Dome throws its sharply cut outline up of 5,000 feet toward the sky, while further on "Cloud's Rest," still higher, earns its name, for a cloud is actually resting on its graceful peak at this moment, while close at hand the Cathedral spires point toward the heaven their names suggest; and but a little way beyond the Bridal Veil Fall pours its volume of water, white and foamy and misty as gauze, from the very top of the cliffs to the basin below. As one watches the great body of water rushing over the precipice one can see it break and separate as it falls, and each fork, trying to fall faster than the other, shoots downward independently like reversed sky-rockets.

Driving on some three or four miles further we come to Cook's Hotel, where we have elected to stop our journey, at 2 P. M. We are tired, of course, but there is a beautiful afternoon before us which it seems a pity to waste in inactivity; so after a few hasty touches to hair that is loaded with dust, a whisk or so at garments whose original color is concealed by the covering of earth, and a dab with a wet corner of a towel at a face that shows high water mark in a distinct line around it for the rest of the day, we go down and get some lunch, and then take a carriage for a circular drive around the valley.

We drive up the valley first past Barnard's Hotel, toward the great Half Dome and Cloud's Rest, across the turbulent Merced

River and down on the other side, past the Yosemite Fall, with its magnificent plunge of 2,548 feet, under the shadow of the stately El Capitan, across the Merced once more, down by the glistening Bridal Veil, past the curiously packed stores of acorns belonging to the Indians, past some camping grounds, where Indian pleasure seekers are to be seen enjoying to the utmost all the inconveniences of camp life, back to the hotel for the night.

We rise in the morning with the lark—or whatever kind of early bird they have in that part of the country—wondering why we don't always get up early and enjoy that loveliest and freshest part of the day. We have selected the drive to Mirror Lake, where, by following up the shadow of the cliffs, we manage to see several reflected sunrises, and after a painful serenade on a cornet and an equally distressing echo of the same we give the Indian torturer of the instrument some small recompense and hasten out of earshot. We find our horses awaiting us where two roads meet, and when the party have been comfortably hoisted, for most of them are amateurs at riding, on to their respective steeds, we start off at a hard trot, each following in the wake of the one before. The horses are small sure-footed beasts that need no guidance or attention even, save an occasional request that he shall postpone his lunch of grass until a more convenient hour and proceed on, at the same time hinting at a desire that he should leave the extreme edge of the precipice and walk just a little nearer to the wall. The short hard trot comes to an abrupt close at the foot of the mountain, where the cavalcade proceeds to climb slowly and surely toward the heights above, the leaders looking down on the heads of those behind and "passing the time of day," while those in the rear anxiously observe the maneuvres in turning the angles in the narrow road of those who have gone before.

There has been a recent washout on this trail, so it is undergoing repair, which makes it more difficult to travel over than usual, the loose, broken rocks slipping from under the horses' feet as they climb.

We stop at one point, and dismounting follow a little path in toward the Vernal Falls which brings us out on to a large flat ledge where we can see the fall tumbling down to us, green as its name suggests, and where we catch the spray it throws out.

The top of this fall is our destination, only 336 feet. To reach it we climb for full two hours over the trail of broken stone. The day before this trail had been impassable; to-day we encounter the laborers hard at work on it, and once or twice are obliged to wait while the men place stones here and there before we can pass over it. Having reached the summit we descend a little way over what seems to us a still more precarious trail, for it runs some distance down over a large smooth rock that offers no security for horses' feet. However, we all get safely down, though each horse's particular efforts are anxiously watched by its rider and those immediately to follow, and then we dismount again and walk across the great rock that forms the ledge of the fall to a natural rocky balustrade, through which the water cuts its way as it plunges into the valley below.

We look at the great rushing, roaring tide of green and foamy, turbulent water, and then below, where we descry the rock we stood upon when we looked up at the fall, and then at the bits of winding trail over which we have traveled, and are disposed to criticise the disparity in distances. We can go down, they say, by the fall by ladder if we don't mind a little spray. We don't mind. We have been told that it is the thing to do, and we have come armed with waterproofs to that end. But we are to climb up a little higher first, take a rest, dine and walk to the foot of the Nevada Fall, which, after its great plunge of 617 feet from the top of the cliff, winds along over a rocky bed until it reaches another ledge and becomes the Vernal Falls.

At "Snow's" we get a good dinner, during which the guardian of the valley is introduced to us. Mr. Denison is a young and handsome man, deeply imbued with enthusiasm about the valley over which he is guardian. He is just building a new trail more comprehensive than any before, which will be open in a few days. He will, he says, take any of the party over it to-day who would like to go, although part of the road would be very difficult, but we will be the first party over the new road, "pioneers," he informs us.

Five of us decide to go, and after a prolonged discussion with the guide as to our respective rights in the case, which ends in his washing his hands of all responsibility in the matter, which suits us exactly, we depart, resuming our upward journey over broken stone.

We have a double corner to turn, a sharp, steep zigzag where the stone is so loose that it slips from under the horses' feet. One horse, struggling for secure footing, is caught up so sharply by his rider, a lady, that he loses his balance and nearly falls backward over the ledge. As I am on the ledge just below her, I am momentarily expecting to receive her, horse and all, on my head, when, as I lay out the programme, we shall all go over the chasm at my elbow and be dashed to pieces on the broken rocks. This programme is, however, not followed out, for her horse, by a brave effort, recovers himself and leaps above to a place just a trifle more secure, scattering with his heels a few large stones that fall at my horse's feet. I begin to feel *de trop*. A man goes up next with a similar struggle, and then it is my turn.

There is a large square block of granite on the edge of the precipice on which my feet have rested while I waited on the corner for the man ahead of me to go up. I might have stepped out of my saddle there so easily that I was tempted to do so; but, being a weak creature when in a company, I deferred to the judgment of the gentlemen against my own sense of caution and kept my seat.

Something disastrous really ought to have happened then, to have proved me sensible instead of merely timorous and fussy, for it was the first time in my life that I had exhibited any timidity of that kind, but I was aggravatingly fortunate. My horse was the surest footed of the lot, and all I had to do was to hang fast to the saddle when he assumed the posture only given to human beings, until he got to a point where he could conscientiously resume his normal attitude. If the horse had only kicked a small stone down on the wise head of the superior man who had insisted on my keeping my seat it would have soothed my sense of justice somewhat.

Once past that bad place, our troubles were over, and soon we found ourselves at the summit looking back on the difficulties we had met and conquered. Our road was now clear and comparatively level as we skirted the tops of the cliffs. We broke into an occasional trot, but the trot of these little climbing beasts is something terrible, so we did not indulge much. Our destination now was Glacier Point, after that the valley. To reach Glacier Point we wound along the top of the granite walls that inclose the valley, getting many a new view of it as we went. For a long while a lofty granite apex, known as the Liberty Cap, from its shape, rose most prominently before us, but later we left it behind us. Our road was fairly level, dipping now and then into a gulch and up again. In one place we found a great square block of stone in the path, on one side was wall and on the other a steep chasm. Each horse hesitated and considered over this obstacle, and then chose his own peculiar method of getting over it and was deaf to the persuasion or entreaty of his rider.

Further on we came to the camp of the men who were at work on the road, where each man's individuality was expressed by the condition of his bunk and kitchen equipment—one man's bed being the ground, with blankets thrown down, looking as if he just crept out, while another was slung hammockwise and neatly made, while his stores were put carefully away beneath it. Dinner was on the fire, while a kettle of cold tea standing near was tasted of by the party. These are the people that really keep open house. Any passing stranger is welcome to help himself to a meal, camper's etiquette only requiring that he shall leave things in as good order as he found them. The really polite thing to do, if you have time, is to prepare the meal for the absent. Payment for this sort of hospitality is an insult.

Continuing on, we look across the tops of the Sierra Mountains, getting a magnificent view of the distant snow-covered peaks, for there is still snow though it is late in July. Far beyond we see the "Little Yosemite," while just ahead of us we have the back of the "Half Dome," looming up above all other peaks, a great solid dome of rock cut sharply off at one side; beyond it is Cloud's Rest, higher, but not so impressive, and further back Star King raises its royal head.

We have an exquisite scene before us now; the sun comes out and glances brightly off the distant snows, while behind the Half Dome a black cloud rises ominously, and an occasional flash of lightning cuts its gloom with a streak of fire. The black cloud was making for us, but the Half Dome caught it on its broad, flat side, and held it back. We could see the rain pouring on its bald, defenseless head until the cloud was spent. We saw far more than we could retain a recollection of at one visit. It was a long trail, and contained many magnificent views in a sublime whole.

At length we reached Glacier Point, where we sat on the veranda of the little hotel perched up there, and looked across the valley at the Nevada Falls, at whose feet we had entered upon this new trail. Exactly how we had managed to get across the valley without descending into it is not altogether clear to me yet. But we did it somehow.

Once more we descended the trail from Glacier Point, so winding, so precipitous and so narrow, bound on one side by a chasm thousands of feet deep, on the other by a wall of granite. Stones thrown from a point half way up the trail are lost to sight and sound long before they reach the valley. The horses feel their way carefully, their feet slipping some inches at every step, so steep is the path. They exhibit a distinct preference for walking on the extreme edge of the precipice, and when they turn the sharp angles that hang out over the valley their heads positively hang over the precipice, while they bring their hind feet down between their fore feet and then turn, using them as a pivot. They are sure-footed little beasts, however, and no accidents occur.

Going over it for the first time two years ago, it seemed to me to be an extremely narrow and dangerous trail. Going up was bad enough, but coming down was terrifying. Going over it for the second time, I was surprised to see what a broad, safe trail it was, and at the third time, I looked upon it as calmly as I would the one that runs so peacefully along the level floor of the valley. This confidence was not altogether due to the "familiarity that breeds contempt," but partly to the constant improvements that are being made in it. These trails are practically rebuilt each succeeding Spring. I was a little disappointed, though people who were new to it seemed to find a sufficient amount of terror in it.

The descent from Glacier Point is long and slow and far more tiresome to both man and beast than the ascent. My stirrup foot and knee were painfully strained long before we reached the bottom, and for once I appreciated a side saddle, for the gentlemen were afflicted with two stirrups and, therefore, two strained feet and knees apiece instead of one. We got to the bottom very much sooner than we should have done with a guide. Our little beasts were pretty tired, for they had an unusually hard day's climb, and so were we; for five straight hours in the saddle are not absolutely restful to an unaccustomed rider, particularly when it is only the finale to a long day's sightseeing.

I was not so tired, however, but that I could spend the evening on the piazza talking indefatigably to a group of questioners about my many travels. When I jumped out of bed at 4.30 the following morning I had occasion to recollect that I had been horseback riding the day before; nevertheless I prepared myself for the stage, for we were to start on the return journey to San Francisco to-day.

We left the valley with many a backward glance at serene Cloud's Rest, at bold, clear cut Half Dome, at the Silvery Bridal Veil and roaring Yosemite Falls, at Sentinel Rock, Cathedral Spires and majestic El Capitan, at the valley below, fresh and green as an emerald, with the Merced sparkling in the morning light, carrying away with us a picture that can never fade or dwindle in comparison with other scenes, for the Yosemite is one of those rare pictures that exceeds all power of words or brush to depict its beauties, that rises in its loveliness and grandeur far beyond human conception. Even the extravagant eulogium of the advertisement fails to reach the standard of actual grandeur and beauty of the Yosemite Valley.

A long hard climb and we are back on the summit, and then down we go to Clark's at a rattling gait, looking out again across the green mountains and the yellow, grainripe valley, observing the big trees as we go—the crooked Mawzanita and richly tinted Madrona that sheds its bark yearly. Here grows the cedar from which the California red wood is obtained, while the rich green pines and graceful firs shoot up, straight and even, to stupendous heights. The silver fir is the most perfect tree in the world in absolute, symmetrical beauty. The silver green of its foliage and the evenness of its branches as they grow smaller and smaller until the top, forming a perfect cone, gives it exceptional grace. And they do grow so tall. When a tree takes a notion to grow in California nothing in heaven or on earth will stop it. It may start a tiny shoot under a rock as big as a church and it will grow right up around it. If it starts from a seed in a crevice in a rock it will eventually split the rock apart. California trees are no joke. They are large, and that's a fact. Any one of the ordinary full grown trees in this forest would create a sensation in a Jersey wood. And we have not come to the grove of large trees yet.

We see doves on the trees and grouse and quail running through the brush, and the streams contain trout, of which we have savory proof every morning at the hotels.

Arriving at Clark's we are set upon by the host and his minions with feather duster and whisk brooms again. And truly we need it this time. The ludicrous appearance of a reverend gentleman from Boston nearly sends me into spasms, although it is Sunday and church is in progress in the adjacent parlors. And one young man with an aristocratic name is so completely disguised with plebian dust that I know him not, although he regards me with reproach. Not the least funny part of the tableau is the intense amusement of one young woman over the laughable appearance of her friends, while she herself is blissfully ignorant of the ant hill of dust resting on her nose and equally dusty mole hills on her cheeks. Having a protuberant face, she caught it in hills and ridges, and when she grins at her friends I walk away where I can sit down and laugh comfortably.

After lunch the stage is at the door again, waiting to take us to the Mariposa grove of big trees. Arrived there big trees kept rising before us as we rode on. Single big trees, with hollow trunks; double big trees, growing up together like giant twins; triple big trees, shooting up straight beside each other, forming immense triangles. We drove on through the giant forest until we reached the largest tree of all—the Grizzly Giant—101 feet in circumference.

We drove on through the giant grove until we came to a tree in which a door had been cut for us to pass through. This was "Wanona," measuring twenty-eight feet in diameter. We drove into the tree, and stopped when our hind wheels were even with the tree. We had a four seated coach with four horses, and we were all inside of the tree but the heads of the leaders. On either side and above us were the red walls of the Cedar King, roughly hewn. We had nothing to say. We drove on past more trees.

Back to the hotel. More dust. More dusters and whisk brooms. Supper, a short lounge on the piazza, a bath and to bed; for in the morning we take the coach at 4. Unearthly hour as it seems it is a lovely time to be out. It was bright moonlight when we started, and we had the pleasure of seeing the "orb of night" fade slowly from the sky before the dawn, and the sun rise from behind the mountain walls, sending shafts of light through the great forests, and then the delicious silence and coolness, the twittered awakening of the birds, and that glorious view of the distant valley bathed in morning light—there is no more lovely time of day than the early morning.

A lady shared the box seat with me this time, and we two sat in utter silence for hours listening to the incessant chatter of two men behind us, until at last they started to tell how to manage babies; then we only smiled at one another with a glance of intelligence and listened more intently, hoping to get some wise suggestions from the stronger sex. But they only said the usual things about not humoring children, and the necessity of teaching them that they must "mind;" so we merely thought "much they know about it anyway," and fell into a deeper silence than before.

Our Pullman sleeper was awaiting us, and we just had time to take lunch in the exaggerated flytrap and get on board, where we had the time and convenience for washing. That was a hot day—106 in the shade—and oh, how grateful for the first breath of the sea that we caught, an hour's journey yet from the coast; and how delightful it was to be obliged to put on an overcoat before leaving the car to cross the bay. Certainly you can have any weather you choose in California. For my part, I like the bracing air of San Francisco best.

I have been to the Yosemite twice, and I shall have to go once more in order to see the valley at the best season. Before I went at all they told me the Spring was the best time to see it, before everything was burned up, and to avoid the great dust and heat, and see the falls when they were full. So I went in June and was nearly frozen. Then they told me it was pleasanter in the valley later when it was warm and the roads were in good condition. I have now tried the midsummer plan and have been nearly roasted and suffocated with dust. Now they say the Fall is the time of year of all others to see the valley.

October, when the leaves are changing, is a brilliant month, without heat or dust or cold or rain. So I shall have to go in October. How people do delight to tell one that the one thing one has missed is the one thing worth seeing. I presume they will say next time that the really best time to see the valley is at Christmas.

In sober truth, I think the Yosemite Valley is always beautiful, whether white and glittering with snow and ice, rich and green with rain, bright and fair under the midsummer sky, or flaming with the brilliant tints of Autumn.

THE COLUMBIA RIVER.

I went on board the steamer State of California with many misgivings in regard to the pleasure to be derived from the trip to Portland, firstly, because every one I had heard express themselves on the subject said I should encounter the most disagreeable kind of sea, and *mal de mer* would be the inevitable result, if not at sea, then on the bar at the mouth of the Columbia River surely. The sea was always rough, and everybody was always sick on that particular route. Secondly, the delegates returning from the recent convention at San Francisco of the Grand Army of the Republic, had also taken passage on the State of California, and, patriotic as I am, and owning to the feminine weakness for uniforms and decorations, I felt that there would be too much of a good thing for comfort in this instance.

And so it proved for others, for the decks and passages were strewn with blankets and mattresses of unfortunate people who could get no better accommodations, owing to the crowd. My usual good luck had, however, placed me in a most comfortable cabin on deck, where I could look out on the restless sea while sitting comfortably on my own sofa, with Miss Sherman as a most agreeable roommate, while her illustrious father, who was returning from the G. A. R. Convention, was on guard next door.

At table I found myself in good company, for the captain was on one hand, a judge on the other, while the man who "marched to the sea" sat opposite and told many stories in response to our eager questions about his former experiences in this part of the world. Under these circumstances I had every reason to enjoy myself, and when, after a few hours out, I noted a conspicuous absence of any symptoms that could be construed into coming illness, my forebodings took flight.

We might have had an opportunity to be seasick on the bar if the tide had been higher.

As it was the State of California fairly walked over the bar. That was the first time I ever saw a ship climb hills. We could feel her go scraping up the sandy undulations of the bottom and down again on the other side, and into the water again. Some of the hills seemed to be pretty steep and long, and I had grave doubt about her ever getting off again, but she always reached the top eventually and slid off as if freshly launched into the deeper water of the following valley.

From Astoria, following up the Columbia River, we saw the deep wooded hills of Oregon, and at their base many salmon canneries. As we approached Portland we hoped to see the famous mountains of this coast, but that was not to be. The atmosphere was thick and gloomy with the smoke of burning forests. Here and there the adjacent hills were ugly with bare and blackened tree stumps, relics of previous fires.

Reaching Portland at night I took the hotel stage at seven the next morning along with a regiment of school girls and boys under the charge of one or two older people. The girls filled the interior completely, while the boys were piled up on the roof. After two false starts, which were brought hastily to a stop by girlish shrieks as to forgotten articles, and long waits while the said articles were being diligently hunted for, we got off and were half way to the depot when another shriek, shriller than either before, told of another and more serious loss. This time it was a watch left under a pillow by its youthful owner. And the whole stage load of people were turned about and driven hastily back, while the elderly lady told her charge the only safe recipe for keeping a watch while traveling. "Never put your watch under your pillow, my dear," she said, "unless you put it in your stocking; then when you come to dress you will be sure to take it out, because you will want the stocking." After a prolonged search, the watch was found and we set off once more for the boat.

A very pretty, neat little boat it was, but built on a plan entirely new to me—flat bottomed and having one paddle wheel at the stern. Boats built in this way run very fast and are very easily handled. They can do what a side wheeler can't in the way of landings. They are the most independent little craft I ever saw, running right up on shore at any sand bank they choose to stop at to get a passenger. We did not always have to run ashore in this way, however; there were little wharves sometimes, but I rather fancy that the vessel liked to climb the beach better.

Stopping at one of the numerous canneries, the captain of the steamer kindly took me through it. We saw here the different tables where the fish were cleaned and cut and put in cans, the operation of making the cans, filling and sealing them. All was very neat and nice and the result highly satisfactory to the world in general.

Returning on board, the captain took me into the engine room of the boat. I wouldn't mind being an engineer on that style of boat at all, for instead of being a black hot hole in the "cellar" of the ship, the engine room is almost as high above the water as the deck of an ordinary ferry boat, and takes the full width of the vessel, only leaving a narrow passageway between it and the bulwarks, occupying more than half the vessel reaching from the stern forward. The machinery is spread around on the deck, with plenty of space to walk around among it, and all is polished to a degree of brightness only known to engineers. Forward are the boilers and the great furnace where the firemen are piling in logs that bear a family resemblance to railway ties.

Speaking of railway ties, reminds me of their manufacture at the tops of these steep cliffs, from whence they are sent down to the river by means of a dry flume, down which they go with lightning-like rapidity, shooting into the river with a force that sends up a splash like a fountain. Indeed, we watched one of these flumes from the boat with an interest that culminated in excitement when each tie made the final plunge. We could see them coming from very near the top and switch around a curve at the lower end before precipitating themselves into the water.

The scenery of the Columbia River is really very fine. It is a beautiful broad river, with green slopes that run high aloft varied by basaltic cliffs and palisades. "Cape Horn," projecting into the water like a promontory, is an imposing and picturesque cliff. These basaltic cliffs resemble in character very much the Giant's Causeway of the northern coast of Ireland, having the same formation of octagonal pillars and honeycombed looking rock that evidently has once been molten.

The Indians say that Mount Hood and Mount Adams, now so many miles away, at one time stood close to the river and were connected by a natural bridge. The mountains grew angry with one another, they say, and threw out fire, ashes and stones, destroying the bridge and choking the river, hitherto navigable. The Great Spirit, getting angry in His turn, hurled the mountains asunder and at their present distance from the river.

At the cascades we left our little steamer, and taking a little train, were transported, bag and baggage, above the cascades, where another little steamer of the same ilk waited us. *En passant* we saw little Indian encampments and Indians out on the water fishing, not as we do with lines, but with spears. Further up we caught a glimpse of the graceful cone of Mount Hood, rising pale and symmetrical from between two hills that rose from the river in the distance. Now and then we saw a forest fire raging, leaving bare and blackened hillsides wherever it passed. The steamer reaches the Dalles in time for its passengers to sup comfortably at the hotel before the train from Portland comes along to pick them up and carry them on toward the East. After a good deal of confusion the "Grand Army" were settled comfortably in their respective berths, too comfortably to be willing to turn out and see the beautiful waterfall we passed but a short time after leaving Dalles.

The following day we discovered that traveling in crowds, though it was certainly jolly and social, had its inconveniences, and there were many thoughtless complaints and considerable bad temper shown by some, while people of happier disposition took it as a joke and managed to extract a good deal of fun from the situation. For my part, when I start out to travel during a specially crowded season I expect a great deal of discomfort will result, and am prepared to take the consequences with equanimity. I observed now that good temper and consideration toward overworked servants was really quite frequently rewarded by grateful thoughtfulness and attention from them, such as they were able to give.

During the day we passed Lake Pond Orielle, a beautiful large body of water lying among the forests of Washington Territory. Later we were given half an hour to ride or walk over to look at an adjacent fall while the train waited. For other amusement we alternately slept and cultivated each other. Every change of cars brings one in contact with new people, and after a great deal of travel one learns to fall easily into acquaintance and comes to enjoy the kaleidoscopic changes of character that pass before one's eyes as they voyage on. Each new acquaintance was to me a study of absorbing interest. One feels, too, that he himself is a novelty to the people he meets and not the old story he is to his friends, and this feeling refreshes him. From time to time one runs across some one of the eminent people of this world, which is always pleasant.

Another night, illumined by forest fires, and another long warm day broken by long stops to investigate and try to cool a box that obstinately remained hot, and other long waits at depots where ice boxes were refilled and where the warm and thirsty passenger risked the integrity of his indigestion in the inordinate consumption of small chunks and slivers of ice, so crystal pure that it excited his admiration at the same time that it quenched his thirst. These stops gave us opportunity to stretch our limbs by a short promenade, after which we returned to the cars somewhat refreshed and rested.

At the end of the third day from Portland and the sixth from San Francisco we reached Livingstone, where those of us who meant to go into the Yellowstone stopped off, bidding good-by to our whilom fellow passengers, who continued on. Here, after a short scramble and rush for tickets, we took another train. Three hours brought us to Cinnaba, where coaches and saddle horses for 150 people awaited us. Another wild rush and scramble followed, during which I climbed up on the front seat of the nearest coach, deserting a learned judge, who had been alternately helping and entertaining me for the last few days.

Our late arrival was not the misfortune that it would seem, for the moon was full and it was far more pleasant to be driving in the cool moonlight than under the hot sun, as we did on the return journey, and Luna manages to invest the scenery with a beauty of her own manufacture. So we did not complain, though between 1 and 2 A. M. were not the hours we had counted on arriving at the mammoth Hot Springs Hotel.

YELLOWSTONE PARK.

You might imagine we were tired after three days of active travel and two consecutive nights on the sleeper. It was very near to 3 A. M. before many of us had succeeded in registering and securing rooms. We were expected to take the stage the following, or rather the same, morning at seven for an all day's drive to the Grand Cañon. For myself, I climbed up on to the box seat feeling decidedly heavy as to eyelids and sore as to brain and achy as to limbs and frame.

After an hour or two of dullness I had managed to become acquainted with my two companions on the box, a very bright, good looking, good natured and intelligent young driver and a very grave and serious, although very amiable and pleasant, senator. And once I got to talking on my favorite subject, my many solitary travels, I was all right. My headache disappeared, my muscles lost the sense of fatigue, and it became patent to the casual observer that I was up for all day.

The hotel at the Mammoth Hot Springs was a very fine and large one, still I particularly admired the management when, at each request for rooms from a gentleman, the manager asked, "Are there any ladies in your party?" and, at the response in the negative, "Register and wait until the ladies have been settled."

A coach load from there on became a party and I was no longer recognized as being alone, and I was put in with from one to the whole number of our ladies at the different hotels, and was not permitted to handle my own baggage nor register my own name thenceforth, two privileges dear to my contrary heart.

These ladies, three in number, had cultivated me on the train, under the delusion shared by many others that I was the daughter of General Sherman, a delusion which arose from my occupying the stateroom with Miss Sherman and going to the dining saloon under her father's escort. At first it gave me a shock when a lady approached me and said, "I had the pleasure of shaking hands with your illustrious father the other day," for my father, who was illustrious, too, in his own way, had been dead but a year. But I soon got used to it and disclaimed the relationship, of which I should have been proud, and the people were pleased to cultivate me for myself, having broken the ice.

After a short drive from the Mammoth Hot Springs we came to a narrow winding cañon known as the Golden Gate, through which the Gibbon River passes with a very beautiful fall. The road winds upon a ledge along the right wall; after that the road is comparatively level until after we have passed the Norris Geyser basin, where we dine at noon. After some feeble attempts at removing the dust we sit down to a nice dinner served by the neatest, deftest and most obliging of waitresses. Dinner is one of the most important questions to the stage traveler, for nothing stirs up the languid appetite like a long and early drive in the crisp, mountain air, so we dine before we look at the wonderful geysers that are before the hotel.

The Norris Geyser Basin is said to be the oldest and the highest in the park. The "Basin" is a broad expanse of dead white lime crust, dotted with geysers and springs, whose special basins vary in color from black to snowy whiteness and sulphurous yellow. From here rises a dense steam and as dense an odor of sulphur.

We pay our respects first to the geyser known as the "Minute Man," who fires off a volley of boiling water regularly once in every sixty seconds "to a height of twenty five or thirty feet," the guide book says, so of course no one need fail to see it in action. The Monarch and the Fearless declined to play for us, so we passed westward to the Constant, the Twins and the Triplets, geysers of the perpetual order.

Higher up the hill we come upon a mud geyser that is just getting ready for action. We sit on a bench and watch it while it bubbles and blubs and sputters like a great bowl of grayish black mush, rising gradually in its basin, boiling more fiercely momentarily until it shoots up a heavy fountain of mud, sending up a drab spray so violently that one instinctively starts and shrinks back at each fresh spurt. It recedes gradually, sinking with a few defiant spurts, as if half inclined to express itself further on the subject. We gather up a few small pointed cones of drab elongated drops of mud that have cooled and hardened as they touched the brink of the geyser, forming an ornamental fringe about its edge.

This is a very queer world, indeed, and its queerness is particularly forced on one's attention in the Yellowstone Park, where, high as it is above the sea level, the nearness to the surface of its inner fires is evidenced all about us.

Further along the winding road and on the left we come to the beautiful Emerald Pool, so called from the rich blue-green tint of the water. When our eyes are sufficiently dazzled by the glare, our minds by the wondrous strangeness, and our hearts are impressed with the beauty of the scene our stage coach drives up and we climb to our respective seats and travel merrily on in search of more wonders.

All the afternoon we drove over good roads and bad roads and indifferent roads, up steep hills, and down deep dales and through partially burnt forests, whose scarred trees still stretched out foliage enough to break the rays of the sun and scratch the unwary passenger's face. Occasionally we climbed or descended hills that called for a dismount from most of the party, which gave our colonels, captains and majors an opportunity to exercise and gather horse and mule shoes as graceful souvenirs for the ladies. Meantime acquaintanceship grew and flourished; there is no place like a steamship on a long voyage for the development of social qualties in people, and no place like the box of a stage coach for the quick growth of friendship.

After sitting shoulder to shoulder on that high and isolated seat for from eight to twelve hours, one is apt to have developed either an interest in one's neighbor or an active hatred. It is not easy to avoid some interchange of thought. For my part, I usually start out and talk my neighbor deaf and dumb and blind in the first half day, first giving the driver permission to "fire" me if I become tiresome. I travel on the supposition that somebody is likely to be bored, and that it's more comfortable to be the borer within limits.

We reach the hotel, at the Yellowstone Falls, at about five in the afternoon, very comfortably tired after our very short night's rest and long day's journey. Here we find those of us who are alone must choose roommates to permit the accommodations to match the demands; under these circumstances I am thankful at getting a very nice and pleasant young lady to lodge with me.

One of the secrets of contentment in traveling is a realization of one's comparative good fortune, and how much worse things might be. The hotel was a simple wooden box, with wooden partitions, but the wood was new and so fresh and sweet that no one could complain. A simple supper served with amiability and goodwill, and eaten with cheerfulness and appetite, re-enforced our energies, and sent us off up the Cañon to see the Falls whose thunder rang in our ears, though they were not in sight.

The upper fall was close at hand. To reach it we plunged into a bit of wood, taking a winding path that led us down a little and out to the verge of the Cañon down which was plunging a magnificent sheet of deep green water turning to foam as it fell. From this upper fall the water rushes impetuously on through the narrow winding cañon preliminary to taking a second and more terrific plunge.

Having that greater fall in view we did not tarry long at this one, beautiful as it was, but retraced our steps to the hotel from whence we took a new departure, striking out with staff in hand on a longer and more laborious climb. Just a footpath worn in the green moss of the woods winding in and out among the trees and up and down hillocks at first, and later, as we approached the verge of the Cañon, narrow sandy slopes hedged sometimes with a prostrate dead branch, up which we scrambled and down which we slid with many a tremor and frequent losses of equilibrium.

At last we descried the Falls, and with a last slip and slide and clutch at empty air, we reached a level that ran out into a little promontory even with the Fall, part, indeed, of that mass of water that was hurling itself in mad haste over a solid wall of rock to the bottom of this rainbow hued cañon. Here we rested, after disposing ourselves at chosen points of vantage, and took in the full beauty of the scene.

The Fall was beautiful indeed, a vast body of rich green water plunging down and turning to whirling foam as it fell into a valley as vari-colored as a painter's pallet. The last rays of the sun shining through the trees, caught the mist that rose from the fall, and transformed it into a bank of rainbow at one point, while at another a veritable bow of brilliant hues spanned the river diagonally, but it was hardly more bright than the cliffs about us, that were literally ablaze with rich and gaudy color.

The Grand Cañon of the Yellowstone River is one of the great scenes of the world—one of the sights worth traveling half around the world to see. It possesses a kind of beauty and grandeur to be found nowhere else. It is not like that gem of America the Yosemite Valley, green and placid in gray walls of towering granite; nor is it like beautiful Switzerland, with its richly verdured valleys and bare gray peaks; still less is it like the Norwegian fiords, richer, greener, more stupendous in massive towering granite; nor is it like the vast, pale tinted valleys and sky reaching snow crowned mountains of the Himalayas.

It is like itself alone—a great cleft in the earth, fissured and ragged, bathed in the rich dyes of Mother Earth's mineral wealth. A narrow winding chasm lies before us, whose steep cliffs lap each other at the base where a glistening turbulent thread of a river winds. The cliffs are gorgeous with every color known, now strongly contrasted, now delicately blended. Colors that are ever being renewed by the mist that rises from the falls, by the vapors that emanate from the earth. Here are greens shading from delicate pale moss to the deep tones of the pines that project down to the verge of the river, in points and ridges of fringe; yellows, pale and deep, shading into pale green; and red from terra cotta to magenta and a bluish purple. At one point the mist that curls up the palisades has favored the growth of delicate green moss and lichen. Surmounting these rainbow cliffs is a forest of pines.

Along the smooth steep slopes of the cliffs castle like crags and pinnacles jut out hanging over the abyss below, and here and there the ridge of a jutting cliff has a bristling spine of pines extending from the top to the river edge, while right up before us rises a huge tower of rock, an elongated cone of dark purplish red, the color and shape of a bunch of sumach.

We took up our line of march again presently and wandered on a little further to a point called "Lookout," a crag that reaches out over the precipice, from whence one can look back on the falls. We waited until the moon came out and added her silvery rays to the general effect. But such beautiful scenes cannot be described adequately in words. When thoroughly steeped in the loveliness and grandeur of the whole we scramble over that sharply undulating path again to the hotel ; there we left orders for the saddle horses for the party to be ready at 5 A. M. and went to bed and to sleep forthwith.

We were awakened in the cold, frosty darkness of early morning, and hastily took coffee and rolls in the pauses of our hasty toilet, and then repaired to the big stove that stood in the center of the office to wait for our horses. We waited an hour, but no horses came ; finally it transpired that the horses were always allowed to run loose during the night, and had wandered away and could not be found. We concluded to walk, and started out over the same hilly trail of the night before past Point Lookout, and on some three miles or more along the verge of the cañons to Inspiration Point, a crag that stands far out over the cañon from where one gets a still more extended view.

Looking eastward, the turbulent Yellowstone River winds along the base of the yellow cliffs, now in full view, now disappearing behind the jutting feet of the palisades, until finally lost altogether in the distance where the cliffs overlap each other. On this side the palisades have a smooth slope up from the river and are wooded with green pines. Looking westward the river comes tumbling toward us over several cascades after its great fall further beyond, and after disappearance for some distance behind the overlapping triangular cliffs, while far above and beyond the upper fall stretches a green forest of pine.

Midway between our dizzy perch and the river rises an inaccessible tower of granite, whereon an eagle has built her nest, and on the edges of the nest we see three young eagles scratching about, occasionally trying their wings or screaming to the old bird who has just left the nest and is soaring smoothly about, apparently on the lookout either for fish in the river or other edibles on its banks. Once she comes with outstretched wings straight toward us, but swerves off and describes a circle after which she spreads her pinions for a higher flight and soon disappears in the distance. The young are pretty large birds and are almost ready to fly from the nest, indeed they do take short flights from time to time, and from where we are they seem to be as large as turkey hens.

Having feasted our eyes on form and color, and seen the sunlight creep up over the brilliant turrets and spires of vari-colored granite and shed her brightest morning rays on the glancing falls and river, forming banks and clouds of rainbow in the rising vapors, we climb back from our branching eminence and go hotelward along the undulating trail, stopping now and then to clamber out on some particularly dizzy and dangerous point that overhangs the river for a fresh view.

After a meal rendered sweet by amiable service and healthy appetites we betake ourselves to the piazza to find that our coach horses are also lost. We settle ourselves to wait indefinitely. They tell us that one boy has been missing three days who went out to search for lost horses!

Finally our driver, who is by the way young and handsome, and fair and amiable, and well informed, and has read Bret Harte, and Dickens, and Mark Twain, and is called Charley, heaves in sight with the horses and we climb gladly back into the coach and proceed merrily, as is our wont, on to the next point. Again we lunch at the Norris Geyser basin and review the geysers there.

Proceeding on our journey we climb some steep hills. On the side of one of them we pass a large basin of boiling water, known as the Queen's Laundry, where most of the party wash a handkerchief, which afterward flutters from the back of a seat as a curtain, where it drys while gathering a thick coat of dust.

We have noted more than once since our entrance in this enchanted park places where streams of cold water and basins or streams of hot water lie so close to one another that a sportsman can, in very truth, catch the trout that inhabits the one, and, without rising, sling his line over and cook it in the boiling water of the other. This sounds almost as utopian as the story of chickens already cooked stalking around with knife and fork sticking in them ready for eating, but it is nevertheless true. However, the visitor to the National Park soon realizes that fact is indeed "stranger than fiction."

We stopped that night near the Lower Geyser basin at a place called Fire Hole. We should at another time have gone on to the Upper Geyser, but at this time the hotel there is already crowded, so we have been notified, therefore we stop at Fire Hole, at the worst hotel in the Park. But here, as well as at the Norris Geyser, large establishments are in process of construction, and in the coming seasons the traveler will be more comfortably housed. At present the most fortunate people are two in a room, and I am among the fortunate. The building is a mere temporary one of lath and muslin, that shakes at a movement, and through which whispers can be heard from end to end, as we discover on retiring. Five or six men are talking with rash frankness in the room next us, and across the hall two women recount their conquests, while from further up the corridor are wafted the angry words of a quarrelsome pair. Later we hear suppressed whispering in a distant chamber, and when that subsides the breathing of the sleepers in the adjoining rooms, punctuated with occasional snores, is distinctly audible. Before the lights are out one room is illuminated with the rays from the next that penetrate the muslin covered cracks. After they are extinguished the sounds make it seem like one large, much-peopled room.

The sound of voices at hasty toilet making arouses me in the morning, and I proceed to dress, and am beguiled the while by an account of myself that is given in a resonant voice in the overpopulated apartment next ours. "Ah," I thought, "now I shall have an opportunity of seeing myself "as ithers see me," but I was disappointed—no opinion either good or bad was expressed, nothing but statements of facts regarding my travels, with which I was already familiar; so I clattered a chair, by way of warning to the talkers that an audience was at hand.

Once more en route, but a short trip this time. We had gone a very short distance before we reached the broad expanse of white lime, dotted with the sapphire blue water orifices of springs and geysers, known as the Lower Geyser Basin. We climb down from our seats, and walk out on the white crust to the Fountain Geyser that is just preparing for action. The exquisite greenish blue color of the water that deepens to sapphire excites our admiration first, and then the corrugated and fancifully indented inner walls of purest white that extend downward in rolls and twisted columns.

The water is just below the edge of the basin, which appears to extend over the mouth of the cavern a little, but it rises as it boils more fiercely until it is even with the surface, and finally it sends up a volume of water to a great height, playing with much force and grace for some minutes. When it subsides, sinking back into the cavern several inches, it is again a basin of rippling blue water, with a little cloud of vapor curling off of it.

There are other geysers and springs in the basin, the Thud group with dark green water, the muffled thud that shakes the ground with each escape of accumulated steam, giving them their name; the Jet Geyser; and eastward across the road, separated by a fringe of trees, the Mud Caldron; and patches of clay of different colors, from pink to gray, known as the Paint Pots.

The next place where we descend from the coach is at Hell's Half Acre, which we cross on foot, walking on a crust that sounds too hollow to inspire confidence, and is covered with hot water at various depths. We are inclined to walk on the ridges that mark it, and are glad when we have reached the opposite bank and climbed up on the solid earth again.

We reach the hotel at Upper Geyser Basin a little before luncheon, having sufficient time to rest and explore the basin before that always welcome meal. We can see the geysers from the veranda very well, but of course one wants to examine them more closely, so we walk down across the little depression that lies between us and the Basin proper, which in this case, like the Norris, rises up mound-like from the center of a large broad valley.

When we arrived the Giantess was playing, and now the Indicator, as a miniature geyser that acts as an escape valve for the Bee Hive is called, is letting off steam at a great rate, indicating thereby that the Bee Hive, which is an irregular operator, means to play soon. The Bee Hive has a very graceful cone, suggesting somewhat its name. The Giantess has no raised crater, its projecting crust overlies its basin, which is filled with the sapphire blue water peculiar to these geysers like unto which I have seen nowhere else in this wide world. The Giant, unlike the Giantess, has a very high large cone, broken down at one side, like a broken column. It plays every four days, and, it would seem, plays to some purpose, for it doubles the usual quantity of water in the river, so the guide book says. The Castle has the largest cone in the basin, and bears some resemblance to a rambling ruin of a castle, while the gem of the geysers, the Grotto of Pearls, gains its name from the group of grotto like arched cones and the opal tinted, pearl like interior walls. These are only a few of the geysers that fill the basin, clouding the air with steam and belching forth hot water.

Old Faithful we visit last. It is the famous geyser of the park because of the regularity of its irruptions. No one need miss seeing this geyser in action, for it plays once in every hour. The crater of Old Faithful rises from the center of a hillock of terraces formed by deposits. Each terrace forms a shallow basin filled with clear warm water. This magnificent natural fountain, this wonderful example of the power of the interior forces of the earth, is put to the very practical everyday use of a washing machine.

It is the delight of the tourist to drop into the crater handkerchiefs and socks and other small articles, washable and otherwise, even that delight of the goat's palate, the tomato can, just before an irruption. This causes the play of the great fountain to present a peculiar appearance, as the bits of muslin and cans are shot up in the air, an appearance not at all poetical. However, the geyser revenges herself for this degradation in true laundry style, by failing to return articles confided to her care with promptitude or regularity. Of the three handkerchiefs dropped in by one unsentimental man of our party but one returned, while on the other hand a sock, one of a pair put in a few days before, came sailing out, only to find its mate and owner had gone and left it to its fate.

A traveler should always take a pair of blue or smoked glasses to the park, for the light is very trying to the eyes in these geyser basins. The vast expanses of dead white crust reflect a dazzling glare.

From our entrance into the park some of us had pined to ride horseback. Personally I had begun to yearn for this delightful exercise before I left San Francisco. It was one of the joys I had promised myself on this trip, and on the first day's coaching I had discovered some other ambitious hearts that beat with mine on this subject. One gentleman of the party really did not care to ride, he had been allotted a horse at first, but made an exchange at the first halt, and congratulated himself thereafter, as he thought of his bruises; but as the other party to the exchange also congratulated himself and expressed his gratitude and pleasure whenever we met at stations, the first man's experience carried no weight. Therefore, we continued to yearn for riding horses.

When we alighted from the coach we knew we were to remain at the geysers five or six hours, so we calculated the time to rest, the time to dine and the time to explore the geysers, and proceeded to the office and ordered eleven horses, four with side saddles and all to be in readiness at three. Before the hour arrived we were informed that only three horses could be had and but two saddles, one being a lady's saddle. Then we held a consultation. It was decided that three ladies should ride the three horses, and that the two biggest men of the party should walk with us as escorts. One of the ladies was a good rider, so she took a horse—what one might call a plain, ordinary horse—unadorned by saddle of any kind. The other lady had never ridden before, so the gentlest animal was chosen for her and combined with the one side saddle. I, myself, figuring as the third lady, took the third and last horse, and, having a littte experience in riding, essayed the animal on the masculine saddle.

We mounted while the assembled tourists looked on and commented and advised. My horse, acting in a somewhat restive manner while I sat uneasily perched sideways on a very slippery and unsupporting saddle, managed ultimately to center the interest on himself. He took offense, it seemed, at the restraining hand of the biggest of the big men on his bridle, and champed and pawed and backed and curveted in the most restless manner. Comments were made on the temper of the animal, and gloomy forebodings were expressed about the prospects of certain disaster to the lady. Advice was hazarded at random about the disposal of the unused stirrup on the off side of the beast. It was thought that if left swinging it would strike the already excited beast and irritate him to further speed, probably rouse his ire and result in a wild stampede. However, others thought the lady looked equal to an emergency, and my escort dropped the bridle and let my horse start. He made a wild break at first, but being caught again was persuaded to walk demurely behind the two spiritless horses of the other ladies for a little way, the colonel keeping at his head.

I, however, having grown a little acquainted with my horse, and discovering that he was more manageable than he at first appeared, and being anxious for a canter, got the lead, and cautioning the colonel to be ready to head him off if he tried to bolt, gave my horse the rein and a touch of the twig that did duty as a riding whip. At first he shot me up sky high at every step of the abominable trot he broke into, but getting him into an easy lope, we went along gayly for a little while, until he dropped back into that atrocious trot of his, when I tried to stop him altogether. Seeing this the colonel, who was keeping up by cutting through the woods, went tearing through the brush of a long wooded point that I was just rounding, and rushing out as we came jouncing along, caught us "on the fly." Meanwhile one of the other ladies' horses ambled steadily along at a grave walk, while the other beast was being continuously belabored with epithets and other things, to keep him from laying down by the roadside.

After this my steed could not be restrained to the sober gait of his companions, so he trotted excruciatingly for short distances, and then we quarrel furiously, he desiring to continue his trot, I insisting that he shall either wait for my friends, or go back to meet them. As we neither are lacking in determination, the struggle lasts until the others have come up. In this way we pass the Devil's Punch Bowl, and eventually reach the edge of the lake, where we see some campers just settling themselves.

On the return journey we did not go so fast, but still we outstripped my companions. Just as we were passing the Punch Bowl again we spied those of our party who were on foot, including the fourth lady, coming along leisurely. The colonel, anxious that I should appear to advantage, said: "Now start on, go up to them with a gallop, and show them how well you can ride," and urged my steed into a lumbering trot; but, alas, for my dignity and pride, the creature no longer desired to hasten, so he settled back at once into a plodding walk, and just as we came up to them stood still, while I slid, saddle, blanket and all to the ground. The girth had broken.

I expressed myself as satisfied with my ride and begged the colonel to ride the horse back, betake myself to a prostrate log, just off the road under a tree, from whence I look meditatively out on the Fire Hole River, sweeping the surrounding scenery with an occasional glance. A pond lies back of me and to my right, at the left the Punch Bowl slopes up to a yawning mouth, while before me and beyond are the river and the lime white geyser crust punctuated with active geysers that look like magnified exclamation points of steam. Then the coach rattled up from the opposite direction, gathered me up with the rest and sped on back to the flimsy hotel.

We were on the back track now. Once more we climbed hills and descended valleys, gathering discarded mule shoes as we went; once more we lunched at Norris'; once more we wound around the narrow ledge through the Golden Gate; once more we saw the silvery fanlike fall of the Gibbon River; climbed the beautiful terraces of the Mammoth Hot Springs, descending, more astonished than ever at the wonders of this world.

The Mammoth Hot Springs are the only springs in the park that can be called beautiful as to scenic effect. These snow-white terraces descending from the hilltop in steps and scallops, look as if they had been carved from marble to represent water frozen as it fell. Climbing up among them, one finds them filled at the top with the beautiful blue water peculiar to the hot geysers. This hot water overflows, and running over the hillside, forms by deposit these graceful terraces with frieze and fretwork and dainty incrustation and arabesque.

Sometimes, in climbing about them, one comes on yawning pits, from whose terrible throats rises steam and the odor of sulphur. Taking it altogether, the prettiest thing of all to me was the peculiar exquisite blue of the water in the geyser basins. I want to go back again to look at that perfect color.

We have seen the park and to-morrow we return. We spend the last evening looking at views and enjoying the baths, rising in the morning early enough to have our pictures taken, coach and all, in a group, before departing. We pass through the great gate of the mountains again, and, reaching Cinnabar, find cars waiting for us, that take us to Livingston, where we board our train for the East.

THE RETURN TO NEW YORK.

One never enjoys the confinement of a sleeping car as one does at the end of a rush of sightseeing and stagecoaching, and one returns to coaching and sightseeing with fresh pleasure and relief after twenty-four hours on the cars. After the closeness and confinement activity and light and air and joy; and the confinement and closeness become rest and comfort after the rush and hurry and glare and bustle. When I was traveling months in and months out in all climates and vehicles I learned to appreciate the restfulness of contrasted pleasures, and to look upon the once abhorred railway cars as parlors of ease, the long journeys as delightful intervals of rest.

Having left the Park we find it exceedingly hot. In the Park the weather was perfect, bright and balmy during the day, with a frosty nip at night that insured refreshing sleep. We found overcoats comfortable early in the morning, but laid them aside as the sun rose higher. It is always best to have heavy wraps with one, for in that region they have frost in every month in the year. Dusters one surely wants, and rubbers if they mean to walk across "Hell's Half Acre," or explore the geysers extensively or closely, as one walks in more or less hot water.

Now, after the coolness and comfort of the park, we find it outrageously hot and grumble accordingly.

In the wee small hours of the early morning I wake to note the glare of the burning forest close to the train. The undergrowth is a mass of fire, while sparks are whirling upward, lighting up the blackened trunks and limbs with at once a weird and picturesque effect.

Quite early in the morning we pass through the Bad Lands, that wonderful region of petrifaction sometimes called Pyramid Park, and quite similar in some of its aspects to the Monument Park and Garden of the Gods of Colorado, while in others the country resembles the Book Cliff region of the Utah desert, the sharply cut cliffs rising abruptly from the rolling plain as if the long basin we are running through had once been a sea.

We see not only cowboys, but cowgirls, as we term the women we see galloping over the plains after their cattle, and I think I wouldn't mind living on a plain in a cabin if I could ride as they do—comfortably, in defiance of civilized customs.

We cross the broad Missouri River, red and muddy as it was when I crossed it at Omaha not many weeks ago. The extreme heat came on as the sun rose higher, and we fell into the old way of eating ice when we stopped at a supply station, hardly affording ourselves time from that refreshing occupation to examine the attractive curio shop at the platform. Some very pretty articles can be picked up at wayside shops of this kind as souvenirs of the country in the way of skins, buffalo horns and Indian fancy work. Then it got hotter, and next morning it was *hotter*, and we were rested too much, and we thought we would not mind walking the remainder of the way. I went out on the platform and sat on the second step and caught all the breeze and cinders going, and so escaped the closeness of the car and avoided fatiguing myself by talking other people to death, and was happy and soiled until we reached Minneapolis, crossed the Mississippi and drew into the depot at St. Paul. Then I gathered up my traps, said good-by to the Northern Pacific Railroad, and proceeded in solitary state to a hotel.

My friends had all stopped at Minneapolis, so I found myself once more alone in a strange hotel, which is just what I am unsociable enough to prefer, when properly tired. And the cozy room and restful bath almost persuaded me to throw away half a day—almost, but not quite. My time is limited and I must see Minnehaha.

The famous little fall of Minnehaha lies at about the same distance from St. Paul that it does from Minneapolis. The proper way to see it is to drive from whichever of the two towns you happen to be stopping at to Minnehaha, and on to the other town and back to the original starting place, describing something like a circle, and including the surrounding country. Starting from St. Paul we drive up several very steep streets to the level country, and then follow the Mississippi River to Old Fort Snelling, past the parade grounds, where some colored soldiers are drilling, and on through an open country over which some very black clouds are creeping rather ominously.

The approaching storm comes very slowly, however, and does not finally break until my carriage draws up at the grounds pertaining to the falls of Minnehaha. At that moment a cyclone sweeps across the country, tearing down some trees close to the fall. I step for shelter under the roof of the lunch platform; at the same moment my carriage disappears and my park friends come running up from the falls and, crossing the open, take refuge in front of a curio bazaar opposite. I stay where I am until the chairs and tables begin to blow away, and then, as the roof of the adjoining building falls down, I run across the open and greet my friends.

We chatter mutual surprise, delight and experiences while we look at the pretty things in the shop, Indian works of art, until the rain slacks a little, and then my friends depart in a wild flurry of umbrellas and waterproofs, while I, with a waterproof lent me by the good-natured master of the shop and umbrella held firmly against the wind, cross the open again, and descend by slide and steps into the little ravine of the falls so aptly christened "Laughing Water."

It is really the prettiest little fall I have seen, a broad, even sheet of crinkled, foaming, white and green, sparkling water. The trees on either side leaning over the gulch were wet with rain, which imparted a richer green to the picture. One tree was prostrate on the ground, broken off by the first hard gust of the cyclone. The trees are willows, and their tiny leaves form a pretty, feathery, fern-like frame for the "Laughing Water."

When I return to my carriage the storm has settled into a steady doleful drizzle. We drive on past miles of fence wholly given over to the advertisement of local shops, miles of brilliantly colored persuasion, adjuration, admonition, even command to go to White's or Jones', while the peculiar virtues of the articles which were to be obtained were set forth in words of many hues.

It was night when I reached Minneapolis, and rain did not set off its vaunted beauty. I have heard many laudations of the town, which are no doubt correct. I only saw muddy streets of straggling outskirts punctuated by a brief vision of glittering shops, grand hotels and theatres in a brilliant flood of electric light. Then we turned a corner, climbed a hill, turned another corner and set out for St. Paul over a country road in the rain, the mud and the dark. The way was long, part of the road ran through some deep woods. The rain fell dismally, while the horses plodded along to the doleful splashing of the mud. I was alone and it was dark and a lonely road without houses for long distances ; but we were too near to a large city for road agents, I expect. Anyway, I didn't see any, though I felt sorry when I thought what a fine opportunity they were losing. When I finally got back to St. Paul, climbed the long, hilly streets and entered the hotel, I was cold, tired, wet and hungry ; but it was 10 o'clock, so I took a warm bath and went to bed, deciding to get my supper for breakfast.

It is really too bad to shoot across the continent on a fast express like a meteor, for there is a great deal to see of interest in each State if one can only take the time to it.

A short trip into Minnesota, to meet my sister, who is visiting friends who live upon a stock farm, proves interesting. Life on a farm is a hard one, especially when the thermometer falls to 52 degrees below zero, but there is some fun to be got out of it. They have all the sleighing parties they like in Winter, and a dance after a brisk drive over the snow in a neat little cutter with one's best girl, is all the livelier, and then the drive home. Really, we city folks do miss a great deal ! Even in harvest time the boys are not too tired for an impromptu dance in the kitchen, if they've a city guest to entertain.

The hostess takes us to drive to the town and look at the work of a recent cyclone, the streets are fenced in with prostrate trees blown down and here and there we see a heap of shingles, all that is left of a house that but yesterday sheltered a family. Now and then we stop and ask a man what damage he has sustained from the wind and are regaled with accounts of roofless houses, broken windmills and ruined crops. After an interchange of experiences and sympathies and decided thankfulness for what is left to them, my hostess says, "bring up your girls this evening, we want to give our visitors a dance."

In the evening a few of the people come, each pair with horse and buggy; two young men are imported from town to supply us with music, one of them "calling off" in a peculiar way of his own, acting as dancing-master as well as leader. He is a nice young man with well oiled hair, which describes a curve that droops gracefully down the middle of his forehead, and an air of superiority and condescension that is not lost on us.

They are not always dependent on fiddlers, however, for on another night we danced with equal zest to a rythmic jingle sung by the hired man. My sister took some of his unique descriptive music down as he sang it, so I am enabled to give a sample. The first quadrille was danced to the tune of "The Grasshopper Sat on a Sweet Potato Vine," and ran thus :

> "First lady swing
> With the right hand gent
> With the right hand around,
> The right hand around,
> Partner by the left,
> With the left hand around
> Lady in the center and seven hands around.
> Swing her out—Allemen left,
> Right hand to your partner
> And grand right and left."

This is danced with great spirit, while the hired man's baritone voice rolls out and his foot beats time.

Another one with another popular air goes :

> "Salute your partners, now don't smile,
> Opposite to the same, in Norfield style.
> First lady give right hand across,
> Mind your eye and don't get lost
> Back with the left, keep hold of hands
> And balance four in a line
> Break and swing half round, balance four in a line,
> Break and spring to place. Allemen left."

Another danced to the tune of a childish chant about Jonah's adventures I once heard, runs in a more romantic strain:

> "With a bow so neat,
> And a kiss so sweet
> Swing opposite lady round and round,
> Swing opposite lady round and round,
> Swing opposite lady round and round
> And then swing with your partner."

But the last one, of which I only caught a line or two, danced to the tune of "The Girl I Left Behind Me," is perhaps the most "fetching."

> "First couple lead to the right,
> And teeter up and down,"

sang the hired man (the Minnesota "teeter" isn't learned in a minute either), then

> "Pass right through
> As I tell you
> And swing that girl behind you."

This goes off with a military dash, and when it is over we cry out "Oh, Hank; sing us some more, do."

Hank can dance, too; the girl he leads out on the floor is proud of having the executor of the fanciest steps in the room for a partner.

The journey from St. Paul to Chicago was marked by a variation from my accustomed habit in traveling. I positively refrained from talking throughout the entire trip. Silence is, however, the distinguishing feature of short trips by rail. One night in a sleeper does not stir up one's social instincts as two or three days and nights do; but after the long sociable journey on the Northern Pacific the extreme silence and constraint of my fellow passengers strikes me strangely. Not that I object; I welcome all changes with equal pleasure. After the incessant chattering I've done for days together I am glad to rest and reflect, and I arrive in Chicago as sedate and solemn as anybody.

We breakfast at Detroit, where, crossing the Detroit River on a boat that takes our train bodily, I am reminded of the time when the passengers were obliged to gather up their baggage and leave the train to take another after crossing, much to their inconvenience; but this is all changed now, and we remain comfortably in our cars and are duly thankful. All day we travel through the British possessions, and toward evening we reach Niagara, and behold the beauty and grandeur of this great work of nature.

Niagara has many aspects. Once I saw it in March, tumbling gray and terrible under a leaden sky, while I stood alone on the suspension bridge and listened to its roar. Sometimes the frost king seizes it and transforms it into a glittering mass of undulating ice with downward pointing spires and frosted drops; then it is a grand and dazzling sight. But just now under the slanting rays of the sun and confined by green banks, it has a softer, more mellow beauty, as its rich green waters rush madly and foamily over the immense precipice. The roar of the falling water sounds less solemn under the bright blue sky of a summer day.

Crossing the famous suspension bridge, looking far up the river toward the falls and down it to see the rapids, we are on American soil again. On we go, and do I imagine it, or is New York State really greener and more beautiful than any other? No, it is not imagination. New York does not suffer from the drought that afflicts the Western and Middle States, and the rich deep tints of green that make the country so beautiful to me are distinctive of the moister climate.

At Buffalo, meeting an old acquaintance in the conductor of the train, I resume my accustomed talkativeness, trying to squeeze the experiences of three months into an hour's chat. Failing that, I take to my berth to wake on the banks of the glorious Hudson, that rolls so majestically toward the sea. One doesn't need to go far from New York to see beautiful scenery. The wooded hills of Spuyten Duyvil and the frowning Palisades with the broad Hudson between are as beautiful as any river scenery I have looked on. And so, I am reflecting patriotically on my native city as we roll into the Grand Central depot, which is the finest depot I have encountered in all my travels.

IN CONCLUSION.

This story of the travels of LILIAN LELAND cannot be more appropriately concluded than by quoting from an article written by her in eulogy of IDA PFEIFFER, in which she said:

I will not dwell upon my own tour, made in all the safety and comfort of recent civilization, but call to mind the adventurous woman who traveled twice around the world before some of the "globe trotters" of to-day were born. I refer to Madame Ida Pfeiffer. I doubt if Ida Pfeiffer's record as a traveler has been broken by any man; certainly no woman has approached her as a far and wide wanderer on the face of the earth.

Madame Pfeiffer was forty-five years of age when she began her travels in 1842, visiting the Holy Land first, and then Scandinavia and Iceland. After these comparatively short trips she sailed for Rio de Janiero. Leaving Rio de Janiero she sailed around stormy Cape Horn to Valparaiso. From there she went to the Society Islands, and thence via the Philippines to Hong Kong. From Hong Kong to Singapore, Ceylon and India. Crossing India she sailed up the Persian gulf, ascending the historic Tigris to Bagdad, and crossed Turkey in Asia and Georgia by caravan to the Sea of Azov. She proceeded next to Sebastopol, Odessa, Constantinople, Smyrna and Athens, and after calling at Corinth and Corfu, returned to Vienna by way of Trieste.

She had spent two years and six months in her tour, and had compassed 2,800 miles by land and 35,000 miles by sea, and was the first woman to accomplish a journey around the world.

In 1851 Ida Pfeiffer started out again with unabated zeal to see the world, going first to London. She sailed for Cape Town, and after rounding the Cape of Good Hope went to Borneo "plunging into the heart of that island."

Sumatra claimed her attention next, and then she sailed to San Francisco, thence to Callao and later to Ecuador, "making the ascent of the Cordilleras, and witnessing an eruption of Cotopaxi." She then proceeded to Panama, crossed the isthmus and went to New Orleans. Ascending the Mississippi, she visited Chicago, the lakes, Canada, Boston and New York, and back to England, completing her second journey around the world without touching a point she had visited on her first tour.

It is not to be supposed that Madame Pfeiffer accomplished all this without some thrilling adventures. She had been set upon by a negro in Brazil, who cut her twice on her left arm before she was rescued, and whom she had cut in the hand in determined self-defense. She had fallen into a river swarming with alligators, had been seized by a Cossack and held a prisoner until the examination of her baggage and passports satisfied him of her harmlessness, and had been surrounded by cannibals in Sumatra, where her own tact and courage saved her from immediate death.

But still she was not satisfied. She went once more to the Cape of Good Hope, sailed from there to Mauritius, and finally went to Madagascar.

Madame Pfeiffer spent several months in the capital of Madagascar, whence she escaped with her life after thirteen days in prison and a long forced journey to the coast, only to die of the disease caused by these trying experiences, October 28, 1858.

No one can hope to rival Ida Pfeiffer as a daring traveler, for the reason that the dangers attending such an expedition as hers are rapidly passing away. Civilization is spreading over every part of the world, and the lawless on land and sea are gradually succumbing to the regulating influences of the American and European people. The traveler who thirsts for such "hairbreadth 'scapes" and dangerous adventures with cannibal and savage as lightened the monotony of Ida Pfeiffer's life will have great difficulty in getting away from the beaten track and finding the haunt of the savage.

To fully appreciate the courage and endurance of Ida Pfeiffer one must consider the disadvantages under which she traveled. The difference that forty years has made in the civilization of the world and the improvement in the various modes of getting about is very great.

To-day we traverse a continent in a few days, sitting comfortably in luxuriously fitted cars, where she spent tedious weeks plodding wearisomely across burning plains and over snowy ranges. Drawn by the deliberate water buffalo, borne by the opinionated donkey, the positive mule, the stately camel, or in palanquin by human hands, she traversed deserts and climbed mountains. The tent and the rude hut of the native sheltered her more often than the hotel. Instead of the record breaking steamer, a floating palace in appointments and size, pursuing a given course in a given time, with little or no reference to wind and wave, she crossed the oceans in sailing vessels, tossed and buffeted by the furious gales of Cape Horn and delayed by the burning calms of equatorial seas.

America leads the world in the speed, comfort and luxury of her railroad service, and there is now an unbroken connection of comfortable steamer and comfortable car right around the globe, with European or American hotels at every junction. If one is possessed of sufficient courage to buy a ticket, hire a porter or cabman, or pay a hotel bill, one has enough to last one around the world.

It is a question in my mind whether after all the advantages are not in favor of the woman who travels alone. To travel, strictly speaking, alone, is impossible, unless one goes afoot or by canoe. The traveler by train or steamer must perforce move along with a crowd. The women who travels with husband, father or brother may be supposed to have one man dedicated to her especial protection, but as the woman who is alone appeals naturally to the heart of every brave and honest man, she becomes the charge of the officials and her fellow passengers as well, and her unprotected condition secures the kindest attention and most considerate care of those who are best able to assist and protect her.

In the event of accident at sea the officers of a vessel take particular care of the lone woman, holding themselves in a measure responsible for her safety. Under ordinary circumstances they will endeavor to entertain her, advise and direct her, and when she passes beyond their own jurisdiction they will bespeak for her the special care of their most trusted friends and strive in every way to secure the future comfort, safety and pleasure of their transient charge.

Of all the pleasant memories of a voyage around the world the most pleasant are of kindnesses received and the most gratifying knowledge acquired is the knowledge of the unselfish kindliness of the heart of man.

LILIAN LELAND.

www.ingramcontent.com/pod-product-compliance
Lightning Source LLC
Chambersburg PA
CBHW020312240426
43673CB00039B/781